Specters of World Literature

For my teachers

Specters of World Literature

Orientalism, Modernity, and the Novel in the Middle East

Karim Mattar

EDINBURGH
University Press

Edinburgh University Press is one of the leading university presses in the UK. We publish academic books and journals in our selected subject areas across the humanities and social sciences, combining cutting-edge scholarship with high editorial and production values to produce academic works of lasting importance. For more information visit our website: edinburghuniversitypress.com

© Karim Mattar, 2020, 2022

Edinburgh University Press Ltd
The Tun – Holyrood Road
12(2f) Jackson's Entry
Edinburgh EH8 8PJ

First published in hardback by Edinburgh University Press 2020

Typeset in 11 / 15 Times New Roman by
IDSUK (DataConnection) Ltd

A CIP record for this book is available from the British Library

ISBN 978 1 4744 6703 2 (hardback)
ISBN 978 1 4744 6704 9 (paperback)
ISBN 978 1 4744 6706 3 (webready PDF)
ISBN 978 1 4744 6705 6 (epub)

The right of Karim Mattar to be identified as the author of this work has been asserted in accordance with the Copyright, Designs and Patents Act 1988, and the Copyright and Related Rights Regulations 2003 (SI No. 2498).

Contents

Preface	vi
Acknowledgments	xv
Note on Transliterations	xix
Introduction: Towards a Spectral Theory of World Literature	1

I The Worlding of "Literature" in the Middle East

1 The *Shabaḥ* of Modernity: World-Systems, the Petro-Imperium, and the Indigenous Trace — 71

2 A Genealogy of *Adab* in the Comparative Middle East — 110

II The Middle Eastern Novel and the Spectral Life-World of Modernity

3 The Revolution of Form: Naguib Mahfouz from the Suez Crisis to the Arab Spring — 177

4 Islam and the Limits of Translation: Orhan Pamuk and the Ottoman Revival — 215

5 Women in the Literary Marketplace: The Anglophone Iranian Novel and the Feminist Subject — 260

Conclusion: Futures of Spectrality	300
Bibliography	308
Index	332

Preface

The image I have selected for the cover of this book—Hans Holbein the Younger's *The Ambassadors* (1533), also known as *Jean de Dinteville and Georges de Selve*—serves to illustrate my overall approach to and ambitions regarding the critical, theoretical, and disciplinary problematic of "world literature" in this project. A masterpiece of early modern European art, the life-sized double portrait was produced by the German artist during his second stay in England, which ran from 1532 until his death in 1543 and coincided with Henry VIII's break from the Roman Catholic Church and the Protestant Reformation that was then sweeping across Europe. As the art historian Mary Hervey discovered in 1900, it was commissioned by de Dinteville—the figure on the left—to commemorate his friend and fellow subject de Selve's visit to London in 1533.[1] The two men—the first a member of the *noblesse d'épée* and ambassador of the King of France and the second the Bishop of Lavaur—were in that year on a diplomatic mission seeking to reconcile Henry with the Pope. Holbein makes sure to weave into the painting a subtle commentary on the political and ecclesiastical conflicts that pervaded the dominions of Christendom at the time and that occasioned its commission and making in the first place—suggesting the discord and schisms of the continent, the terrestrial globe centered around Europe on the bottom shelf of the central display is upside down, the lute adjacent to it has a broken string, and the astronomical and other scientific instruments on the top shelf are misaligned for use in the northern latitude. Although it is of wider spiritual significance, the painting's memento mori—the famous anamorphic skull hidden in its bottom section—has been interpreted as a warning about the vanity of the ambassadors' hopes and the inevitability of further upheaval in the European politico-religious order.

Beyond what it says about its immediate contexts, what interests me in particular about *The Ambassadors* is its registration and representation in precise visual form of what might be considered the incipient *Weltanschauung* of an early modern Europe on the verge of its age of imperial expansion and conquest. Thoroughly anthropocentric, this worldview is one which saw man positioned—or position himself—as sole authority over both the earthly and the heavenly planes, as subject to the object that is the world as such. In the painting, the two figures—one garbed in the luxurious secular attire of wealth, nobility, and power and the other in the more modest clerical attire of devotion and learning—flank and loom over a central display that carries on its shelves a number of meticulously rendered symbols of such domination and its reach. Placed between and below these two epitomes of male accomplishment as conceived during the Renaissance, the display bears on its bottom shelf a German mathematical treatise, a Lutheran hymnal, and a case of flutes in addition to the globe and the lute as previously noted, and on its top a celestial globe, a shepherd's dial, a universal equinoctial dial, a horary quadrant, a polyhedral sundial, and a torquetum. Together, these objects comprise an index of the universal, even transcendental aspirations of the humanistic, scientific, and theological endeavors and inquiries of the time. The oriental rug draped over the top shelf deserves a special mention here. Of Anatolian origin, and with a design that is now referred to by the name of Holbein himself, it suggests not only the influence of the mathematics of the Islamic Golden Age on the development of the contemporary astronomical instruments that are arranged on its surface, but also a history of (imperial) encounter, exchange, and conflict between "West" and "East" that was unfolding at the moment of the painting and that would expand and intensify in the centuries to come. As a whole, the painting absorbs within its frame and focalizes through the figure of early modern

European man the entirety of the world over which that figure was soon to assume near-comprehensive mastery. It is perhaps fitting that the future Queen of England Elizabeth I—who was to grant the British East India Company a royal charter at the close of the same century—was born in the same year that it was produced, and that one of Holbein's sitters—de Dinteville—was present at her christening.

As concept, discourse, practice, institution, and discipline, world literature in my account is defined by precisely the dialectic of appropriation (of worldly content) and projection (of European or "Western" power) that *The Ambassadors* unconsciously inscribes. Further, world literature in all of these senses might and in my view must be traced back to the early modern moment of the painting, which set the scene for what I discuss in this book as global capitalist modernity, its genealogical origin and condition of possibility. However, the implications of the piece for my understanding of world literature do not end here. Most significantly, the anamorphic skull that cuts across its surface cryptically suggests an interruption not only of the content—man and his claims on the world—portrayed *in* the painting, but also of the coherent self-positioning and self-identity of the subject produced *by* the painting. Only perceptible when the viewer positions him- or herself at an oblique angle in relation to the canvas (a point from which the remainder of the content is reduced to inchoate shape and color), this image of death—what Jacques Lacan calls in his well-known reading of the piece its "anamorphic ghost"—undoes the consistency, assurance, and mastery of the "I" / "eye" that is constituted in its field of vision, and thereby that of subjectivity per se.[2] *The Ambassadors*, as Lacan concludes, thus "makes visible" at "the very heart of the period in which the subject emerged [. . .] something that is simply the subject as annihilated"—it "reflects our own nothingness [. . .] in the figure of the death's head."[3]

In this book, I approach world literature from the perspective of the decentered "I" / "eye" of *The Ambassadors*, the subject as disaggregated by its ghost. Over the last twenty or so years, and continuing to this day, the discipline of literary studies in its established institutional forms has been engaged in one of the most prolonged and intensive exercises of self-scrutiny in its history. Literary scholars have been particularly concerned with the internal coherence, social value, and currency of its long-held frameworks of organization and analysis in light of the challenges posed by globalization, the neoliberal restructuring of the university, the devaluation and defunding of the humanities, a collapsed job market, declining enrollments, departmental closures (especially as pertaining to foreign language departments), and so forth. Seeking to attune literary studies to the contemporary world and to make a renewed case for its continued existence as such, they have come to increasingly question the "national literature" paradigm that had served as its backbone since the founding of the first modern literature departments in Britain and the United States in the late nineteenth century. Similarly, that of "comparative literature" as pioneered by figures such as Erich Auerbach and Leo Spitzer in the 1940s and 1950s has been castigated for its Eurocentric heritage and sphere of activity, and that of "postcolonial literature" as spurred by the work of Edward Said, Homi Bhabha, and Gayatri Spivak in the 1980s and 1990s for its anglo- / francophone orientation, theoretical abstruseness, and reliance on a delimiting historiographical model. Amounting to a drive to "world" literary studies, these developments have resulted in the crystallization and consolidation of "world literature" as a new—or newly revived—paradigm for the discipline in this period.

Evoking the Goethean dream of *Weltliteratur*, advocates of world literature such as David Damrosch, Franco Moretti, and Pascale Casanova have highlighted its promise of coverage and comparison on a global scale. Foundational, their work has prompted the comprehensive reframing of questions of literary history, canonicity, language, translation, literary exchange and circulation, and pedagogy that we have witnessed in recent years. At the same time, however, there has been a strong critical backlash against the fledgling field. Detractors including Djelal Kadir, Aamir Mufti, and Emily Apter have stressed its appropriating, homogenizing, and commodifying implications, its imperialistic absorption (via translation) of the world's literary resources as examples of fashionable multiculturalism to be included in anthologies and syllabi. In this book, I attempt to mediate between these two broadly defined positions. I hold onto the early promise of the field, and I do so precisely *via*, rather than despite, a sustained focus on the complicity of world literature in processes of cultural and other forms of globalization. I argue that as concept, discourse, practice, institution, and discipline, world literature produces local literature as an "other" that nevertheless haunts its universalizing, assimilative imperative with the force of the uncanny. Best understood according to a Derridean logic of spectrality, the manifestation of otherness in the domain of world literature is thus constitutive of world literature. By drawing attention to the other, the specter in its midst, I hope in this book to contribute productively and compellingly to the continuing debate on world literature.

At the heart of this book is what I call a "spectral" theory of world literature. I develop this theory with reference to the world-systems analysis of Immanuel Wallerstein, Terence Hopkins, Samir Amin, and others, and by deploying Edward Said's and Aamir Mufti's readings of Orientalism as a site of the codification and classification of world textualities as "literature" in the modern, European sense of the late eighteenth to mid-nineteenth centuries. I argue that the historical process by which the peripheries of the world-system are incorporated into the logic and parameters of global capitalist modernity is *facilitated by* as well as *enacted in* the export, internalization, and reproduction of this notion of literature there. Giving rise to the forms of modernity—paradigmatically, the novel, the lyric poem, and the stage play—in the periphery, this process results in the superseding of local forms and the life-worlds of which they are the expression. In this way rendered other to modernity, yet never altogether assimilated in or excised from its narrative, the local thereby manifests as what Jacques Derrida calls a "specter," a "trace" that infects and inflects the forms of modernity. Thus redefined as the worlding of the concept of literature attendant on modernity, world literature, I show, is constituted in the logic of spectrality.

I take the Middle Eastern novel as both metonym and metaphor of a spectral world literature. I start by considering its current worldly manifestations in English, translation, the global publishing industry, global award culture, literary reviews and criticism, and the (anglophone) academy. Typically explained in relation to a post-9/11 upsurge of public interest in the region, I trace a deeper genealogy of its rise to prominence. Drawing on recent developments in the field of Middle East studies—as in the work of Roger Allen, M. M. Badawi, Muhsin al-Musawi, Jeffrey

Sacks, Nuha Alshaar, Waïl Hassan, Zachary Lockman, Rashid Khalidi, Abdelfattah Kilito, and others, I argue that the Middle Eastern novel is premised on and reproduces a trajectory of modernity in the region which saw the reinscription of the classical Arabic-Islamic concept of "*adab*" in terms of the modern, European concept of literature. Precipitated by the colonial encounter and its accompanying heritage of an internalized Orientalist philology, such an overturning of literary tradition occurred in remarkably similar ways across the region. In what I consequently posit as "the comparative Middle East," I explore how the origin of the Middle Eastern novel in modernity continues to determine its production, translation, circulation, and reception in the world. I focus on the pivotal sites of Middle Eastern modernity—Egypt, Turkey, and Iran, and argue that lost to the worlding of novels from these countries is their constitution in the logic of spectrality. With the intention of redressing this imbalance, I thus critically restore their engagements with the others of Middle Eastern modernity. I locate such engagement in form, in the inf(l)ection of novelistic form by the spectral trace of the political, religious, and gender life-world most generally designated and expressed by *adab*. Read in this light, the Middle Eastern novel comprises what I call a revolution of form. All in all, I seek in this book to demonstrate through a new reading of the Middle Eastern novel that world literature is always-already haunted by its others, the ghosts of modernity.

My primary texts include novels and other literary works by Abdelrahman Munif, Naguib Mahfouz, Orhan Pamuk, Azar Nafisi, Yasmin Crowther, and Marjane Satrapi. Throughout, I read these texts alongside classic statements of world literature from Johann Wolfgang von Goethe and Karl Marx to the present, the discourse of the modern novel as initiated by Miguel de Cervantes, and landmarks of Middle Eastern literary history such as the *Mu'allaqāt* and *Alf Layla wa Layla*. In each case, I assess how their appearance in the world is mediated by various strategies of containment and domestication, and then provide a counter-reading focalized around questions of form. In so doing, I cumulatively show how the Middle Eastern novel traverses and reconfigures the aesthetic forms definitive of the modern novel—realism, modernism, postmodernism, postcolonialism, and cosmopolitanism—from the perspective of its others. Across my five main chapters, the Middle Eastern novel is thus critically conceptualized as expressive of the spectral life-world of modernity.

In undertaking this analysis, I have made a number of methodological and stylistic choices that require clarification from the outset. Methodologically, I have developed and deployed a broad global framework for my reading of the Middle Eastern novel, turned extensively to secondary sources at various points in my discussion, and relied on available translations for in-text citations from my primary sources. Regarding my global framework, I have found that world-systems theory and its core / periphery orientation provides the most thoroughgoing and comprehensive basis for understanding the rise of the novel in the Middle East in the first place, and thus for its imbrications with the wider process of modernization in the region. Clearly laid out in the Introduction, the modifications or additions I have made to world-systems analysis in its approach to the question of incorporation might help further entrench its value for literary studies. Regarding my use of secondary sources, I have found the expertise of other scholars indispensable when dealing with the pre-modern Middle Eastern literary heritage and with the comparative histories of political, social, cultural, and economic modernization in Egypt, Turkey, and Iran. As is the case especially in Chapter 2, drawing on the work of specialists in the relevant national literary traditions is necessary and in my view reasonable when attempting the sort of historically and geographically expansive comparisons that will increasingly define world literature in the years to come. And regarding my use of translations, the worlding of the Middle Eastern novel via translation (among other means) is *itself* an object of analysis in this study, and so assessing primary sources in this format becomes part and parcel of my wider project. As I demonstrate in Chapter 1 and especially Chapter 4, however, I read these translations alongside the originals, and conduct comparative linguistic analyses that seek to evoke the limitations of the former and thereby of translational approaches to world literature in general.

Stylistically, I have employed a slow, patient method of exposition in especially the Introduction and Chapter 2, where I develop my critical, theoretical, and historical framework. While perhaps against the grain of much recent writing in literary studies, I thought it best in the Introduction to introduce the familiar (such as Marx's theory of the commodity and Derrida's of spectrality) in as much detail as what I have assumed to be the relatively less familiar (such as Wallerstein's and Hopkins's theory of incorporation and Edmund Husserl's of the life-world), so as to ensure as clear and coherent a presentation of the material as possible. The same principle applies to my discussion of comparative Egyptian, Turkish, and Iranian literary histories in Chapter 2. Although the background on the individual national literary traditions that I have provided will be self-evident to specialists therein, what might be less so is that on all three of these traditions alongside one another (which I assume on the basis of dearth of literary scholarship on what I call in this book the *comparative* Middle East). The style for which I have opted seems to me appropriate to the syntheses of existing scholarship that I am attempting in these chapters.

Apart from the point about style (as he tends towards a more flamboyant and deliberately provocative prose than myself), all of the above will sharply and specifically bring to mind the work of Franco Moretti, in particular his article "Conjectures on World Literature" (2000).[4] As I discuss in the Introduction, his proposals about world-systems theory, secondary sources, and translation vis-à-vis world literature and its study have strongly—though not uncritically and far from exclusively—guided this project. This brings me to something of a quandary. Given the credible allegations of serious sexual assault—rape—that have been levelled against Moretti in the wake of the #MeToo movement (allegations which Moretti has denied and which have not been brought before a court of law), I find it ethically unjustifiable to implicitly contribute to his professional reputation and standing by engaging with his work in as much depth as I do.[5] Yet at the same time, given the extent and specificity of its influence on my own, I also find it academically irresponsible not to do so. I have no satisfactory resolution to this dilemma. Instead, I will reiterate here what I say to my students—undergraduate and graduate alike—when I present Moretti's writings in the classroom. If for whatever reason you object to reading and discussing this material, then I welcome you to skip over it, and I will happily provide you with alternatives (in the case of this book, I also deal with the work of Damrosch and Casanova, who are often cited in the same breath as Moretti for their contributions to the world literature debate). Otherwise, let it provide us with the opportunity to reflect together not only on its important content, but also on the very serious questions its presence in our midst raises about professional, scholarly, and pedagogical responsibility when it comes to the work of objectionable figures. It seems to me that Gerald Graff's imperative—"Teach the conflicts"—applies as much to this and similar cases as it does to the internal disciplinary history of literary studies to which he is referring.[6]

Returning now to the subject matter proper of this book, I will close this brief preamble by suggesting that world literature must now be regarded as inevitable. As critics, scholars, and practitioners continue to engage this paradigm, it seems to me that our *responsibility* is to the others produced in its wake. In this book, I call for renewed attention to these others, to the specters of world literature.

Notes

1. Hervey was the first to definitively identity the two subjects of the painting, and her work has served as the basis for later interpretations. See Hervey, *Holbein's "Ambassadors."*
2. Lacan, *The Seminar of Jacques Lacan, Book XI*, p. 89.
3. Ibid. pp. 88, 92.
4. See Moretti, "Conjectures on World Literature."
5. For the allegations, see Mangan, "2 Women Say Stanford Professors Raped Them Years Ago."
6. Graff, *Professing Literature*, p. viii.

Acknowledgments

This book is dedicated to my teachers. First and foremost, I would like to thank Elleke Boehmer, Aamir Mufti, Jennifer Wicke, and Nicholas Royle for their guidance, support, and inspiration over the years. My D.Phil. supervisor at the University of Oxford from 2009 to 2013, Professor Boehmer oversaw the beginnings of this book as a doctoral thesis and has guided me through my early academic career with remarkable care and attention. Her work ethic, mentorship, and friendship have not only made this book possible, but have also come to model for me a professional and personal ethos to which I continue to aspire. In his writings, conversation, and seminar at the Institute of World Literature in Istanbul in 2012, Professor Mufti has shaped my thinking on Edward Said, Orientalism, and world literature in innumerable ways. I am grateful in particular for his thorough engagement with my work from an early stage, especially in his role as my doctoral examiner. From our very first meeting during my M.A. in English at the University of Virginia in 2007, Professor Wicke has helped instill in me—as is the case with all of her students—the rigorous professional sensibility required for survival let alone success in this increasingly fickle business of ours. I owe the attitude with which I approached my graduate studies and which was foundational to my success in securing a tenure-track assistant professorship out of my D.Phil. largely to her influence and the selflessness of her support and encouragement. My first meeting with Professor Royle during my M.A. in English Literature and Critical Theory at the University of Sussex in 2004 was similarly inspirational. Happening to coincide with the death of his great friend and mentor, his seminar on Jacques Derrida was infused with a passion and an affectivity that deconstruction rarely elicits, and that has stayed with me ever since. In a word, he taught me how to read Derrida—and by extension "theory" per se—in the fullest sense, a difficult lesson that I hope I am able to impart to my own students.

I would also like to thank Sinan Antoon, Emily Apter, Anna Ball, Anna Bernard, Walter Cohen, miriam cooke, Hamid Dabashi, Sarah D'Adamo, David Damrosch, David Fieni, Nouri Gana, Erdağ Göknar, the late Barbara Harlow, Salah Hassan, Waïl Hassan, R. A. Judy, Djelal Kadir, David Lloyd, Stephen Morton, Mohamed-Salah Omri, Wen-chin Ouyang, Bruce Robbins, Jeffrey Sacks, and Ella Shohat. In their generosity, the ways in which these colleagues and friends have engaged with and responded to this book and related projects over the last ten or so years have been central to their framing and refining; in their intellectual and other pleasures, our collaborations around topics from or related to it at various points have been extremely rewarding. I am grateful to Mona Baker, Joseph Allen Boone, Erdağ Göknar, Salah Hassan, David Lloyd, Luiza Moreira, and Aamir Mufti for inviting me to present material from this book at various national and international conferences, symposia, and special events.

At the University of Colorado at Boulder, I thank my colleagues Thora Brylowe, Jane Garrity, David Glimp, Raza Ali Hasan, Cheryl Higashida, Janice Ho, Karen Jacobs, Ruth Ellen Kocher, William Kuskin, Laura Winkiel, and Sue Zemka for their mentorship, professional support, and camaraderie since I began my Assistant Professorship in the Department of English in 2013; and my students Damian Borovsky, Eun Cho, Kevin Dibb, Theodor Hamstra, Anahita Khorsand, Andrew Lindquist, Caci Pippin, Hope Ruskaup, Allison Shelton, Allegra Upton, and Travis Zimpfer for the inspiration and gratification that working with them on their undergraduate and graduate theses has provided. At the University of Oxford, I thank faculty members including Ros Ballaster, Christine Gerrard, Patrick Hayes, Laura Marcus, Ankhi Mukherjee, Karma Nabulsi, Seamus Perry, Matthew Reynolds, and Avi Shlaim for their always helpful advice on matters pertaining to my research and teaching as well as our occasional collaborations; and my fellow students including Alex Bubb, Ruth Bush, Dominic Davies, Peter Hill, Charne Lavery, Erica Lombard, Nisha Manocha, Tamara Moellenberg, Eleni Philippou, Mezna Qato, Asha Rogers, Charlotta Salmi, the late Konstantin Sofianos, Edward Sugden, Justin Tackett, Scott Teal, Vincent Van Bever Donker, Stephanie Yorke, and Manmay Zafar for fostering and being part of the always supportive and stimulating graduate community that we shared. In the Modern Language Association Global Arab and Arab American Forum, my fellow executive committee members Hatem Akil, Ala Alryyes, Rasha Chatta, Carol Fadda-Conrey, Pauline Homsi Vinson, Ahmed Idrissi Alami, and Shaden Tageldin have since 2016 been wonderful interlocutors and co-conspirators on matters of shared interest at this most important of scholarly associations.

Since my days in graduate school, a number of editors have supported my work. Thank you to Paul Bové, Peter Boxall, Stuart Gillespie, Rashid Khalidi, Luiza Moreira, Lucian Stone, Janet Wilson, Laura Winkiel, and Robert Young for shepherding my journal articles, book chapters, and reviews to press, and to their anonymous external readers for their insightful comments and suggestions. Thanks also to Duke University Press, Edinburgh University Press, and Taylor & Francis for granting me permission to reproduce previously published material. Material from Chapter 1 originally appeared in my journal article "The *Shabaḥ* of World Literature: Bedouin Cartographies in Abdulrahman Munif's *Cities of Salt*," *English Language Notes*, 52:2 (2014), pp. 35–52. Material from Chapter 4 originally appeared in my journal article "Orhan Pamuk and the Limits of Translation: Foreignizing *The Black Book* for World Literature," *Translation and Literature*, 23:1 (2014), pp. 42–67. Material from Chapter 5 originally appeared in my journal article "Re-Reading the 'Rogue State': The Politics of Gender in Anglophone Iranian Literature," *Interventions: International Journal of Postcolonial Studies*, 14:4 (2012), pp. 551–68.

This book has been generously supported by a number of fellowships, grants, and awards. At the University of Colorado at Boulder, thanks are due to the Department of English, the College of Arts and Sciences, and the Office of Diversity, Equity, and Community Engagement for the "First

Monograph Grant" (2015–6), the "Arts and Sciences Fund for Excellence Award" (2016), the "Dean's Summer Research Grant" (2017), the "IMPART Faculty Fellowship" (2018), and the "Kayden Research Grant" (2018). At Columbia University, where I conducted the research for and wrote much of Chapter 1, to the Department of Middle Eastern, South Asian, and African Studies for furnishing me with a Visiting Scholarship in the Spring of 2014. And at the University of Oxford, to the Faculty of English Language and Literature and Lady Margaret Hall for the "Meyerstein Award for Graduate Research" (2009–11) and the "Barbara Johnstone Award for Graduate Research" (2009–12). The doctoral thesis from which this book is partially derived was funded by an Arts and Humanities Research Council "Doctoral Award" from 2010 to 2012.

The editorial team at Edinburgh University Press has been outstanding, and it has been a genuine pleasure to work with them. I would like to express my thanks to Nicola Ramsey, Adela Rauchova, Kirsty Woods, Eliza Wright, and Christine Barton in particular for their enthusiasm for this book from the outset and their detailed guidance on its production and finalization at every stage. Their attention to my concerns, no matter how small, has been exemplary. My gratitude also to EUP's anonymous external readers for their many excellent and well-taken recommendations.

Finally, my deepest and most heartfelt thanks go out to Awni, Hala, and Mira Mattar for their tireless support and endless patience with me while I have been working on this project. It is literally the case that it wouldn't have been possible without their having taught me how to be a person. Hopefully, I can return to being one now that it is complete.

Note on Transliterations

In this book, I have transliterated numerous names, titles, and terms from the Arabic, Ottoman Turkish, and Persian languages. I have followed the general transliteration guidelines provided by the *International Journal of Middle East Studies* for each of these languages, with a few exceptions based on personal preferences. First, I have indicated the letters *hamza / hemze* and *'ayn* with, respectively, closing and opening single quotation marks rather than modifier letter right and left half rings (' and ' rather than ʾ and ʿ). My reason for this choice is that this appears to be the standard usage in the majority of the translated primary texts (as well as many of the secondary sources) from which I have cited when these have been available. Second, I have included diacritical marks in transliterations of titles of books, journals, newspapers, articles, and so forth (e.g. *Mudun al-Milḥ* rather than *al-Milh*), in order to aid the reader in identifying the correct sources and terms. Third, I have capitalized the definite article "al-" when this occurs at the beginning of such a title (e.g. *Al-Nafṭ wa al-Tanmiyya* rather than *al-Nafṭ*), so as to remain consistent with the English translations that I also provide in the main text. Fourth, I have separated prepositions, conjunctions, and prefixes from their objects (e.g. *wa al-Tanmiyya* rather than *wa-l-Tanmiyya*), for the same purpose. And finally, I have transliterated proper names of individuals (except in bibliographical citations, where I have reproduced the author's name as it appears in the text), places, and historical events in their commonly cited romanized forms for ease of reference—that is, omitting their diacritical marks (e.g. Munif rather than Munīf, Dhahran rather than Ẓahrān, and *Nahda* rather than *Nahḍa*). For such references in literary texts, I have followed the usage of the English-language translations from which I have cited when these have been available. As the names of many of the regional organizations to which I refer (e.g. Al-Maṭbaʻa al-Amiriyya) are less familiar, I have retained their diacritics.

Introduction: Towards a Spectral Theory of World Literature

No justice [. . .] seems possible or thinkable without the principle of some *responsibility*, beyond all living present, before the ghosts of those who are not yet born or who are already dead, be they victims of wars, political or other kinds of violence, nationalist, racist, colonialist, sexist, or other kinds of exterminations, victims of the oppressions of capitalist imperialism or any of the forms of totalitarianism.

Jacques Derrida, *Specters of Marx*

No worker said it outright or pronounced his name out loud, but his specter filled the whole desert.

Abdelrahman Munif, *Cities of Salt*

In much of the contemporary critical debate on "world literature," the onus in the compound has fallen on "world" rather than on "literature." This is to be expected. After all, "literature" is a more or less transparent concept, whereas what is at stake in the discussion is the remit, scale, scope, objectives, and disciplinary dimensions of a literary studies expanded from the nation unto the "world." This tendency is evident in the writings of David Damrosch, Franco Moretti, and Pascale Casanova, the "Holy Trinity"—to borrow Robert Young's ironic but affectionate quip about the founding figures of postcolonial studies—of world literature.[1]

For instance, Damrosch opens *What is World Literature?* (2003)—the grouping's pivotal text—by abjuring any close and explicit attention to the concept of literature itself: "[i]n this book," he explains, "I will have relatively little interest in attempting any firm definition of literature as such."[2] Damrosch suspends this question in order to facilitate his definition of world literature as "a subset of the plenum of literature," and to thereby develop a groundwork for his now vastly influential theory of and methodology for a world literature that "encompass[es] all literary works that circulate beyond their culture of origin, either in translation or in their original language."[3] Intended at least in part to assuage anxieties about what would otherwise be the "sheer scope" of world literature among scholars, this theory and methodology proceeds by way of a series of spatial metaphors—most notably, that of "elliptical" or "double refraction"—that purport to describe the nature of the production, translation, circulation, and reception of works of literature in the world.[4] In other words, it proceeds by way of a novel and sophisticated worldly cartography of an object that is by and large given or assumed.

Moretti also dismisses the assumption that world literature is merely "literature, bigger" in his equally influential article "Conjectures on World Literature" (2000).[5] Searching for "a new critical method," he proposes instead that world literature be understood according to a world-systems model, as "[o]ne, and unequal": "*one* literature (*Weltliteratur*, singular, as in Goethe and Marx)" or "one world literary system," he elaborates, "but a system which is [. . .] profoundly unequal."[6] Despite the novelty of this approach, it again presupposes a unified and homogenous notion of literature—indeed, "*one* literature"—that, universally applicable, will serve as the basis for what Moretti proceeds to outline as his "distant reading" strategy, his "trees" and "waves" models of global literary exchange, and his understanding of literary form in terms of a "compromise" between the local and the global.[7] In Casanova's *The World Republic of Letters* (1999; trans. 2004), the situation is somewhat more complex. Casanova does in fact attend to what she calls "the invention of literature" in Western Europe from the mid-sixteenth to the nineteenth centuries in some detail, but then dubiously attributes the quality of literarity solely to metropolitan centers such as Paris, London, and New York in her account of an abstract but hierarchized world literary space.[8] I discuss the issues in this account in more detail below.[9]

It seems to me that before we ask "what is world literature?," we must first ask the apparently more basic question, "what is literature?" Specifically, we must inquire into the concept of literature on which Johann Wolfgang von Goethe and Karl Marx relied in their initial formulations of a *"Weltliteratur."* This is because Goethe and Marx have been widely cited as points of origin for the various critical approaches to this matter that have recently emerged, including those mentioned above. Indeed, although the term *Weltliteratur* was coined several decades earlier by Christoph Martin Wieland, Goethe's pronouncement to his secretary and disciple Johann Peter Eckermann in January 1827 that "[n]ational literature is now rather an unmeaning term; the epoch of World-literature is at hand" has been taken as something of a rallying cry for the recently revived field.[10] Similarly, Marx's (writing with Friedrich Engels) pronouncement in the *Manifesto of the Communist Party* (1848) that "from the numerous national and local literatures, there arises a world literature" has spurred a number of attempts to ground the field on a materialist basis attentive to its imbrications with capital.[11] Drawing on the worldliness of these projections without a thorough critical interrogation of the object they are worlding is problematic. This sort of gesture potentially reproduces whatever assumptions about or ideologies of the literary Goethe and Marx might have carried through into their ideas of *Weltliteratur* even as it builds on, enhances, or deviates from these. In my approach to world literature, I have therefore found it necessary to begin by going back to the basics and taking a closer look at the object to which this formula is referring in its original articulation.

Goethe first forwarded his idea of a *Weltliteratur* late in his career, in a series of "Conversations" conducted with Eckermann in the 1820s and published by the latter in 1836.[12] Discussing there his reading of an unnamed "Chinese novel," Goethe notes against his interlocutor's objection regarding the unfamiliarity of this material that "the Chinese," in fact, "think, act, and feel almost exactly like us" and that "we are perfectly like them."[13] He then draws a comparison between this novel and his own literary works as well as those of Samuel Richardson, Pierre-Jean de Béranger, and others, and from this point surmises that "poetry is the universal possession of mankind."[14] In this way founded on an ideal of literary universality, the "World-literature" that results from this act of comparison provides Goethe a grounds for relating or connecting German and more generally Western European literature to that of "the East" and, by extension, to the world at large. This was particularly urgent for the aging master due to his concerns about the disposition of German intellectual, cultural, and political life at the time. For in the 1820s, prior to the era of unification initiated by Otto von Bismarck, Germany remained a loose confederation of largely independent states and German literature, in his view, was correspondingly lacking in a sense of national cohesion. Finding the Romantic nationalism then being promulgated by (near-)contemporaries such as Johann Gottfried Herder, Friedrich Schlegel, August Wilhelm Schlegel, Friedrich Schleiermacher, Novalis, and others parochial and often chauvinistic, he, as John Pizer argues, thus sought through World-literature an alternative means to "imaginatively compensate" for such fragmentation.[15] In his thorough and detailed exposition of Goethe's reflections at this stage of his career, Pizer persuasively demonstrates that his notion of World-literature is therefore to be understood as "a transnational cultural ideal" that, "dialectical," is constituted "at the [. . .] interstice between the universal and the particular on the one hand, and the subnational and the transnational on the other."[16]

Goethe, as Damrosch reminds us in his editorial commentary on the relevant conversations, never produced a fully fledged theoretical account of World-literature.[17] However, a more precise sense of what he meant by this term as well as of the assumptions or ideologies by which it is undergirded might be gleaned from a consideration of his *West-Eastern Divan* (*West-östlicher Divan*, 1819). Goethe's last major collection of lyric poems, the *Divan* is inspired by the fourteenth-century Persian poet Hafiz and draws on the literary, cultural, and religious heritage of "the Orient" for both its form and its subject matter. As such, it comprises his richest *literary* exemplification and evocation of the ideals associated with his otherwise abstract concept of World-literature. Furthermore, as Edward Said has noted, the philological inquiries that prompted its composition were to infuse his later thinking on this matter.[18] In it, we find what might be considered a non-elective affinity between Goethe and his peers, one that hinges on what the text suggests to be his late (re)turn to an essentially Romantic understanding of the nature of the literary object itself.

As Goethe explains in the "Notes and Essays" he appended to the *Divan* in order to clarify his intentions, his project there is at its core one of gathering and assimilating the literary and cultural material of the Orient for the enrichment of his native German culture. Positioning himself as a "traveller" or "merchant" who displays through his poetry the "greatness, beauty, and excellence" of his foreign discoveries to his audience, he keenly seeks to contribute to a culture that has seen "so many things from the Orient [. . .] integrated into our language" as part of what Raymond Schwab has called Europe's "Oriental Renaissance" of the seventeenth to nineteenth centuries.[19] He does so not just through his comprehensive references and allusions to the Orient—its historical figures and events; its religions, especially Islam; its mythologies; its governing sensibilities regarding love, drink, and war; and so on, but also through his use of poetic form. Hafiz in particular emerges for Goethe as a paradigm for what he intends as a renewed and genuinely intercultural poetics. Referring to his model and inspiration, he writes in the "Book of Háfiz" (as translated by Martin Bidney [2010]):

> I'm hoping that I learn to write with ease
> Using your rhyme-form, repetition, too.
> First meaning, then the word I'll seek, to please;
> Let any end-tone that returns to view
> Deepen the meaning innovatively.
> No one more gifted at this feat than you.[20]

It is thus through Hafiz as Goethe strives to emulate him that he is able to "invent" for German culture a "redeeming form," and through the "eternal glowing gold" that pours forth from his quill that a specifically "German heart" is reawakened to the world.[21] In other words—those, actually, of Said in his discussion of the collection—Goethe's project in the *Divan* is less one of faithfully representing the culture of which he is clearly in awe, and more one of the "completion and confirmation" of the specifically European lyric "I" as enacted via the formal appropriation of the poetics of the displaced Oriental other to which this "I" is returning.[22] The *Divan* must therefore be read in terms of what Said calls a "Romantic redemptive project," one that in this case looks towards the world rather than the nation for the source of its redemption.[23] As its literary embodiment, it suggests that Goethe's understanding of World-literature is premised on the Romantic notion of literature as a site of sublime, transcendental self-realization and that it is comprised of the mapping of this notion onto the world in a dialectic of self and other, West and East, the local and the global. Goethe's World-literature is, then, indeed what Pizer calls "a universalized poetic framework."[24] But it is one, it is crucial to underline, that is based on a particular and, at least in the early nineteenth-century context in which he was writing and conversing, particularly *European* concept of literature.

As Pizer points out, and as confirmed by S. S. Prawer and Martin Puchner, among others, Marx almost certainly derived his ideas on *Weltliteratur* from Goethe.[25] The passage in question occurs in *The Communist Manifesto*, and is worth quoting (again) at length:

> The bourgeoisie has through its exploitation of the world-market given a cosmopolitan character to production and consumption in every country. To the great chagrin of Reactionists, it has drawn from under the feet of industry the national ground on which it stood. All old-established national industries have been destroyed or are daily being destroyed. They are dislodged by new industries, whose introduction becomes a life-and-death question for all civilized nations, by industries that no longer work up indigenous raw material, but raw material drawn from the remotest zones; industries whose products are consumed, not only at home, but in every quarter of the globe. In place of the old wants, satisfied by the productions of the country, we find new wants, requiring for their satisfaction the products of distant lands and climes. In place of the old local and national seclusion and self-sufficiency, we have intercourse in every direction, universal interdependence of nations. And as in material, so also in intellectual production. The intellectual creations of individual nations become common property. National one-sidedness and narrow-mindedness become more and more impossible, and from the numerous national and local literatures, there arises a world literature.[26]

In his fascinating and painstaking study *Karl Marx and World Literature* (1976), Prawer speculates that what was particularly congenial to Marx in Goethe's *Weltliteratur* is the latter's emphasis not on global cultural homogenization, but rather on the maintenance of the "distinctiveness and difference" of national literatures in the grand "symphony of world literature."[27] This observation corresponds well with the author's celebration of the immense creative-destructive energies of the bourgeoisie as evident in this passage and throughout the *Manifesto*. By launching an all-out assault on the national isolationism ("seclusion," "self-sufficiency," "narrow-mindedness," etc.) that would delimit production both material and intellectual to the nation, these energies force a world market and thus a world literature—both of "a cosmopolitan character"—into being, and thereby instigate the next stage of universal revolutionary history.

Puchner expands on this insight in *Poetry of the Revolution: Marx, Manifestos, and the Avant-Gardes* (2006). Discussing the *Manifesto* as itself an example of world literature, he argues that Marx was to borrow from Goethe—"the very personification of the literary bourgeoisie"—an economistic understanding of the literary text as "translatable and thus exchangeable."[28] He then, Puchner explains, radicalizes this conception: "[w]here Goethe envisions a mercantile world literature dominated by the craft of translation and captured by the image of circulating coins, Marx envisions a capitalist world literature dominated by the circulation of capital."[29] While, as I elaborate below, an interrogation of the relationship between world literature, the world market, and the circulation of capital is central to my argument as I proceed, for now I would like to point out what has thus far remained an unstated premise in the critical readings of Marx's *Weltliteratur*. Namely, Marx's reliance—the same as Goethe's—on an unexamined, uncritical concept of literature that, taken as a universal, he then maps onto the world in his account of the arising of the same therein. It is only by understanding "the numerous national and local literatures" qua "literature" that Marx's version of world literature attains its coherence. This is an issue that demands further consideration among those interested in the genealogical origins of this idea.

As a first step in this direction, it is important to bring to the surface and state unequivocally the network of unconscious suppositions regarding literature and, more broadly, the aesthetic that mediated Goethe's and Marx's formulations of a *Weltliteratur*. Further, these suppositions must be contextualized with reference to the conditions of Western European society at the time when they were thinking their ideas through. A few general and relatively uncontroversial remarks might here be made. What might be considered the prevailing structure of feeling in Western Europe during the late eighteenth- to mid-nineteenth-century epoch that saw the birth of *Weltliteratur* is, I would say, best encapsulated by Marx himself, in the dictum "[a]ll that is solid melts into air" that immediately precedes his comments on literature and culture in *The Communist Manifesto*.[30] Marx is of course referring in this passage to the dynamic, world-historical force of a bourgeoisie that had overthrown or was in the process of overthrowing the entire political, social, cultural, and economic order of the European *ancien régime*—its "fixed, fast-frozen relations," its "train of ancient and venerable prejudices and opinions"—and replaced it with the new global order of capitalist modernity.[31] Extrapolating from Marx, Marshall Berman identifies a number of other related causes and effects of this revolutionary upheaval, including: the largescale industrialization and commodification of production; a sweeping demographic shift from the country to the city; unprecedented and disorienting urban growth; the further entrenchment of the nation-state and its bureaucratic structures of power; the rise of new social movements clamoring often violently for the rights of marginalized class, race, gender, and other groupings; the further spread of European empires and anti-colonial nationalisms around the world; the establishment of a capitalist world market; and new, often world-changing intellectual, scientific, and technological innovations and discoveries.[32] As Raymond Williams, Terry Eagleton, and others have powerfully argued, it is in and only in this specific historical milieu—in Williams's words that of "capitalism and especially industrial capitalism" as it begins to implicate itself in every aspect of European and then global life— that what Eagleton describes as "[t]he modern sense of the word 'literature,'" our own, "really gets under way."[33]

It is no coincidence that the period under question saw the flourishing of Romanticism across Europe as well as the high-water mark of European aesthetic theory, and—as per M. H. Abrams in his famous account—the definitive, continent-spanning shift from a "mimetic" to an "expressive" understanding and practice of literature.[34] Indeed, these developments have been and, I think, must be read as ideological reflexes of the very same capitalist modernity against which their proponents were chafing. In Romantic poetry from England (as in William Blake, William Wordsworth, and Samuel Taylor Coleridge, etc.) to France (François-René de Chateaubriand, Alphonse de Lamartine, Gérard de Nerval, etc.) to Germany (Johann Gottfried Herder, Friedrich Schiller, Novalis, Friedrich Hölderlin, etc.), we find similar and often symbiotically influenced figurations of the individual, the sublimity of nature, and the prelapsarian past against the shortcomings and outright abuses of modern industrial society. Literature is thus (often explicitly) posited in such writings as the sole remaining enclave of a sovereign and autonomous creative imagination unfettered by the violent, alienating banality of the real. There, it achieves its apotheosis as what Eagleton calls "a whole alternative ideology" to that of modernity.[35]

This sense of literature is supported by the aesthetic theory of Immanuel Kant, Schiller, Johann Gottlieb Fichte, Friedrich Wilhelm Joseph Schelling, Georg Wilhelm Friedrich Hegel, and Coleridge, among others, then in wide circulation throughout Europe. As with literature, the aesthetic itself as well as aesthetic experience is posited by such thinkers as at a remove from the external world, as a locus of distance and differentiation in which the free play of the imaginative and cognitive faculties is kindled. Instilled by representatives of this class, this insistence upon the autonomy of the imagination (as well as on related concepts such as freedom, individuality, self-determination, legality, ownership, universality, and so forth) in the aesthetic thought of the time must be read as a function of the modern European bourgeoisie's investment in and dependence on its own autonomy from the deep-seated class, property, and production relations of the *ancien régime*. As such, to quote Eagleton at length, "[t]he construction of the modern notion of the aesthetic [...] is [...] inseparable from the construction of the dominant ideological forms of modern class-society, and indeed from a whole new form of human subjectivity appropriate to that social order."[36] As a paradigm of the aesthetic, it might thus be said that the concept of literature established in European thought and practice in the late eighteenth to the mid-nineteenth centuries is a paradigmatic ideological form of capitalist modernity.

It is this concrete and specific concept of literature born in modernity that constitutes the unconscious foundation of Goethe's and Marx's formulations of a *Weltliteratur*. As I have argued, Goethe's *Weltliteratur* hinges on a Romantic—which is to say, modern and European—understanding of the literary object, and Marx derived his ideas on literature from Goethe. In its original conception, *Weltliteratur* might thus be defined as *the projection of a reified modern notion of literature onto the world*. Or, *Weltliteratur* is *the worlding of the concept of literature attendant on modernity*. I have also argued that in the contemporary critical debate on world literature, scholars have tended to draw on the worldliness of their forbears' ideas while stopping short at an interrogation of the object they are worlding. In effect, they thereby replicate the assumptions and ideologies harbored by the earlier conceptions. As the upshot of the genealogy critique that I have outlined, I therefore propose that global capitalist modernity be identified as the unconscious—the repressed origin and condition of possibility—of world literature as concept, discourse, practice, institution, and discipline in the present day.

* * *

To thoroughly grasp world literature in relation to its origins in global capitalist modernity, it is necessary to draw on world-systems theory. Certainly, the link between world literature and modernity is suggested in Goethe and Marx. As we have seen, Goethe's emphasis on the translatability and exchangeability of literary texts is taken up by Marx and Engels in their conception of a market-oriented, cosmopolitan world literature anchored in and orchestrated by capital. Yet despite his many forays into fields of inquiry beyond the literary such as the natural sciences as well as his interventions into the political and religious controversies of his day, Goethe is not considered to have been a significant economic thinker. And Marx's own writings on non-Western politics, societies, and economies amount to a few brief passages on "the Asiatic mode of production" in the *Grundrisse* (1857–8) and elsewhere as well as a mere (!) 400 or so pages of journalism on international matters in venues such as the *New York Daily Tribune*.[37] Moreover, their accounts of literature and thus of world literature are themselves premised on modernity as their unconscious condition, and so fall short of attending to it critically and reflexively. World-systems theory provides the fullest and richest reading of capitalism in its genuinely global dimensions, and is therefore foundational to an understanding of world literature in relation to its historical contexts.

World-systems theory as developed most influentially by Immanuel Wallerstein (who actually prefers the term "analysis" over "theory") is a macro-scale and interdisciplinary perspective in the social sciences that seeks to comprehend and explain the nature of the political, social, cultural, and economic totality over the *longue durée* with reference to the world rather than the nation-state as its primary unit of analysis. It originated in the early 1970s, in response to what Wallerstein and others found to be the deeply objectionable political and intellectual climate of the United States during the post-1945 / Cold War era. Of special concern were the ramifications of this climate in and for the US university. As a corollary to the country's newfound global primacy and its associated efforts towards global statecraft in light of the Soviet "threat," this period saw massive public (via the US federal government) as well as private (via corporate foundations) investment in the establishment and promotion of the new discipline of area studies there. Sharply inflecting the social sciences in particular, the outcome was a widespread ideological privileging of modernization and development theory in regard to the Third World. Against these trends, and spurred by the revolutionary momentum of 1968, Wallerstein drew on a combination of *Annales* school historiography (especially its figurehead, Fernand Braudel), Marxism, and dependency theory in order to reinvent the social sciences and provide a more incisive and substantial account of the global predicament, past, present, and future. Coming to monumental fruition in his four-volume opus *The Modern World-System* (1974–2011), the result was a radical theoretical and methodological framework for social research conducted on a genuinely global scale that is among the most powerful currently available to thought. Today, world-systems theory is firmly established in the US academy, and its research agenda is actively pursued at the Fernand Braudel Center for the Study of Economies, Historical Systems, and Civilizations at SUNY Binghamton as well as in a number of scholarly publications (including the *Journal of World-Systems Research* and the Braudel Center's *Review*).³⁸

As Wallerstein explains, and as indicated by his hyphenation of "world" and "system," world-systems theory is concerned not with "systems, economies, empires *of the* (whole) world, but [with] systems, economies, empires *that are* a world."³⁹ That is to say, it conceives of a world-system as "a spatial / temporal zone which cuts across many political and cultural units, one that represents an integrated zone of activity and institutions which obey certain systemic rules."⁴⁰ Or, as he puts it in his landmark study *The Modern World-System I: Capitalist Agriculture and the Origins of the European World-Economy in the Sixteenth Century* (1974):

> A world-system is a social system, one that has boundaries, structures, member groups, rules of legitimation, and coherence. Its life is made up of the conflicting forces which hold it together by tension, and tear it apart as each group seeks eternally to remold it to its advantage. It has the characteristics of an organism, in that it has a life-span over which its characteristics change in some respects and remain stable in others. One can define its structures as being at different times strong or weak in terms of the internal logic of its functioning. [. . .] [L]ife within it is largely self-contained, and [. . .] the dynamics of its development are largely internal.⁴¹

Specifically, world-systems theory is interested in the *modern* world-system, what Wallerstein calls the capitalist world-economy. Wallerstein dates the origin of this system to the long sixteenth century, a period which saw the European discovery of the Americas (1492), the transition in the majority of Europe from a feudal to a (proto-)capitalist economy, and the establishment there of an interstate arrangement (the "European world-economy") based on the notion of the sovereign state as enshrined in the Peace of Westphalia (1648).⁴² This combination of factors (capitalism, the sovereign state, global territorial reach), he argues, was to eventually encompass the rest of the world *as* the modern world-system.⁴³

As a capitalist world-economy, the modern world-system is defined by Wallerstein as "a large geographic zone within which there is a division of labor and hence significant internal exchange of basic or essential goods as well as flows of capital and labor."[44] It is not overseen by a single political institution or ideology, but rather comprises "many political units" which are connected to one another in the interstate compact.[45] Likewise, it contains "many cultures and groups" which speak many languages, practice many religions, and differ in their everyday rituals and routines.[46] That is, both political and cultural heterogeneity are constituent features of the modern world-system. What unifies the system on a global scale is what Wallerstein calls the "worldwide division of labor" on which it was built.[47] By this, he means the forces and relations of production of the world-economy as relationally distributed across the world-economy as a whole. Divided between capital-intensive production and labor-intensive production, the world-economy is thus divided between what he, following Argentinian dependency theorist Raúl Prebisch, calls "core" and "peripheral" zones. Interdependent, each of these zones has a distinct economic role within the system, and thereby develops different structures and institutions of class, labor, production, and political organization. Each profits unequally from it. Precisely, the power hierarchy that ensues between the core and the periphery as determined by their relative degrees of industrial, intellectual, scientific, technological, military, and other forms of development ensures "a constant flow of surplus-value from the producers of peripheral products to the producers of core-like products" in a process that, extrapolating from Marx, Wallerstein calls "unequal exchange."[48] The core thus dominates and exploits the periphery in an endless process of capitalist accumulation on a global scale. In this book, I refer to this process as "global capitalist modernity."

In this usage, I allude to Fredric Jameson's notion of "a singular modernity" in his 2002 book of the same title. There, Jameson takes aim at the contemporary resurgence of the discourse of modernity. He identifies its "ideologues" as not just the rebranded modernizers-of-old (such as Anthony Giddens) whose Third Way politics had recently come to the fore, but also as the sorts of postmodernist and postcolonialist intellectuals who insist upon the formula of "'alternate' or 'alternative' modernities."[49] His issue with this sensibility is that by suggesting that "there can be a modernity for everybody which is different from the standard or hegemonic Anglo-Saxon model" and that "you can fashion your own modernity differently" as, for example, "a Latin-American kind," "an Indian kind," "an African kind," and so forth, it effaces the universal and univocal logic of global capitalism by which all such modernities are initiated in the first place.[50] This is *not* to say that modernity doesn't manifest differently in the different contexts in which it takes root (a qualification also evident in Wallerstein's "many political units," "many cultures and groups," and so on). Only that the emphasis must be placed on the capitalist imperative at the heart of modernity per se as it spreads across and infiltrates the remainder of the globe. Hence, a "singular" modernity that is global in reach and capitalist in orientation—or, "global capitalist modernity."

Before moving on, it is important to underline, as Wallerstein repeatedly does, that "core" and "periphery" are not absolute, reified concepts, but rather *"relational,"* and can only be understood in relation to one another in the context of the whole.[51] This point is important to emphasize because much of the criticism that has been levelled against world-systems theory by humanists in particular has tended to assume that each of these terms refers to a specific, unchanging set of states (Western European and North American on the one hand, Third World on the other), one of which exerts perpetual dominance and authority over the other. Such reference, the argument goes, discursively reproduces the hegemony of the core, and thus acts as an ideological bolster for structures of global inequality and exploitation. This is not the case. Firstly, "core" and "periphery" refer not to states but rather to production processes, and therefore allow for the relative position of states within the world-economy to vary over time. Secondly, the entire state-centric basis of these and other attacks is misguided. As discussed above, world-systems theory as originally devised by Wallerstein and company was intended to move research in the social sciences away from a narrow, state-centered focus and towards a global perspective whereby the widescale and deep historical movements of capital could be understood both in themselves and for their impact on the individual constituents of the system. Much new scholarship in the humanities—not least in the field of world literature itself—has been moving in a similar direction. It seems to me that humanities scholars would be well served to shed any residual assumptions they might have about world-systems theory, and explore with fresh eyes the benefits that might accrue for their own work from engagement with such a powerful, flexible, and encompassing model. As David Palumbo-Liu, Bruce Robbins, and Nirvana Tanoukhi put it in their major recent volume on this matter, *Immanuel Wallerstein and the Problem of the World: System, Scale, Culture* (2011), world-systems theory provides "a well-developed vision of what the world scale means" at a moment when the "gravitational pull" of such a scale has become nigh inescapable.[52]

Of particular relevance to my argument as it unfolds is the account world-systems theory provides of the "incorporation" of the periphery into the logic and parameters of global capitalist modernity. Wallerstein and Terence Hopkins provide a useful overview of this process in a special issue of the Braudel Center's *Review* on "Incorporation into the World-Economy: How the World-System Expands" (1987). Following Wallerstein's description of the origins of the modern world-system in the sixteenth century as summarized above, when the world-system consisted of Western Europe and Iberian America, Hopkins and Wallerstein recount in this text that it consequently expanded to North America and the Caribbean in the seventeenth century; Russia, the Ottoman Empire, the Indian subcontinent, and West Africa in the late eighteenth century; and other parts of Asia, Africa, and Oceania in the second half of the nineteenth century. The purpose of this expansion, they continue, was "to 'incorporate' the [hitherto unincorporated] zone" into the capitalist world-economy, "to make what was external internal," so that productive and other activity there was made to conform with and fully participate in the ongoing functioning of the capitalist world-economy—to, that is, enlarge the territorial compass of capitalist productive activity and thus of potential sources of surplus-value as necessary for the global accumulation of capital.[53] In order to effect this incorporation, two things were necessary: "to transform the sphere of production, such that there were created some major production activities which became integrated into, 'essential' to, the axial division of labor" and "to transform the sphere of governance, such that there were created state structures that functioned as members of, and within the rules of, the interstate system."[54] As Hopkins and Wallerstein proceed to elaborate with their co-authors via a range of real-world examples including the Caribbean, the Ottoman Empire, and southern Africa, the incorporation of the periphery is thus historically achieved.

Samir Amin, perhaps the foremost world-systems theorist of the periphery, has accentuated the violence and disruption brought about there through incorporation, which for him are inherent features of this process. In *Unequal Development: An Essay on Social Formations of Peripheral Capitalism* (1973; trans. 1976), one of his early classics, he charts the general lineaments of this upheaval in nine theses. In what for my purposes are the most important of these, he describes trade as an "onslaught from without," one that causes "certain crucial retrogressions" to take place in the economies of pre-capitalist formations; the resultant prioritization of export activities there as a "distortion" that leads to the "ruin" of traditional local economies and industries; the possibility of new economic, industrial, and other forms of development and growth as severely delimited, in a perpetual state of "underdevelopment" due to the same prostration before the export market; and the levels of unemployment, income inequality, national disunity, state bureaucracy and autocracy, and so forth that stem from these mutations as correspondingly "extreme."[55] In short, Amin describes the fate of the periphery as it undergoes incorporation—what, following Andre Gunder Frank, he calls "the development of underdevelopment"—as quasi-apocalyptic in severity.[56]

Naturally, the process of incorporation is an extremely complicated affair. It takes place in different ways in each distinct zone of incorporation, according to the specificities of the local political, social, cultural, and economic contexts that are being subjected to its demands. Each instance has its own history and its own narrative, and is mediated by the varying practices and institutions of its various agents. In the historical span of the modern world-system, such agents have included trade in general, through the exertion of economic power by stronger (capitalist) over weaker (pre-capitalist) zones; colonial and imperial hegemons, through the exertion of direct political and military power; their neocolonial and neoimperial variants, through the exertion of indirect political and military power; modernizers-from-within, through the political and military authority of autocrats, comprador classes, local elites, and others; and international entities like the World Bank and the International Monetary Fund, through "structural adjustment programs" and other financial mechanisms that are often themselves considered neoimperialist in effect, among many other examples. Even today, the discourse of "austerity" that came into wide circulation in the wake of the Global Financial Crisis of 2007–8 might be read in this light, given its deployment among especially European governments as a thin veil for the privatization and thus capitalization of hitherto nationally owned industries (most flagrantly, in Greece). Despite the multiplicity of routes this process has taken, world-systems theory teaches and history itself seems to verify that the end result is the same—the incorporation of the periphery into global capitalist modernity. While further theoretical consideration of the intricacies of incorporation as detailed by world-systems theorists is outside the scope of this book, I return at various points to this work as it pertains to the Middle Eastern contexts that I primarily address.

* * *

Beyond what has been covered in the existing world-systems scholarship, I would now like to suggest that the process whereby the periphery is incorporated into the logic and parameters global capitalist modernity is *facilitated by* as well as *enacted in* the domain of literature. By this, I mean that in addition to the restructuring of political, social, and economic life in the periphery as highlighted by world-systems theorists, the incorporation process also comprises the restructuring of, broadly, intellectual and cultural life. Just as "the sphere of governance" and "the sphere of production" require transformation according to the needs of the world-economy, so too does what might be considered "the sphere of culture."[57] Specifically, I locate the transformation to which this sphere is subject in the shifts in the definition of literature witnessed in historical instances of incorporation. As I proceed to demonstrate, intrinsic and, most radically, *essential* to the incorporation process is the export, internalization, and reproduction of the modern, European concept of literature discussed above in the periphery. Its establishment there helps lay the ideological and institutional foundations of modernity in the periphery, and it thus acts as a support structure for the "modernization" and "development" of other spheres of activity. Furthermore, it is also representative of the wider workings of incorporation per se; through it, we might perceive the conflicts and contradictions, the dialectical thrust of its machinations as these pertain to political, social, cultural, and economic life in its totality. In short, what I am proposing is that the definition of world literature forwarded above—the worlding of the concept of literature attendant on modernity—identifies not just the implications of an idea as originally conceived, but moreover a *world-historical process* by which that idea was made possible in the first place and which that idea further advances. This process is best understood through or as an extension of the account of incorporation provided by world-systems theory. Finally, I am correspondingly claiming and I aim to demonstrate that world literature today is in its many senses and manifestations undergirded by this specific historical process.

In making this argument, I take my cue and my inspiration from the recent work of Aamir Mufti. In his article "Orientalism and the Institution of World Literatures" (2010) and book *Forget English!: Orientalisms and World Literatures* (2016), Mufti discusses the process of the codification and classification of world textualities as literature in the modern, European sense of the late eighteenth to mid-nineteenth centuries. He identifies this as an offshoot of colonial history, specifically of the accompanying heritage of Orientalist philology as practiced by figures such as Johann Gottfried Herder, William Jones, August Wilhelm Schlegel, and Goethe and as analyzed by Said, Schwab, and others. Acting as an ideological complement to colonialism as it sought to refashion societies around the world, the role of Orientalist philology in this regard, he continues, was to produce and establish "a method and a system for classifying and evaluating diverse forms of textuality, now all processed and codified uniformly as *literature*."[58] Mufti sees this Orientalist system of knowledge production at the heart of the Goethean and Marxian concept of *Weltliteratur*, a concept which from its very inception was thus deeply imbricated with the project of colonial modernity. As he puts it, "world literature had its origins in the structures of colonial power and in particular the revolution in knowledge practices and humanistic culture more broadly initiated by Orientalist philology in the late eighteenth and early nineteenth centuries, which developed in varying degrees of proximity to the colonial process."[59] Contemporary world literature, he concludes, is premised on this repressed heritage. Destined to repeat the moment of its formation, it therefore functions as a sort of compulsive sorting algorithm or interface whose end is to render the world's vast and heterogeneous range of practices of writing across the millennia universally legible as literature. Ever-expanding, it is a mechanism of global cultural appropriation, homogenization, and commodification. In both texts, Mufti expounds this argument with reference to South Asia as his primary case study, where he reads the philologically induced division between Hindi and Urdu during the colonial period as the linguistic and literary platform for the national, ethnic, and religious divisions that were to lead to the Partition of India in 1947.[60]

It is difficult to overstate the centrality and significance of Mufti's insight that world literature is based on the production of world textualities as literature to my argument as I proceed. Indeed, I consider Mufti's work here to be the linchpin of my own. However, in my account, I diverge from his in one crucial respect. Whereas for Mufti world literature is a product of Orientalism per se—as he says, "a genealogy of world literature leads to Orientalism"—for myself, it is a product of what world-systems theory delineates as the broader, more encompassing analytical and historical category of global capitalist modernity.[61] This distinction is most clearly illustrated by considering Mufti's comments on the world-systems approach in *Forget English!* There, he identifies a schism, often hostile, in the world literature debate between proponents of the "center-periphery" model furnished by world-systems theory and those more reliant on an "empire-colony" model drawn from postcolonial theory, one which stems from their different relationships to the historical as well as their distinct disciplinary backgrounds.[62] He then suggests that this tension be considered "a productive one," and proposes in his own work to "alternate between these usages, using each one to modify and enrich the perspectives made possible by the other."[63]

This resolution demonstrates a characteristic intellectual flexibility and generosity on Mufti's part. The problem with it, however, is that it appears to gloss over or downplay what from the world-systems perspective at least is the fundamental incommensurability between its own and the alternate historical model of, broadly, a postcolonial studies that posits "empire-colony" as its primary unit of analysis. As we have seen, world-systems theory comprehends the history of empire only within the wider purview of capitalism's millennial trajectory of global self-replication, as but one of many agents—albeit uniquely momentous—of this process. It seems to me that "alternating" between the world-systems and the postcolonial frameworks is conceptually as well as historiographically unsustainable, and that the prior confers the substantial advantage of not just allowing for, but also *necessitating* comprehensive research into imperial history (as in the work of the several theorists discussed above) as a key aspect of a trajectory that stretches to the present, when capitalism's global ascendency is all but secured.

More to the point, it is only within the historical unfolding of global capitalist modernity that world literature as I have defined it can be understood in its properly global remit. Certainly, Orientalism plays a pivotal role in this process, in the incorporation as literature of various practices and modalities of textual and indeed oral expression from at least parts of non-Western world. This is as much the case in the Middle Eastern contexts that I address as it is in the South Asian ones that Mufti addresses. However, Orientalism as classically evaluated by Edward Said, for one, refers to a Western European, principally British, French, and German academic discipline and intellectual-institutional discourse that is concerned with, well, the Orient, meaning first and foremost the Middle East and India in the eighteenth to nineteenth centuries, and then expanding to the Far East in the twentieth.[64] What, we might ask, of sub-Saharan Africa, or of Meso-America, or of indigenous communities from North America to Oceania? How can the incorporation of their modes of textual and oral expression be accounted for by an analysis focalized around the heritage of a discipline dedicated to an entirely different part of the world?

I of course acknowledge that Mufti is discussing Orientalism as a "cultural logic," a "system of cultural mapping" that, as grounds for the concept of world literature, determines the manifestation as literature of textualities and oralities from parts of the world not traditionally associated with the Orient.[65] My point, though—and this is where I deviate from Mufti—is that world literature is also a historical process that saw in concrete and verifiable ways the diffusion and establishment of literature all over the world as part of a wider process of incorporation into modernity. The Orientalism argument cannot concretely account for the mechanisms and intricacies of world literature's historical constitution beyond the Orient, as the attention of the Orientalists Mufti foregrounds rarely directly stretches there. Even in the Middle East itself, literature, as I will show, emerged in a substantially different way—rather, in many different ways—than in South Asia, as more an *internalized* appropriation among local elites intent upon modernization than as the external imposition of Orientalist scholars and colonial administrators that Mufti traces. World-systems theory, especially its account of incorporation, helps us perceive in its totality the process whereby literature is projected onto the world—*including the role that Orientalism plays in this process*—and to recognize it as constitutive of world literature.[66] In my view, world-systems theory thus provides a more powerful and comprehensive framework for continued research in this direction.

* * *

As indicated above, I map the incorporation of the periphery into modernity as facilitated by and enacted in literature in three moments, what I call the moments of "exchange," "internalization," and "reproduction." Again, it is important to emphasize that the process I am describing is not a literary analogue or superstructural by-product of incorporation understood as a fundamentally economic phenomenon; rather, it is an intrinsic or essential element of incorporation. Before detailing this process as it pertains to literature in the Middle East, I will first outline its constituent moments in the abstract, in terms of something like what Moretti calls the "law[s] of literary evolution" (though, as will become clear, I strongly contest some of the implications of the "evolution" metaphor).[67] Finally, it should also be noted that I do not consider these moments to operate in a self-identical manner in every historical instance of incorporation, or even that each is necessarily valid in or applicable to the process. In any particular instance, the sequence of moments might conceivably be different, the brunt of the process might be placed on one or another of these moments, or one or another of them might be altogether absent. Derived primarily from my Middle

Eastern case studies, across which it does appear to work in remarkably similar ways, what I am presenting here is perhaps more a set of principles than a set of "laws" that offers a general framework for analysis of the literary dimensions of incorporation on a global scale and that may be fine-tuned in light of variations in this process on a case-to-case basis.

By *exchange*, I refer to the trade in literature between the core and the periphery as precipitated by and as an extension of the histories of exploration; political, social, cultural, and economic interaction; colonialism; imperialism; Orientalism; and so forth. Profoundly unequal, literary exchange is like its economic correlate dominated by the core. It comprises on the one hand the export of the literature and literary products of the core to the periphery, and, on the other, the extraction, refinement, and import as literature of the raw textual and oral material of the periphery to the core. For literary exchange to be possible, there must be a unit of equivalence or common currency between core and periphery. Introduced, unsurprisingly, by the core, this unit of equivalence is the concept of literature itself.

Although he doesn't use this term (at least not the sense that I am using it), Mufti has provided the most thoroughgoing illustration of what I am calling literary exchange between core and periphery in the texts mentioned above. Focusing on South Asia, Mufti chronicles in these texts how India's multiple cultures of writing across the millennia were amalgamated into a single idea of (Indian) literature in the late eighteenth to mid-nineteenth centuries, and then transmitted and sold to the West via representative works such as Kalidasa's *Śākuntala* (*Abhijñānaśākuntalam*, c. fifth century) as part of the Oriental Renaissance there. This process, he continues, was instigated by Orientalists and colonial administrators such as, most notably, William Jones, and also including Warren Hastings, Nathaniel Bradley Halhed, Henry Thomas Colebrook, and Charlie Wilkins, among others. Upon his arrival in Bengal as Supreme Court Judge for the East India Company in 1783, Jones encountered what Mufti calls a "philological sublime" in the apparently infinite diversity of textual matter (reflecting multiple languages, cultures, and religions) on the subcontinent.[68] For the effective functioning of a unified colonial legal and administrative apparatus, he had therefore to unify such disparate matter in an "idea of

Indian literature" and thus in that of "India" as "a unique *national* civilization."[69] In this way, Mufti identifies the birth of what he calls "nation-thinking" in the subcontinent in the domain of literature.[70] Through his analysis, we can clearly perceive the relationship between literary exchange and the wider process of incorporation as delineated by Wallerstein et al. as a *reciprocal* one, as one of interdependence and intertwinement rather than of base / superstructure determinism.

By *internalization*, I refer to the appropriation, adoption, and, often, adaptation of the modern, European concept of literature in the periphery as a feature of the wider project of nation- and state-building associated with incorporation. Driven by local political and intellectual elites under the influence of the core whether direct (as in, most clearly, colonial contexts such as India and Nigeria) or indirect (as in non-colonized yet relatively "underdeveloped" contexts such as early Republican Turkey), internalization establishes literature as a pivotal site of modern national identity, community, and coherence that gives distinctive shape to the nation-state among its peers in the modern interstate system. Often in coordination or collaboration with other institutions of the emergent state, it establishes literature as an institution of the state. In so doing, it displaces local practices of textual and oral expression as remnants of what is consequently rendered the pre-modern past that the state is striving to transcend. In short, the internalization of literature there contributes not insignificantly to the laying of the ideological and institutional foundations of modernity in the periphery.

At this point, I part ways most explicitly with Casanova and what has thus far been in some respects her comparable model of global literary relations. In *The World Republic of Letters*, Casanova, as noted above, maps an abstract but hierarchized world literary space dominated by metropolitan centers such as Paris, London, and New York. While autonomous, independent of their relative political, economic, or military power, the "literary domination" of these centers, she argues, is nevertheless founded on their accumulated cultural capital as well as on the global reach of French and English as ensured by their nations' colonial histories.[71] Home to the most prestigious literary institutions—the major publishing houses, the major-language translation industry, the global review and criticism industries, it is through one or more of these centers that texts by writers on the margins of world literary space (those that are written in a minor language or otherwise embedded within their national culture) must pass in order to attain international recognition. In a process of what Casanova calls "consecration" or "*littérisation*," it is there, and only there, she claims, that these sorts of texts first come into existence as literature per se, that they attain "the condition of literature."[72] In contrast to commentators who dismiss Casanova's topography of world literary space as too oriented around Paris or, more generally, Europe, I tend to agree with Mufti's counter-intuitive critique that her account is in fact *not Paris- or Eurocentric enough*.[73] That is to say, Casanova radically underestimates the world-historical role of the literature she elsewhere discusses as having been "invented" in Europe.[74] As I have suggested, it is precisely this concept of literature that is internalized in the periphery as part of the incorporation process. As I will show, it is this process rather than metropolitan "consecration" that determines the manifestation and legibility of what is thereby *already* the literature of the periphery in the world.

By *reproduction*, I refer to that of the forms of modernity—paradigmatically, the novel, the lyric poem, and the stage play—in the periphery as made possible by and on the grounds of the establishment in literature of the ideological and institutional foundations of modernity there. In other words, I am suggesting that it is in the literature established in and as (an aspect of) the incorporation process that modern literary forms first arise in the periphery. Crucially, these forms do not cohabit and coexist in the periphery with what their emergence renders as their pre-modern predecessors, local forms of textual and oral expression. Rather, and just as the form of the nation-state supersedes earlier forms of political, social, and economic organization (indeed, as part of this process), they *supersede* local forms in a dialectical struggle over culture and representation that, both facilitating and enacting its wider dialectic, leads inevitably to modernity.

It is here that the implications of my focalization of the contemporary world literature debate through the lens of literature become perhaps most pronounced. For this analysis reveals a dimension of violence, a struggle for domination and supremacy in and as inherent to the global spread of modern literary forms that thus far appears to have been occluded or skirted in the work of the foremost theorist of world literature as a system, Franco Moretti, as well as, to some extent, in the world literature debate more generally. Borrowing from Jameson, Moretti explains in the article noted above that such spread and the formal variations that accrue from it are to be accounted for in terms of "compromise," specifically "compromise" between "foreign form, local material[,] and local form."[75] From the perspective of the argument that I have set out, this account is quite problematic. "Compromise" requires—and Moretti does conduct his brief though illustrative readings of a range of novels from around the world on the assumption that this is the case—that parties are on somewhat of an equal footing, that each at least in principle is able to participate in and contribute to reaching an agreement or middle ground between otherwise conflicting positions. As I have tried to argue and as I will soon substantiate, the forms of modernity hold no quarter for their predecessors—as its functionaries and embodiments, it is their world-historical charge precisely to overthrow and overtake them in the dialectic of modernity as it unfolds across the world. Furthermore, "compromise" seems a dubious term from the world-systems perspective both conceptually (insofar as world-systems theory emphasizes the carnage wrought upon the periphery in the incorporation process that I am arguing extends into the domain of literature) and empirically (insofar as historical instances of incorporation corroborate this point).

So then, instead of "compromise," we have in the global spread of modern literary forms a hitherto underexplored history of violence whose end is their worldwide hegemony. In the Middle Eastern contexts that I address, literature thus supersedes the classical Arabic-Islamic concept of "*adab*," and its forms—the novel, the lyric poem, and the stage play—those that have traditionally issued from and been embedded within the life-world of the latter. In its classical sense, *adab* and its forms elide the modern distinction between "literary" (fictional, imaginative, creative, etc.) and "non-literary" (factual, historical, biographical, scholarly, instructional, informational, etc.) writing. However, among the multitude of the forms of writing encompassed by this concept that we would today consider more explicitly "literary"—those that were specifically overtaken and rendered obsolete by their modern variants—are: various forms of poetry (such as the *qaṣīda*, the *ghazal*, the *mathnawī*, and so forth); the genre of fictional prose narrative known as the *maqāma*; the folk tale (or *qiṣṣa*), whether realistic (the *ḥikāya*) or in the shape of a fable featuring animals or mythological creatures (the *mathal*); the fictional or otherwise embellished travelogue (the *riḥla*); the philosophical or mystical allegory; other genres of Sufi literature, most prominently poetry; and many others.[76] While consideration of the concrete historical process of literary incorporation as it pertains to other parts of the world is beyond the scope of this book, it seems to me important and worthwhile to pursue this sort of analysis along the lines that I have set out.

Through the moments of exchange, internalization, and reproduction, it is possible to reconstruct in outline the process by which the worlding of the concept—and, now, *forms*—of literature attendant on modernity is historically achieved. I would like to propose that as concept, discourse, practice, institution, and discipline, contemporary world literature is both *premised on* and *reproduces* this process. For something like world literature to be a coherent category of scholarship, education, publishing, and even writing, of the literary and academic industries, it must necessarily assume its object—literature—as a universal. This assumption, I have argued, has been prompted by a history which has seen precisely the universalization of this object. It seems to me that the unreflexive deployment of this paradigm in the many professional and institutional venues where it is currently advocated reproduces and perpetuates the assumption of universality, and thereby further entrenches its logic around the world and as a lens for *reading* "the world."

It also seems that much of the criticism that has been levelled against the world literature paradigm by its opponents registers, whether explicitly or not, an anxiety about this same assumption and the historical process by which it has been enabled. For Djelal Kadir, world literature is defined by a transitive practice of "worlding" that is equivalent to "imperial moves that circumscribe the world into manageable global boundedness"—we "who do the worlding," he observes, "arrogate to ourselves not only the verb's subject agency but [also] the world itself."[77] For Aamir Mufti, it, whether conceived as a body of literary works or as a category of research and scholarship, is defined by "the global relations of force that historically the concept has put in play and simultaneously hidden from view."[78] And for Emily Apter, it, relying upon "a translatability assumption" and the "endorsement of cultural equivalence and substitutability," is defined by "the entrepreneurial, bulimic drive to anthologize and curricularize the world's cultural resources."[79] While these lines of attack might be taken as reason enough to abandon world literature altogether, I (along with many of those who articulated them in the first place), however, see an opportunity to push the paradigm towards a more rigorously reflexive, critical, and engaged plateau. As I have argued, world literature understood as a world-historical process illuminates in novel and fascinating ways the workings of global capitalist modernity in all of its dimensions, from its origins to the present. Through it, we might glean not only new insight into modernity, but also new frameworks for critical thought and practice in response to its unrelenting crusade.

* * *

To offer a brief recap of my argument thus far, I have defined world literature as the worlding of the concept of literature attendant on modernity. As a world-historical process, it is constituted in the superseding of the local and particular in favor of the global and universal, specifically in that of local forms by the forms of modernity—the novel, the lyric poem, and the stage play. As these forms take root in the periphery, world literature facilitates and enacts in literature the incorporation of the periphery into global capitalist modernity. From these premises, it follows that in world literature as an agent of modernity, the forms of modernity *produce* local forms as *pre-modern, external, other*. Local forms are excised from the narrative of modernity altogether, reinterpreted and rewritten in terms of literature, and / or preserved as artifacts of a pre-modern past. The nature of this process and its significance for our understanding of world literature is elucidated by an analysis of form.

In undertaking this analysis, I take my bearings from the broadly Hegelian Marxist tradition of Georg Lukács, Theodor Adorno, Walter

Benjamin, Fredric Jameson, and Franco Moretti. I find this tradition to be the most seriously and methodically invested in questions of form vis-à-vis the political, social, cultural, and economic totality from which it arises and of which it is the expression. My starting point is Adorno's injunction in *Aesthetic Theory* (1970; trans. 1997) that "form" be recognized "as sedimented content."[80] Form, he continues, is produced in what amounts to a threefold dialectical movement of *abstraction, mediation,* and *crystallization* in relation to content. With content understood as "the world" as such—"empirical experience," "empirical reality," "the empirical," the "external," "what simply exists," form engages with and gives shape to its content at a remove from it.[81] It is in a movement of "stepping back"—or, abstraction—from the world that form adopts its stance towards it.[82] In this movement, form mediates the conflicts that, definitive of the world, appear "immediate and as absolute cleavages" there (in Marxism, those of social antagonism in general and of class conflict in particular).[83] Indeed, the mediation of conflict in form "becomes the for-itself of consciousness [. . .] by the act of stepping back from it."[84] This is what Jameson, in *The Political Unconscious: Narrative as a Socially Symbolic Act* (1981), describes as "the imaginary resolution [in form] of a real contradiction" or, more generally, as the "symbolic enactment of the social within the formal and the aesthetic."[85] Form, to return to Adorno, is thus "crystallize[d]" in and as its abstraction from and mediation of "[t]he unsolved antagonisms of reality."[86]

To flesh out this rather abstract and intentionally generic account of form derived from Adorno, I turn to the classic example in the Marxist tradition, the commodity as analyzed by Marx in *Capital, Volume I* (1867). In this example, the threefold dialectical movement I have sketched can be seen in action, as it were. In the very first sentence of *Capital*, Marx identifies the commodity as the "elementary form" (*Elementarform*) of the capitalist mode of production.[87] In what might be regarded as a mapping of the form / content dialectic outlined above onto this form, the commodity is distinguished from its physical body—the mere "thing" or "object" that is produced for consumption—by means of its exchangeability on the open market.[88] Exchange requires a unit of equivalence between the things being exchanged—a "third thing, which is itself neither the one nor the other," and it is with reference to this thing that the commodity acquires its market-, or, exchange-value, its very existence as a commodity.[89] As the commodity's exchange-value is determined not by the usefulness of its body but rather by its substitutability for others of its kind, its exchange— and, by extension, exchange in general—is premised on an "abstraction" from its use-value.[90] Abstraction from its use-value leads to abstraction also from the material determinants of its use-value—namely, the labor that has gone into producing it and thus the relations of production within which labor is embedded. So it is that in the commodity form, "the definite social relation between men [. . .] assumes [. . .], for them, the fantastic form [*die phantasmagorische Form*] of a relation between things."[91] As *the* form of capitalist society, the commodity is thus crystallized in and as its abstraction from and mediation of the relations of production that pertain under capitalism. Its role is to mystify the social antagonism at the heart of capitalism, and to thereby bind the system into a coherent totality in ideological as well as economic terms. Generalizing from Marx, Lukács describes the social totality that emerges from the commodity form in terms of "reification."[92]

As a model for the analysis of form in general, Marx's analysis of the commodity seems beset by an inbuilt limitation—that it is pertinent only to the social formation, capitalism, wherein the commodity is dominant. As Lukács puts it, the commodity is "a *specific* problem of our age, the age of modern capitalism."[93] Furthermore, Marx's focus on the commodity's function of mystifying the specific social antagonisms of capitalism appears to have infiltrated the conceptual apparatus and very language developed by his heirs in their otherwise wider-ranging approaches to form, including its literary and cultural varieties. I have indicated something of the privilege accorded to the language of "conflict," "contradiction," and "antagonism" in the accounts of form provided by Adorno and Jameson. This seeps quite explicitly into their readings of literary and cultural texts. Moretti partakes in the same in the "Conjectures" article, where, alluding to Jameson, he discusses "forms" as "the abstract of social relationships" and "formal analysis" as "an analysis of power."[94]

It would obviously be untenable to claim that these accounts stem exclusively from Marx's of the commodity, and therefore from the conditions particular to capitalist modernity. Yet their overriding emphasis on form as a site of the mystification or resolution of conflict does give one pause. Does form always function in such a way and towards such ends? Specifically, is an account of form seemingly rooted in and certainly acquiring it contours from the critique of capitalism sufficiently general to understand its workings in the pre- or non-capitalist social formations of the periphery identified and investigated by world-systems theory? By raising this question, I do not intend to suggest that conflict, contradiction, and antagonism are not constituent features of the sorts of peripheral zones considered by Wallerstein, Amin, and others. I do, however, want to distance myself from the assumption that an analysis of form in one way or another related to its capitalist manifestations can be retrospectively deployed for the reading of form in contexts that precede or are otherwise external to capitalism. In my own, I therefore wish to retain what I have delineated as the threefold dialectical model of abstraction, mediation, and crystallization derived from Adorno (hence my stress on these terms in the foregoing summary), but at the same time to de-emphasize the capitalism-specific critique into whose service this model has hitherto been put. In other words, I want to expand the definition of form beyond (though also including) mystification or resolution, so as to be able to theoretically encompass other expressive possibilities suggested by the concept—if any are in fact conceivable—in especially peripheral contexts.

In developing this account of form, I have found recourse to Edmund Husserl's concept of "life-world" (*Lebenswelt*) particularly useful. Husserl presents this concept late in his career, in his last book *The Crisis of European Sciences and Transcendental Phenomenology: An Introduction to Phenomenological Philosophy* (1936; trans. 1954). Through it, he seeks to resolve a contradiction he had come to see in his earlier method of phenomenological reduction (which, highly influential, had helped establish phenomenology as a distinct branch of philosophy)—namely, that positing a "bracketed" consciousness and its intentionality as the foundation for experience and knowledge is incoherent in light of what he realized to be the essential embodiment, intersubjectivity, and historicity of consciousness. Bearing comparison with near-cognates like "Being-in-the-world" (Martin Heidegger), "form of life" (Ludwig Wittgenstein), "habitus" (Pierre Bourdieu), and others, the idea of the life-world is thus forwarded by Husserl as a means to provide a new ontological grounding for consciousness. As he explains:

> [T]he life-world [. . .] is always already there, existing in advance for us, the "ground" of all praxis whether theoretical or extratheoretical. The world is pregiven to us, the waking, always somehow practically interested subjects, not occasionally but always and necessarily as the universal field of all actual and possible praxis, as horizon. To live is always to live-in-certainty-of-the-world. Waking life is being awake to the world, being constantly and directly "conscious" of the world and of oneself as living *in* the world, actually experiencing [. . .] and actually effecting the ontic certainty of the world. The world is pregiven thereby, in every case [. . .].[95]

In Husserl's conception, the life-world, like the Kantian transcendental ego, is the universal condition of possibility for consciousness that grounds consciousness in space and time, or extension; that is shared by all, or intersubjective ("we, each 'I-the-man' and all of us together, belong to the world as living with one another in the world; and the world is our world, valid for our consciousness as existing precisely through this 'living together'"); and that is consequently the ultimate horizon of "all [historical] [sic] periods and peoples" and, moreover, "the entire spatio-temporal world."[96] As such, the life-world is in his view *singular*—"the plural," he underlines, "makes no sense when applied to it."[97]

Of course, Husserl in particular and phenomenology more generally have come under attack from, not least, the same Marxist tradition I have highlighted as central to my thinking on form. Adorno was himself at the forefront of these attacks in the 1950s and 1960s, when phenomenology had become firmly entrenched in the terrain of Continental philosophy.[98] Broadly, the problem with the (Husserlian) phenomenological method from a materialist perspective is its underpinnings in the tradition of transcendental idealism. By positing experience, knowledge, and, later, history itself as grounded in the transcendental, it, the argument goes, radically obscures the material base that for Marxists mediates the actually existing structures of experience and knowledge in the world as well as the actual unfolding of history. This line of critique can clearly be seen to extend to Husserl's concept of the life-world.

Against this critique, I would like to suggest that a materialist retrieval of the life-world concept is both feasible and desirable for an analysis of form. Indeed, Jürgen Habermas, Adorno's successor as Director of the Frankfurt Institute for Social Research, has attempted precisely such a retrieval in his two-volume study, *The Theory of Communicative Action* (1981; trans. 1984, 1987), the second volume of which is subtitled *Lifeworld and System: A Critique of Functionalist Reason*. There, Habermas takes explicit aim at the basis of Husserl's approach to the life-world. He argues that this approach is unsound as it, "in contrast to the historical shapes of particular lifeworlds and life-forms," is premised on an ontology that is put forward as "invariant."[99] He then reconsiders the life-world concept along more materialist lines—"[i]f we now relinquish the basic concepts of the philosophy of consciousness in which Husserl dealt with the problem of the lifeworld," he elaborates, "we can think of the lifeworld as represented by a culturally transmitted and linguistically organized stock of interpretive patterns."[100] That is to say, he reimagines the life-world as the "*sociocultural*" ground of experience, knowledge, and history for a given group or society, as the shared set of political, social, cultural, and, indeed, economic coordinates that gives meaning and coherence to experience as mediated by these coordinates and as thus rendered *specific* to that group.[101] In short, Habermas *pluralizes* our understanding of the life-world concept (as indicated by his consistent pluralizing of the term), and, in so doing, reclaims it for materialist thought.

Formulated in this way, the life-world concept is valuable for my account of form insofar as it provides a materialist foundation for the form / content dialectic that is not limited to capitalism and its critique. Through it, we can read form as the abstraction, mediation, and crystallization of the experience of multiple social formations, both of and beyond those of capitalism. Further, the multiple expressive possibilities of form become apparent when delinking its analysis from a critique that is ultimately directed against capitalism. In addition to its function of mystifying or resolving social antagonism, form can be interpreted as a site of the more or less transparent embodiment of a society's self-consciousness; of the enactment not just of antagonism, but also of other modalities of social experience such as desire, reproduction, sustenance, care, cooperation, craft, barter, dialogue, community, environmental relationality, and conservation; of the articulation of affect both subjective and intersubjective; of the preservation of historical memory and the registration of dreams for the future; of the condensation, structuring, and refinement of socially accumulated knowledge; of the ritual repetition of the social; and so on. In the expanded account I have set out, form in general might thus be defined as the dialectical expression of the life-world whence it arises.

* * *

The implications of this account of form for my argument about world literature are many and substantial. Pivotally, it suggests that if in world literature as an agent of modernity the forms of modernity produce local forms as pre-modern, external, and other, they, by the same token, produce the *life-worlds* of which these forms are the expression as pre-modern, external, and other. This process is best understood according to a Derridean logic of spectrality. Jacques Derrida develops this figure of thought during what has been dubbed his ethical and political turn of the early 1990s, in his book *Specters of Marx: The State of the Debt, the Work of Mourning, and the New International* (1993; trans. 1994). Originally presented as a series of lectures for a conference on "Whither Marxism?" held at the University of California, Riverside in 1993, this book engages with the heritage of Marx and Marxism in the post-communism era proclaimed by Francis Fukuyama as the "end of history."[102]

In *Specters of Marx*, Derrida argues that in this period of capitalism triumphant, of the ascent of neoliberalism and the universalization of Western liberal democracy, Marx—himself, his testament, his inheritance—has been declared dead and has thus been reduced to a "specter" or "shadow."[103] As per the logic of spectrality that Derrida proceeds to set out, this specter—"a power held to be baleful in itself," a "demonic threat" which continues to haunt the century—must be conjured away or exorcised by capitalism's proponents in order to ensure capitalism's intellectual, political, and ideological consistency and hegemony.[104] Yet, he continues, this project is doomed to failure due to the unprecedented worldwide violence and savagery that has resulted from the rise of this same capitalism in this period. Against those who would neo-evangelize in its name, he reminds us that "never have violence, inequality, exclusion, famine, and thus economic oppression affected as many human beings in the history of the earth and of humanity," that "never have so many men, women, and children been subjugated, starved, or exterminated on the earth."[105] In what he calls a "counter-conjuration," Derrida thus calls forth the specter of Marx from these "innumerable singular sites of suffering," and posits a "New International" whose critique is based upon the notion of radical *responsibility* to capitalism's others as well as to the spirit from which it borrows its name.[106]

Derrida derives his thinking of the specter from a reading of the language of "specters," "spirits," "ghosts," "phantoms," and "phantasms" as distributed across and insinuated in Marx's texts (as well as from a range of literary texts such as, most notably, William Shakespeare's *Hamlet* [c. 1599–1602]). Homing in on *The Communist Manifesto*, *Capital*, and *The German Ideology* (1846) in particular, he detects in this usage a residuum of otherness, of non-presence or non-being that Marx, in his reliance on the metaphysics of presence that has dominated the Western philosophical tradition, attempts—unsuccessfully—to banish. The specter thus manifests for Derrida as a figure of thought for simultaneous presence and non-presence, being and non-being, one which is "neither" and yet "both" of these diametrically opposed concepts and which thereby undoes the opposition between them as established in Western philosophy.[107] Properly irreducible to a mere concept or idea, let alone a *logos*, the specter is the immaterial trace of the past as manifest in the material reality of the here and now. It is that by which this reality and the spatial, temporal, and ontological foundations on which it is built is rendered "out of joint," or haunted.[108] As Derrida elaborates in what he consequently proposes as a "*hauntology*," or spectral traversal and deconstruction of ontology:

> If there is something like spectrality, there are reasons to doubt this reassuring order of presents and, especially, the border between the present, the actual or present reality of the present, and everything that can be

opposed to it: absence, non-presence, non-effectivity, inactuality, virtuality, or even the simulacrum in general, and so forth. [. . .] [O]ne must perhaps ask oneself whether the *spectrality effect* does not consist in undoing this opposition, or even this dialectic, between actual, effective presence and its other.[109]

As such, the logic of spectrality might be considered a variation—one derived from the particularities of his reading of Marx—of that of the "trace," of "*différance*," or of any of the network of other affiliated and near-substitutable terms (such as the "supplement," "archi-writing," the "*pharmakon*," the "unnameable," the "tympanum," the "hymen," the "fan," and so forth) that Derrida pursues elsewhere in his writings.

The two terms to which I have drawn attention are of special relevance for an understanding of spectrality. In her Translator's Preface to *Of Grammatology* (1967; trans. 1974), Gayatri Spivak helpfully explains that "trace" refers to "the mark of the absence of a presence, an always already absent present."[110] Further underlining its spectral resonances, Derrida continues that it indicates "[t]he absence of *another* here-and-now, of another transcendental present, of *another* origin of the world appearing as such, presenting itself as irreducible absence within [. . .] presence."[111] Thus linked with spectrality, both trace and specter might be referred to *différance* in an endless chain of substitutions-with-variation. Neither a word nor a concept, "*différance*", Derrida teases in "Différance" (1968; trans. 1973), might be understood as a spatial and temporal "interval," "distance," or "spacing"—a "middle voice"—between the terms of a conceptual binary (such as of the intelligible and the sensible, concept and intuition, culture and nature, and so on), one by which their difference is constituted and thus through which each is defined.[112] Unthinkable, unnameable, it is the "origin of differences" for which the designation "origin" is unsuitable.[113] Supplemented by trace and *différance*, the logic of spectrality can now be articulated in terms of the ontological difference and deferral of another world that is nevertheless present-in-its-absence as trace in *this* world.

Since its publication in English, *Specters of Marx* has prompted a widespread and wide-ranging "spectral turn" in literary and cultural studies. As María del Pilar Blanco and Esther Peeren note in their editorial introduction to *The Spectralities Reader: Ghosts and Haunting in Contemporary Cultural Theory* (2013)—an excellent companion to this turn, the particular fecundity of Derrida's thought for literary and cultural studies scholars is that it allows for the liberation of the figure of the specter from its "occultist" or "obscurantist" implications and its redeployment "as a conceptual metaphor signalling the ultimate disjointedness of ontology, history, inheritance, materiality, and ideology."[114] Through Derrida, that is, the specter becomes "a figure of clarification with a specifically ethical and political potential."[115] As indicated by the breadth, depth, and structure of this volume, this potential has been realized by scholars from across the humanities, and often beyond—in American studies, post/modernist studies, postcolonial studies, gender and sexuality studies, media studies, critical historiography, critical geography, critical theory, and trauma theory, among other fields and disciplines.

Thus far, however, the spectral turn has not extended to the critical debate on world literature in a substantial way. While Vilashini Cooppan does draw on its language in her article "Ghosts in the Disciplinary Machine: The Uncanny Life of World Literature" (2004), her concern, somewhat characteristic of the early 2000s, is with the influence of its "ghostly forefathers" on the pedagogical and scholarly practices of world literature as a discipline.[116] She in fact doesn't mention Derrida and his thought on spectrality at all. It is part of my intention in this book to expand the spectral turn to the world literature debate, and, as I will momentarily clarify, to think through world literature as in itself constituted in the logic of spectrality. For now, though, it is important to highlight, and explain my deviation from, two texts associated with this turn that have perhaps come closest to something like a "spectral world literature," Jean-Michel Rabaté's *The Ghosts of Modernity* (1996) and Pheng Cheah's *Spectral Nationality: Passages of Freedom from Kant to Postcolonial Literatures of Liberation* (2003).

As indicated by his title, Rabaté's project in *The Ghosts of Modernity* is one of rereading the history of modernity from the perspective of a spectral analysis derived from a range of psychoanalytic and poststructuralist theorists. Against accounts that see it as a site of the erasure of ghostly doublings and returns, he seeks to demonstrate that modernity is actually "systematically 'haunted' by voices from the past," by "the ineluctability of spectral returns."[117] Yet in what amounts to a rereading of *modernism* rather than modernity per se, all of his textual case studies are of familiar figures from the late nineteenth- to mid-twentieth-century Western, especially Western European canon—namely T. S. Eliot, Ezra Pound, James Joyce, Stéphane Mallarmé, Maurice Blanchot, Hermann Broch, and Samuel Beckett. It doesn't require pointing out that while Rabaté's core intervention, conceptual machinery, and language have been influential on my own project, my interest is in the spectral dimensions of modernity as a global phenomenon, which leads me to a distinct understanding of spectrality as well as to a distinct canon.

Cheah, on the other hand, does attend to the world beyond the West—at least that which is represented by the postcolonial canon—in *Spectral Nationality*. In this book, Cheah takes issue with a contemporary theoretical climate—including the Derrida of *Specters of Marx* and the New International—that has been overly hostile to the claims of the nation as well as of nationalism. A dismissal considered by the author "too hasty," he seeks against this prevailing current of thought to refigure the nation—specifically, the postcolonial nation—as a spectral other to neoliberal globalization and its endemic abuses, as a site of resistance that holds out a "spectral promise" for "the living nation-people" otherwise caught within the deathly grasp of global capital.[118] The problem with this account is that it, while brilliantly argued and expertly developed with reference to postcolonial writers such as Pramoedya Ananta Toer and Ngũgĩ wa Thiong'o, radically underestimates what world-systems theory teaches is the central and, indeed, *essential* role of the nation-state form in the emergence and continued functioning of the capitalist world-economy. As discussed above, the nation-state (including nationalism as its ideological by-product) is not the other of capital, but rather a site of the organization of productive activity in conformity with the demands of the global economy. As reflected by my emphasis on "world" rather than "postcolonial" literature, my interest in this project is therefore in the spectral other produced by the forms (literary and cultural as well as sociopolitical) of the nation-state itself as part and parcel of its irrevocable trajectory towards modernity.

To return to my argument about world literature, then, it can now be said that in the forms of modernity, the life-worlds modernity produces as other to itself manifest as spectral. By producing local forms and the life-worlds of which they are the expression as other, the forms of modernity render them incongruous, incompatible, and, in the end, inconceivable within the logic and parameters of modernity. They obviate their perpetuation within the political, social, cultural, and economic coordinates of modernity. They extricate them from the space and time of modernity, from the ontological plenitude of such as the here and now of *this* world. They, in short, declare them dead, and buried in the space and time of another world.

As per the logic of spectrality that I have set out, the dead, though, always return as immaterial traces of the past, as specters, that haunt the present and its self-constitution as the entirety of presence or being. Banished by them from modernity as a metaphysics and an ontology, from its narrative of incorporation on a global scale, yet retaining its being in and of another world, the life-world of the other thus *necessarily* manifests in the forms of modernity, and does so in—only in—a spectral manner. It thereby *haunts* the forms of modernity as specter, as trace, with haunting understood as the uncanny return of the other produced by form. Unseen, unheard, unthought, it *infects* and *inflects* form as its displaced, transliminal origin, rendering form always-already out of joint and striving impossibly to reconstitute its unity against the force of a cryptic foe. In this way, the forms of modernity can be understood to be produced in a dialectic of the abstraction, mediation, and crystallization of what I call *the spectral life-world of modernity*. I distinguish this designation from Walter Benjamin's comparable notion of "phantasmagoria" insofar as the latter, derived from Marx's analysis of the commodity as "*die phantasmagorische Form*" of capitalism, purports to describe capitalism as an ideological dream-world that is mediated by the commodity form.[119] "Spectral life-world of modernity," on the other hand, refers to the phantasmagoria, as it were, of global capitalist modernity vis-à-vis its *external* others. As in modernity per se, these have been occluded in Benjamin's as well as the Marxist account of form more generally. It can now be proposed, therefore, that, as an agent of modernity whose forms are the dialectical expression of the spectral life-world of such, *world literature is constituted in the logic of spectrality*.

* * *

My spectral theory of world literature amounts five interrelated theses:

- World literature is the worlding of the concept of literature attendant on modernity.
- World literature is constituted in the superseding of local forms by the forms of modernity.
- The forms of modernity are haunted by the spectral trace of the life-world of the other.
- The forms of modernity abstract, mediate, and crystallize the spectral life-world of modernity.
- World literature is constituted in the logic of spectrality.

Thus far, these theses have been presented in a highly abstract, condensed manner. It is the purpose of this book to flesh them out with reference to Orientalism, modernity, and the novel in the Middle East. Before introducing the subject matter proper of the book, though, a note on the implications of my spectral theory is necessary.

As mentioned in the Preface, I intend this book in its widest remit to contribute productively and compellingly to the ever-expanding debate on world literature. This debate, I suggested, has been riven between advocates of a field that promises coverage and comparison on a global scale and critics of this field's appropriating, homogenizing, and commodifying implications. It seems to me that the spectral theory I have outlined suggests a promising mediation of these broadly defined positions. It allows for comparatism on a global scale, and it does so precisely *via*, rather than despite, a sustained focus on the complicity of world literature in what I have identified as global capitalist modernity. This is indeed precisely the ambition of my spectral theory of world literature.

Like global capitalist modernity itself, world literature must now be regarded as inevitable. As critics, scholars, and practitioners continue to engage this paradigm, it seems to me that as per the epigraph from Derrida above, our "*responsibility*" is to the others it produces in its very existence as concept, discourse, practice, institution, and discipline.[120] I thus call for renewed attention to these others, to the specters of world literature.

Cide Hamete's *Quixote*: The Novel and the Oriental Other of Modernity

In this book, I focus on the novel as *the* paradigmatic embodiment of modernity in the domain of literature. I understand the novel as an exemplary case study of the spectral constitution of the forms of modernity and thus of world literature. My argument implies that variations in novelistic form around the world are to be accounted for not in terms of "compromise," but rather in those of spectrality. That is, as the novel is reproduced in the periphery via the process of its incorporation into modernity, its variations accrue not from the more or less transparent, intentional, and surface-level negotiation of local and global form, but rather from the spectral infection and inflection of the global by the local form that the former itself produces as its other. As local forms and the life-worlds they express vary across distinct peripheral contexts, the form that the novel assumes therein is likewise subject to variation according to the specificities of the contexts where it takes root. Spectral inf(l)ections of form can be detected in and traced through any and all of the formal features of a novel—in its language (choice, use, etc.), style, modes of characterization, dialogue between characters, plot, narrative, structure, historical and geographical setting, spatio-temporal locus, ontological and epistemological underpinnings, and so forth. While, as is apparent, the figuration of "ghosts" and related phenomena such as haunting, the uncanny, magic, witchcraft, folklore, myth, and, broadly, the supernatural in literary texts is not the primary concern of my spectral theory of world literature (to clarify this distinction, I will henceforth refer to the former as "ghosts" and to the latter in terms of "specters" and "spectrality"), such representations might nevertheless be regarded as privileged sites for exploring the operation of what I have called "spectral inf(l)ection" more generally.

Given these concerns, it is important to start with a brief discussion of Miguel de Cervantes Saavedra's *Don Quixote* (*El ingenioso hidalgo don Quijote de la Mancha*, 1605–15) as a point of origin for the modern novel. Across the centuries, major critics, theorists, and philosophers—as well as a vast range of novelists from around the world—have emphasized the seminal role of Cervantes's novel in this regard. Those who have cited *Don Quixote* as "the first modern novel," "the first great novel of world literature," or even "the first modern work of literature" include Friedrich Schlegel, Arthur Schopenhauer, Hermann Cohen, Miguel de Unamuno, José Ortega y Gasset, Erich Auerbach, Georg Lukács, Mikhail Bakhtin, Michel Foucault, and Harold Bloom, among many others.[121] These sorts of observations have led Bloom to conclude of Cervantes that "he is the only possible peer of Dante and Shakespeare in the Western Canon."[122] Even Ian Watt, whose influential account of "the rise of the novel" traced the genre's origins to the social conditions particular to England in the eighteenth century, later identified that of Don Quixote—along with those of Faust, Don Juan, and Robinson Crusoe—as one of the four founding "myths of modern individualism."[123]

Why has *Don Quixote* been accorded such a privileged position in the (Western, world) canon, in the narrative of modernity in its literary dimensions? Rachel Schmidt has provided the most exhaustive and methodical response to this question in her recent book, *Forms of Modernity:* Don Quixote *and Modern Theories of the Novel* (2011). There, Schmidt traces how it was precisely with reference to *Don Quixote* as exemplar that such pivotal thinkers as many of those listed above first devised their theories of the novel, their novelistics, and how their theories—so foundational to the modern understanding of the novel per se—were consequently informed by their readings of Cervantes's engagement with and problematization of the question of modernity in this work. In the neo-Kantian and Romanticist philosophical terrain of the nineteenth to early twentieth centuries within (or against) which most of these thinkers were working, of special concern were issues of the individual's relation to an increasingly alienating and disenchanted world; his or her agency, autonomy, and freedom; the role of the artwork and of the aesthetic; and the appeal of the past—its ideals, its heritage, its culture—as a source of redemption for the profane present. It is not difficult, therefore, to see why *Don Quixote* should have emerged as an exemplary text, and why the novelistic form *necessarily* deployed by its author as a means to traverse these issues should have become, in Schmidt's phrasing, *the* literary "form of modernity."

In this novel about an impoverished Spanish gentleman whose imagination had become so riddled with tales of chivalry that he loses his sanity, reinvents himself as a knight errant, and sets out to restore the ideals of the past to his fallen world, Cervantes explicitly seeks to distance himself from the genre of the chivalric romance ascendant in European literary culture during the previous centuries. As he explains in his Prologue to the "first part" of the novel, published in 1605 (and as rendered by Edith Grossman in her widely acclaimed recent translation [2003]), his intent is one of "demolishing the ill-founded apparatus of these chivalric books, despised by many and praised by so many more."[124] In so doing, he establishes a new "apparatus" or form—the novel, one whose very identity as discussed in the Prologue and realized throughout the narrative is at its core thus defined by the concerns characteristic of modernity, including those of the individual and society, the internal and the external, illusion and reality, the artwork, and past and present. Furthermore, he also thematizes these concerns throughout the novel, in especially his depiction of his protagonist's constant chafing against a world that in his "age of iron" is rapidly being transformed all around him.[125] Most famously illustrated by the "Adventure of the Windmills" episode, this is also suggested in passages which feature Don Quixote decrying the new institutions and developments of early modern Spain, ranging from the professionalization of the military to the centralization of political and legal authority to the commodification of social relations.[126] So it is that *through Don Quixote*, the form of the modern novel has been (and continues to be) read in terms of its constitutive irony (Schlegel); its playful engagement with genre as well as the individual / society relationship (Cohen, Ortega y Gasset); its (always-already *post*modernist) disavowal of literary authorship and authority (Unamuno); its melancholy dialectics of inside and outside, past and present (Lukács); its dialogical interfacing, even interweaving of diverse genres, styles, voices, and perspectives (Bakhtin); and so on.[127]

Central to all of these accounts of *Don Quixote* and the modern novel is the notion that their modernity is comprised of the radical formal break they enact with the past, its literary and cultural traditions, and the lifeworlds that these traditions express. Whether explicitly or implicitly, and with varying degrees of urgency, this point has been made by all of the thinkers mentioned above. However, I find it to have been most powerfully articulated by Lukács (covered by Schmidt) and Foucault (not covered, presumably because his discussion of *Don Quixote* doesn't take place in the context of a more encompassing theory of the novel). For Lukács, *Don Quixote* signals a watershed between two historical epochs. At the moment of the novel's composition, with the life-world of medieval Europe in full decline, the romance had lost what he (writing during his neo-Kantian period) calls its "roots in transcendent being," its connection to a world that had acted as its historico-philosophical condition of possibility.[128] It had thereby been reduced to an "empty shell" or "dead form."[129] In his parodic inversion of the romance, Cervantes—the "intuitive visionary" of this moment—inscribes the melancholy historical process which had seen the death of a world and which had left man alone, unhomed, and forsaken by God, struggling to forge from the abyss of his isolated soul a meaning for that which had been rendered immanently meaningless.[130] This, Lukács calls the "full flowering" of the novel as "form."[131] For Foucault, *Don Quixote* marks an epistemic rupture from the epoch by which it was preceded. As its "negative," the novel inverts the episteme of the romance and its world (what he calls the Renaissance), one in which events are recounted as literal truth and where there is no division between the word and the thing, the signifier and the signified.[132] In his quest to restore or recreate this world, Don Quixote must project onto his own the language, the signs, and the narrative of its predominant form. Of course, this attempt—profoundly ironic—presupposes in its exigency and thus reproduces *as* his narrative the very chasm that Don Quixote is hoping to bridge. As the first work of literature to have charted this chasm, the novel, then, ushers in a new age—our inheritance—in which language has finally broken off its "old kinship" with things and has attained its "sovereignty" as sole legislator of the real.[133]

In my parlance, these and other accounts suggest that *Don Quixote* establishes the logic and parameters of modernity, however defined, in novelistic form. In many ways its progenitor, this, it might be said, is the precedent that *Don Quixote* has set for the entire novelistic tradition. Indeed, taking into consideration only the novelists who have been *directly* influenced by the formal devices, thematic foci, narrative structures, modes of characterization, and / or philosophical conundrums of this text (of whom many have referenced or intertextually engaged with it or its author in their own writings), it seems to me that they comprise something of a backbone of the history of the form. Such authors include: Henry Fielding, Laurence Sterne, Tobias Smollett, Charlotte Lennox, Gustave Flaubert, Fyodor Dostoyevsky, Miguel de Unamuno, G. K. Chesterton, Franz Kafka, William Faulkner, Jorge Luis Borges, Graham Greene, Samuel Beckett, Gabriel García Márquez, Milan Kundera, Kathy Acker, Paul Auster, and Salman Rushdie, among many others.

On the whole, though, these readings have neglected to address or have outright obscured the question of the (possible) Arabic-Islamic shaping of the form of *Don Quixote*, and thus of that of the modern novel. This question hinges on Cervantes's metafictional introduction (and regular reminders and discussions) of the figure of Cide Hamete Benengeli, an "Arab Historian," as the "first author" of the text of which (most of) his novel is purportedly the translation.[134] In his role as first-person frame narrator (or, as Foucault might say, "author function"), Cervantes first encounters Cide Hamete in Chapter IX of the first part.[135] At this juncture, the sources he had been relying upon for his reconstruction of his protagonist's narrative had dried up, leaving him at somewhat of a loss as to how to proceed. Not inconveniently, he soon comes across an Arabic manuscript in the Alcaná market in Toledo bearing the title "*History of Don Quixote of La Mancha. Written by Cide Hamete Benengeli.*"[136] He then commissions "some Morisco" to translate this manuscript, and the result—a *mise en abyme* comprising Cervantes's framing of the Morisco's translation of Cide Hamete's text (including each author-figure's editorial mediation of and commentary on the embedded text[s] with which they are working as well as its / their author[s])—is the first part of the novel, *Don Quixote*.[137] This metafictional gesture is redoubled in the "second part," published in 1615. There, Cervantes introduces the first part as an element in the world of his characters, as a book that has been published and that is being widely read by them (he also frequently refers to the so-called "false *Quixote*," published in 1614 under the name of one "Alonso Fernández de Avellaneda.")[138] Adding, to borrow a term from Gérard Genette, another layer of "metaleptic" complexity to the text (not to mention a chronological paradox), this twist also prompts new comic misadventures as characters—notably, the duke and duchess—exploit what they have learned from reading about the deluded knight and his squire for their own amusement.[139] While the device of a discovered and translated originary text is a familiar feature of the romance (one intended to indicate its authenticity), the very vigor by which Cervantes pursues it and the complications to which he subjects it in fact further his project of subverting of the genre.

Don Quixote's metafictional box of tricks has certainly intrigued and inspired critics, theorists, and writers alike over the centuries. This is perhaps most vividly evinced by the (proto-)postmodernist aesthetic tradition that the novel appears almost single-handedly to have spurred, one that ranges from Sterne to Unamuno to Borges, and beyond. All Cervantine scholars have considered this aspect of the text in one way or another, and those who have focused specifically on Cide Hamete and the formal implications of his "authorship" include E. C. Riley, Américo Castro, Francisco Márquez Villanueva, Robert Alter, James Parr, and others.[140] Likewise, the Arabic-Islamic content of the novel—especially that featured in "The Captive's Tale" and other episodes or passages such as "Ricote's Exile / Return," "The Puppet Show," and the "*albogues*" translation—has come under increasing scrutiny among *cervantistas* in the last several decades.[141] Those who have written significantly on this topic in this period include John Rodenbeck, María Antonia Garcés, Antonio Medina, E. C. Graf, Frederick de Armas, and others.[142] What has not received any substantial attention (or not until very recently), however, is the idea of a potential relationship *between* the novel's form and its content. In light of Cervantes's identification of the original author of *Don Quixote* as an "Arab" as well as of his evident consciousness of the Arabic-Islamic world and its heritage in Spain in this text (not to mention his own earlier five-year experience of captivity in Ottoman Algeria), this seems an apposite area of inquiry.

In their recent work, Walter Cohen and Nizar Hermes have offered some fruitful guidance on this issue. For the first of these critics, *Don Quixote* indeed registers the Arabic-Islamic world, and it primarily does so in its form. Of course, Cohen is cognizant of the novel's Arabic-Islamic content as in the episodes mentioned above, as well as of the impact of the early modern imperial imbroglios in and around the Mediterranean between Christendom (as represented by Spain, Portugal, and Italy) and Islam (as represented by the Moorish legacy of al-Andalus and the Ottoman Empire) on Renaissance literature more generally. As per his overarching argument about the "nonrepresentation" of empire in the Renaissance canon, though, his point is that this material—comprising only about 5 percent of the text—is relegated to the background.[143] In *Don Quixote*, it is by virtue of Cervantes's stated intention of discrediting the romance that he must turn away from the grand matters of imperial and religious conflict, and towards those of ordinary, everyday life in Spain. As such, Cohen suggests, the novel's (and, thereafter, literary realism's) logic "*entails* the relegation of empire to the margins."[144] Cervantes's engagement with the Arabic-Islamic world and the Spanish / European imaginary of the Orient, then, re-enters the text through the figure of Cide Hamete, the Arab original author—"[b]lessings" upon him!—to whom he grants ultimate authority over the narrative.[145] Unrepresentable, the "former foe" is thus "incorporat[ed]" into the text at the level of form.[146]

Hermes pushes this line of inquiry further.[147] Noting that a thorough critical interrogation of the Arabic-Islamic influences on *Don Quixote* has yet to appear in the scholarship, he homes in on "The Captive's Tale" and the novel's overall picaresque disposition as particularly telling sites for exploring this topic. Regarding "The Captive's Tale," he perceives a striking thematic and structural overlap between its central narrative and that of the so-called "Frankish Tale"—also known as "The Love Tale of 'Ali Nur al-Din the Cairene and Princess Mariam, Daughter of the King of France"—from the *One Thousand and One Nights* (*Alf Layla wa Layla*, c. ninth–fourteenth centuries).[148] Both narratives comprise a love-induced religious conversion, though the former—for obvious ideological purposes—reverses the Christianity to Islam dynamic that drives the latter. With the novel's picaresque components, he suggests that these might very well have been inspired—whether directly or indirectly—by the Arabic genre of the *maqāma*. In many ways comparable to *Don Quixote*, the *maqāma* as established by Badi' al-Zaman al-Hamadani and al-Hariri of Basra in the tenth to eleventh centuries typically features a wandering rogue or trickster figure—one, it has been argued, on whom the early Spanish *picaro* was modelled—who captivates crowds of onlookers with his feats of rhetorical prowess, only to end up swindling them.[149] While no definitive evidence about Cervantes's knowledge of these sources is available, the circumstances of his Algerian experience and of their wide circulation and popularity in al-Andalus (at least prior to the denouement of the Reconquista in 1492)—in addition to the formal similarities that have just been outlined—strongly support Hermes's case. What finally brings this case together, though, is Cervantes's deployment of none other than Cide Hamete. Enthralled by his "Arabian tales," what Hermes calls Cervantes's "positive interaction" with the Arabic culture to which he was exposed throughout his life is crystallized in and as his author-surrogate.[150]

Clearly, much work remains to be done in this area among *cervantistas*. For now, on the grounds of Cohen's and Hermes's important recent interventions, it seems apparent that Cervantes's engagement with the Arabic-Islamic world in *Don Quixote* runs much deeper than his passing references to it in the content of the novel, that it mediates its very form. Crucially, this subtle structuring effect is hinted at or teased through the figure of Cide Hamete, but never overtly foregrounded—Cervantes never discusses it in his otherwise wide-ranging meditations on literary history and aesthetics, and no concrete evidence of his familiarity with the relevant source material exists. Due, no doubt, to the demands of his time—literary and cultural as well as ideological—it *must* remain hidden, undisclosed, something of an Oriental unconscious of the text. Might it be surmised, therefore, that *from its origins, the form of the modern novel is inf(l)ected by the specter of its Oriental other*?

This account offers significant new purchase on our understanding of the novel form per se. Franco Moretti—the most likely contemporary candidate as heir to the "theory of the novel" tradition outlined above—has sought to extend this understanding in light of the world literature debate. In his two-volume edited collection *The Novel* (2006), he and his contributors collectively and collaboratively reinterpret the form according to the theoretical and methodological models developed in the world literature scholarship, as a genuinely global phenomenon that in the millennial course of its self-constitution has cut across many more histories and geographies than hitherto acknowledged.[151] As he puts it in his purposively brief and open-ended editorial introduction, he conceives of the novel as "the first truly planetary form," one whose history spans "two thousand years" and whose geography overlaps with "the advent of world literature."[152] This vision is admirably borne out by the collection proper. Divided into volumes on "History, Geography, and Culture" and "Forms and Themes," its contributions—authored by among the most prominent of literary critics and theorists working today—cover seemingly every major narrative tradition from classical antiquity to the present, and, indeed, from all over the world.[153] There is no other way of saying it—Moretti's is a beautiful work, one whose every page is as entertaining as it is enlightening, a veritable treasure trove for those interested in as expansive a comprehension of the novel form as possible. However, I worry that under such an all-embracing definition, the category of "the novel" loses all of its specificity and coherence. It loses its contours as a *specific* form that originated in a specific time and place. It loses its distinctiveness from *other* (narrative) forms, and thus its *raison d'être* of absorbing and amalgamating them as per its role in the wider trajectory of modernity that I have delineated. It loses its world-historical function as a form of modernity. In short, what is lost to this definition is any sense of the violence and upheaval from which the novel was born and which it has been historically complicit in perpetuating as it has spread across the globe—the power dynamic at its core.

It is unquestionably the case that many if not most of Moretti's contributors attend to these more, say, political concerns in the history of the novel. My qualm is more with the basic conception of his project. It seems to me that in his quest to expand the breadth and depth of our understanding of this form vis-à-vis world literature—to "world" it, as Djelal Kadir might say, Moretti must due to the paradoxical constraints imposed by this conception necessarily elide some of the fundamentals by which the term "novel" attains any sort of workable, localizable, and commonly agreed-upon definition. As I hope to have demonstrated, the spectral approach I have pursued seems to allow for a worldly, transhistorical scope while retaining, perhaps even consolidating the consistency of "novel" as a category of analysis.

The Middle Eastern Novel in Modernity

Specifically, my interest is in the Middle Eastern novel. I take the Middle Eastern novel as both metonym and metaphor of what I have delineated as a spectral world literature. I read its origins, development, and current worldly prominence in relation to the nation- and region-specific unfolding of the wider trajectory of the periphery's incorporation into modernity via literature that I have charted as definitive of world literature. That is to say, I assess how it was initially forged in the furnace of world literature; how its rise resulted in certain significant sociopolitical as well as cultural occlusions and marginalizations; how it has been and continues to be constitutively haunted by its others, its specters; and how its contemporary standing is premised on this heritage. All this, I trace through its form, which I argue is—in the context of the history of the novel—revolutionary. This account, I demonstrate, makes for a new, radical conceptualization of the Middle Eastern novel in its national, regional, and global contexts, as well as, by extension, a new, comparative understanding of Middle Eastern literary and cultural modernity per se. In undertaking this analysis, I draw on and further critically develop some of the major insights that have been forwarded and trends that have emerged in the field of Middle East studies in recent years.

As in all other instances of the arising of modern literary and cultural forms in the periphery, the formation of the Middle Eastern novel was mediated by the specificities of modernity—its local and particular historical, institutional, and ideological manifestations and variations—as these took root in its national and regional contexts. In the Middle East, the three moments of literary incorporation into modernity that laid the groundwork for the novel there play out, in outline, as follows (I more fully expound this process as it pertains to the key sites of Middle Eastern modernity in Chapter 2):

- First, the moment of *exchange*. As indicated by my discussion of *Don Quixote* above, and as I further elaborate by means of a range of examples throughout the book, the history of literary exchange between Western Europe (as core) and the Middle East (as periphery) is a long and complex—indeed, millennial—one. In this book, however, I focus on modern literary exchange between the regions as precipitated by the French Campaign in Egypt and Syria (1798–1801) and as attendant on the subsequent practices and discourses of Western—primarily British, French, and Zionist—colonialism and imperialism in the Middle East from the nineteenth to the mid-twentieth centuries. This is because it was precisely the colonial / imperial dynamic at the heart of political, social, cultural, and economic interaction between the regions in this period that prompted the modernity particular to the Middle East; that instigated the wholesale re-envisioning of the Middle Eastern literary and cultural sphere; and that eventually led to the emergence of the Middle Eastern novel. As I discuss with reference to the historiographical scholarship of Edward Said, Albert Hourani, and Eugene Rogan and the literary historical work of Roger Allen, M. M. Badawi, Muhsin al-Musawi, Jeffrey Sacks, Nuha Alshaar, Stephen Sheehi, Tarek El-Ariss, Kamran Rastegar, and Abdelfattah Kilito, among others, this dynamic—anchored in Orientalist philology as a system of discursive and thus practical order and control in the multiple spheres of interaction—spurred what is (problematically) known as the "*Nahda*," or cultural renaissance, of the Arab world in the mid-to-late nineteenth century. I interpret the *Nahda*—comprising, as it did, the influx and adoption of new, especially Western literary forms and genres, philosophical and political worldviews, sciences and technologies, languages, translations, and so forth—as the originary blueprint of literary and cultural modernity in the Middle East at large.

- Second, the moment of *internalization*. In this specific historical terrain, I continue, the modern, European notion of literature was internalized in the Middle East as a feature of the region's more general incorporation into modernity. Following the lead of scholars such as those listed above, I trace how the classical Arabic-Islamic concept of "*adab*" (which encompasses a plethora of "literary" as well as other genres of writing, and which in my parlance is expressive of multiple modalities of experience in the classical to medieval Arabic-Islamic life-world) was systematically reinscribed as "literature" according to the European model across the region during this period. While of course remaining closely attentive to distinctions in distinct national contexts, I demonstrate that in its underlying structure and momentum, this process occurred in remarkably similar ways across what I identify as the key sites of Middle Eastern modernity—Egypt (where its architects included figures such as Rifaʻa al-Tahtawi, Ahmad Faris al-Shidyaq, Butrus al-Bustani, and Taha Husayn); Turkey (İbrahim Şinasi, Ziya Pasha, Mehmet Akif Ersoy, Ziya Gökalp, Nurullah Ataç); and Iran (Mirza Fathʻali Akhundzade, Mirza Aqa Khan Kermani, Mirza Malkam Khan, ʻAli Akbar Dehkhoda, ʻAref Qazvini, Mohammad Taqi Bahar, Taqi Rafat). Finally, I show that this act of literary and cultural reinscription was central to the projects of state- and nation-building that were taking place across the region from the *Nahda* to the postcolonial (or, "post/colonial") period, and thus to the wider project of modernity in the Middle East.[154]

- And third, the moment of *reproduction*. I conclude that it was in and only in the newly rewritten concept of literature that the novel first arose in the Middle East. As a form of modernity, it was reproduced across the region as part of a wider process of incorporation into modernity that was facilitated by and enacted in literature. I track the historical impetus by way of which the novel emerged in the Middle East in general with the aid of the work of Allen, Badawi, Salma Jayyusi, Waïl Hassan, Kilito, and others, and in its specific national contexts by turning to scholarship more oriented around the relevant national literary histories. I show that as the novel became established as a—or, *the*—predominant modern literary form in the region, its effect was to supersede the local narrative and other literary forms associated with *adab* (such as those listed above as well as others) that had been in wide circulation there and that had enjoyed widespread popularity for centuries and more. This, I call the dialectic of Middle Eastern (literary and cultural) modernity.

According to and further substantiating my spectral theory of world literature, I argue in this book that in world literature as an agent of modernity, the Middle Eastern novel has its origins as a form of modernity particular to the Middle East. As such, it has played (and continues to play) a crucial role in producing the Arabic-Islamic life-world most broadly designated and expressed by *adab* as other. From its inception, therefore, it has been haunted by the spectral trace of the life-world of *adab*, and its form might thus be read in terms of its abstraction, mediation, and crystallization of the spectral life-world of Middle Eastern modernity. As metonym and metaphor of world literature, it can now be understood to be constituted in the logic of spectrality.

This approach to the Middle Eastern novel gives rise to, and perhaps even necessitates a critical re-evaluation of the historical and geographical umbrella term "the Middle East" itself, as well as of the field of study to which it lends its name. As is widely acknowledged, the idea of a "Middle East" was first forwarded by the American naval strategist Admiral Alfred Thayer Mahan in 1902 to refer to an area of British strategic interest in and around the Persian Gulf.[155] As Anna Ball and I explain in our co-edited volume *The Edinburgh Companion to the Postcolonial Middle East* (2019), it therefore serves as "a reminder of the overt role that British and French imperialism played in the charting of the region's political geography over the course of the 20th century."[156] These implications, we continue, are consolidated when taking into account the formation of Middle East studies, an offshoot of area studies, during the Cold War period, as well as the more recent deployment of "Greater Middle East" by the US administration following the events of September 11, 2001 as a means to justify and expand—to universalize—the "War on Terror."[157] As such, and due to its underpinnings in Euro-American imperialism; its Orientalist epistemologies and ontologies; and its homogenizing functions with respect to a vast and diverse region stretching across the Levant, the Gulf, North Africa, Iran, Turkey, and beyond, the unselfconscious usage of this term among scholars has often been considered problematic and, indeed, deeply objectionable (not least, of course, by Said himself).[158]

As is evident, I wish in this book to retain "Middle East" as an analytical lens for the comparison of the literatures and cultures of the countries that have typically—if for mistaken or misguided reasons—been situated within its domain. I, though, also seek to provide a more solid, comprehensive, and reflexive critical framework for such comparison based on the closely aligned and similarly structured trajectories of modernity—its sources, influences, and effects—in these countries. On these grounds, and in negotiation with the work of Said, Zachary Lockman, Rashid Khalidi, and others on the history, ideology, and implications of both the term and the field, I thus propose a new, comparative Middle Eastern literary and cultural studies.

The Middle Eastern Novel in the World

More specifically yet, my interest is in the Middle Eastern novel in the world today. In the last several decades, the Middle Eastern novel has enjoyed a massive upsurge of visibility and popularity on the world stage. Certainly, a number of Arab and other Middle Eastern writers both anglo- / francophone (such as Ameen Rihani, Khalil Gibran, Albert Memmi, Kateb Yacine, Assia Djebar, and Waguih Ghali, etc.) and in translation (Naguib Mahfouz, Jabra Ibrahim Jabra, Yaşar Kemal, Tayeb Salih, Sonallah Ibrahim, etc.) did attain a degree of international recognition—which was sometimes considerable—in the earlier part of the twentieth century. Also, the field of modern Arabic literature did begin to establish itself in the Anglo-American academy during this period (M. M. Badawi, the first Lecturer of Modern Arabic at St. Anthony's College, Oxford from 1967, was the central, galvanizing figure of the fledgling discipline). I argue, however, that it was not until the 1980s that the Middle Eastern novel really began to receive the sort of attention in the global literary and academic industries—in publishing, award culture, reviews and criticism, scholarship, and elsewhere—that its European and North American forerunners had been granted for at least a century. Indeed, even as late as 1980, as Edward Said anecdotally recounts, New York-based publishers would refuse to bring out translations of Mahfouz and other regional writers on the grounds that "Arabic is a controversial language."[159] I address the Middle Eastern novel's global contexts of production, translation, circulation, and reception with reference to a range of representative examples throughout this book, in especially Chapters 1, 3, 4, and 5.

The Middle Eastern novel's rise to worldly prominence in this period has typically been explained in relation to contemporaneous political, social, and cultural developments. In their accounts of its recent flourishing, scholars of its anglophone (such as Layla Al Maleh, Waïl Hassan, Nouri Gana, Carol Fadda-Conrey, and Steven Salaita) and translational

(Salih Altoma, Said Faiq) varieties have cited the following contributing factors: the increased institutional recognition and legitimation of the postcolonial, the multicultural, and the ("Third") worldly in general across the literary and academic industries from the early 1980s; the high-profile awarding of the Nobel Prize in Literature to Mahfouz in 1988 and to Orhan Pamuk in 2006; the sharpened public and media interest in—and thus commercial viability of—the region and its literatures in the wake of 9/11 and the "War on Terror"; and the continuance of the same in light of new conflicts and upheavals there (most conspicuously, those of or associated with Iraq, Iran, Palestine, Egypt, Syria, the Arab Spring, the Islamic State, and the Middle Eastern refugee crisis in Europe). My reading suggests a vastly different interpretation of the Middle Eastern novel's current worldly status. It suggests that while the period under discussion did indeed provide the conditions necessary for the Middle Eastern novel's *accelerated* global production and consumption, these processes were made possible in the first place by its establishment as a modern literary form in the region on the basis of what I have charted as the trajectory of literary incorporation there. That is, the Middle Eastern novel is legible as literature in the literary and academic industries (where it can thereby be commodified on a mass scale) only by virtue of its origins as a form of modernity. It follows from this argument that it can only manifest in the world according to the logic and parameters of modernity. As I demonstrate, this point is evidenced by what I call the strategies of containment and domestication that largely mediate its production, translation, circulation, and reception among publishers, award bodies, reviewers and critics, and scholars today. I conclude that under these conditions, what is *lost* to the worlding of the Middle Eastern novel is its constitution in the logic of spectrality.

In this book, I seek to redress this imbalance and foreground spectrality as constitutive of the Middle Eastern novel. I do so by closely and critically attending to the worlding of novels and other literary works from the key sites of Middle Eastern modernity. From Egypt, I focus on those of Mahfouz; from Turkey, those of Pamuk; and from Iran, those of Azar Nafisi, Yasmin Crowther, and Marjane Satrapi. Throughout, I read these texts alongside classic statements of world literature from Goethe and Marx to the present, the discourse of the modern novel as initiated by Cervantes, and landmarks of Middle Eastern literary history such as the *Muʿallaqāt* and *Alf Layla wa Layla*. Against their containment and domestication, I aim to critically restore these novels' engagements with the others of Middle Eastern modernity. I locate such engagement in form, in the haunting of the form of the Middle Eastern novel by the spectral trace of the life-world of the other, its spectral inf(l)ection by the political, religious, and gender experiences of the life-world designated and expressed by *adab*. I argue that in its traversal of the realism–modernism–postmodernism–postcolonialism–cosmopolitanism aesthetic lineage that has defined the history of the novel, the Middle Eastern novel brings the modern novel full circle. That is, it brings to the surface and fully expresses the Oriental other that, as I suggested in my discussion of *Don Quixote*, has acted as the unconscious condition of possibility of the form of the modern novel itself. In this way, it might (somewhat exactly) be said that the Middle Eastern novel comprises a *revolution* of the form of the novel, and that it thereby expresses the spectral life-world of modernity per se. This, I conclude, is its most expansive implication for our understanding of a spectral world literature.

Overview of Parts and Chapters

This book is comprised of five chapters distributed across two parts, and a conclusion. In **Part I, "The Worlding of 'Literature' in the Middle East,"** which includes two chapters, I establish the critical, theoretical, and historical framework of the book. **Chapter 1, "The *Shabaḥ* of Modernity: World-Systems, the Petro-Imperium, and the Indigenous Trace**," provides a condensed and largely self-contained illustration of the critical and theoretical methodology, inquiries, and interventions that undergird the remaining chapters. It does so through a reading of Abdelrahman Munif's five-volume epic of Gulf petro-modernity, *Cities of Salt* (*Mudun al-Milḥ*, 1984–9; trans. 1987–93). Focusing on its first volume, and taking my cue from John Updike's infamously dismissive review, I start by considering how this novel has been framed for international audiences since its translation into English. Rather than contesting it, I am interested in the conditions of Updike's response to Munif as "insufficiently Westernized" to have produced a novel. This response, I argue, is symptomatic of a world literature that conceives of "the literary" only according to "Western" norms and models, and that is thereby constitutively unable to perceive inf(l)ections of the literary as enacted by its others. I then offer a corrective based on what I show to be Munif's spectral characterization of Bedouin resistance leader Miteb al-Hathal. A *"shabaḥ"* (specter), this figure hovers at the interstices of modern oil state that had overwritten or incorporated his world, and, unassimilable, haunts it—indeed, the novel—with the revolutionary memory of its own abuses. Drawing on a wide range of primary and secondary sources, I trace Munif's spectral inf(l)ection of novelistic form through a discussion of questions of indigeneity in the world (literary) system; the textualization of Bedouin oral poetic tradition in Orientalism; and the dialectics of what I call Gulf (especially Saudi Arabian) "petro-modernity" in relation to Bedouin history, politics, and culture. In sum, this chapter articulates the linkage between world literature, Orientalism, modernity, the novel, and spectrality at the heart of this book.

Chapter 2, "A Genealogy of *Adab* in the Comparative Middle East," sets the historical scene of the book by charting the emergence of the modern concept of "literature" in the Middle East. After surveying the range of terms for the literary that are currently in use across the Arab world, Turkey, and Iran (especially *"adab," "edebiyat,"* and *"adabiyāt"*), I raise a series of questions pertaining to their origins, constitution, ideological content, and functions in their national and regional contexts. I argue that in their contemporary deployment, each is premised on the reinscription of the classical Arabic-Islamic concept of *"adab"* that took place in tandem with the incorporation process in their national milieus from the nineteenth to the mid-twentieth centuries. Against the long-held view in Arabic literary studies that *adab* is equivalent to "belles-lettres," I, following the lead of the more recent scholarship, reinterpret it as an expression of the multiple modalities of political, social, and cultural experience of the classical to medieval Arabic-Islamic life-world. With reference to the relevant primary and secondary sources, and paying particular attention to the influence of an internalized Orientalist philology, I then trace how *adab* was systematically reinscribed as "literature" in the modern,

European sense in Egypt, Turkey, and Iran during the period under discussion. Comprising a wholesale re-envisioning of the Middle Eastern literary and cultural sphere, this act laid the groundwork for the novel and other modern literary forms in the Middle East. I thus posit the Middle Eastern novel as founded on the occlusion and marginalization of literary and cultural tradition in the region, which thereby returns to haunt it according to the logic of spectrality. Based on what I will have identified as the overlapping trajectories of (literary and cultural) modernity across the region, I close the chapter by forwarding the idea of a "comparative Middle East."

In **Part II, "The Middle Eastern Novel and the Spectral Life-World of Modernity,"** which includes three chapters, I explore the Middle Eastern novel in the world today. In each of these chapters, I assess how the Middle Eastern novel's production, translation, circulation, and reception in the world is mediated by a variety of strategies of containment and domestication that obscure its spectral engagements with the others of Middle Eastern modernity. Focusing respectively on novels from Egypt, Turkey, and Iran, and paying special attention to form, I then provide a series of counter-readings that seek to redress this imbalance. In each case, I demonstrate the spectral inf(l)ection of novelistic form by the political, religious, and gender experiences of the life-world designated and expressed by *adab*. In so doing, I cumulatively show how the Middle Eastern novel traverses and reconfigures the aesthetic forms definitive of the modern novel from the perspective of its others. Across these chapters, the Middle Eastern novel is thus critically conceptualized as expressive of the spectral life-world of modernity.

Chapter 3, "The Revolution of Form: Naguib Mahfouz from the Suez Crisis to the Arab Spring," considers how Naguib Mahfouz—the only Arab Nobel laureate for literature to date—has been co-opted in global and in national literary cultures alike. I argue that while the Swedish Academy's decision to award Mahfouz the Nobel Prize in 1988 was based on universalist principles that obscure what I regard as his more local aesthetic and formal sensibilities, his subsequent recognition by the Egyptian state as a national writer similarly obscures his lifelong critique of that same state for its authoritarianism, corruption, and political violence. Both acts, I continue, have the same effect—they inscribe Mahfouz and his work into their narratives of (global, national) modernity, and thus undermine or negate his actual significance for world literature. In this chapter, I aim to restore this significance.

I start by surveying what Rasheed El-Enany has described as the four main phases of Mahfouz's novel-writing career (those of historical romance, realism, modernism, and, finally, the return to "indigenous" or "traditional" form), which I suggest provide a useful introduction to the history of the Arabic novel in general. I then turn more exclusively to the novels of his late, indigenous / traditional phase. First, I offer a reading of *Arabian Nights and Days* (*Layālī Alf Layla*, 1979; trans. 1995). Against the Orientalist construction of the *One Thousand and One Nights* as a work of world literature, I argue that Mahfouz's novel draws on the frame narrative, folklorish elements, and magical devices of this ur-text of the Arabic popular tradition in order to reinvent the novel as a world literary form. Second, I look into *Morning and Evening Talk* (*Ḥadīth al-Ṣabāḥ wa al-Masā'*, 1987; trans. 2007). Mahfouz's last major literary engagement with Egyptian political history, this novel, I argue, adopts and adapts the classical Arabic genre of the *ṭabaqāt* in order to reinterpret the 200-year trajectory of modernity in the country (which comes to its crux in the Suez Crisis and its aftermath) from the perspective of its political, social, cultural, and economic margins. I round off the chapter by considering the implications of what I call Mahfouz's "revolution of form" for literary, cultural, and scholarly discourses of the Egyptian Revolution of 2011. In contrast to the cultural outpouring of Tahrir Square and to what has been termed the "1990's generation" of Egyptian writers, and overlooked in the scholarship on the Arab Spring, I propose that Mahfouz's engagement with form enacts a more deeply rooted, organic, and historically conscious *form of revolution* against the abuses of (Egyptian) modernity.

Chapter 4, "Islam and the Limits of Translation: Orhan Pamuk and the Ottoman Revival," addresses the carefully (self-)cultivated image of Orhan Pamuk—the only other Middle Eastern Nobel laureate for literature to date—as a worldly, cosmopolitan, and secular-liberal writer. Best encapsulated by Rebecca Walkowitz's "born translated" paradigm of world literature, this image, I argue, has come to define the aesthetics and politics, the ethos, of his novels as these have made their way into the world. It has functioned to undermine the nature and extent of his engagement with the local (especially his native city, Istanbul, and its Ottoman, Islamic heritage), and, by extension, the ways in which such engagement is reflected in his manipulation of novelistic form. In this chapter, I contest the "born translated" idea, and demonstrate that Pamuk and his work are better understood as *untranslatable* in the many senses proposed by Emily Apter.

I do so via a sustained focus on *The Black Book* (*Kara Kitap*, 1990; trans. 1994, 2006), Pamuk's opus of 1990, as this novel has been translated and read in Britain and the United States. I start with a detailed critical introduction to the novel in relation to the history of the Turkish modernity that serves as its ultimate horizon, and with reference to important recent scholarship on Pamuk. Next, I inquire into its English translations. Offsetting Güneli Gün's (1994) and Maureen Freely's (2006) respectively foreignizing and domesticating translation strategies against my own literal translations of select passages, and drawing on the translation theory of Lawrence Venuti, I show that both are by definition unable to capture the logic and significance of Pamuk's culturally specific use of language. This translational limitation, I suggest, has strongly influenced the novel's Anglo-American reception, which has tended to emphasize its worldly postmodernism at the expense of its rich and nuanced investment in the local. In the counter-reading I then pursue, I argue that anything but a postmodernist deconstruction of the myths of national and religious identity, *The Black Book* in fact comprises an evocation of Istanbul's (and Turkey's) Ottoman, Islamic heritage in the face of a Turkish secular modernity by which this heritage has been and continues to be repressed. I detail this argument through close attention to Pamuk's treatment of Islam, especially the Sufi and Hurufi orders, as this is indicated by the imagery of the mannequin, the face, and the writer that saturates and even structures the novel. *The Black Book*, I conclude, inscribes what I call "cultural neo-Ottomanism" as form. I end the chapter by considering the implications of Pamuk's cultural neo-Ottomanism for questions of the Islamic Revival in the Middle East and the postsecularism / secularism debate.

Chapter 5, "Women in the Literary Marketplace: The Anglophone Iranian Novel and the Feminist Subject," turns to the anglophone—specifically, the recent upsurge in the production and visibility of English-language novels authored by Middle Eastern writers in Britain and the United States—as an increasingly important site of and mechanism for the discursive and representational worlding of the region. While the majority of scholarly attention in this area has fallen on the anglophone *Arab* novel, I suggest that the anglophone *Iranian* novel might well be considered alongside the former within the "comparative Middle East" framework that I have set out. In this chapter, I investigate how and to what ends the anglophone Iranian novel mediates Iran in and for the world. I look into the material and political contexts of its production, circulation, and reception in the English-speaking world, and zoom in on its engagement with questions of gender in Iran (especially after the Revolution of 1979) as a means to address the ensuing geopolitical tensions between this country and "the West." Through this analysis, I weigh the possibilities and limitations of the (post-postcolonial) "global anglophone literature" model that has come to the fore within the disciplinary nexus of English in recent years.

I start with a historical overview of diasporic Iranian literary production after the Revolution, paying particular attention to autobiographies / memoirs and novels written by women in this period. Drawing on the work of Max Saunders, I forward the notion of "autobiografiction" as critical lens through which these most prominent of anglophone Iranian literary genres might be read alongside one another. Next, I assess how the US discourse of Iran as a "rogue state" has deployed the rhetoric of gender repression there in order to further US geopolitical interests in the region. This discourse, I suggest, has come to define the Anglo-American publishing industry's approach to Iranian literature. Having thus established the political and material contexts of the anglophone Iranian novel, I then delve more deeply into its representations of gender. Following Hamid Dabashi and others, I argue that the massive popular and critical acclaim by which Azar Nafisi's memoir (or, in my terms, autobiografiction) *Reading Lolita in Tehran: A Memoir in Books* (2003) was met was based on its conformity to and reproduction of the "rogue state" idea of Iran, and its related disavowal of any form of feminism—especially Islamic feminism—other than the secular-liberal or universal. Yasmine Crowther's and Marjane Satrapi's likewise autobiografictional (graphic) novels *The Saffron Kitchen* (2006) and *Persepolis* (2000–3; trans. 2003, 2004), I continue, work against the cosmopolitan literary and political ideals to which Nafisi's text subscribes, and instead plot trajectories of feminist agency in Iran rooted in and taking their contours from a sense of *multiple belonging* in nation, religion, family, and profession. Individually and together, they thus remap the cosmopolitan novel's characteristic narrative of flight from the "Third World" as what I identify as a narrative of return to and active participation in the world. In so doing, they, I conclude, articulate new and compelling visions of Iranian modernity for their global audiences, and bring important Iranian perspectives to bear on the contemporary discussion of Islamic feminism in literature and culture.

In my **Conclusion, "Futures of Spectrality,"** I consider the wider implications of the book. Addressing the question of whether "spectrality"—and by extension (Derridean) theory per se—has a future in literary studies given the "postcritical" turn that scholars such as Rita Felski have recently called for, I suggest that it indeed does. This book, I affirm, is nothing if not a contribution to and expansion of the project of critique for the world literature debate. Through its reading of the Middle Eastern novel as metonym and metaphor of such, it will have sought to reorient world literature around the paradigmatic critical figure of the specter. Moving forwards, our task and indeed responsibility is one of expanding this analysis to the world in endless critique.

Notes

1. Young, *Colonial Desire*, p. 163.
2. Damrosch, *What is World Literature?*, p. 14.
3. Ibid. p. 4.
4. Ibid. pp. 4, 283.
5. Moretti, "Conjectures on World Literature," p. 55.
6. Ibid. pp. 55, 56. Emphasis in original.
7. Ibid. pp. 56, 66, 64. For a more detailed discussion of "distant reading," including Moretti's response to the controversy that has surrounding this term since he proposed it, see Moretti, *Distant Reading*.

8. Casanova, *The World Republic of Letters*, p. 45.
9. Many other contributions to the world literature debate have also tended to prioritize questions of the remit, scale, scope, and so forth of a literary studies organized around the concept of "world," and often similarly at the expense of a thorough investigation of the object being worlded. Among the most prominent of these contributions are Spivak, *Death of a Discipline*; Tanoukhi, "The Scale of World Literature"; Thomsen, *Mapping World Literature*; Hayot, *On Literary Worlds*; and Cheah, *What is a World?*
10. Goethe, "Conversations with Eckermann on *Weltliteratur* (1827)," p. 19.
11. Marx, "The Communist Manifesto," p. 225.
12. For an unabridged translation of Eckermann's original volume, see Goethe, *Conversations of Goethe with Johann Peter Eckermann*.
13. Goethe, "Conversations with Eckermann on *Weltliteratur* (1827)," p. 18.
14. Ibid. p. 19.
15. Pizer, *The Idea of World Literature*, p. 40.
16. Ibid. pp. 35, 45.
17. See Goethe, "Conversations with Eckermann on *Weltliteratur* (1827)," p. 15.
18. See Said, *Orientalism*, p. xviii.
19. Goethe, *West-East Divan*, p. 176. See Schwab, *The Oriental Renaissance*.
20. Goethe, *West-East Divan*, p. 24.
21. Ibid. p. 24.
22. Said, *Orientalism*, p. 167.
23. Ibid. p. 154.
24. Pizer, *The Idea of World Literature*, p. 30.
25. See Pizer, *The Idea of World Literature*, pp. 65–6; Prawer, *Karl Marx and World Literature*, pp. 143–5; and Puchner, *Poetry of the Revolution*, pp. 48–53.
26. Marx, "The Communist Manifesto," pp. 224–5.
27. Prawer, *Karl Marx and World Literature*, p. 144.
28. Puchner, *Poetry of the Revolution*, pp. 49, 50.
29. Ibid. pp. 50–1.
30. Marx, "The Communist Manifesto," p. 224.
31. Ibid. p. 224.
32. See Berman, *All That Is Solid Melts Into Air*, p. 16.
33. Williams, *Marxism and Literature*, p. 50; Eagleton, *Literary Theory*, p. 16.
34. See Abrams, *The Mirror and the Lamp*, pp. 70–99.
35. Ibid. p. 17.
36. Eagleton, *The Ideology of the Aesthetic*, p. 3.

37. See Marx, *Grundrisse*, pp. 471–513.
38. For a useful overview of the intellectual history of world-systems theory in its wider contexts, see Wallerstein, *World-Systems Analysis*, pp. 1–22.
39. Wallerstein, *World-Systems Analysis*, pp. 16–7. Emphasis in original.
40. Ibid. p. 17.
41. Wallerstein, *The Modern World-System I*, p. 347.
42. Ibid. p. 66.
43. Regarding the issue of periodization, there is some disagreement among Wallerstein's colleagues and collaborators. For Giovanni Arrighi, the world-system originates not in the sixteenth, but rather in the fourteenth century, when the Mediterranean trade hegemonies of the city-states of Venice, Genoa, and Florence produced the first of a succession of "systemic cycles of accumulation" or "long centur[ies]" that precipitated the later Dutch, British, and US cycles. Arrighi, *The Long Twentieth Century*, pp. 6, 7. For Janet Abu-Lughod, the world-system first arose not as what she considers to be these "Eurocentric" approaches would have it, but rather in the thirteenth century, when, prior to the European hegemony, there existed a vast trading network that stretched across Eurasia and that was stitched together by the Mongol Empire. Abu-Lughod, *Before European Hegemony*, p. ix. Despite these differences, the core structural features of the world-system as defined by Wallerstein as well as his account of its specifically modern and capitalist manifestation—the central concern of my own appeal to this theory—remain largely consistent among the majority of its practitioners. I will therefore outline these with reference to the work of the field's progenitor.
44. Wallerstein, *World-Systems Analysis*, p. 23.
45. Ibid. p. 23.
46. Ibid. p. 23.
47. Wallerstein, *The Modern World-System I*, p. 163.
48. Wallerstein, *World-Systems Analysis*, p. 28.
49. Jameson, *A Singular Modernity*, p. 12.
50. Ibid. p. 12.
51. Wallerstein, *World-Systems Analysis*, p. 17. Emphasis in original.
52. Palumbo-Liu et al., "Introduction": pp. 5, 4. This volume comprises an excellent discussion of the possibilities and limitations of a world-systems theory / humanities, especially literary studies, rapprochement.
53. Hopkins and Wallerstein, "Capitalism and the Incorporation of New Zones into the World-Economy," p. 776.

54. Ibid. p. 776.
55. Amin, *Unequal Development*, pp. 200, 202, 201.
56. Ibid. p. 203.
57. Of course, world-systems theorists have addressed the question of culture within their frameworks of analysis. For a useful overview of the relevant debates about culture in world-systems theory, see Wallerstein, *World-Systems Analysis*, pp. 60–75. However, the question of literature in particular has not come under significant consideration in this work, and certainly not in relation to the incorporation process as I am discussing.
58. Mufti, *Forget English!*, p. 80. Emphasis in original.
59. Ibid. p. 19.
60. See also Mufti, "Orientalism and the Institution of World Literatures." In his recent book *Archaeology of Babel: The Colonial Foundation of the Humanities* (2017), Siraj Ahmed makes a very similar argument about the constitution of the category of world literature in Orientalist philology and colonialism. However, he also takes Mufti to task for remaining indebted to the philological tradition and its endemic structures of power and hegemony even while attempting to correct its Eurocentrism. See Ahmed, *Archaeology of Babel*, p. 47. I discuss Ahmed's work as well as his critique of Mufti at greater length in Chapter 1.
61. Mufti, *Forget English!*, p. 19. Emphasis in original removed.
62. Ibid. p. 32.
63. Ibid. pp. 32, 33. Emphasis in original removed.
64. See Said, *Orientalism*, pp. 1–4.
65. Mufti, *Forget English!*, pp. 19, 20. Emphasis in original removed.
66. Wallerstein himself regards Orientalism as essentially a modernizing endeavor. Assessing their project as one of explaining why "these 'high civilizations' [of the Orient] were not 'modern' like the pan-European world," he argues that "[t]he answer the Orientalists seemed to put forth was that there was something in the composite culture of these civilizations which had 'frozen' their history, and had made it impossible for them to move forward [. . .] to 'modernity.'" "It followed," he concludes, "that these countries thus required assistance from the pan-European world if they were to move forward to modernity." Wallerstein, *World-Systems Analysis*, pp. 8, 9.
67. Moretti, "Conjectures on World Literature," p. 58. Emphasis in original removed.
68. Mufti, *Forget English!*, p. 105. Emphasis in original removed.

69. Ibid. p. 109. Emphasis in original.
70. Ibid. p. 97. See also Mufti, "Orientalism and the Institution of World Literatures."
71. Casanova, *The World Republic of Letters*, p. 115.
72. Ibid. pp. 127, 126.
73. See Mufti, *Forget English!*, pp. 96–7.
74. See Casanova, *The World Republic of Letters*, pp. 45–81.
75. Moretti, "Conjectures on World Literature," pp. 64, 65. Emphasis in original removed.
76. I more fully discuss *adab*, its genres, and its reinscription as "literature" in the modern sense across the Middle East in Chapter 2.
77. Kadir, "To World, To Globalize," p. 7.
78. Mufti, *Forget English!*, p. 94.
79. Apter, *Against World Literature*, p. 3, 2.
80. Adorno, *Aesthetic Theory*, p. 5.
81. Ibid. p. 5.
82. Ibid. p. 145.
83. Ibid. p. 145.
84. Ibid. p. 145.
85. Jameson, *The Political Unconscious*, pp. 62, 63.
86. Adorno, *Aesthetic Theory*, p. 6. For a wider-ranging introduction to the question of form in the Marxist tradition, see Jameson, *Marxism and Form*.
87. Marx, *Capital*, p. 125.
88. Ibid. pp. 126, 125.
89. Ibid. p. 127.
90. Ibid. p. 127.
91. Ibid. p. 165.
92. See Lukács, *History and Class Consciousness*, pp. 83–110.
93. Ibid. p. 84. Emphasis in original.
94. Moretti, "Conjectures on World Literature," p. 66.
95. Husserl, *The Crisis of European Sciences and Transcendental Phenomenology*, pp. 142–3. Emphasis in original.
96. Ibid. pp. 108, 147.
97. Ibid. p. 143.
98. See especially Adorno, *Against Epistemology*.
99. Habermas, *The Theory of Communicative Action, Volume 2*, p. 119.
100. Ibid. p. 124.

101. Ibid. p. 136. Emphasis in original.
102. See Fukuyama, *The End of History and the Last Man*.
103. Derrida, *Specters of Marx*, p. 96.
104. Ibid. p. 96.
105. Ibid. p. 85.
106. Ibid. pp. 86, 85, 84. For an excellent discussion of the resonances of Derrida's reading for Marxist theory more generally, see Sprinker (ed.), *Ghostly Demarcations*.
107. Derrida, *Specters of Marx*, p. 6.
108. Ibid. p. 3, *passim*.
109. Ibid. pp. 10, 39–40. Emphasis in original.
110. Spivak, "Translator's Preface," p. xvii.
111. Ibid. p. 47. Emphasis in original.
112. Derrida, *Margins of Philosophy*, pp. 8, 9. Emphasis in original removed.
113. Ibid. p. 11.
114. Blanco and Peeren, "Introduction," pp. 5, 7.
115. Ibid. p. 7.
116. Cooppan, "Ghosts in the Disciplinary Machine," p. 16.
117. Rabaté, *The Ghosts of Modernity*, p. xvi.
118. Cheah, *Spectral Nationality*, pp. 393, 394.
119. Benjamin's main presentation of capitalism as a "phantasmagoria" occurs in his unfinished masterpiece, *The Arcades Project* (1972; trans. 1999). He cites Marx's analysis of the commodity in "Convolute G," and introduces his project in the "Exposé" of 1939, "Paris, Capital of the Nineteenth Century," as one of "show[ing] how, as a consequence of this reifying representation of civilization, the new forms of behaviour and the new economically and technologically based creations that we owe to the nineteenth century enter the universe of a phantasmagoria." Benjamin, *The Arcades Project*, p. 14 (see also pp. 181–2, *passim*). For excellent discussions of this concept as it resonates throughout Benjamin's work, see Buck-Morss, *The Dialectics of Seeing* and Cohen, "Walter Benjamin's Phantasmagoria."
120. For the epigraph, see Derrida, *Specters of Marx*, p. xix. Emphasis in original.
121. Schmidt, *Forms of Modernity*, p. ix; Lukács, *The Theory of the Novel*, p. 103; Foucault, *The Order of Things*, p. 54. The foregoing list is an expanded version of that provided by Schmidt in *Forms of Modernity*.
122. Bloom, *The Western Canon*, p. 127.
123. See Watt, *The Rise of the Novel* and Watt, *Myths of Modern Individualism*.

124. Cervantes, *Don Quixote*, p. 8.
125. Ibid. p. 76.
126. For the "Windmills" episode, see Cervantes, *Don Quixote*, pp. 58–65. For an excellent, historically contextualized overview of Don Quixote's response to these and other developments in early modern Spain, see Schmidt, *Forms of Modernity*, pp. 17–29.
127. For her overview of each of these thinkers' approaches to *Don Quixote* and the novel form, see Schmidt, *Forms of Modernity*, pp. ix–xvi.
128. Lukács, *The Theory of the Novel*, p. 101.
129. Ibid. p. 101.
130. Ibid. p. 130.
131. Ibid. p. 130. Emphasis in original removed.
132. Foucault, *The Order of Things*, p. 53.
133. Ibid. p. 54.
134. Cervantes, *Don Quixote*, pp. 67, 916. Emphasis in original removed.
135. For Foucault on "author function," see Foucault, "What is an Author?"
136. Cervantes, *Don Quixote*, p. 67. Emphasis in original.
137. Ibid. p. 67.
138. For the introduction of the first part, see ibid. pp. 472–3. For Cervantes's most extensive discussion of the "false *Quixote*," see ibid. pp. 453–8.
139. For Genette on "metalepsis," see Genette, *Métalepse*. For the introduction of the duke and duchess, see Cervantes, *Don Quixote*, pp. 653–7.
140. With the exception of Parr, this list is provided by Walter Cohen. See Cohen, *A History of European Literature*, p. 269.
141. For "The Captive's Tale," see Cervantes, *Don Quixote*, pp. 330–74; for "Ricote's Exile / Return," see ibid. pp. 809–16, 875–83; for "The Puppet Show," see ibid. pp. 620–36; and for "*albogues*," see ibid. pp. 900–1.
142. This list is derived from the survey of relevant scholarship recently conducted by Nizar Hermes. See Hermes, "Why You Can/'t Believe the Arabian Historian Cide Hamete Benengeli."
143. Cohen, *A History of European Literature*, p. 239.
144. Ibid. p. 266. Emphasis added.
145. Cervantes, *Don Quixote*, p. 474.
146. Cohen, *A History of European Literature*, p. 272.
147. It should be noted, though, that Hermes's contribution on form in *Don Quixote* appeared before Cohen's. See, respectively, notes 142 and 140 above for the relevant bibliographical information.

148. For an unabridged English version of the "Frankish Tale," rendered there as "The Tale of Young Nur and the Warrior Girl," see Mardrus, *The Book of the Thousand Nights and One Night, Volume III*, pp. 297–341.
149. For an overview of the scholarship on Arabic influences on early Spanish literary culture, including the *maqāma / picaro* linkage, see Hermes, "Why You Can/'t Believe the Arabian Historian Cide Hamete Benengeli," pp. 213–6.
150. Ibid. p. 216.
151. In its original Italian, this collection is actually comprised of five volumes.
152. Moretti, "On *The Novel*," p. ix.
153. See Moretti (ed.), *The Novel, Volume 1* and Moretti (ed.), *The Novel, Volume 2*.
154. In our co-edited volume *The Edinburgh Companion to the Postcolonial Middle East* (2019), Anna Ball and I forward the concept of "post/colonial modernity" in relation to the Middle East, and define it "a broad intellectual and historical horizon for analysis" that suggests "both the impact of diverse colonial encounters on the modern history of the region and the forging of complex postcolonial positionalities against continued manifestations of local and global hegemony." Through this concept, we intend to underline the continuity of colonialism and its multifaceted structuring effects in the region even after formal decolonization. Ball and Mattar, "Dialectics of Post/Colonial Modernity in the Middle East," p. 8.
155. See Mahan, "The Persian Gulf and International Relations."
156. Ball and Mattar, "Dialectics of Post/Colonial Modernity in the Middle East," p. 4.
157. See ibid. p. 4.
158. See Said, *Orientalism*, pp. 1–28.
159. Said, *The Politics of Dispossession*, p. 372.

I
THE WORLDING OF "LITERATURE" IN THE MIDDLE EAST

I

The *Shabaḥ* of Modernity: World-Systems, the Petro-Imperium, and the Indigenous Trace

The abodes are desolate, halting-place and encampment too,
at Minà; deserted lies Ghaul, deserted alike Rijám,
and the torrent-beds of Er-Raiyán—naked shows their trace,
rubbed smooth, like letterings long since scored on a stony slab;
blackened orts that, since the time their inhabitants tarried there,
many years have passed over, months unhallowed and sacrosanct.
[. . .]

So I stood and questioned that site; yet how should we question rocks
set immovable, whose speech is nothing significant?
The Muʿallaqa of Labid

Stay—Let us weep at the remembrance of our beloved[.]
The Muʿallaqa of Imruʾ al-Qais

In a recent retrospective assessment of his translation of this novel some twenty-five years earlier, Peter Theroux recounts that with the appearance of Abdelrahman Munif's *Cities of Salt* (*Mudun al-Milḥ*, 1984–9; trans. 1987–93) in Arabic and then English, "[t]he Oil Encounter was to be woven into Arab and world literature."[1] This sense of *Cities of Salt* as singular—or at least pioneering—in its engagement with oil within the domain of world literature is supported by Edward Said. Writing in 1990, he identifies it as "the only serious work of fiction that tries to show the effect of oil, Americans, and the local oligarchy on a Gulf country."[2] Munif was uniquely equipped to chart these effects. For in the composition of his novel, the Jordanian-born Saudi writer (whose citizenship was revoked in 1963, for political reasons) was able to draw on a lifetime of hands-on experience in the Middle Eastern oil industry. He earned a Ph.D. in Petroleum Economics from the University of Belgrade (1961); worked for the Syrian Oil Ministry for a decade (1964–73); consulted for the Organization of Petroleum Exporting Countries (OPEC) from 1975 to 1980; and, in the same period, served as editor-in-chief for the Baghdad-based monthly periodical *Oil and Development* (*Al-Nafṭ wa al-Tanmiyya*). Further, and also well before *Cities of Salt*, he wrote an influential politico-economic treatise—his first book—that criticized the United States' involvement in the Gulf oil industry and called for the nationalization of this industry in especially Iraq (*The Principle of Partnership and the Nationalization of Arab Oil* [*Mabda' al-Mushāraka wa al-Ta'mīm al-Bitrūl al-'Arabi*, 1972]).[3] All this was to feed into *Cities of Salt*, a novel that depicts the oil encounter in the fictional Gulf state or Sultanate of Mooran (which closely resembles Munif's native Saudi Arabia), and that details its effects on a nomadic Bedouin community that is violently and traumatically incorporated into the particular form of modernity—what I call "petro-modernity"—that is constituted in its wake.

The transition of *Cities of Salt* into the world via its (English) translation was, however, far from easy or straightforward. Indeed, it was met with an immense degree of antagonism upon its English-language publication. Most famously—or infamously—encapsulated in a review authored by John Updike for *The New Yorker* in 1988 (and collected in his *Odd Jobs: Essays and Criticism* [2012]), this sense of hostility and dismissiveness came to define the discursive parameters within which the novel has been and continues to be read in the (Anglo-American) world. In this review, Updike portentously explains that Munif "appears to be [. . .] insufficiently Westernized to produce a narrative that feels much like what we call a novel"—a rather "unfortunate" circumstance, in his estimation.[4] The specific problem with what he thereby implies is merely the text, he continues, is that it, concerned with "men in the aggregate," lacks a "central figure" with "enough reality to attract our sympathetic interest."[5] That is, it falls short of the paradigm of "individual moral adventure" as established by Miguel de Cervantes in *Don Quixote* (*El ingenioso hidalgo don Quijote de la Mancha*, 1605–15) and Daniel Defoe in *Robinson Crusoe* (1719), and as thus rendered characteristic of the European novel.⁶ While Updike's conclusions have of course been vigorously contested, his gesture of weighing *Cities of Salt* against its European forerunners and judging its merit, its status, even, as a novel according to its conformity or nonconformity to them has in no small measure come to frame its worldly reception.

In much of the critical debate on *Cities of Salt*, the prime motivating factor has been the (perceived) obligation to respond to Updike. As such, the overriding tone of the debate has been one of defensiveness. In their important recent interventions, Issa Boullata, Ilana Xinos, and Peter Hitchcock, for instance, all readily concede the point that the text lacks a typical protagonist in the European fashion. Against Updike, however, each seeks to reclaim its status as a novel by arguing that it does in fact contain a protagonist (and therefore remains consistent with the European model), though one with a different identity, location, and function in the narrative than is usually the case. For Boullata, Munif positions not any specific character, but rather "society as a whole [as] the protagonist of [his] novel"—a conscious formal decision on the author's part, in that "this juncture of historical circumstance in Arabia" demanded of Munif that he turn his literary attention towards the social aggregate or collectivity.⁷ For Xinos, it is the "specific community" of alienated, working-class Bedouin in Harran (one of Munif's archetypal "cities of salt," based on the real-world Saudi city of Dhahran) that arises as "the novel's protagonist."⁸ Beyond Boullata's, this argument alludes to Munif's lifelong investment in the cause of socialism in the Arab world (as indicated by his membership in and brief stint working for Ba'ath Party in the early 1960s, until he was ostracized and forced to resign in 1965 due to political differences)—through it, Xinos is able to detect in the novel a strong reflection of this sensibility. And for Hitchcock, it is because Bedouin self-identification is inherently collective that Munif avoids standard European modes of characterization, and opts instead to transcribe their lived experience of community through his use of "timeshifts, repetitions, formal (classical Arabic) and colloquial narration (local/regional dialects), lengthy transgressions, and transnational locations."⁹

In their counter-readings, these critics have provided a valuable grounds for understanding and appreciating *Cities of Salt* despite the objections of its naysayers. However, it seems to me that in their rush to rescue the novel from Updike's myopic disavowal of its very being, they, by the same token, have fallen into an interpretive trap unwittingly laid by him. That is, their ripostes are all premised on and all reproduce what might be regarded as the "protagonist-assumption" that mobilizes Updike's approach to the novel and that structures his notion of novelistic form in general—unreflexively taking it on, they merely define "protagonist" more expansively than as a "central figure" in their attempts to recast *Cities of Salt* as a novel. As is clearly seen to be the case in Updike, this is an issue because this assumption is derived from the European novel and might therefore be considered a Eurocentric one. As I will show, its adoption in critical readings of the novel obscures certain crucial facets of Munif's engagement with novelistic form, the challenge he poses to the European novel and his attempt to reconfigure it against its complicity in the very process of the Bedouin's incorporation into petro-modernity that emerges as the central concern of his narrative. So then, instead of contesting Updike, I wish to take his reading at face value, and identify it as symptomatic of a world literature that can only conceive of the novel—and, by extension, of "the literary"—within a Eurocentric framework. It might appear excessive to make such a claim on the basis of a single (and widely disputed) viewpoint. Nevertheless, I think that it is brought home by the fact that even those who have been most outspoken in their opposition to Updike have tended to perpetuate his underlying assumptions in their own approaches to the novel, which I take to be at least partly representative of its wider reception in the world.

In this chapter, I argue that *Cities of Salt* is illegible to world literature precisely because Munif deconstructs the inherited European notions of "protagonist" on which his novel's worldly reception has been based. This argument hinges on what I show to be Munif's spectral characterization of Bedouin resistance leader Miteb al-Hathal. Having disappeared from his desert oasis village Wadi al-Uyoun upon the arrival of American corporate agents and the discovery of oil there, this figure intermittently resurfaces as a "*shabaḥ*," a specter, at the interstices of the modern oil state that had subsequently been installed, and that had overwritten or incorporated his world. Refusing incorporation, and expunged from the newly erected state and its political, religious, military, and economic hegemony (what I call its "petro-imperium"), yet retaining his connection to and identification with another world, he thereby haunts it—indeed, the novel—with the revolutionary memory of its own abuses. Thus figuring the unassimilable other of (petro-)modernity as it seeks to inscribe the Bedouin into its polity and its metaphysics, Miteb's ghostly trace also comes to suggest the infection and inflection of one of its forms—the novel—by the local, indigenous life-world that this form has been complicit in displacing. This, I demonstrate, is what is lost to world literature due to its reliance on a Eurocentric understanding of the novel.

After providing a detailed critical introduction to *Cities of Salt* (specifically, its first volume), I trace Munif's spectral inf(l)ection of novelistic form in four steps or stages. First, I frame the novel in relation to the big-picture question of indigeneity in the world (literary) system. With reference to the *Prolegomena* (*Al-Muqaddima*, 1377) of Ibn Khaldun as well as to more recent scholarship (as in Halim Barakat, miriam cooke, and others), and looking into the fate of the Naqab Bedouin in Israel as a contemporary case study, I suggest that the millennial dialectic of nomadism and civilization in the Middle East continues to unfold as the region's states strive ever more aggressively to incorporate their vestigial indigenous communities into their structures and strictures. Assessing Munif's contribution to what Chadwick Allen proposes as a "global indigenous literary studies," I foreground his uniquely spectral traversal of and engagement with this process in *Cities of Salt*. Second, I consider the apparent contradiction of Munif's depiction of a traditionally oral indigenous culture in the textual form of a novel. Drawing on the work of Aamir Mufti and Siraj Ahmed, I contextualize this issue with reference the textualization of Bedouin oral poetry in the Orientalist philology of William Jones (specifically, his translation/transcription of the *Mu'allaqāt* [c. sixth–seventh centuries; trans. 1782]). Once more, I forward his use of spectrality as a unique means of working through the orality / textuality paradox. Third, I address his representation—or non-representation— of oil in the context of a global culture that has failed to significantly register this most vital of resources—its origins, role in, and pervasive effects on the contemporary world—in its imaginary (a point that has variously been made by Amitav Ghosh, Imre Szeman, Rob Nixon, Peter Hitchcock, Timothy Mitchell, Robert Vitalis, and others). I show that despite ordering and controlling the totality of the world that is born in its image, oil remains an absent signifier in Munif's text—its effects are seen and felt throughout, but never is its black viscosity exploited for its ready metaphoric appeal. This, I argue, is intentional on Munif's part— its non-representation indicates something of the reason why oil and the shadowy, corrupt conditions of its production in especially Saudi Arabia and its partner, the United States, have been, and must be, excluded from culture. Finally, bringing the foregoing discussion to its crux, I home in on Miteb al-Hathal as a figure of spectrality who most fully expresses the remit and ambition of Munif's novel. I closely follow his disappearance from Wadi al-Uyoun and his multiple spectral reappearances, and argue that by the end of the novel, his spectrality holds out the only possible promise of what Jacques Derrida calls a "democracy to come" in (Saudi) petro-modernity.

In undertaking this analysis, my aim is to provide an illustration of the critical and theoretical underpinnings of this book as a whole, and to demonstrate the link between world literature, Orientalism, modernity, the novel, and spectrality at its heart.

Abdelrahman Munif's *Cities of Salt*: An Introduction

In its original Arabic, the title of the first volume of Munif's five-volume novel is not "*Cities of Salt*" (the title of the quintet as a whole), but rather "*Al-Tīh*" (1984). Meaning "the wilderness," this term is intended to indicate the wilderness of the soul as well as that of forced migration. While the subsequent volumes turn more to the intrigues of Mooran's royal family as it strives to consolidate its power both before and after the discovery of oil, *Al-Tīh* (which I henceforth refer to as "*Cities of Salt*," after its English translation [1987]) maintains a tight focus on a community of indigenous Bedouin in Mooran as it is exposed to, impacted by, and eventually incorporated in the modern oil state that overtakes its habitat and its way of life.[10] After evoking the quiet, pastoral life of this community in the prelapsarian oasis of Wadi al-Uyoun ("Valley of the Water Springs"), and then detailing its destruction at the onset of petro-modernity, it charts the scattering of its inhabitants—now displaced, and increasingly cut off from one another—across the Arabian Peninsula. Many end up in the newly founded coastal export town of Harran, a "city of salt" that—as the author once explained in an interview with Tariq Ali—"offer[s] no sustainable existence" due to its inorganic, capital-driven, and alienating nature.[11] As such, *Cities of Salt* provides what the Arab intellectual Mansur from Munif's first novel *Trees and the Assassination of Marzuq* (*Al-Ashjār wa Ightiyāl Marzūq*, 1973) describes, in Sabry Hafez's translation, as "not the history of the kings, hucksters[,] or pimps who try to look like roosters, but of simple people who went unnoticed, whose names no one mentioned in a book, or bothered to inscribe on a piece of marble."[12] It is, in short, a counter-historical novel that seeks to re-inscribe the story of the Bedouins' doubled material and historiographical dispossession, and to pry open a space in the (global) cultural imaginary for the losses, the violence and disruption that have been written out of or overwritten by official (Saudi, American) narratives, those wrought by petro-modernity.

Cities of Salt opens with what is sometimes dismissed as an overly idealizing, romantic tropology of Wadi al-Uyoun. Munif introduces the Wadi as "an outpouring of green amid the harsh, obdurate desert"; as "one of those rare cases of nature expressing its genius and willfulness, in defiance of any explanation"; as a "phenomenon," a "miracle," an "earthly paradise."[13] It is figured by Miteb al-Hathal, a community paterfamilias of sorts, and his tribe, the Atoum, as the center-point around which their world turns—the landmarks of the surrounding desert are mapped in relation to their proximity from it, and the caravan trails of the nomadic, trading members of the tribe extend from, and always back to the Wadi. Further, the Wadi's water-based ecology instills a sense of social and environmental relationality among the more settled, farming Atoum— the existential necessity of maintaining a balanced usage of this scarce resource mediates their symbiotic relationship to the land, and thereby their inherently collective social, economic, and cultural practices. Idealized though it may be, this description aims to capture the nature and rhythms of the Bedouins' pastoral world; their cyclical, cosmic sense of time; and their localized, tribal sense of space. The Wadi, in a word, represents not just a physical place with its accompanying customs and traditions, but also a metaphysics that undergirds the Bedouins' relationship to their world.

Into this landscape "three foreigners" suddenly appear, raising Miteb's and the tribe's suspicions as to their intentions.[14] They are American geologists who, armed with a working knowledge of the Arabic language and the Qur'ān (c. 609–32), initiate the search for oil.[15] Suggesting a historical parallel with the Crusades, these figures, though, can only be perceived by the Atoum as "Franks" and "Christians" given the tribe's localized and delimited sphere of knowledge.[16] Their mythified first encounter with the agent of petro-modernity is for the Atoum thus defined, to paraphrase Ian Watt, by "suspended decoding"—the trauma of the encounter doesn't just "delay" interpretation in this case, it proscribes it altogether as the concepts of "America," "geology," and even "oil" have yet to take shape or place within the Atoum's epistemology, their worldview.[17] The Americans' ensuing survey, involving going "to places no one dreamed of going," collecting "unthinkable things," writing "things no one understood," and using strange "instruments," manifests, then, as magic—"witchcraft," "sorcery"—in the Atoum's folkloric imagination: as Miteb puts it, "[t]he jinn took possession of the whole place from the day the infidels came—it's haunted."[18] And, as might by now be expected, the cognitive dissonance produced by the irruption of the modern into what is presented as the authentic, rooted, and organic culture of Bedouin pre-modernity soon mutates into violent physical upheaval. Despite Miteb's protests, the powerful local emir Abu Radwan is blinded by the "oceans of oil, oceans of gold" promised by the Americans, and tractors—"maddened machines"—descend to oversee the "butchery" of Wadi al-Uyoun, leaving this once-idyllic habitus of the Atoum to vanish "under the soil of another time."[19] Thus begins the story of what Hafez calls Mooran's "cruelly perverted" modernization, a story that although most closely parallelling that of Saudi Arabia, also extends to the entire Gulf region.[20]

In these opening hundred or so pages, *Cities of Salt* doesn't only delineate the collapse of the Bedouin way of life and the fragmentation of Bedouin community in petro-modernity. In what might be regarded as an allegory of the structural basis of this history, it also demonstrates, in outline, how this sort of devastation (inevitably) issues from the alliances between foreign corporate interests and corrupt local political elites that have to some extent defined the global oil industry per se. More broadly yet, it suggests that as global capitalist modernity intersects a single-resource economy such as Saudi Arabia's, a skewed, peripheral version of modernity results, one that establishes a hierarchical structure of power directed entirely towards the production and commodification of that resource for the international market. In the remainder of its 600-plus pages, the volume, with characteristic attention to its historical correlates, details how Mooran's increasingly wealthy ruling elite consolidates its power with the aid of its Desert Army, religious dogma, and American support, and how the Bedouin—now deprived of their (social) identity as well as their home—are consequently re-scripted as alienated labor in the modern oil state, or petro-imperium.[21] It shows, as Timothy Mitchell says of what he calls contemporary "carbon democracy," "the networks through which oil flows and is converted into energy, profits[,] and political power."[22] The scene thus shifts from the Wadi, now an oilfield, to the coastal export town of Harran—there, the Wadi's former inhabitants, reduced to construction workers, build both the modern American compound ("large and well-ordered," replete with asphalt streets, palm trees, and swimming pools) and the Arab compound, which is segregated from the American, and built from the "remnants" of crates, zinc sheets, and stones imported for the other.[23] Insulated by his wealth, and distracted by new American technologies such as the telescope, the automobile, the radio, and the telephone, Harran's emir—Khaled al-Mishari—is unable to identify with the fate of his people. Suffering the mounting degradations of exploitative labor, inhuman living and working conditions, Orientalist American stereotyping, and police brutality, the once proud Bedouin workers eventually organize and strike, only to be subdued by force in a final act of incorporation.

 As the story of the existential decentering of the Bedouin and their life-world, it is fitting, then, that the narrative of *Cities of Salt* itself becomes radically decentered after the levelling of Wadi al-Uyoun, their original habitus. It is not only that the scene shifts from the Wadi to the new oil town of Harran, but also that the characters with whom the reader has lived and breathed for the first hundred pages largely drop from view, to be replaced by a succession of new generations from all over the Arabian Peninsula. This refusal of realist focalization through setting and character as established by the European novel and thus rendered characteristic, even definitive of the novel form is most dramatically embodied by Miteb. Once the focal point of the narrative and the sole remaining trace of Bedouin territorial, tribal, and cultural attachments, he likewise falls through the cracks of the narrative in a gesture of formal destabilization that upends the more traditional protagonist-figure's (partial) function of eliciting identification and empathy on the part of the reader and channelling his or her intimate relationship with the text. Along with the narratological structure of the text more generally, he therefore suggests something of what I'll call Munif's peripheral engagement with and reconfiguration of the form of the global novel. Drawing on Immanuel Wallerstein, Fredric Jameson, and Franco Moretti, the postcolonial critic Neil Lazarus reminds us that "[t]he specific modes of appearance of modernity in different times and places [. . .] ought then to be thought about not as 'alternative' but as 'coeval . . . modernities or, better yet, peripheral modernities . . . in which all societies shared a common reference provided by global capital and its requirements.'"[24] On these grounds, he then proposes that "world literature" be understood as "the literature that registers and encodes the social logic of modernity."[25] In the case of *Cities of Salt*, it seems to me that Munif "registers" through his manipulation of novelistic form the social logic of the modernity particular to Saudi Arabia and the Gulf region, a peripheral modernity in which the dynamic of global capitalism is mediated by the local and specific contexts of single-resource economics, centralized political power, and alienated social and cultural relations. In short, Munif invents—or at least compellingly and uniquely contributes to a longer history of such—Arabic peripheral modernism as form.

Yet Miteb doesn't vanish altogether. Terrifying the emirs and the Americans alike, he intermittently resurfaces as a desert resistance leader who can only manifest in the ambiguous form of a "ghost" or "specter"—in that of the *shabaḥ*—within the political and metaphysical parameters of the modern oil state.[26] As such, he points towards spectrality as a site of resistance to both the state and the novel as a global cultural form. This is because his spectrality is suggestive of the trace left in the world (literary) system by its other, the local culture, the local form otherwise lost to the machinery of modernization. While documenting the displacement of the Bedouin by reshaping the form of the global novel, *Cities of Salt* thus also deconstructs itself, the political baggage carried by its novelization of Bedouin culture, via the spectrality effect. And just as world literature might well be read to register the social logic of (peripheral) modernity, Munif's spectral characterization of Miteb also invites us to explore the trace of the other that the world literary system can never altogether assimilate or erase. In a word, *Cities of Salt* foregrounds spectrality as a constitutive feature of world literature, and, in so doing, articulates the critical thesis at the heart of this book.

Understood in this way, in its full formal as well as contextual specificity, *Cities of Salt* prompts new reflection on a range of issues in contemporary Arabic, Middle Eastern, and global literary studies. I now consider its implications for questions of indigeneity in the world (literary) system, the orality / textuality double bind in Orientalism, and the representation of oil in the global cultural imaginary.

Traces of Indigeneity in the World (Literary) System

As I have discussed, *Cities of Salt* presents the confrontation between Bedouin indigeneity in (a fictionalized) Saudi Arabia and the modern world as one of its central thematic and formal concerns. While within its narrative setting this encounter is played out against the specific backdrop of the Saudi oil industry in the twentieth century, the novel nevertheless taps into and evokes—or at least prompts consideration of—a longer history of tension and antagonism oriented around the figure of the Bedouin in relation to the gradually unfolding dialectic of modernity in the Middle East. A millennial one, this history pertains not only to Saudi Arabia and the Gulf, but also to the region at large. It is chronicled at least as early as the *Prolegomena* of Ibn Khaldun, the Tunisian historian and father of Islamic sociology. As he pursues his universal philosophy of history in this treatise, authored in 1377, Ibn Khaldun establishes a dichotomy—one which favors the latter—between the nomadic, pastoral life (*badawa*) of the Bedouin (*al-badawī*) and the settled, sedentary life (*ḥaḍara*) of civilization (*al-ḥaḍāra*). He argues that Arab society and culture had naturally advanced from the nomadic to the settled, and that the Bedouin represent an earlier, more primitive phase of pre-agricultural development: "[c]ompared with sedentary people," he emphasizes, "they are on a level with wild, untamable animals and dumb beasts of prey."[27] Through his analysis of the Bedouin, then, nomadism and civilization are posited by Ibn Khaldun as irreconcilably at odds, with the former—its "wandering and movement"—"the antithesis and negation" of the "civilization" towards which he wishes to usher the Arab world.[28]

In the modern states of the Arab world and the Middle East more generally, Ibn Khaldun's precepts about the Bedouin appear to have been widely adopted and instituted as policy. Indeed, it might be said that the nomadism / civilization dialectic first formulated by him has to some degree undergirded the evolution of the modern state system itself in the region. This is because nomadism—or, in the terms of Gilles Deleuze and Félix Guattari, "nomadology"—represents a structural threat to the state's very possibility, and must be incorporated to ensure the self-legitimation of the state via clearly defined boundaries.[29] As social interaction, relationship to nature, and metaphysics, it constitutes not a transgression of the state border (of the sort that can be policed or otherwise contained), but rather a far more dangerous force—a sensibility, one that undermines the very spatio-temporal foundations on which the state is built, that precedes and refuses to register the imposition of the border on the infinite and timeless desert, the metaphysical habitus of the Bedouin. As the noted Arab sociologist Halim Barakat has explained, this is the core structural reason why "[m]odern nation-states and political movements have used every sort of pressure and enticement to encourage bedouin to abandon 'their primitive way of life' and settle down."[30] Such measures, widespread across the Middle East, include: the subsidization of sheep over camel herding, the accompanying encouragement of a settled agricultural rather than a mobile trade economy, the state appropriation and redistribution of land, the conscription of youth into national armies, and the administration of education and healthcare provision.[31]

In her assessment of what she calls the "tribal modern" in the Gulf states of the United Arab Emirates, Qatar, Bahrain, and Kuwait, miriam cooke has suggested that the contemporary upshot of this process is less devastating for the Bedouin than would seem to be the case from the foregoing overview. Drawing on a range of "neo-Bedouin" case studies from across this area including language, dress, public ceremonies, vernacular architecture, national museums, and tribal sports, she—alluding to the Qur'anic notion of *"barzakh"* ("undiluted convergence")—argues that the tribal has made a resurgence in the Gulf of the twenty-first century, and that today's Gulf states have been able to successfully combine or integrate their hitherto conflicting "tribal and modern identities and cultures."[32] While compelling in its logic and especially readings, this argument, however, is problematic for a few reasons. It tends to downplay the sort of violence and disruption enacted upon the tribal when these oil states were originally being constituted that Munif, for one, has taken pains to restore to historical memory (though cooke does acknowledge that the tribal was "repressed" in the mid-twentieth century due to the demands of the nascent oil industry).[33] More to the point, it elides what Munif as well as the historical record have shown to be the radical political and metaphysical incommensurability between the life-worlds of the tribal and the modern. Today, given the history of the Bedouin's incorporation into the modern state that I (and Munif) have delineated, the tribal can only manifest—if at all—*within* the terrain of the very same modernity by which it was evacuated of its essential identity in the first place, its distinctive and unique relationship to and being in the world. To the extent that it has made a comeback or return, the tribal, then, has done so not in the terms of an "undiluted convergence" (with the modern), but rather in those of spectrality.

I now turn to the case of the Naqab Bedouin in contemporary Israel in order to demonstrate that the nomadism / civilization dialectic through which the modern Middle Eastern state has been structured and the violence by which it has historically been propelled are ongoing today. In September 2011, the Israeli government announced the so-called "Prawer Plan," the "Bill on the Arrangement of Bedouin Settlement in the Negev" ("Negev" is Israel's Hebraized name for *al-Naqab*, the Arabic name by which this desert region in the south of historical Palestine was known for centuries and more). According to Ehud Prawer, its architect and the head of policy planning in the Prime Minister's Office, the Plan was intended to address the "increasing gaps between Israeli Bedouin and Israeli society as a whole," and was based on four "cornerstones":

> 1) Providing for the status of Bedouin communities in the Negev; 2) Economic development for the Negev's Bedouin population; 3) Resolving claims over land ownership; and 4) Establishing a mechanism for binding, implementation and enforcement, as well as timetables.[34]

Its stated overall goal was to develop this region in (what became) Israel, and "to bring about a better integration of Bedouin in Israeli society."[35]

As with most Israeli state policies regarding its minorities, official explanations are often a thin veil for practices that are otherwise observably discriminating and disenfranchising. Bringing to mind the longer history of Palestinian displacement, and bearing specific comparison with the "Absentees' Property Law" of 1950, the Plan was in fact a policy of territorial and, correspondingly, social and cultural dispossession by other means.[36] Tantamount to ethnic cleansing as defined by the United Nations, its immediate consequences included the forced relocation of 30,000 Bedouin living in the Naqab to government sanctioned townships under the authority of the Abu Basma Regional Council; the demolition of up to thirty-five Bedouin villages "unrecognized" by the state; the uprooting of a further 40,000 members of these communities; and the permanent erasure of historical Bedouin ties to the land.[37] It is not by mere oversight that Prawer avoids mention of the fact that as it sought to shunt the Bedouin from their land, the Israeli government continued to pursue what British journalist Ben White describes as "initiatives for the creation of new Jewish communities in the Negev"—communities such as Hiran, which was built in the place of the levelled Bedouin village Umm al-Hiran.[38]

Spearheading the international campaign against it, Adalah—The Legal Center for Arab Minority Rights in Israel condemned the Plan for how it "legitimizes the displacement, dispossession, and eviction of tens of thousands of Arab Bedouin citizens of Israel," how it "establishes a legal framework to implement [discriminatory] government policies."[39] Taking this critique a step further, Ahmad Amara, a Palestinian human rights lawyer and scholar, has shown that the Israeli government derived its approach from Ottoman and British colonial policy, and has, since

1948, systematically "outlawed" the "very existence" of the Bedouin—their "villages, habitation, and centuries-old presence"—in the Naqab.[40] These arguments, and the accompanying legal challenges and protests orchestrated by Adalah, the International Solidarity Campaign, and other advocacy organizations both in Israel and around the world in the 2012–3 period had a substantial effect. They prompted the UN Office of the High Commissioner for Human Rights, the European Parliament, and the NGO Human Rights Watch to place, for the very same reasons, increasing pressure on the Israeli government to abandon its plans. Indeed, Navi Pillay, in her capacity as UN human rights chief at the time, officially stated that "[i]f this bill becomes law, it will accelerate the demolition of entire Bedouin communities, forcing them to give up their homes, denying them their rights to land ownership, and decimating their traditional cultural and social life."[41] While Israel's policies towards the Naqab Bedouin have continued in a less formal, more incremental and surreptitious manner, and are—to this day—very much in progress in the form of evictions, home demolitions, revocations of citizenship, and so forth, the Israeli government did at least make an appearance of ceding to this global backlash. In December 2013, it announced that the Plan will be halted.

At first glance, this narrative appears to signify a successful international campaign against a state's neocolonial designs regarding territories inhabited by its indigenous population. Without doubt, the campaign incisively exposed the slippage between official state discourse and its underlying motivations, and was, at least ostensibly, a political success. However, the basis on which it was launched might give us pause. In their critiques of the Plan, NGOs, IGOs, and scholars alike have all relied on the language—sometimes framed in relation to Israel's colonial history—of human rights and international law. In so doing, they have brought to the surface, or demystified, the Plan's otherwise occluded and indeed highly objectionable humanitarian ramifications and legal contraventions. Certainly, this language has been effective, and its appeal to principles commonly accepted in the international community is strategically sound, if not necessary in this scenario (given the difficulties that typically accompany attempts to forge international consensus in response to Israeli policy). But might it (as an ideological by-product of logic by which it has attained global currency) be masking *another* unsavory truth? What can we learn if we take the official Israeli justification at face value?

I return, then, to the overall intention of the Plan as stated by Prawer—to bring about "a better integration of Bedouin in Israeli society." The Plan's critics have dispelled the seeming innocuousness by which this objective was (deliberately) couched—its reference to the well-documented scarcity of education, healthcare, employment, and infrastructure provision in small, often makeshift villages that have yet to be assimilated into the state grid. What they have missed in their attempts towards a demystification, though, is the tragedy *already explicit* in Prawer's use of the term "integration." For "integration"—which, as I have comprehensively discussed, amounts to what Immanuel Wallerstein and others call "incorporation" into the modern world-system—has been the primary threat to the Bedouin way of life throughout the history of the region since, at the very least, Ibn Khaldun. While Israel's policies towards the Naqab Bedouin comprise a specific neocolonial variant of this process, then, Prawer's use of "integration" suggests what I have outlined as the more deeply rooted dialectic at the very heart of state formation not only in Israel, but also throughout the modern Middle East. Impelled not just by neocolonialism, but also by the forces of modernization, development, authoritarianism, and globalization, the Middle Eastern state has over the course of the last century systematically sought to incorporate the Bedouin into sedentary, localized, and accountable forms of sociopolitical existence as a condition of both its emergence in the first place, and its (sustained) hegemony. Continuing to unfold today (as I hope to have shown through the case of the Naqab Bedouin), the nomadism / civilization dialectic has thus determined the fate of Bedouin indigeneity in the modern Middle East. By extension, it might also be said to define the very nature and being of the indigenous in relation to the modern world-system.

Focalized through a consideration of the Bedouin in the Middle East, this account of indigeneity vis-à-vis the world-system offers significant new purchase on what Chadwick Allen has proposed as a "global indigenous literary studies." In his recent work, Allen has singularly and with remarkable energy sought to develop a framework for the critical, decolonized comparison of indigenous literatures and cultures from around the world—in his words, a "global literary studies (primarily) in English that [is] *trans*-Indigenous."[42] Allen is of course acutely aware of the critical as well as political risks involved with adopting a global comparative lens for such literatures and cultures when those of specific indigenous individuals, communities, and nations have for so long been marginalized, if registered at all, within the dominant critical paradigms of the (anglophone) academy. Eliding the specificity of the local (once more), this sort of approach—according to many indigenous and other scholars and intellectuals—potentially reproduces the top-down, homogenizing perspective of settler-colonialism itself as its basis for comparison. Nevertheless, he sees—and I strongly agree—the possibilities afforded by a more nuanced and reflexive comparatism as far outweighing the costs. He thus posits the prefix "*trans-*" (evoking *trans*lation, *trans*nationalism, *trans*formation, and so on) as a means to denote the importance of maintaining an emphasis on particular "traditions and contexts," while also acknowledging "the mobility and multiple interactions of Indigenous peoples, cultures, histories, and texts."[43] In this way occasioning new methodologies of critical thought and practice both within and across the local, the notion of "transindigenous" also precipitates a new politics of affiliation and engagement in response to settler-colonialism as this has impacted indigenous communities around the world.

Given his disciplinary background, it is understandable that Allen should orient his model of a global indigenous literary studies around literatures that are written "(primarily) in English." However, what many consider to be such an anglophone bias might be contested on numerous fronts. One might argue that it remains indebted and further contributes to the (exclusionary) disciplinary paradigms within which "the literary" is studied in the Anglo-American academy (even while expanding their canons); that it consolidates the primacy of English as a "literary" language, as well as its historical role as a tool of colonization in the very (settler-)colonial contexts under critical discussion; that it undermines the deployment of their own languages among indigenous writers, whether for the purposes of cultural self-expression or for those of resistance; and / or that it results in the critical neglect of indigenous literatures from parts of the world that have not been (directly) historically subjected to the imperium of English. While appreciating all of these concerns, for me, though, the most serious with Allen's anglophone approach is that it seems to invite a specific—and therefore delimited—historiography of the indigenous, one that is grounded in the admittedly widespread, but far from ubiquitous experience of settler-colonialism. That is, his anglophone model leads Allen to an exclusive focus on indigenous literatures and cultures from the anglophone settler-colonial contexts of North America, Hawaii, Aotearoa New Zealand, and Australia, which, in turn, requires a general indigeneity / settler-colonialism historiographical framework for the coherent comparison of (or readings across) such literatures and cultures. As I have shown, this simply does not apply to the case of (Bedouin) indigeneity in Saudi Arabia and the Gulf, where fully fledged settler-colonialism never took place, and also in much of the Middle East (with Palestine and Algeria being the obvious major exceptions). As I have also covered (in terms of global capitalist modernity), a more encompassing critical and historiographical framework and a correspondingly modified politics are thus necessary in order to compare indigenous literatures and cultures on a genuinely global scale.

All this, Munif directs us towards via his spectral traversal of and engagement with the process of the Bedouin's historical incorporation into (petro-)modernity in *Cities of Salt*. Suggesting something of the lot of indigeneity per se in the world (literary) system, his novel invokes what the Lebanese ethnographer Jibrail Jabbur notes as the traditional Bedouin poetic practice of "reading" the "remains" of the provisional desert campsite (the pre-Islamic / classical Arabic poetic form of the *qaṣīda* typically features as its opening motif or *nasīb* the poetic speaker engaged in such an act of reading or deciphering, known in Arabic as *al-wuqūf ʿalā al-aṭlāl*—"stopping" or "standing by the ruins").[44] Later described as a "trace," the remains—which comprise "a book written without a pen and unintentionally by the people who had camped there"—are perhaps all that is left for us to read of the Bedouin way of life.[45] The task—inherently political—that Munif sets out for us, then, is one of properly interpreting this trace. Carefully steering us away from the nostalgia it might otherwise tempt for a utopian, but irrecoverable past of man-nature symbiosis, he demands that we identify the trace as a locus of revolutionary memory, of otherness by which the world-system is haunted, and through which the world-system might be interrupted and reshaped.

Bedouin Poetics in Orientalism: From Orality to Textuality

According to the foregoing analysis, Munif's intent in *Cities of Salt* might be summarized as one of charting a revolutionary counter-history of Bedouin indigeneity in the context of petro-modernity and, by extension, the modern world-system. If this is the case, then might it not be argued that this project—by virtue of its expression in and as a novel—is premised on an internal contradiction, one that threatens it with incoherence and even collapse? That is, isn't the representation of a traditionally oral indigenous culture in the textual form of a novel a function of, and doesn't it reproduce, the very process, the logic of the Bedouin's historical incorporation into the modern oil state that Munif seeks to dismantle, or at the very least denaturalize? More generally, isn't the novel as a modern literary form itself complicit with a global modernity that saw the wholesale absorption and codification of the oral through a practice and a system—one primarily associated with the discipline of (Orientalist) philology—of textualization, resulting in the worldwide hegemony of the written word? In this section, I consider the implications of Munif's deployment of the novel form and its ineluctable textuality for his depiction of the Bedouin, and the unique means by which he works through its apparent contradictions.

To start, a little background on Bedouin oral literature is in order. In both its form and function, this tradition has exhibited a remarkable continuity from its pre-Islamic origins to the present day. Although proverbs, riddles, and other genres are also widespread among the Bedouin tribes of the Middle East and North Africa, the most prevalent are the *qaṣīda* (ode) and the *qiṣṣa* (folk tale). The pre-Islamic to classical Arabic poetic form par excellence, the *qaṣīda*—whose metrical pattern is conventionally comprised of half lines of two feet—aims to glorify the poet's tribe, extol its virtues, and celebrate its customs. Among the war poems, panegyrics, elegies, and admonitions that might be taken to best fulfill these roles are also more playful erotic lyrics, and those that detail rituals characteristic of everyday life (such as coffee drinking, pasturage, and so on). In all cases, whether about love or war, the paramount emphasis of the *qaṣīda* is the life of the tribe. The *qiṣṣa*, while similarly concerned with the values of virtue, pride, generosity, and the honor of the tribe, often mobilizes them for a more direct, explicit moral agenda. Whether in the shape of a realistic tale about tribal wars or agriculture, or in that of an allegory featuring animals or mythological creatures, the *qiṣṣa* seeks to instill these values in its audience, and, in so doing, to provide a quasi-ideological support structure for the tribe. In both the *qaṣīda* and the *qiṣṣa*, then, the life-world of the Bedouin is given expressive form. Moreover, it is in both—by virtue of their traditionally oral performance (in public settings ranging from the familial to the communal)—that the life-world of the Bedouin is also collectively *enacted, embodied*, and, indeed, *lived*. In this way, and as most immediately carried across by these forms, its orality has played a fundamental role in the preservation and reproduction of Bedouin culture as a living one across the centuries.[46]

It is precisely the orality of Bedouin literature that, in the words of Siraj Ahmed, rendered it for the eighteenth-century Orientalist and colonial administrator William Jones so powerful an expression and enactment of "the nomad's love of freedom."[47] In my Introduction, I, with reference to the work of Aamir Mufti, highlighted the role of Jones's philological inquiries into the languages of the Indian subcontinent in the British colonial enterprise there after his arrival in Bengal in 1783.[48] In his recent investigations into this figure (a polymath and polyglot of the highest order), culminating in his book *Archaeology of Babel: The Colonial Foundation of the Humanities* (2017), Ahmed has sought to trace Jones's seminal influence on the discipline of philology—and, by extension, on comparative literature, world literature, and the humanities per se—back even further. In contrast to Mufti's primary focus on his South Asian period (though Mufti does also briefly discuss Jones's earlier poetics and aesthetics), Ahmed locates Jones's contribution to the European philological revolution and to the popularization of the Indo-European language hypothesis in the series of translations / transcriptions from the Persian (specifically, of Hafiz in 1771), the Arabic (of the *Mu'allaqāt* in 1782), and the Sanskrit (of *Śākuntala* in 1789) that he embarked upon beginning in the early 1770s.[49] It was by way of Jones's translations / transcriptions, and the method of Orientalist philology by which he undertook them, that what Ahmed identifies as the "colonial foundations of the humanities" were laid. Bringing what he calls his "archaeology" home for us in our contemporary moment, Ahmed reminds us that it was none other than Jones—via his rendition of Hafiz—who inspired Johann Wolfgang von Goethe's turn towards "the East" in his *West-Eastern Divan* (as discussed in the Introduction), and thereby his (indeed, our) concept of *Weltliteratur*.[50]

Of special interest to me here, of course, is Jones's translation / transcription of the *Mu'allaqāt* (loosely translated as "The Hanging Poems" or "The Suspended Odes"), the collection of seven golden *qaṣā'id* (plural of *qaṣīda*) of the pre-Islamic sixth to seventh centuries that was to become established as a—or, *the*—cornerstone of the classical Arabic poetic tradition.[51] For Jones, the *Mu'allaqāt*—like Bedouin literature more generally—reflected the essence of all poetic language. It was what he regarded as their original "extempore" form that so fascinated him—intended to be performed in a singular, fleeting event of self-revelation and self-annihilation, they conveyed not only the transience of all human experience, but also the Bedouin's particular contempt for and autonomy from the "stately pillars," the "solemn buildings of the cities" that would otherwise circumscribe their society and contain the unbridled outpouring of their passions.[52] As such, he—as Ahmed succinctly concludes in an earlier essay—considered the Bedouin's poetry to exist "in ethical, political, and ontological opposition to the state-centered empires that surrounded them."[53] Through this poetry (as well as his studies of and translations from the Persian and Sanskrit literary traditions), then, he was to develop the concepts of language and literature on which his early philology was based—the notion of language as a sacred, material force that possesses no "reference, foundation, or origin outside itself," and that is manifest in its purest being only in the moment of its utterance.[54]

However, and in an augury of the more direct apprenticing of his philological method to the colonial endeavor when he went to South Asia, the very act of translating / transcribing the *Mu'allaqāt* on Jones's part—of putting to paper a language that was originally unwritten, of imprisoning in text a poetry that was originally in the wind—disrupts and in fact negates what he himself so clearly perceived to be the exact equivalence, the correlation between their oral form and their expressive / enacting function vis-à-vis the Bedouin life-world. As Ahmed notes, "the printed texts we now call the *Mu'allaqāt* constitutively misinterpret the aesthetic phenomenon they name [. . .] and [. . .] the culture from which they are said to descend[,] because these poems did not originally take textual form."[55] A paradigm of his Orientalist philology, Jones's translation / transcription of the *Mu'allaqāt* (as well as of Hafiz and *Śākuntala*) might, then, be interpreted as an act of textualizing a practice of (oral) self-expression from the non-Western world that, properly speaking, is ethically, politically, and ontologically antithetical to its manifestation in this form. A worldly one (directed towards their dissemination in the wider world), this act thus further contributes to (or even establishes, according to Ahmed) the process of rendering legible or appropriating as *literature* raw expressive practices—specifically, those of the non-West—that had hitherto been excluded from its domain. Having in this way played a foundational role in the field of world literature, this is the heritage that Jones and his Orientalist philology have bequeathed to us today.

In his book, Ahmed takes Mufti (among many others) to task for supposedly "remain[ing] trapped within the trajectory of philological power" even while attempting to correct philology's Eurocentric origins and turn it against its colonial history.[56] While there are some major distinctions between Ahmed's and Mufti's approaches (the former develops an "archaeological" method to unearth the constitution of the humanities per se in colonialism, whereas the latter deploys a genealogy critique to expose the constitution of the more specified field of world literature in colonialism), it seems to me that at their core, their projects are in closer alignment and even affinity than Ahmed for one appears to be willing to acknowledge. That is, and in contrast to Ahmed's characterization, Mufti is—very much like his peer—first and foremost motivated by and engaged in the *critique* rather than the *recovery* of (Orientalist) philology in his work in this area (as discussed in the Introduction, his project is one of charting "a genealogy of world literature [that] leads to Orientalism").[57]

Given these similarities, Ahmed's work might well be reconsidered along the lines of what I explained as my divergence from Mufti in the Introduction. As with Mufti's, this is primarily directed towards uncovering how the network of concepts and categories regarding the languages, literatures, and cultures of the non-Western world established by colonial philology has structured and continues to shape a number of scholarly fields and disciplines, as well as the possibilities and limitations of critical thought within them—it is directed, ultimately, towards *our own* inheritance from this tradition in the contemporary (anglophone) academy. As such, it to some degree forestalls any critical inquiry into these languages, literatures, and cultures that seeks to move beyond the logic and implications of their internalization in and for philology. In the case of the *Muʿallaqāt*, it pre-empts an interrogation of the continuity or at least correspondence between Jones's translation / transcription and the broader historical process of the Bedouin's incorporation into the modern Middle Eastern state that I have outlined. As I have sought to emphasize, this latter process is by definition one of inscription (of the Bedouin into modernity)—it might well be regarded as having been precipitated or at least prefigured by Jones's more literal act of arrogating, codifying, and reproducing Bedouin culture in textual form. From the perspective of the argument that I have set out, Jones's practice of Orientalist philology might, then, be understood in relation to the more general trajectory of Middle Eastern modernity for which it (partially) laid the groundwork, and which continues to directly encroach upon the Bedouin and their communities across the region today. In this light, Orientalist philology can be seen to comprise (or to have been pivotally involved in) a Middle East-specific practice of (literary and cultural) incorporation, and thus read alongside other distinct but comparable histories of incorporation from around the world within a more encompassing model of world literature.

It is just such a history and the orality / textuality contradictions on which it has hinged that Munif has sought to grapple with in *Cities of Salt*. In his deployment of spectrality—the subtle subversion of textuality through the unassimilable trace of the oral other, he refuses the logic of incorporation to which the indigenous communities of the Middle East have historically been subject, and destabilizes the very textual foundation on which the novel form is built for its collusion in the process by which modernity has overwritten and continues to overwrite the oral languages, cultures, and communities of the world. As suggested by his novel, spectrality—while acknowledging the current global hegemony of the written word—can thus also express and enact a form of resistance to it, and thereby relay the possibility, utopian it may be, of an accountability, a justice that is as yet unforeseeable.

The Bedouin in Petro-Modernity

As indicated by the citations from Peter Theroux and Edward Said above, *Cities of Salt* is concerned with the fate of Bedouin indigeneity in the specific context of the Middle Eastern oil encounter. As such, it stands as an exemplar of what Amitav Ghosh coined as "petrofiction" in a review first published in *The New Republic* in 1992 (and collected in his *Incendiary Circumstances: A Chronicle of the Turmoil of Our Times* [2006]).[58] It is, though, a rather rare example of this genre. For, as Ghosh continues, the oil encounter "has produced scarcely a single work of note"—a circumstance all the more startling given that "[i]t would be hard to imagine a story that is equal in drama, or in historical resonance" to that of oil.[59] "[W]hy," he pointedly asks, "has this encounter proved so imaginatively sterile?"[60] In this section, I think through the implications of Munif's representation of oil in relation to a global cultural imaginary that indeed appears to have widely neglected or obscured the story of one of the most pervasive features, even structuring mechanisms of the modern world, one that has impacted and continues to shape seemingly every major aspect of contemporary reality—energy, manufacturing, consumption, transportation, migration, geopolitics, warfare, state formation, environment, crisis, and so on. Highly ambiguous, this representation—in fact a *non*-representation, I show, itself reveals why oil has been, and must be excluded from culture.

In a *PMLA* "Editor's Column" on "Literature in the Ages of Wood, Tallow, Coal, Whale Oil, Gasoline, Atomic Power, and Other Energy Sources" published in 2011, Patricia Yaeger suggests energy—the different forms it has taken across history—as a Jamesonian horizon for the production of the literary. Her intent is to foreground energy production and consumption as an alternate possible grounds for literary history, one that would "sort texts" not by the artificial constructs of "period," "genre," or "nation," but rather "according to the energy sources that made them possible."[61] In his entry for the column, "Literature and Energy Futures," Imre Szeman elaborates further on the benefits of what with Dominic Boyer he has elsewhere forwarded as an "energy humanities."[62] He argues that the pay-off of humanistic inquiry oriented around energy would be to draw new and much needed critical attention to "one of the key conditions of possibility of human social activity [. . .] whose significance and value [is] almost always passed over, even by those who insist on the importance of modes and forms of production for thinking about culture and literature."[63] In our contemporary moment, oil remains the dominant energy source, accounting—according to the International Energy Agency—for a total of approximately 31.7 percent of the global energy supply as of 2015 (this is the highest proportion of any single source, though it has been falling since its peak in the 1970s).[64] This fact gives one significant pause when it comes to Szeman's proposed "energy humanities." For how can such a project properly attune itself to the present, and emerge as a worthwhile and feasible nexus of contemporary inter- or transdisciplinary critical inquiry when—given what Szeman himself confirms is a "dearth" of oil in twentieth- to twenty-first-century literature and culture—it lacks an identifiable object of analysis?[65] Seeing oil's lack of representation as more of a challenge than a limitation, Szeman continues that in this case, an emphasis on energy "bring[s] to light a foundational gap to which we have hitherto given little thought."[66] From this perspective, our critical task—now seen to be urgent in itself—becomes one of *explaining* oil's relative invisibility in modern literature and culture, and *exposing* the social, political, and ideological determinants of this circumstance. The driving force of modern political economy, oil might in this way be understood to implicitly *subtend* the cultural imaginary, its constitution as well as its depictions—ubiquitous as these are—of modernity's other, second-order phenomena (such as those listed above).

The majority of critics who have attended to the question of oil in modern literature and culture have likewise noted its less than overwhelming representation. Rob Nixon comments that "not since [Upton] Sinclair's California saga *Oil!* appeared in 1927 has any author hazarded writing the great American oil novel," before moving on to *Cities of Salt* as an exception.[67] Continuing his analysis, Ghosh suggests that this is because "oil smells bad"—for Americans, it "reeks" of "overseas entanglements," "foreign dependency," "economic uncertainty," "military enterprises," and "dead civilians"; for Arabs, it "chose to be discovered in precisely those parts of the Middle East that have been most marginal in the development of modern Arab culture and literature—on the outermost peripheries."[68] Peter Hitchcock offers a more symptomatological analysis—it is, he argues, "oil's saturation of the infrastructure of modernity that paradoxically has placed a significant bar on its cultural representation."[69] Szeman and Boyer further underline this point—"[i]f it has been so difficult to grasp and grapple with so important an element," they remark, "it is [. . .] because fossil fuels are saturated into every aspect of our social substance."[70] If one looks hard (and sometimes imaginatively) enough, one can, naturally, identify exceptions to the rule of oil's non-representation beyond Sinclair and Munif. Texts that might be seen to comprise something like a global petrofiction canon include: Edna Ferber's *Giant* (1952) and its film adaptation by George Stevens (1956); Ghassan Kanafani's *Men in the Sun* (*Rijāl fī al-Shams*, 1962; trans. 1999); the *Mad Max* films, all directed by George Miller (1979–2015); Ken Saro-Wiwa's *A Forest of Flowers* (1995); Sam Mendes's (dir.) *Jarhead* (2005); Cormac McCarthy's *The Road* (2006); and Paul Thomas Anderson's (dir.) *There Will Be Blood* (2007), among others. However, and apart from their being few and far between, a focus on such texts in attempts towards a "petro-criticism" draws attention away from what seems to me the far more interesting underlying issue of oil's general non-representation.

This is what Nixon, Ghosh, and Hitchcock, among others, appear to have done in their otherwise solid readings of *Cities of Salt*, all of which see it as an exception to the rule. In their approaches to the novel, these critics have concentrated on its portrayal of the oil encounter, paying special attention to themes of cultural and ecological disenfranchisement under "petro-despotism" (Nixon); labor and authoritarianism in the "oil sheikdoms" (Ghosh); and social and class relations as mediated by oil's "logic of objectification" (Hitchcock).[71] In so doing, they have overlooked Munif's wry dramatization of the logic by which oil has necessarily been repressed in the cultural imaginary, and his satirical inversion of the ideologies of (Saudi, American) representation. Yes, Nixon, Ghosh, and Hitchcock all productively foreground his novel as a corrective, but they miss the point that the impetus of this corrective is his awareness—which is embedded in the novel both thematically and formally—of Szeman's "foundational gap." Read in this light, *Cities of Salt* can be seen to articulate the dialectic of oil's non-representation in modern literature and culture, the most significant issue facing the field of energy humanities as it continues to inquire into and engage with petro-modernity.

As discussed above, Munif goes to great lengths to demonstrate the social effects of the burgeoning oil industry in Mooran throughout *Cities of Salt*. From Wadi al-Uyoun to Harran, he traces the social and cultural displacement of the Bedouin, the levelling of their original habitus, their reinscription as alienated labor in the modern oil state, and the emergence of a political and economic infrastructure specific to that state. Yet while every conceivable outward manifestation of the state—from its ruling dynasty, military, and working classes to its cities, buildings, and roads—is richly detailed, never is the engine that drives Mooran's particular form of modernization directly represented in itself. In *Cities of Salt*, oil orders and controls the totality of the world born in its image, but, for all its dense, symbolic materiality, it remains an absent signifier. Why? A closer look the novel's historical correlates is necessary in order to shed some light on this question.

Mooran is of course most closely modelled on the Kingdom of Saudi Arabia. Like Mooran, Saudi Arabia was founded in the early twentieth century (specifically, 1932) by a wealthy ruling elite, in this case the dynastic ruling family the House of Saud and its autocratic figurehead Ibn Saud (Abdulaziz ibn Abdul Rahman ibn Faisal ibn Turki ibn Abdullah ibn Muhammad Al Saud), the first monarch of the Kingdom. Again as with Mooran, this process was facilitated and the ruling elite's power consolidated by means of three essential factors, the military, religion, and foreign support. Starting in 1902, and under Ibn Saud's leadership, the Saudi Arabian Army—specifically, the Royal Saudi Land Forces (cf. Munif's "Desert Army")—embarked on a series of territorial conquests across the Arabian Peninsula, which were to culminate in the unification of the Kingdom in 1932. In this period, Ibn Saud maintained his family's long-standing alliance with the conservative Wahhabi religious establishment (one which stretches back to the eighteenth-century origins of this movement under Muhammad ibn Abd al-Wahhab). With his military successes, Ibn Saud was able to grant the Wahhabis control over the religious institutions of his newly founded state, leading, in turn, to the creation of a strict moral and legal order as necessary for instilling discipline and subservience among his subjects (though unnamed, religious dogma plays a similar role in Munif's novel). At the same time (and just before the July 1933 episode of the American geologists recounted in note 15), he also signed an oil concession agreement granting exploration, drilling, extraction, and export rights to the parent company of the infamous Arabian American Oil Company (ARAMCO), the Standard Oil Company of California (SoCal, legally renamed Chevron in 1984). Established shortly thereafter (in 1944) with exclusive rights over Saudi oil, ARAMCO was to proceed to build the infrastructure of the oil economy—its oilfields, refineries, and pipelines—that the Saudi royal family has exploitatively depended upon (as it continues to do) for the augmentation of its wealth and the safeguarding of its authority.[72]

Even from this cursory overview, oil can be seen to have functioned in Saudi Arabia—as in Mooran—as more than a mere lubricant for the state, its economy and institutions. In its production, exchange, and consumption, it has, so to speak, underwritten the very constitution of the state. Indeed noxious, an obscenity (as per Ghosh), it is what Timothy Mitchell calls "a form of politics" that has structured Saudi Arabia's political economy from the ground up.[73] As such, it has also significantly impacted the political economy of oil importing and consuming states including, most notably, the US (the world's largest consumer of oil, accounting for approximately 20 percent of total global consumption as of 2015 according to the US Energy Information Administration); the relations between these major exporters / importers, producers / consumers; and thus the entire international order.[74]

Back in Saudi Arabia, oil and the form of modernity attendant on it were very much as devastating for the Bedouin as Munif stresses. As mentioned in note 15, Wadi al-Uyoun is based on the real-world Bedouin village of 'Ain Dar, which was located in the eastern part of the Arabian Desert. Oil was discovered there in 1948, a finding which precipitated that of the Ghawar oilfield, the largest in the world. As might be expected, nothing of 'Ain Dar's Bedouin heritage remains, not even what Labid might have called its "blackened orts"—only the new, "best in class" rigs that Saudi Aramco has made sure to showcase on its website (ARAMCO was renamed "Saudi Aramco" in 1988, after the Saudi government acquired a 100 percent stake in the company in 1980).[75] Likewise, and as mentioned in note 23, Harran is also based on a real-world Saudi city, Dhahran. As with Harran, this city was founded in the 1930s by an American oil company, SoCal, as its center of operations, and further developed from the 1940s by its subsidiary, ARAMCO (in its contemporary embodiment as Saudi Aramco, the company's headquarters are still located there). And again, most abhorrently like its analogue, it was so on the basis of a strict segregation between its American community (the engineers, administrators, and executives brought in by SoCal and later ARAMCO from the US to oversee their enterprise) and its Arab community (the menial laborers, builders, roughnecks, and others, often Bedouin, brought in from around the Arabian Peninsula to carry out its grunt work). Indeed, Robert Vitalis has described the city as "a Jim Crow enclave on the eastern shore of Saudi Arabia."[76] In an irony that is perhaps characteristic of empire, an American corporation was—and in this it was certainly backed by successive US administrations from the 1930s to the 1950s—thus directly involved in a foreign segregationist enterprise at the very moment when the Jim Crow laws were being challenged and then dismantled closer to home.[77]

Given this background, it should come as no surprise that both the Saudi and the American political establishments have made every effort to keep the history of oil out of their official discourses of state sovereignty, the rule of law, economic inequality and the distribution of wealth, energy production and consumption, trade, and international relations. Furthermore, this account might help us explain why oil has been largely excluded from the global cultural imaginary. As the primary determinant of the Saudi state structure (its polity, institutions, and economy) as well as of Saudi-American geopolitical relations, it *must* be repressed or marginalized in modern Arabic and modern American literature and culture alike in order to sustain an ahistorical—and thus naturalized—sense of the status quo, one on which the powerful in these countries have depended for their legitimacy, authority, and other, more mercenary interests. In other words, oil must not be represented due to the threat this would pose to the hegemony and reproduction of a state system that serves the powerful—if it were, and if the root cause of the inequality, disenfranchisement, and historical violence that define this system was exposed, then it might realistically be contested on a mass scale. By not representing oil in itself—a quite conscious formal decision on his part—Munif indicates in the form of his novel something of the logic of oil's non-representation in modern literature and culture. A corrective to this circumstance, *Cities of Salt* might therefore be understood as based on and structured around Munif's awareness—reflexively embedded into the text—of this gap between representation and reality, of the political, social, and cultural conditions both in Saudi Arabia and elsewhere in the world that made his corrective so urgent in the first place. In this sense, *Cities of Salt* can be seen as much more than a possible object for the energy humanities, or as an exception that proves the rule of non-representation. In what I have argued is its traversal of the cultural logic of petro-modernity, it also provides a clear and compelling response to the central question that this field must address as it strives to critically engage the present.

The Spectrality Effect and the Democracy to Come

As I have demonstrated, *Cities of Salt* is a counter-historical novel about Bedouin indigeneity in the context of (Saudi) petro-modernity. As such, it hinges on Munif's characterization of the figure of Miteb al-Hathal. Without doubt, Miteb acts as the primary focal point and voice of the narrative for its first hundred pages—he articulates and embodies the Atoum's rooted, collective sense of social and cultural identity, their life-world, as well as the effects of its loss as their village is threatened and then destroyed by foreign interlopers. Correspondingly, the reader is drawn to strongly identify with him. The pathos of his disappearance is made all the more acute given this identification. It evokes not only readerly empathy for a character and a world subjected to injustice and violence, but also nostalgia for a narrative syntax that—derived from and oriented around the experience of the local—is displaced and ultimately overwritten by that of modernity. As I have suggested, it is because Miteb and what he represents are incommensurable with modernity that they must necessarily be excised from its polity and its metaphysics, and thus from its own, ulterior narrative logic.

The remainder of the novel is driven by this logic. Within its parameters, Miteb's many subsequent reappearances are imbued with a disturbing, uncanny sense of ambiguity, of uncertainty. First, he is sighted by his son Shaalan on the outskirts of Wadi al-Uyoun, their village, late one night shortly after it had been razed to make way for an oilfield. In a pattern which repeats itself over the course of the next several nights, he retreats back into the darkness as soon as Shaalan approaches. Unable to confirm his father's sudden manifestations, Shaalan is—like the reader— left unsure as to whether these events had indeed taken place, whether what he had seen was "a vision or a real thing."[78] Next, Miteb is spotted by another of his sons, Fawwaz, at Rawdhat al-Mashti, a campsite where the Atoum had paused to rest during their resulting exile and flight. Likewise unverifiable, he is in this apparition—which again takes place at night— eerily distorted, almost grotesque. Seeming "enormously tall and rather white skinned," and bearing a staff in one hand, he recites prophecies of doom into the darkened, tumultuous sky—"[t]his is the last of your happiness," "[f]ear is from things to come."[79] Much later in the novel, and after a long absence, Miteb surfaces once again. In Harran, the epicenter of Mooran's oil industry, rumours of a fledgling desert revolution led by none other than "Miteb al-Hathal himself" and backed by the "armed bedouin" he had apparently enlisted to his cause start to circulate, giving rise to panic among the emirs and their American collaborators.[80] And finally, the "ghost" does indeed "burst on the scene," that of the H2 or Askar work camp that had been erected to support the construction of a pipeline between Wadi al-Uyoun and Harran.[81] In the commotion of "gunshots," "roars of camels," and "whinnying horses" that ensues, the pipeline is destroyed and the camp is burned down.⁸² As if circling the void of his unspeakable name and being, of—properly—his unnameability, the Arabs and the Americans alike can only gesture towards or hint at who might have initiated this highly symbolic act of resistance:

> All the cryptic whispers and queries had but one answer: Miteb al-Hathal. He was the only person conceivably willing or able to do such a thing. No worker said it outright or pronounced his name out loud, but his specter filled the whole desert.⁸³

In his reading of these episodes, the postcolonial critic Stefan Meyer has argued that Miteb is to be understood as a figure of "the paradox of presence and absence."⁸⁴ Through this character, he continues, Munif "connects the notion of disappearance with both the tradition of bedouin guerilla warfare as well as Muslim messianic traditions such as that of the *Mahdi*."⁸⁵ While the link he seeks to make here between Miteb's disappearance and Bedouin and Muslim traditions is telling, Meyer, though, somewhat downplays the narrative significance of the "paradox" that he himself points out. For in *Cities of Salt*, Miteb's simultaneous presence and absence (as played out in the passages cited above) amounts to a narrative figuration of what I have delineated as a Derridean logic of spectrality. In terms of his position within the narrative, its spatiality and temporality, Miteb inhabits precisely the undefined, undefinable border zone between presence or being (the ontological plenitude of the here and now as what actually exists) and its other that is charted—of course, by way of approximation—by this logic. That is, he—as a figure of Bedouin indigeneity who refuses to dissever himself from an identity, a community, and a culture that are annulled in and for petro-modernity, who resists the violence that would bury his life-world "under the soil of another time"—cannot be incorporated into the space and time of the modern oil state, the actual here and now that comprises the world of the narrative. In this way unrepresentable, unidentifiable, and unnameable, he therefore manifests in the narrative, in the state, as—and only as—a *shabaḥ* (in its original Arabic, this term—"الشبح"—more faithfully expresses the particular form of Miteb's spectrality, its sources, resonances, and implications).⁸⁶ In so doing, he infects the logic of categorical disjunction between past /

present, desert / town, nomadism / civilization, orality / textuality, and, indeed, poetry / novel contrived and installed by modernity, and inflects the latter term of each of these binaries with the trace of the former. In a word, Miteb is the unassimilable trace of its lost oral other that haunts the text of modernity.

In *Specters of Marx: The State of the Debt, the Work of Mourning, and the New International* (1993; trans. 1994), Jacques Derrida makes an important connection between spectrality and what he calls "the democracy to come." He argues that the very concept of "democracy" is and has always been in itself haunted. Constituted in the paradoxical suturing of "*cratos*" (the rule, might, or force of the sovereign) and "*demos*" (the people), it is defined by a "*diastema*"—a "failure, inadequation, disjunction, disadjustment, being 'out of joint'"—by which those whom it claims to represent are in their plurality or multitude rendered necessarily other to the singularity of power, and thus spectral.[87] As he elaborates in *Rogues: Two Essays on Reason* (2003; trans. 2005):

> Democracy is what it is only in the différance by which it defers itself and differs from itself. It is what it is only by spacing itself beyond being and even beyond ontological difference; it is (without being) equal and proper to itself only insofar as it is inadequate and improper, at the same time behind and ahead of itself, behind and ahead of the Sameness and Oneness of itself; it is thus interminable in its incompletion beyond all determinate forms of incompletion, beyond all the limitations [. . .].[88]

As such, democracy is always-already a "promise," something that is "*to come*" (not in the sense of a future possibility, but rather in that of its designation of an ideal that it internally contradicts—its aporetic structure).[89] Substantiated with reference to its historical instances (all of which he suggests have been haunted by various forms and various degrees of political, social, racial, ethnic, gender, religious, economic, and other exclusion and marginalization), it is this understanding of democracy as by definition an unfinished project that Derrida aims to indicate through his supplementary "to come." Accordingly, democracy translates into and calls for a specific response, a "militant and interminable political critique" that—comprising "justice"—is oriented around "the infinite secret of the other."⁹⁰ It demands, in short, the recognition of and faithfulness to its ghosts.

In *Cities of Salt*, Miteb in his spectrality articulates this imperative, and thus points towards the only possibility of a democracy to come in (Saudi) petro-modernity. It is through what Derrida might consider to be the "event" of his unaccountable irruption into the narrative and the state that the limitations of both are exposed, and that some semblance of redress might be imagined as the world they represent—our own—hurtles towards its otherwise rather bleak petro-futurity.[91]

Notes

1. Theroux, "Abdelrahman Munif and the Uses of Oil."
2. Said, *The Politics of Dispossession*, p. 376.
3. See Munīf, *Mabda' al-Mushāraka wa al-Ta'mīm al-Bitrūl al-'Arabi*. No information about its publisher is provided in this book, suggesting that it was independently published.
4. Updike, *Odd Jobs*, p. 618.
5. Ibid. p. 618.
6. Ibid. p. 618.
7. Boullata, "Social Change in Munīf's *Cities of Salt*," pp. 213, 212.
8. Xinos, "Petro-Capitalism, Petrofiction, and Islamic Discourse," p. 3.
9. Hitchcock, "Oil in an American Imaginary," pp. 84–5.
10. At the time of writing, only three of the five volumes of *Mudun al-Milḥ* have appeared in English. All translated by Peter Theroux, Volume 1, *Al-Tīh* (1984), was released as *Cities of Salt* (1987); Volume 2, *Al-Ukhdūd* (1985), as *The Trench* (1991); and Volume 3, *Taqāsīm al-Layl wa al-Nahār* (1989), as *Variations on Day and Night* (1993). See Munif, *Cities of Salt*; Munif, *The Trench*; and Munif, *Variations on Day and Night*.
11. Ali, "A Patriarch of Arab Literature."
12. Hafez, "An Arabian Master," p. 43.
13. Munif, *Cities of Salt*, pp. 1, 2. In his discussion of this passage, Rob Nixon has most clearly articulated the sense of critical hesitation provoked by such a description. It suggests, he argues, a reliance on Munif's part on the troubling and widely criticized postcolonial "trope" of "conjoined ecological integrity and cultural authenticity." Nixon, *Slow Violence and the Environmentalism of the Poor*, p. 84.

14. Munif, *Cities of Salt*, p. 28.
15. Like much of the novel, this episode is modelled on and closely parallels the actual history of oil—in this case, its exploration and discovery—in Saudi Arabia. Specifically, it recalls the arrival of two American geologists at the village of Jubail on the country's east coast in July 1933. Wadi al-Uyoun, however, is based on the inland village of 'Ain Dar, located in the eastern part of the Arabian Desert. Conflating the histories of Jubail and 'Ain Dar into the single fictional narrative of Wadi al-Uyoun allows Munif a unified aesthetic and narratological focus on the experiential structure of petro-modernity per se, and thus lends to his narrative a more universal scope than would have been apparent were he to have adhered to his historical sources à la lettre. I discuss the novel's historical background in more depth in the section on "The Bedouin in Petro-Modernity" below.
16. Munif, *Cities of Salt*, p. 26.
17. Watt coined the term "delayed decoding" to describe a narrative device in Joseph Conrad's *Heart of Darkness* (1899) whereby the protagonist, Marlow, is shown to experience a disorienting temporal lapse between his immediate sensations and his ability to interpret or understand them. See Watt, *Conrad in the Nineteenth Century*, pp. 169–80, *passim*. Like Chinua Achebe's *Things Fall Apart* (1958) before it, *Cities of Salt* inverts the "Westerner in the (colonial) world" dynamic that elicits the delayed decoding effect in *Heart of Darkness*, and locates it instead in the experience of the subjects of Western (colonial, capitalist) interventions as they are being subjected to these. Beyond *Things Fall Apart*, though, and as I have tried to indicate through the notion of "suspended decoding," it seems to me that Munif also radicalizes this effect in order to express something of the epistemological quandary or void of the East / West encounter attendant on petro-modernity when experienced at a point that precedes or is otherwise outside of modernity.
18. Munif, *Cities of Salt*, pp. 30, 31, 44, 45.
19. Ibid. pp. 86, 106, 96.
20. Hafez, "An Arabian Master," p. 54.
21. In this case, the real-world correlate is of course the House of Saud and its consolidation of power in the early twentieth century, culminating in the founding of the Kingdom of Saudi Arabia in 1932. See below for further detail on this background.
22. Mitchell, *Carbon Democracy*, p. 5.

23. Munif, *Cities of Salt*, pp. 207, 237. As with Wadi al-Uyoun, Harran is also based on a real-world Saudi city, Dhahran. See below for further detail on this background.
24. Lazarus, "Cosmopolitanism and the Specificity of the Local in World Literature," p. 123.
25. Ibid. p. 122.
26. Munif, *Cities of Salt*, pp. 510, 511.
27. Ibn Khaldûn, *The Muqaddimah*, p. 93.
28. Ibid. p. 118.
29. For their most extensive discussion of this concept, see Deleuze and Guattari, *Nomadology*. In this text (extracted from their *A Thousand Plateaus: Capitalism and Schizophrenia* [*Mille plateaux*, 1980; trans. 1987]), the poststructuralist thinkers deploy the figure of the nomad as a metaphorical apparatus for a "'nomad' or 'minor science'" that contests the hegemonic claims, imperialism, and sovereignty of "State science." Ibid. pp. 17, 19. Against this sort of abstract and generalized appropriation of the nomad figure, my interest here lies more in the actual, ongoing history of the incorporation of (Bedouin) nomadism in the modern Middle Eastern state, and what *Cities of Salt* suggests are the revolutionary possibilities afforded by a regional counter-history charted from this perspective. In other words, I aim to develop what might be considered a more localized, materially grounded, and politically focalized nomadology.
30. Barakat, *The Arab World*, pp. 53–4.
31. For a detailed exposition of the methods by which the Bedouin have been incorporated into the modern Middle Eastern state, see Chatty, *From Camel to Truck*.
32. cooke, *Tribal Modern*, pp. 14, 10. Emphasis in original.
33. Ibid. p. 9.
34. "Cabinet Approves Plan to Provide for the Status of Communities in, and the Economic Development of, the Bedouin Sector in the Negev."
35. Ibid.
36. The "Absentees' Property Law" was established by Israel in 1950. It transferred ownership of any property in the newly founded State of Israel (1948) legally belonging to a Palestinian (or an Arab citizen of any Arab state) not in residence there between 29 November 1947 and 19 May 1948 to the custodianship of the state. It was effectively a policy of racialized property theft in the guise of a legal procedure, and has contributed significantly to the decades-long Palestinian refugee crisis.

37. Ethnic cleansing has not been recognized as an independent crime under international law (it is prosecuted by the International Criminal Court and the International Court of Justice as a "crime against humanity"). However, it was defined by a United Nations Commission of Experts charged with investigating war crimes in the former Yugoslavia as the "rendering [of] an area ethnically homogeneous by using force or intimidation to remove persons of given groups from the area" and "a purposeful policy designed by one ethnic or religious group to remove by violent and terror-inspiring means the civilian population of another ethnic or religious group from certain geographic areas." "Ethnic Cleansing."
38. White, "Israel."
39. "The Arab Bedouin and the Prawer Plan: Ongoing Displacement in the Naqab," n.p.
40. Amara, "The Negev Land Question," p. 29.
41. "UN rights chief urges Israel to reconsider bill that would displace thousands of Bedouins."
42. Allen, *Trans-Indigenous*, p. xiv. Emphasis in original.
43. Ibid. p. xiv.
44. Jabbur, *The Bedouins and the Desert*, p. 396. See the epigraph "The Muʿallaqa of Labid" on p. 71 above for one of the most prominent examples of the *aṭlāl* motif in the Arabic literary heritage (this citation is from Arberry, *The Seven Odes*, p. 142).
45. Ibid. p. 396.
46. For a detailed overview of Bedouin oral literature, including numerous examples and readings, see Jabbur, *The Bedouins and the Desert*, pp. 391–420. For more focused studies of orality, performance, intertribal conflict, and, in the case of the latter, gender relations in this tradition, see Meeker, *Literature and Violence in North Arabia* and Abu-Lughod, *Veiled Sentiments*.
47. Ahmed, *Archaeology of Babel*, p. 34.
48. See pp. 22–3 in the present volume.
49. For his discussion of Jones's poetics and aesthetics in this timeframe, see Mufti, *Forget English!*, pp. 67–72.
50. See Ahmed, *Archaeology of Babel*, p. 1.
51. For the full text of his translation, see Jones, *The Moallakát*. For a short excerpt, see the epigraph "The Muʿallaqa of Imruʾ al-Qais" on p. 71 above (this citation is from ibid. p. 5).
52. Jones, *Poems Consisting Chiefly of Translations from the Asiatick Languages*, p. 179. Cited in Ahmed, *Archaeology of Babel*, p. 130.

53. Ahmed, "Notes from Babel," p. 314.
54. Ahmed, *Archaeology of Babel*, p. 34.
55. Ibid. p. 134.
56. Ibid. p. 47.
57. Mufti, *Forget English!*, p. 19. Emphasis in original removed.
58. Ghosh, *Incendiary Circumstances*, p. 138.
59. Ibid. pp. 138, 139.
60. Ibid. p. 139.
61. Yaeger, "Editor's Column," p. 305.
62. See Szeman and Boyer (eds), *Energy Humanities*.
63. Szeman, "Literature and Energy Futures," p. 323.
64. See "Key World Energy Statistics, 2017," p. 6.
65. Szeman, "Literature and Energy Futures," p. 324.
66. Ibid. p. 324.
67. Nixon, *Slow Violence and the Environmentalism of the Poor*, p. 73. Emphasis in original.
68. Ghosh, *Incendiary Circumstances*, pp. 139, 140.
69. Hitchcock, "Oil in an American Imaginary," p. 81.
70. Szeman and Boyer, "Introduction," p. 6. Other recent scholarly works on this topic include: Barrett and Worden (eds), *Oil Culture*; LeMenager, *Living Oil*; and Wilson, Carlson, and Szeman (eds), *Petrocultures*.
71. Nixon, *Slow Violence and the Environmentalism of the Poor*, p. 73; Ghosh, *Incendiary Circumstances*, p. 148; Hitchcock, "Oil in an American Imaginary," p. 85.
72. For an excellent discussion of how Saudi political history in the twentieth century was mediated, even defined by oil, see Mitchell, *Carbon Democracy*, pp. 204–14.
73. Ibid. p. 5.
74. See "Frequently Asked Questions."
75. "'Ain Dar rig sets new course."
76. Vitalis, *America's Kingdom*, p. xx.
77. For a useful overview of the relationship between ARAMCO and the US government in this period, see ibid. pp. 1–26.
78. Munif, *Cities of Salt*, p. 141.
79. Ibid. p. 152.
80. Ibid. p. 380.
81. Ibid. p. 510.

82. Ibid. p. 510.
83. Ibid. p. 511.
84. Meyer, *The Experimental Arabic Novel*, p. 81.
85. Ibid. p. 81. Emphasis in original.
86. Munīf, *Mudun al-Milḥ: Al-Tīh*, p. 495.
87. Derrida, *Specters of Marx*, p. 64. Emphasis in original.
88. Derrida, *Rogues*, p. 38.
89. Derrida, *Specters of Marx*, p. 64. Emphasis in original.
90. Derrida, *Rogues*, pp. 86, 88.
91. See ibid. p. 87.

2

A Genealogy of *Adab* in the Comparative Middle East

[W]e are the guests of language.
                    Abdelfattah Kilito, *Thou Shalt Not Speak My Language*

This book of mine to the sophisticate will be sophisticated
And smooth-tongued, while to the foolish it will be foolish.
                    Ahmad Faris al-Shidyaq, *Leg over Leg*

In the contemporary Middle East, the range of terms used to designate "literature"—"*adab*" (the Arab world), "*edebiyat*" (Turkey), and "*adabiyāt*" (Iran), among others—bear a striking resemblance.[1] Indeed, they share a common linguistic root, the Arabic word "*adab*" (أدب). Etymologically speaking, this word harbored a number of distinct but overlapping connotations in the classical to medieval Arabic-Islamic life-world. Broadly, it referred to the highly esteemed virtues of propriety, custom, etiquette, courtesy, civility, decency, discipline, refinement, urbanity, education, and so forth of that historical and geographical terrain (i.e., as rooted in Arab sociocultural traditions and undergirded by Islamic precepts), *and* to a specified field of literary and cultural practice by which these values were expressed and reproduced. Today, however, *adab* and its Turkish and Iranian correlates signify something quite different. They now refer directly and specifically to the modern, European concept of "literature" discussed in the Introduction to this book, and encompass, act as the conceptual grounds for the modern literary forms—the novel, the lyric poem, and the stage play—associated with the latter as these have become ascendant in the national and regional cultures of the Middle East. How did this transformation in the meaning of *adab* and its variants come about? In their current definition and usage across the Arab world, Turkey, and Iran, what are their origins, how were they constituted, what ideological content do they carry, and what functions do they serve? How do they relate to the wider trajectory of modernity in the region?

In this chapter, I trace a genealogy of *adab*'s reinscription as literature in the Middle East. I argue that in their contemporary deployment, the terms *adab*, *edebiyat*, and *adabiyāt* alike are all premised on the concerted efforts undertaken by elite scholars, intellectuals, and writers in their respective national contexts to modernize and develop their literary and cultural spheres in the nineteenth to the mid-twentieth centuries. Under the influence of the Western European (read: Orientalist) philological models and methods to which they were newly exposed, and in tandem with the modernization and development of other spheres of political, social, and economic activity in this period (what I have outlined in terms of incorporation), these cultural practitioners specifically targeted what they came to see as the stultified and outdated literary traditions of the Arabic-Islamic past. In their various national milieus, they therefore endeavored—by and large successfully—to revise the very language of that heritage, to rewrite it in accordance with the demands of their time(s) and place(s). All this came to a head in the classical Arabic-Islamic concept of *adab*—evoking precisely the dead literary culture that they sought to bury, they systematically and with detailed attention to its philological implications reinscribed it as literature in the modern, European sense. Through this pivotal act of reinscription (one from which *adab*, *edebiyat*, and *adabiyāt* as they are now understood derive), the philological groundwork for literary and cultural modernity in the Arab world, Turkey, and Iran—in the Middle East—was thus in large part laid. Indeed, it was in its shadow that the modern literary forms—most notably, the novel—that have come to dominate literary and cultural production in the region arose in the first place.

In light of the argument that I have set out in this book, it might be said that the reinscription of *adab* as literature both *facilitated* and *enacted* the wider dialectic of modernity in the Middle East. That is, as a process that was structured by *exchange* (with primarily Western Europe as core), *internalization* (of the literary concepts of the core), and *reproduction* (of the literary forms of the core), it in essence comprised the wholesale re-envisioning of the Middle Eastern literary and cultural sphere from the perspective of the modernity from which these concepts and forms were born and which they smuggle with them in their very bodies as they migrate around the world. In the historical and geographical contexts under discussion, it was—in ways that were of course specific to each case—carried out within the boundaries of the distinct modern nation-states that were newly being erected across the region. As such, it contributed significantly to establishing the sense of an *individual* national literary heritage (as suggested by the now differentiated Arabic, Turkish, and Iranian terms for literature)—and thus of an individual national identity and culture—in each. (Recall that according to Immanuel Wallerstein, the modern world-system in part depends upon the universalization of the notion of the state as autonomous, independent, and sovereign.)[2] It was, in a word, an act of *incorporation* played out in the domain of literature, one that in no small measure helped lay the ideological and institutional foundations of modernity in the new nation-states of the region.

Enter the novel. As a form of modernity, the novel, I propose, was rendered legible in the Middle East—and thus imported, translated, adopted, adapted, and eventually enshrined there—only by way of the now internalized concept of literature associated with and representative of modernity. To put it another way, I am suggesting that the reinscription process I have delineated acted—among its other roles—as a necessary, historical condition of possibility for the emergence and eventual predominance of the novel in the region. As literature was installed in the various national contexts of the Arab world, Turkey, and Iran, so too were varying national novelistic traditions in those countries, each with its own major influences, figureheads, and aesthetic lineage (not to mention language, socialpolitical concerns, cultural content, and so on as mediated by local specificities). These traditions, though, were all closely aligned in (at least) one respect. By virtue of their stature as representative of their newly modernized national literary cultures (if not necessarily in terms of the content of their individual texts), they all at least implicitly—and in similar and comparable ways—provided what Benedict Anderson has famously described as "the technical means of 're-presenting' the *kind* of imagined community that is the nation [specifically, the modern nation-state]," that on which the latter depends for its ideological cohesion and consistency.³ In their individual contexts, they all served as loci for the formal and symbolic arrangement of the otherwise fragmented elements of their national communities, and thereby for the self-expression and consolidation of these communities as unique, united (even in their divisions), and distinctively modern. As such, these traditions—which together make up what I have called "the Middle Eastern novel"—brought to its culmination and further expanded the project of the modern concept of literature of which they were the extension. They—along with the other modern literary forms that accompanied them—displaced the literary heritage of the Arabic-Islamic past as encapsulated by *adab* in its classical sense, producing it as other to the Middle Eastern literary and cultural modernity of which they were and continue to be the embodiment. I thus posit the Middle Eastern novel as founded on the occlusion and marginalization of literary and cultural tradition in the region, which—as I aim to demonstrate in this book—returns to haunt it according to the logic of spectrality.

In the following, I develop this argument step by step. I start by detailing the nature and remit of *adab* in the life-world of classical to medieval Islam. I dispute the long-held view in Arabic literary studies—one that was brought into popular critical currency by Roger Allen and Hilary Kilpatrick—that this concept is equivalent to "belles-lettres." The latter, I argue, is a Eurocentric notion that was retrospectively and therefore questionably projected onto an incompatible context. Following the lead of scholars such as Muhsin al-Musawi, Jeffrey Sacks, Nuha Alshaar, Abdelfattah Kilito, and others, I thus reinterpret *adab* as an expression of the multiple modalities of political, social, and cultural experience in an area that—stitched together under the impetus of successive regional empires—historically spanned most of what we today refer to as "the Middle East." With reference to the relevant primary and secondary sources, and paying particular attention to the influence of an internalized Orientalist philology, I then trace how *adab* was systematically reinscribed as literature in the modern, European sense across the Middle East during the nineteenth to the mid-twentieth centuries. I focus on the key sites of Middle Eastern literary and cultural modernity—Egypt, Turkey, and Iran, and show through close attention to each that this act was a pivotal one as modernity was being forged within their respective national contexts. Next, I—engaging with the work of Allen, M. M. Badawi, Salma Jayyusi, Waïl Hassan, Kilito, and other scholars of the Middle Eastern novel—argue that it was only through the lens of this new concept of literature that the novel (as well as other modern literary forms) could be registered and was therefore propagated in the region. Extrapolating from this point, I round off this section by positing what I hope will be apparent as the Middle Eastern novel's constitution in the logic of spectrality. In dialogue with the work of Edward Said, Zachary Lockman, Rashid Khalidi, and others on this issue, and based on what I will have identified as the overlapping trajectories of (literary and cultural) modernity across the region, I close this chapter by forwarding the idea of a "comparative Middle East."

Overall, my aim here is to establish in its most expansive dimensions the historical setting for my readings of the Middle Eastern novel in this book.

Adab in the Life-World of Classical to Medieval Islam

In Arabic literary history, *adab* in its classical sense is conventionally defined as "belles-lettres." Roger Allen—one of the most distinguished and widely read Arabists of recent times—consolidated this understanding for a wide scholarly and popular audience in his now classic survey of the field, *An Introduction to Arabic Literature* (2000). In a section on "Questions of Definition: *Adab* and Belles-Lettres," he unambiguously states that "[t]he origins and development of a corpus of belles-lettres in Arabic are directly linked to the concept of *adab*."[4] Intended to distinguish its classical from its narrower, modern sense (as literature), the notion of belles-lettres, he continues, indicates that *adab* comprised a more expansive field of writing, one that encompassed "grammar, poetry, eloquence, oratory, epistolary art, history, and moral philosophy" and that reflected the "love of learning and urbanity" characteristic of the intellectual community of its practitioners, the *udabā'* (the plural form of *adīb*).[5] As such, *adab*, in Allen's account, served as an umbrella term for a plethora of the genres of writing that were widespread in classical Arabic-Islamic culture, beyond (though also including) what we would today consider the more strictly "literary."

Among the many genres that are typically associated with *adab* (by most Arabists, not just Allen) are:

- The compilation, the reference work, and the anthology (as initiated by al-Jahiz, an eighth- to ninth-century pioneer of the *adab* tradition).
- The courtly manual on topics such as bureaucracy, rulership, etiquette, eloquence, and so forth, loosely referred to as the "mirrors for princes" genre (working in around the same period, Ibn Qutayba was a leading figure here).
- The scholarly monograph on similar topics as well as, prominently, those of (divine) love, desire, and sexuality (al-Jahiz is again noted for his groundbreaking contributions to this genre, though the latter set of themes was more vigorously pursued by a range of his successors—most famously, Ibn Sina—from the eleventh to the fifteenth centuries).
- The historiography (*tārīkh*), the biographical dictionary (*ṭabaqāt*), the memorial (*tadhkira*), and the travelogue (*riḥla*) (often intermixed, these genres were developed by figures such as al-Baladhuri, al-Ya'qubi, and al-Tabari in the ninth to the tenth centuries, and brought to their culmination by Ibn Khaldun and Ibn Battuta in the fourteenth century).
- The mystical (Sufi) treatise and its poetic variants (al-Misri was a major forerunner of this genre in the ninth century, best exemplified by Ibn al-'Arabi and Rumi in the thirteenth century).
- The philosophical or mystical allegory (as pursued by Ibn Tufayl in the twelfth century).
- And finally, the *maqāma* (as noted in the Introduction, this genre was established by al-Hamadani and al-Hariri in the tenth to the eleventh centuries).[6]

Casting a wide net indeed, *adab* is along these lines to be regarded as the epitome, the most accomplished and complete expression of Arabic-Islamic culture during its classical period.

In her entry on "*Adab*" in *The Routledge Encyclopedia of Arabic Literature* (1998)—a likewise foundational guide to the field, Hilary Kilpatrick adopts a similar approach to the concept. She starts with a general definition of *adab* as "'good breeding,' 'manners,' 'culture,' 'refinement,' '*belles-lettres*,'" and proceeds to discuss its various genres and proponents as mentioned above on the basis of this understanding.[7] *Adab*, she concludes, is best thought of not as a genre in itself, but rather as "an *approach* to writing [. . .] in which the themes and aims mentioned here have their place."[8] Certainly, there has been and continues to be much heated debate among classicists about a concept that appears to bear so many referents, that was practiced in varying ways by a vast array of influential figures, and that spanned an equally immense historical and geographical terrain.[9] However, and as suggested by the overarching, cumulative accounts that Allen and Kilpatrick have sought to provide, it seems to me that the interpretation of *adab* as belletristic in orientation has to some extent acted as a baseline or universal in these deliberations.[10] Indeed, it would not be too great a stretch to claim that this reading of *adab* has largely mediated and even defined how the Arabic-Islamic past per se is viewed in modern Arabic literary studies.

The ramifications of this reading are considerable for our inquiries into the past, the present, and everything in between. For belles-lettres is a characteristically European notion, one that was derived from the new, Enlightenment discourses of literature, aesthetics, and criticism in circulation throughout Europe in the seventeenth to eighteenth centuries. It originated in France around the beginning of this period, and was brought into currency in the English-speaking world by figures such as Jonathan Swift, Henry Home, and Hugh Blair in the eighteenth century. Literally meaning "beautiful" or "fine writing," it referred to the qualities of style, originality, elegance, taste, beauty, sublimity, wit, and so on that for its proponents defined this writing as well as to the emergent discipline of literary criticism by which it was to be judged. And in this, it was quite explicitly related to, even based on the Englightenment humanism then being promulgated by philosophers such as, most relevant here, John Locke and David Hume.

For instance, Home discusses belles-lettres—what, with painting, music, sculpture, architecture, and other examples, he calls "the fine arts"—in terms of its capacity to elicit the "moral sense" that he, following these thinkers, regarded as "rooted in human nature" and "governed by principles common to all men."[11] In his account, its practice and its criticism alike went hand in hand with the pursuit of this humanistic goal, and were for this paramount (though not exclusive) reason therefore to be "cultivated to a high degree of refinement"—"no occupation attaches a man more to his duty," he concludes, "than that of cultivating a taste in the fine arts."[12] For Blair—though more focused on its practical composition than its aesthetic and ethical implications in his work in this area—belles-lettres and its study were likewise essential for the development of "good taste," "good sense," and "human reason," for "the dignity of the human mind."[13] In this, its original sense, belles-lettres was thus very much continuous with the aesthetic thought—and, by extension, the new conceptions of the literary—abroad in Europe at the time. Correspondingly, its deployment by Allen, Kilpatrick, et al. as a means to distinguish classical from modern *adab* has the paradoxical and self-defeating effect of attributing to its classical variant precisely the qualities and implications harboured by the concept in its modern manifestation. In other words, this usage is deeply problematic, as it projects onto classical *adab* and its world a notion of literary and cultural practice from another, with all of its sedimented historical, philosophical, and ideological content.

In this light, the definition of *adab* as belles-lettres might be seen to critically replicate in the field of Arabic literary studies the process by which *adab* was historically reinscribed as literature in the new nation-states of the Middle East (even while registering this background). Indeed, the former act might be interpreted as an *extension* and even a *derivative* of the latter, insofar as it seems to take up and renew the latter's characteristic procedure of re/writing the history of Arabic-Islamic culture according to the concepts and categories of modernity. While, unlike the latter, it of course does not imply the critical relegation of that heritage to a condition of stagnation and decay, it remains troubling due to its underlying critical assumptions and its more explicit impact on our understanding of literary history. As such, it exacerbates what Muhsin al-Musawi—discussing the *Nahda* in particular and the modernization process in the Arab world more generally—describes as the "failure on the part of the architects of modernity to connect effectively with a rich culture of their past."[14] It underscores what Jeffrey Sacks—considering the transformations to which the Arabic language was subjected in the nineteenth century—calls "the destruction of the terms of language in an older, Arabic-Islamic logocentrism."[15] It imposes what Nuha Alshaar—engaging with recent scholarship on this issue—identifies as "a secular context" on *adab*, reproducing and reinforcing what she continues is the "artificial boundary" between religion and literary and cultural practices installed by modernity.[16] In his provocative and powerful book *Thou Shalt Not Speak My Language* (2002; trans. 2008), the Moroccan literary historian Abdelfattah Kilito suggests that we—the "guests of language" (as per the epigraph above)—must during "our residence in its realm" assume "the respectful manners [in Kilito's original Arabic, '*al-adab*'] required of guests toward their host."[17] It seems to me that by defining *adab* as belles-lettres, we fall short of our outsider's obligation towards the concept and the literary and cultural world it articulates that it—as Kilito is here insinuating—has in itself always-already named.

If we are to thoroughly understand the significance of *adab*'s modern reinscription as literature (which I have argued is at least echoed by its contemporary designation as belles-lettres), it seems to me necessary, then, to begin by reconstructing this concept in its full contextual specificity. In his groundbreaking recent study *The Medieval Islamic Republic of Letters: Arabic Knowledge Construction* (2015), al-Musawi—a Professor of Arabic Literature at Columbia University—has provided the most exhaustive depiction of the classical to medieval Arabic-Islamic world to date. In his account, this world historically spanned the seventh to the eighteenth centuries (though al-Musawi's main interest is in the postclassical period, loosely signposted by the Siege of Baghdad in 1258); stretched from al-Andalus to Anatolia to India; and was constituted primarily through Arabic as the language of the Qur'ān (c. 609–32). He argues that in it, Islam—Islamic theology, metaphysics, epistemology, logic, law, rhetoric, and poetics—acted as the episteme or condition of possibility for knowledge production as most comprehensively manifest in the *adab* of the region throughout this period. As such, and much as that of medieval Europe was underwritten by its own clerical orthodoxies, its literary and cultural sphere—an expression of what al-Musawi calls the "pervasive Islamic consciousness" of this world—was anchored in Islam from its beginning to its end.[18] This, for al-Musawi, was the singular defining trait or common denominator of the Arabic-Islamic world. It was what rendered its literary and cultural practices to a reasonable degree consistent as the empires of the region rose and fell, and as successive metropolitan centers—Cairo, Baghdad, Damascus, Aleppo, Isfahan, Mashhad, and Istanbul, among others—took, in turn, their place at the vanguard of political and cultural influence there. It was what mediated the many complex interactions between the Arabic, Persian, and Turkish languages in this period as the cartography of imperial power—with its associated linguistic incursions and hegemonies—was constantly being drafted and redrafted, allowing for works originally written in these languages to gain in their translation and circulation throughout an otherwise hostile landscape. It was what furnished figures such as Ibn al-'Arabi, Rumi, Ibn Battuta, Ibn Khaldun, and many of the others listed above as well as their works a home as they—often itinerant by vocation—traversed the extent of this region, from its nodal points (where the *udabā'* frequently came into contact) to its outermost limits and beyond. Though multifarious, and distributed across a massive historical and geographic terrain, the individuals, texts, and languages that al-Musawi brings into critical conjunction in his description of the Arabic-Islamic world were all held together by Islam as episteme. Hence the specifically *Islamic* republic of letters that he identifies.

It is precisely Islam as a context for *adab* that is largely lost to its definition in terms of the secular notion of belles-lettres (a point that Alshaar has most vigorously pursued and attempted to remedy in her recent edited volume *The Qur'an and* Adab: *The Shaping of Literary Traditions in Classical Islam* [2017]).[19] For instance, while Islam does of course feature in Allen's (and any other) account of the concept, it does so more as a general historical backdrop rather than an episteme by and through which *adab* was constituted.[20] In light of the arguments that al-Musawi and others have set out, it seems a matter of increasing urgency in the field of Arabic literary studies that *adab* be reinterpreted against the grain of *both* its modern and its contemporary conscriptions (which amount to the same thing).

To begin, one might note that in its early usage it was (near-)synonymous with the term "*sunna*"—literally, the Way or Path of the Prophet Muhammad, and more broadly the body of traditional social and legal customs and practices of the Islamic community as derived from his influence. On these grounds, one might then trace how it expanded in sense through the Umayyad Caliphate (661–750), when it came to designate the sum of knowledge required for cultured and urbane as well as ethical conduct in Islamic society. It was with this specific context very much taken as a given that *adab* incorporated the humanistic pursuits and genres of writing by which it is commonly identified—the religious sciences, ancient poetry, tribal lore, history, geography, statecraft, philology, rhetoric, oratory, music, fashion, and so on—in this period. Next, one might assess how what might now be considered its specifically *Islamic* humanism was further consolidated via its (translational) assimilation of Hellenic, Indian, and Persian influences— notably, the genre of the didactic fable—during the subsequent Abbasid (750–1258) and Fatimid (909–1167) Caliphates, and how its other genres were to flourish in the cross-cultural but profoundly religious matrix of its ever-expanding world. One might conclude by recalling the known Cairo-based scholar Ibn al-Akfani. By the fourteenth century, well into the medieval period, this figure was able to summarize *adab* as—in George Makdisi's gloss—an "ornament of both tongue and fingertips," as a literary and cultural practice that encompasses the totality of the Arabic-Islamic heritage with the aim of guiding the devout Muslim subject (the resolute, or "*al-qāṣid*") towards what he called "the most supreme principles" ("*asnā al-maqāṣid*").[21]

In sum, *adab* in its classical sense might from the perspective of the argument I have attempted to put forward in this section be redefined as an expression of the multiple modalities of political, social, and cultural experience in the life-world of classical to medieval Islam.

Articulations and Disarticulations of *Adab* in Modernity: Orientalism, Philology, *Nahda*

Adab in this sense no longer exists. Indeed, this term was one of the foremost objects of modernization and development in the Arab literary and cultural sphere during the *Nahda* (or cultural renaissance) of the mid-to-late nineteenth century. In Arabic historiography, the *Nahda* is conventionally traced back to the French Campaign in Egypt and Syria (1798–1801). While short-lived, Napoleon Bonaparte's invasion and occupation of

Egypt (his Syrian adventure was less successful)—intended to establish a French imperial presence in the Middle East against the backdrop of waning Ottoman influence and continuing geostrategic conflict with the British Empire—was of monumental significance for the region and beyond. In *Orientalism* (1978), Edward Said identifies the Campaign—specifically, the contingent of *savants* (historians, archaeologists, philologists, scientists, etc.) that Napoleon brought with him in order to set up the Institut d'Égypte (1798–1801) in Cairo, and whose endeavors eventually resulted in the field-defining work of Egyptology, the *Description de l'Égypte* (1809–28)—as having set the "keynote" of the relationship between the West and the Middle East in the modern period, of modern Orientalism.[22] "Quite literally," he writes, "the occupation gave birth to the entire modern experience of the Orient as interpreted from within the universe of discourse founded by Napoleon in Egypt."[23] However, the impact of this episode was just as—if not more—pronounced in the region itself as it was for the European discourses and institutions in which Said is primarily interested.

It was in the power vacuum that resulted from what the lauded historian of the Middle East Albert Hourani calls this "intrusion of a European power into the heart of the Muslim world" that Muhammad 'Ali—the Khedive of Egypt from 1805 to 1848, whose dynasty endured until the Egyptian Revolution of 1952—was able to rise to power.[24] This is crucial, in that Muhammad 'Ali—widely regarded as the founder of modern Egypt—initiated during his reign precisely the modernizing and westernizing reforms in the political, social, cultural, and economic spheres that would eventually blossom into the *Nahda* not just in Egypt, but also in the Arab world at large (his grandson Isma'il, Khedive from 1863 to 1879, is particularly noted for consolidating and further advancing Muhammad 'Ali's vision in this regard). As I discuss in more detail below, it was he who sent Rifa'a al-Tahtawi—perhaps the single most important forerunner of the *Nahda*—to Paris in 1826, where as part of the education mission for which he was enlisted he was to begin assimilating the wealth of modern French and European culture (its literary and philosophical masterpieces, its scientific and technological advances, its Englightenment values, etc.) for the enrichment of his own (as would take place in the coming years). As Eugene Rogan explains, what spurred Muhammad 'Ali's fascination with and investment in European modernity during his rule, what prompted his view of Europe as a model for his own country's modernization, was his exposure to "the customs and manners of the French, the ideas of the Englightenment, and the technology of the Industrial Revolution" during Napoleon's occupation.[25] So it was that in the wake of the French Campaign, Muhammad 'Ali oversaw the beginning of the process of the importation and adoption of new, Western literary forms and genres, philosophical and political worldviews, sciences and technologies, languages, translations, and so forth in the Arab world that would find its fullest realization in the *Nahda*. As Hourani concludes in his 1983 preface to his classic, *Arabic Thought in the Liberal Age, 1798–1939* (1962), this was how the Arab world began to be "drawn [. . .] into the new world-order which sprang from the technical and industrial revolutions," that of modernity.[26]

In Arabic literary history, the literary and cultural developments associated with the *Nahda* are likewise generally traced back to the French Campaign and the new, galvanizing cultural encounters and exchanges with Europe that it instigated. In his *Introduction*, Allen, for instance, also highlights the pivotal roles played by Muhammad 'Ali, al-Tahtawi, and other comparably prominent figures in such developments. While acknowledging the internal or indigenous cultural interactions that were ongoing within and across the Middle East during the *Nahda*, he stresses that "increased contact with the West was clearly a very important part of [this] process."[27] In his edited volume on *Modern Arabic Literature* (1992), M. M. Badawi—quite as well respected as Allen for his work in this area (the latter was in fact one of his doctoral students at Oxford)—similarly underlines "the profound influence exercised by western literature on the *Nahḍah*," and indeed, for this reason, structures the volume into chapters on what this influence rendered as the discrete traditions of "poetry, the novel, short story, drama[,] and literary criticism" in the Arab world.[28] As he tellingly summarizes:

> Modern Arabic literature is obviously the literature of the modern Arab world, and this is generally assumed to begin with the French campaign in Egypt in 1798. The date is significant, for it marks the dramatic open-

ing of the Arab world, which was then part of the Ottoman Empire, to the west, ultimately with momentous consequences for its political, economic, social[,] and cultural development.²⁹

In recent years, the *Nahda* in particular and Arab and Middle Eastern literary and cultural modernity more generally have been subject to much renewed critical interest and interrogation. In addition to al-Musawi and Sacks (whose interventions here, most relevant to my own, I discuss in more detail below), scholars such as Stephen Sheehi, Tarek El-Ariss, and Kamran Rastegar, among others, have provided major new readings of this period and have reassessed the questions it poses for literary history. Broadly, they have sought in their work to challenge the model of unidirectional, "West" to "East" cultural influence hitherto predominant in the scholarship on the *Nahda*, and—with the aid of new developments in postcolonial, comparative, and other branches of literary / critical theory—to reorient critical attention towards (literary expressions of) the local and particular modern*ities* emergent across the region in the nineteenth to twentieth centuries.

For Sheehi, who focuses on issues of identity formation and subjectivity in the modern Arab world, it is how Arab "intellectuals, literati, and activists of all confessions" *themselves* "generated and reconstituted" the paradigms of modernity during the nineteenth century that is key to unpacking the sense of civilizational inferiority that continues to pervade this world.³⁰ Turning more explicitly to the literary as itself a site where modernity is performed and contested, El-Ariss aims through close readings of instances of affective "rupture and collapse" in Arabic literary texts that deal with the encounter with the West to "displace Europe as the origin of Arab cultural, political, and literary modernity."³¹ Expanding his scope to the as yet unexamined network of literary interactions between Arabic, Persian, and English in the nineteenth century, and looking to dispute readings of the Middle Eastern novel that see it as the inevitable telos of modernity there, Rastegar aims to tease out a sense of the region's "contingent modernities" via a literary history attentive to "interlinguistic subjectivities, ambiguous imaginative geographies, and dynamic shifts in cultural register."³² Clearly, this work cumulatively represents a major new departure in the literary historiography of the *Nahda*, and suggests an understanding of Middle Eastern modernity that conforms to what probably the majority of scholars interested in these issues today agree to be a more flexible, heterogeneous, and, indeed, "deprovincialized" model of global literary and cultural relations.[33]

It seems to me, though, that the accounts of modernity forwarded in this work (more so in the cases of El-Ariss and Rastegar than that of Sheehi) to some degree downplay just how pivotal Europe and its influence were in establishing the conceptual framework, the foundations on which what I concur are the modernities specific to the Middle East and their literary and cultural expressions would unfold from the beginning of the nineteenth century. For the encounters and exchanges these scholars describe, the literary texts they address, and intellectual debates they reconstruct were all situated within—and must be contextualized with reference to—a literary and cultural sphere whose very identity was being comprehensively reconstituted and redefined in this period according to precisely this influence. As I have suggested—thus far only in outline—in this chapter, all this hinged on the reinscription of *adab* as literature in the modern, European sense that took place across the Middle East in this period. As al-Musawi puts it, "with the arrival of European modernity through colonization or incorporation," "*adab* became institutionalized [in Egypt, Greater Syria, and Iraq, his primary referents here] as a term referring specifically to literary writing."[34] Sacks pushes this line of inquiry further. He details the role of the European (that is, Orientalist) discipline of philology in particular in "the installation of a series of colonial, Orientalist categories"—including literature—"in [the Arabic] language," as key proponents of the *Nahda* were exposed to and then internalized it.[35]

In the terms of the argument I have set out in this book, the reinscription of *adab* as literature might thus be regarded as a process of exchange, internalization, and reproduction by which modernity (yes, the same hegemonic, European modernity that most scholars working today have sought to discredit as a horizon for critical analysis) was facilitated and enacted in the Middle East. Furthermore, when viewed in these terms, this process can be understood to have occurred in remarkably similar ways across the Middle East. It might thus serve as a new and powerful lens for the critical comparison of the modern literatures and cultures of the region. I now turn to what I have identified as the key sites of Middle Eastern (literary and cultural) modernity—Egypt, Turkey, and Iran—in order to demonstrate the specificities and intricacies of this process in its national contexts, as well as its overlapping trajectories across the region.

Egypt

The crucible of the *Nahda* (which spread from there to the Ottoman-ruled territory of Greater Syria in the latter part of the nineteenth century), Egypt is an apposite starting point for considering the transformations to which the Arab and the Middle Eastern literary and cultural spheres were subject in the nineteenth to the mid-twentieth centuries. As noted above, it was under Muhammad 'Ali that many of the reforms that would come to define modern Egypt began to be instituted. What particularly enthralled the soon-to-be Khedive upon his exposure to European modernity during the French occupation of his country was what he regarded as the evident superiority of its military forces and its (associated) new technologies. It was for this primary reason—to learn the secrets of an army that had so rapidly overwhelmed those of Egypt's defending Mamluks (as in the Battle of the Pyramids [1798])—that he started dispatching delegations of students, scholars, and intellectuals on education missions to Europe (he also brought in scores of European advisors and administrators for similar as well as other ends, notably those of political bureaucratization, education reform, and industrial development). The first of these delegations was sent to Italy in 1809, and was directed towards the acquisition of printing technology as necessary for the large-scale publication of the military and other technical handbooks and manuals that would serve as a basis for the new military and technical schools that Muhammad 'Ali began to establish from 1816 (thus overhauling Egypt's traditional religious or Azhar education system). Many more were to follow.

A perhaps inevitable consequence of such accelerated contact and exchange with the West in this period was the exposure—often highly appealing—to other aspects of its political, social, and cultural life. This is perhaps most vividly evinced by al-Tahtawi's *rihla* of his five-year sojourn in Paris, where—as mentioned above—he was sent by Muhammad 'Ali in 1826 to serve as Imam for one of his delegations. In this account of his Parisian experience—known in English as *The Quintessence of Paris* or *A Paris Profile* (*Takhlīṣ al-Ibrīz fī Talkhīṣ Bārīz, aw, al-Dīwān al-Nafīs bi Īwān Bārīs*, 1834)—al-Tahtawi records with admiration (though not always uncritically) his impressions of a French and European culture that had exceeded the Egyptian in many ways, including in its Enlightened, rational thought; its burgeoning sense of national identity, community, and duty; its advanced forms of political organization and participation; its progressive (sometimes overly so) social attitudes towards especially women; and much of its literary and cultural output.[36] Indeed, the text even includes numerous fragments of French poetry that—though mostly unattributed—were translated by al-Tahtawi himself, in among the earliest known such translations into Arabic.[37] As he concludes of Paris, it is "filled with all intellectual sciences and arts, as well as astounding justice and remarkable equity"—qualities that he emphasizes "must once again find a home in the lands of Islam and the territories subject to the law of the Prophet."[38] This is highly significant, in that al-Tahtawi—regarded by scholars such as Hourani, Badawi, Allen, and many others of comparable stature as "the father of modern Arab thought" (in Badawi's phrase)—came upon his return from Paris in 1831 to play an indispensable role for Muhammad 'Ali and his reformist, modernizing agenda.[39]

Of the many European or European-modelled innovations that Muhammad 'Ali pursued, those with perhaps the most radical and far-reaching impact on the Egyptian (and thus Arab) literary and cultural sphere in particular were the printing press, journalism, and professionalized / institutionalized translation. Though not the first of the Arab world or even Egypt (Napoleon had brought one with him in order to disseminate his proclamations in Arabic), the Arabic printing press that Muhammad 'Ali established in 1821—which came to be known as the Government Press (Al-Maṭba'a al-Amiriyya)—was essential for his program, intended, as it was, to print the translated scientific and technological works necessary for his new education system. However, it soon came to encompass the Arabic literary heritage as well, making texts such as those of Ibn Khaldun more readily available to and accessible for Egypt's increasingly literate middle-class reading public. It also printed Egypt's first newspaper, an official gazette—*The Egyptian*

Chronicle (Al-Waqā'i' al-Miṣriyya)—which was founded by Muhammad 'Ali in 1828 and, by the Khedive's appointment, edited by none other than al-Tahtawi from 1841. Of course, journalism (another of Benedict Anderson's "technical means" for representing the imagined community of the nation) functioned in the Arab world not only to facilitate the circulation of information and ideas (with important political and other ramifications), but also to drive the simplification and standardization of the Arabic language itself, a process which was to eventually result in the universalization of Modern Standard Arabic in literary and other forms of writing across the region. To this, al-Tahtawi made a noteworthy early contribution in his role as editor of this gazette. Furthermore, it was in newspapers that, a little later, the Arabic novel was to first make its appearance—what is often cited as the very first of these works, Muhammad Husayn Haykal's *Zaynab* (1913), was originally published in serialized form in the Egyptian *Al-Jarīda* (1912), as were many of Naguib Mahfouz's early offerings in other prominent venues (notably, *Al-Ahrām*).

Another post to which al-Tahtawi was assigned by Muhammad 'Ali was that of Director of the School of Languages (Madrasat al-Alsun) in Cairo upon its foundation by the latter in 1835. As with the press, and in tandem with the Translation Bureau (Dār al-Tarjama) that was set up in 1841, this School—which provided training in European languages including English, French, and Italian—was intended to aid in the massive translation enterprise required by Muhammad 'Ali for his education reforms. And also like the press, it soon came to encompass European literary as well as technical writings, leading to a translation movement that saw for the first time the appearance in Arabic of thousands of novels, works of poetry, and plays from the European languages. For my interests, a particularly resonant instance is the translation of Daniel Defoe's *Robinson Crusoe* (1719). This is not only because the anonymous 1835 version published in Malta was the first novel of any kind to come out in Arabic, but also because another key figure of the *Nahda* who I discuss below—Butrus al-Bustani—attempted a version of his own in 1861.

So then, while this effect was far from the forefront of his mind when putting his reforms into place, Muhammad 'Ali's fostering of the modern, European(-derived) institutions of printing, journalism, and translation was truly transformative for the literary and cultural sphere not just in his native Egypt, but also in the Arab world at large. In a word, it set the stage for the *Nahda*. It is especially this aspect of his grandfather's legacy that Isma'il— perhaps Egypt's most dedicated westernizer—is noted to have further developed during his own, otherwise largely disastrous tenure as Khedive (which saw massive governmental overexpenditure in modernization projects and the related sale of Egypt's stock in the Suez Canal Company to the United Kingdom, leading—after his ouster in 1879—pretty much directly to the British occupation of his country from 1882 to 1956). Among his significant cultural achievements were Egypt's National Library (Dār al-Kutub), which he founded in 1870, and its Teachers' Training College (Dār al-'Ulūm), founded in 1872. With the political turmoil that would engulf his country from the 'Urabi Revolt of 1879 to 1882 to the Egyptian Revolution of 1919 to the Egyptian Revolution of 1952, and beyond, it might well be said that the period of Isma'il's reign was the high-water mark of the *Nahda* (at least in Egypt).

It was on the new literary and cultural terrain most thoroughly cultivated in Egypt that the modern, European concept of literature associated with the *Nahda* would begin to grow, and that what Sacks calls "the institution of literature in Arabic" would eventually flourish.[40] I now turn to two figures from elsewhere in the Arab world—Ahmad Faris al-Shidyaq and Butrus al-Bustani—so as to detail the specific, philology-induced pressures to which the Arabic language was subject during the *Nahda*, culminating in the reinscription of *adab* as literature. While neither of these figures was originally from Egypt (both were from what was in the nineteenth century the Ottoman territory of Greater Syria, specifically present-day Lebanon), the process to which they both so substantially contributed was in itself transnational in its origins, reach, and repercussions, and might be considered to have occurred both within and between the overlapping cultures of the Arab world (especially those of Egypt and Greater Syria). Underlining this point, al-Shidyaq in fact migrated to Cairo in 1825, where he primarily lived and worked for more than two decades (until 1848), and al-Bustani was provided with financial support by Khedive Isma'il for the compilation of the seven volumes of his *Kitāb Dā'irat al-Ma'ārif* (1876–1900)— the first modern Arabic encyclopedia—that he was able to publish in his lifetime (the remaining four were completed and published by family members after his death in 1883).

Al-Shidyaq—in whom critical interest among Arabists seems to have exploded over the last decade or so—was a prolific scholar, writer, journalist, translator, and linguist whose life as well as work appears to have spanned the extent of his nineteenth-century world and its major intellectual and sociocultural debates. In addition to Lebanon and Egypt, he spent considerable time in Malta, England (where he became a British citizen), France, Tunisia, and Turkey, and famously converted from Protestantism to Islam in 1860 (upon which he adopted the given name Ahmad). He is perhaps best remembered for having been a keen advocate of and participant in the modernization of the Arabic language and its literature, and for his defense of Arab culture against the incursions associated with Ottoman imperial dominance in this period. These interests are reflected in many of the projects in which al-Shidyaq was involved over the course of his life—during his residence in Cairo, he served for a while as editor of Muhammad 'Ali's *Al-Waqā'i' al-Miṣriyya*; during his stay in England, he contributed significantly to Samuel Lee's Arabic translation of the Bible (eventually published in 1857); and throughout his life, he published numerous works on issues in modern Arab (and European) art and society, including language.

The single work for which al-Shidyaq is best known, however, is a sprawling, semi-autobiographical *riḥla* known in English as *Leg over Leg* or *One Leg over Another* (*Kitāb al-Sāq 'alā al-Sāq fī mā huwwa al-Fāriyāq, aw, Ayyām wa Shuhūr wa A'wām fī 'Ajam al-'Arab wa al-A'jām*, 1855).[41] In this narrative, al-Shidyaq follows the often highly comical (mis)adventures of his fictional alter ego Fariyaq (whose name is a concatenation of the author's own given and family names) as he travels from Lebanon to Egypt to England to France and relives, with much embellishment, many of his creator's experiences and encounters in these locales. The device of a travelogue based on his life affords al-Shidyaq the opportunity to essayistically and satirically reflect on many of his own long-standing hobby horses (the Shandean allusion is intentional). These concerns include: the contemporaneous political, social, and religious controversies of these countries; the similarities and differences between Arabs and Europeans;

women, their bodies, and their sexuality; and, perhaps most prominently, the Arabic language itself (as he says in his Author's Notice, "everything that [he has] set down in this book is determined by one of two concerns. The first of these is to give prominence to the oddities of the language, including its rare words" [the second is women and their qualities]).[42]

In her "Foreword" to the English translation, Rebecca Johnson suggests that *Leg over Leg*—a text which she considers to be "generically impossible to characterize" or "multigeneric"—proceeds by way of "an omnivorous textuality" that "absorb[s] texts and literary forms through juxtaposition, quotation, imitation, and parody" and that "incorporates [European influences such as Laurence Sterne] into Arabic literary categories [such as the *maqāma*]."[43] As such, it stands for her as an exemplar of an Arabic literary modernity that, following recent scholarship, she defines not by its "import[ations] from the West," but rather "through [its] interaction with Europe" (the very same modernity as that forwarded by Sheehi, El-Ariss, and Rastegar, whom she regularly cites).[44] Along the lines of the critique that I set out above, it seems to me, though, that this sort of reading radically underestimates and even obscures the extent of al-Shidyaq's specifically philological borrowings from "the West."

In the case of *Leg over Leg*, it is al-Shidyaq's deployment of an authoritative narratorial "I" to order and control the entirety of his protagonist's story that indicates this inheritance (and that undermines Johnson's observation that "there is no stable position of narrative authority" in the text).[45] From the very first sentence of the text, and throughout, we find the narrator referring to himself and his work in the first person ("know that I embarked upon the composition of this four-book opuscule of mine during wearing, grinding nights [. . .]"); addressing his readers and thus setting their expectations ("If, on the other hand, you say, [. . .] I say to you"); and focalizing his narrative through the lens of this perspective ("This now being known, I declare: the Fāriyāq was born [. . .]").[46] As Sacks has powerfully argued in his recent, award-winning book *Iterations of Loss: Mutilation and Aesthetic Form, al-Shidyaq to Darwish* (2015), this usage on al-Shidyaq's part can be traced back to his career-spanning investment in and reliance on an Englightenment, specifically Kantian notion of "man" (one that might indeed be regarded as gendered given al-Shidyaq's running commentary on "woman" throughout the text).⁴⁷ Inscribing it in *Leg over Leg* in and as his narratorial "I," this notion— "a figure of sovereignty and autonomy in language"—provides al-Shidyaq what Sacks continues is a new, "anthropocentric" grounding for language that jolts language out of what in the life-world of classical to medieval Islam, of *adab*, had been its "theocentric" grounding.⁴⁸ As a pivotal text of Arabic literary modernity, it might thus be said that *Leg over Leg* marks in its very constitution (its philological underpinnings as inscribed in form) the beginning of a shift away from *adab* in its classical sense, and towards literature as derived from and intimately related to modern, European ideas of humanism, rationality, sovereignty, autonomy, and authorship.

This trajectory of *adab*'s reinscription as literature was further advanced by al-Bustani. Although he spent most of his life in his native Lebanon (Greater Syria), al-Bustani might be seen to have followed in al-Shidyaq's figurative footsteps in the range of his pursuits and the magnitude of his contributions to the *Nahda*. Like al-Shidyaq, he was a powerhouse writer and intellectual, one who over the course of his career almost single-handedly revolutionized the Lebanese / Syrian literary and cultural sphere (with further-reaching implications). Among the many fields and activities in which he was pivotally involved are: Arabic language and literature, through his encyclopedic knowledge of and writings on these topics, past, present, and future (including an Arabic dictionary and several grammar books); the Arab cultural heritage, through his actual encyclopedia and other scholarly endeavors; journalism, through the several newspapers and journals that he founded (which reflected his ideologies); translation, through his participation in another Arabic version of the Bible (the Smith-Van Dyck Version [1860–5]) and, notably, his rendition of *Robinson Crusoe* (1861); education reform, through his work as a teacher for the American Protestant Mission in Beirut and his establishment of Lebanon's secular National School (Madrasa al-Waṭaniyya) in 1863; and Lebanon's public life, through the roles he played in a number of elite cultural and scientific associations. Inspired by the Tanzimat reforms of the Ottoman Empire in the mid-nineteenth century as well as his work with the Protestant Mission (he converted from the Maronite Church to Protestantism in the early 1840s), al-Bustani's vision—one which he sought to actualize in all of these areas—was of a modern Arab literary and cultural sphere based on the principles of secularism and (Syrian) nationalism. In his view (as Hourani and Sheehi have most comprehensively demonstrated), it was only through the implementation of these principles in literature and culture that a coherent and distinctive Arab cultural identity attuned to the modern world could be fashioned.[49]

Most significant for my purposes here, al-Bustani carried his ideas about Arabic literature and culture through into his engagement—which was quite direct—with the concept of *adab*. His most expansive treatment of *adab* is contained in a lecture he delivered to what Sheehi surmises was the Syrian Scientific Society (Al-Jam'iyya al-'Ilmiyya al-Sūriyya) in 1859, entitled and published later in the same year as *Lecture on the Literature of the Arabs* (*Khuṭba fī Ādāb al-'Arab*, 1859).[50] In this talk, al-Bustani presented his views on Arabic intellectual history over the last millennium, and his proposals for its advancement in his contemporary moment (indeed, when al-Bustani published it in one of his journals and then as a book, he divided the text into sections on the state of the Arabs' knowledge or learning—*'ilm*—before Islam, after Islam, and in the present). His argument was a sweeping one—as he saw it, Arabic knowledge production had reached its peak under the Abbasid Caliphate, when the Arab world experienced a scientific revolution as well as an efflorescence of literary and cultural output (and when Europe was mired in darkness). Since then, its only progress had been towards its own collapse, which al-Bustani took to be a fait accompli by the time that he was developing and presenting his thought on this matter. As he puts it (in Sheehi's translation), "culture [in al-Bustani's original Arabic, '*al-adab*'] among the Arabs these days is in a complete state of decay ['*ḥālit inḥiṭāṭ*']."[51]

The task for al-Bustani, then, was to reclaim the heritage of the Islamic Golden Age so as to ensure the Arabs' proper place at the forefront of world history. However, achieving this goal required not a reversion to or consolidation of Islam as the episteme that undergirded the glories of the past, but rather exactly the opposite. As Europe had superseded the Arab world in its intellectual and other developments, and as its own Enlightenment in its many manifestations was spurred by a rationalism attendant on the increasing separation of church and state in especially the sixteenth to eighteenth centuries, the Arabs had to learn from this model and reorganize their intellectual world around a new, rational and secular form of knowledge. As Sheehi concludes in his detailed reading of the *Khuṭba*, it is precisely this form of knowledge, of *'ilm*—one that was derived from al-Bustani's modern European influences, and unambiguously "positivist, empirical, secular, and scientific"—that came to act as a basis for this figure's propositions regarding and thus redefinition of *adab* in the Arab world.[52] As such, the text might be understood as what Sacks calls "a program statement for Enlightenment in the field of language," one that hinges on the reinscription of *adab* according to the internalization of European influences.[53] This sense of *adab* is further underlined elsewhere in al-Bustani's work. As Sacks argues, al-Bustani's entry on this topic in his two-volume Arabic dictionary *Book of the Ocean of Oceans* (*Kitāb Muḥīṭ al-Muḥīṭ, ay, Qāmūs Muṭawwal li-Lughat al-'Arabiyya*, 1867–1870) presents it—"a language event that is communicable, formally monadic, temporally coherent, and legible"—in relation, ultimately, to "man" (as opposed to God or Allah), the master signifier of the Enlightenment tradition.[54]

The developments in the conceptualization of *adab* signposted by al-Shidyaq and al-Bustani were to come to their culmination back in Egypt in the early-to-mid twentieth century, in the work and thought of Taha Husayn. This figure, who came to be regarded as "the elder statesman of Egyptian letters" (in Hourani's phrase), was at the very heart of Egypt's literary and academic life in this period.[55] Upon his return from Europe in 1919 (where he had studied at the University of Montpellier and the Sorbonne, earning a Ph.D. at the latter), he secured a number of increasingly prestigious academic and other appointments including Professor of History at Cairo University, Rector of the University of Alexandria, and, later, Minister of Education for the Wafd government (before its dissolution in 1952). His productivity was immense—in addition to his scholarly works on a vast range of topics in Islamic literature, philosophy, and history (including a monograph that provoked quite a controversy in the Arab world, *On Pre-Islamic Poetry* (*Fī al-Shi'r al-Jāhilī* [1926]), he wrote an internationally renowned three-volume autobiography entitled *The Days* (*Al-Ayyām*, 1929–67); six novels; and innumerable articles as well as longer texts on issues in contemporary Egyptian politics and society. While diverse, and encompassing many genres and intellectual registers, it might be said that these writings were all driven by a prevailing, career-spanning sensibility on Husayn's part regarding his native Egypt, its history and culture, and its place in the world. His views on these matters are most comprehensively and systematically laid out in his book *The Future of Culture in Egypt* (*Mustaqbal al-Thaqāfa fī Miṣr*, 1938).

In this text, a polemic calling for Egyptian independence (in the face of continuing British imperial influence) as well as the universalization of education, Husayn makes the impassioned argument that for Egypt to be part of the modern world, it must follow the example of its paradigm, Europe. "In order to become equal partners in civilization with the Europeans," he writes (in Sidney Glazer's translation), "we must literally and forthrightly do everything that they do."[56] He goes further. He emphasizes that from Pharaonic times, Egypt has actually *always* been part of European—or, Mediterranean—civilization, a fact that the country has lost sight of due to its relatively recent religious, linguistic, and other alignments with the rest of the Middle East. Emulating Europe, then, becomes a matter of reclaiming Egypt's own repressed or sedimented cultural identity, a task which requires the modernization and development of not only its military and economy, but also its "scientific, artistic, and literary" production as well, so that Egyptians may be able to "study[. . .], feel[. . .], judg[e], work[. . .], and organiz[e] [their] lives the way they [Europeans] do."[57] As with al-Bustani on *'ilm*, Husayn is unambiguous as to what this entails: "I am [. . .] asking that the preservatives of defense, religion, language, art, and history be strengthened by the adoption of Western techniques and ideas."[58]

The impact of Husayn's prescriptions regarding Egyptian culture—including, as indicated above, its literature—was considerable. For as the institutional face of modern literature and its study in Egypt (as per the wide circulation of his literary critical works as well as his many important and influential professional appointments), he was in a unique position to implement his ideas in practice. And he indeed did so, by establishing and institutionalizing an "idea" of the literary object, a "technique" for literary criticism, and what Michael Allan calls a "literary curricul[um] for the modern Egyptian state" which—together amounting to the modern discipline of literary studies in Egypt—were all very much adopted from the West.[59] In his reading of Husayn's *On Pre-Islamic Poetry*, Sacks highlights the following particularly telling passage: "I," Husayn writes (in Sacks's translation), "want to follow in literature [al-adab] [sic] the philosophical method that Descartes invented for research into the reality of things at the beginning of this modern era."[60] The Cartesian allusion here serves a number of functions. It works to identify the object of analysis—*adab*, literature, or, indeed, *adab as* literature—as an isolatable one, as one that is to be understood and assessed devoid of its grounding in context, in world, in Islam. It therefore sets out a program for literary criticism oriented around the reading of literary texts in their individuality, one that bears an uncanny resemblance to the "New" or "Practical" critical methodologies then being espoused in the West (uncanny because no indication of Husayn's familiarity with the relevant material is provided in the text). And furthermore, it sets up and projects onto Arabic literature and its study a historicizing distinction between its "modern era" (a notion associated with René Descartes, Enlightenment philosophy, and Europe) and what is consequently rendered its pre-modern past. In a word, it inscribes *adab* as literature in the modern, European sense, and thus provides Husayn the conceptual groundwork for the project he was to more fully elaborate in *The Future of Culture in Egypt*, that of connecting Egypt—by way of what can now be seen as the shared heritage of its Arabic literature—to the European civilization that for him stood as the pinnacle of modernity and the model for Egypt's future. As Allan neatly summarizes in his recent book *In the Shadow of World Literature: Sites of Reading in Colonial Egypt* (2016), Husayn was in this way to play a foundational role in situating Arabic literature alongside the "Greek, Latin, French, English, and German" traditions, as one among many of "the literary traditions of an emergent world literature."[61]

Most expansively undertaken in Egypt, the reinvention of *adab* in modernity and the institutionalization of the modern concept of literature in Arabic that I have sought to trace in this section was of momentous consequence not just in the Arab world, but also further afield.

Turkey

I would like to suggest that the account of the *Nahda* in Egypt and the Arab world I have set out serves as a useful model for understanding the process of literary and cultural modernization undertaken in Turkey (as well as Iran, for that matter) in around the same period. Of course, one must recognize and be attentive to local specificities when carrying out such a comparative analysis. In Turkey as in any other context, the modernization process was mediated by the conditions particular to its national terrain at the time of its implementation—in this case, broadly, the declining fortunes of the Ottoman Empire from the early nineteenth century, its attempted reform along Western lines during the Tanzimat era (1839–76), and its eventual collapse in the aftermath of the First World War (1914–18), leading to the founding of the Republic of Turkey under Mustafa Kemal Atatürk in 1923. As perhaps most vividly illustrated by the comprehensive program of language reform underway in Turkey throughout this period and beyond, all of these circumstances impacted the Turkish literary and cultural sphere in ways that were unique to it.

What I am arguing, however, is that in its underlying logic and momentum, this process occurred in a remarkably similar way in Turkey as it did in Egypt and elsewhere in the Middle East. As in Egypt, it comprised the importation and adoption of new, Western literary forms and genres, philosophical and political worldviews, sciences and technologies, languages, translations, and all of the other features of European modernity (even more of them, in fact) typically associated with the *Nahda*. Further, as indicated by the episode of al-Shidyaq's move to Istanbul once his reputation had become established in the Arab world (he worked as a translator at the behest of the Ottoman government there, and launched the Arabic-language newspaper *Al-Jawā'ib*) as well as by al-Bustani's stated admiration of Tanzimat ideologies, it was to a degree informed by—and it correspondingly informed—the *Nahda*, as is only fitting given the religious, linguistic, cultural, and other links between the Ottoman Empire and the Arab territories (historically) subject to its control. And finally, bringing this comparison home, it likewise involved, even pivoted around an act of reinscription whereby the Turkish / Ottoman correlate of *adab*—*edebiyat*—was rewritten in terms of the modern, European concept of literature.

By the turn of the nineteenth century, the Ottoman Empire was in a state of severe disarray. As Erik Zürcher explains in his authoritative history of modern Turkey, the Empire—which at that point encompassed the Anatolian heartland, the Balkans, and most of the Arab world—appeared to have reached its structural limitations in this period. Organized around a small, decentralized political system (which was overseen by the Sultan, a figure of absolute authority, and run by a ruling elite of *'askerī* and *'ulemā* based out of an Istanbul governmental apparatus known as the Sublime Porte [Bāb-ı 'Ālī]); an increasingly ineffective military (which was comprised of the shrinking and technologically obsolete Janissary and Sipahi corps); and a pre-capitalist, largely agricultural economy (which was in permanent fiscal crisis due to military overexpenditure and a corrupt, inefficient taxation system), it was no longer able to sustain itself and exert its singular authority over territories that were as racially, ethnically, religiously, and nationally heterogeneous as they were vast. Due to these internal shortcomings, and most dramatically manifest in a series of catastrophic military and territorial losses at the hands of its Western and Northern European rivals (especially Habsburg Austria and Russia under Catherine the Great) in the preceding centuries, it had quite clearly been "surpassed" by Europe "economically, technologically[,] and militarily."[62]

And so began an era of reform in the Ottoman Empire, during which the Empire attempted to modernize itself according to the model so immediately and imposingly embodied by Europe. Under Selim III, Sultan from 1789 to 1807, a "New Order" ("Niẓām-ı Cedīd") was proclaimed whereby the Ottoman army would be professionalized (with the aid of foreign military advisors and new military schools, much as in Muhammad 'Ali's Egypt); a new treasury and tax system installed; and other administrative changes made. While in itself short-lived, effectively ending in 1807 with Selim's ouster (and later assassination) by the Janissaries (whose interests were directly threatened by his plans), the spirit of the New Order was very much resuscitated and consolidated by his successors. Under Mahmud II, Sultan from 1808 to 1839, the conservative Janissary order that had forestalled earlier efforts towards especially military reform was finally abolished (in 1826), an act which paved the way for the realization of Selim's vision regarding the army as well as other, related areas of Ottoman political and economic life. As Zürcher summarizes, "[a]ll his [Mahmud's] reforms can be understood as a means to that end: building a new army cost money; money had to be generated by more efficient taxation, which in turn could only be achieved through a modern and efficient central and provincial bureaucracy."[63]

These developments were to culminate in the Noble Edict of the Rose Garden (Gülhane Hatt-ı Şerīf)—also known as the Imperial Edict of Reorganization (Tanzīmāt Fermānı)—issued in 1839 by Mahmud's son, Abdulmejid I (Sultan from 1839 to 1861), and whose agenda was further pursued by his successor, Abdülaziz (Sultan from 1861 to 1876). Promising to establish guarantees for the life, property, and equality before the law of all subjects of the Ottoman Empire (whatever their race, ethnicity, religion, or national background) as well as major overhauls in just about every aspect of its infrastructure (its bureaucracy, administration, economic policies, financial institutions, industrial activities, trade, commerce, transportation systems, communications networks, civil society, legal code, educational institutions, military, and even national symbols), this decree came to serve as the founding statement of the Tanzimat that would transform the Empire into, eventually, a modern nation-state. Once more, Zürcher sums up the pivotal role played by its European sources on this, "the first phase of the emergence of modern Turkey," well:

> The European influence was exerted in three different, but interrelated spheres: the incorporation of a growing part of the Ottoman economy in the capitalist world system; the growing political influence of the European great powers, which expressed itself in attempts both to carve up the Ottoman Empire without causing a European conflagration and to dominate it while maintaining it as a separate political entity[;] and finally, the impact of European ideologies such as nationalism, liberalism, secularism[,] and positivism.[64]

Naturally, the developments I have outlined had a huge effect on the Ottoman literary and cultural sphere, where they were advanced, advocated, enabled, and registered in a number of highly significant ways. Like much of the Ottoman Empire, its dominant literary forms and genres—not to mention the Ottoman Turkish language in which these were written—had become largely defunct by the nineteenth century, increasingly divorced from the realities of the modern world to which the Empire was striving to attune itself. From the beginnings of the Empire in the fourteenth century, its literature—*edebiyat*—had been by and large continuous with that of its Arab and Persian neighbours (or colonies).[65] Indeed, it had been based on and oriented around what the Turkish literary historian Talat Halman describes as "the forms and aesthetic values of Islamic Arabo-Persian literature."[66] As such, *edebiyat* might be considered an Ottoman variant of *adab*, one that assumed a shape that though specific to the Empire and its political, social, and cultural life (including its language), was still very much analogous to that of *adab*.

As with its Arabic predecessor and prototype, *edebiyat* encompassed a spectrum of genres of writing, from the "literary" to the "non-literary" (as we would at present have it) and everything in between. The most prominent of these genres in Ottoman culture was, of course, Divan poetry. Halman estimates that two thirds of the Sultans were themselves poets, and often quite adept, though the sixteenth century poets Fuzuli and Baki are widely regarded as the masters of this tradition.[67] As Halman elucidates, Divan poetry was "[f]rom beginning to end" modelled on that of the Arabic and Persian traditions, from which it borrowed its major forms—the *ḳaṣīde* (the Ottoman Turkish version of the Arabic *qaṣīda*), the *ğazel* (*ghazal*), the *mesnevī* (*mathnawī*), various forms of religious or mystical (Sufi) verse, and several others.[68] To further underline this linkage between *adab* and *edebiyat*, it is worth recalling a few major Ottoman prose genres (which were mainly non-literary) as well. Among those with the most immediate correlation to *adab* and its genres as listed above are: the *siyāsetnāme* (which corresponds to the Arabic courtly manual or "mirrors for princes" genre); the *tārīh* (*tārīkh*); the *tezkıre* (*tadhkira*); the *siyāḥatnāme* and the *sefāretnāme* (which both correspond to the Arabic *riḥla*, though the latter is specific to the ambassadorial travelogue); and other genres of especially theological and philosophical writing.

As with *adab*, *edebiyat*—its status, its underpinnings, its very definition—was to undergo a sea change in the nineteenth century. As in Egypt, the European or European-modelled innovations that were to most significantly impact Ottoman literature and culture in particular in this period were the printing press, journalism, and professionalized / institutionalized translation. In the words of Nergis Ertürk, the introduction or further advancement of these ventures from the reign of Sultan Selim III to the Tanzimat amounted to nothing less than a "communications revolution" in the Ottoman Empire.[69] The first printing press for Ottoman Turkish (that is, its modified version of the Arabic script) was introduced to the Empire in 1726, by one Ibrahim Muteferrika. It is estimated that throughout its dominions, only 142 books in the language were actually produced by this and other presses between 1727 and 1838, though—importantly—among these were translations of the Arabic and French technical works required for Selim's new military schools.[70] Printing was to really come into its own in the Empire towards the end of this period and into the Tanzimat. In 1831, the Empire's first newspaper—an official gazette called the *Almanac of Facts* (*Takvīm-ı Vekāyi'*)—was launched. It was followed by the English expatriate William Churchill's government-funded *Chronicle of Events* (*Cerīde-ı Ḥavādis*) in 1840 and İbrahim Şinasi's independent *Interpreter of Situations* (*Tercüman-ı Aḥvāl*) in 1860, both of which contributed in their editorial policies to the simplification of the language as was necessary for their wide circulation and accessibility in the expanding Ottoman public sphere.[71]

Concomitant with the birth of journalism in the Ottoman Empire was the emergence of a literary translation movement. While an official Translation Office (Tercüme Odası) was set up by the Sublime Porte in 1833 to aid in its international diplomacy, it was not until the newspaper became established as a popular medium for the circulation of ideas and information that specifically literary translations (from the European languages, especially French) started to appear on a mass scale. As Ertürk surmises, this is because book production remained prohibitively dear, and newspapers were able to publish and disseminate translated works to a mass audience by means of the more cost-efficient serial format.[72] Şinasi was at the forefront of these efforts—apart from himself translating works by figures such as Alphonse de Lamartine, Jean Racine, Jean de La Fontaine, François Fénelon, and others, it was via his newspaper (as well as others that were influenced by his) that those of François-René de Chateaubriand, Victor Hugo, Jacques-Henri Bernardin de Saint-Pierre, Alexandre Dumas, Charles Paul de Kock, Eugène Sue, and so on were to first make their way to Ottoman readers.[73] The first novel to be translated into Ottoman Turkish was Fénelon's *The Adventures of Telemachus* (*Les aventures de Télémaque*,1699), a feat that was accomplished by Yusuf Kamil Pasha—who became Grand Vizier for Sultan Abdülaziz shortly thereafter—in 1859 (though this translation was not published in book form until 1862). As might be expected, the first native Turkish novel—Sami Frashëri's (Şemseddin Sami Bey) *The Love of Talat and Fitnat* (*Ta'aşşük-ı Tal'at ve Fitnat*, 1872)—followed hard on its heels.

What we see in Ottoman literature and culture during the Tanzimat is, then, very much as we have seen in Egypt during the *Nahda*—in a word, a process of modernization based on the European forms and genres, print media, ideas, and institutions that advocates of literary and other reforms wholeheartedly championed. While as in Egypt this trend of course did not go unchallenged (it was met with strong opposition by more conservative factions in the *'ulemā* religious establishment from the moment Selim introduced the modernizing imperative to the Empire, and the state attempted regain control over the media via widespread censorship under Abdülhamid II [Sultan from 1876 to 1909]), it—as retrospectively suggested by the history of Turkish literature in the twentieth century—was certainly the dominant, driving force in the literary domain throughout this era.[74] Bringing to mind al-Tahtawi and others, the highly influential Tanzimat poet, journalist, translator, and statesman Ziya Pasha (Abdul Hamid Ziyaeddin) captures the prevailing reformist sentiment of his time well in a well-known elegy for his fallen civilization ("Gazel," 1870). As he writes (in Nermin Menemencioğlu's translation):

> In the land of the infidel, I have seen cities and mansions,
> In the dominions of Islam, ruin and devastation.[75]

Although he was active at a later period than Ziya Pasha, the likewise esteemed and reform-minded man of letters Mehmet Akif Ersoy picks up on and productively develops this strand of thought in his "The Secret of Progress" ("Sirr-ı Terakī," 1912). After similarly lamenting the predicament in which the "Arabs, Persians[,] and Tartars"—"[a]ll the components of the Muslim world"—have found themselves, he, considering what he calls "the Japanese ascent" (presumably the Meiji period [1868–1912]), seeks to learn its "secret" so as to prompt that of his own culture.[76] And what he discovers and puts to paper in the following stanza is perhaps the clearest, most self-contained (poetic) expression we have of the Tanzimat in its literary and cultural dimensions—a program statement in verse, as it were, of the project of Turkish literary modernity. As Menemencioğlu translates once more:

> Do not go too far for such a quest,
> The secret of your progress lies in you.
> A nation's rise comes from within itself,
> To imitate does not ensure success.
> Absorb the art, the science of the West,
> And speed your efforts to achieve those ends,
> For without them one can no longer live,
> For art and science have no native land.
> But bear in mind the warning that I give:
> When reaching through the eras of reform,
> Let your essential nature be your guide—
> There's no hope of salvation otherwise.[77]

In these lines, Ersoy can clearly be seen to be endorsing and looking to further stimulate the impulse to "absorb"—or, internalize—the art, science, and so forth of the West that had been prevalent throughout the Ottoman Empire's "eras of reform." More importantly, though, he also betrays an absorption of a specific notion of the literary that has *already* taken place in the text itself. In his "art and science have no native land," he inscribes into the text an assumption of aesthetic and intellectual universality that—derived from the very (European, Enlightenment) models he warns against too-closely "imitating"—appears to be at odds with what he claims is to be nurtured, the "secret" that lies within the Ottoman subject (the individual "you" to the poetic speaker's "I") and the Ottoman nation (the collective "you"). For what can this "secret" amount to if not the contextual specificity of Ottoman thought on these matters as encapsulated by *edebiyat*, which is in turn defined by its Islamic character and connections to the Arabo-Persian (rather than European) world? Representative of the Tanzimat, the poem might thus be read as a literary act by which a *European* "essential nature"—an Enlightenment idea pertaining in this case to both "man" and the modern nation-state—is projected onto the Ottoman subject and nation alike, one that is played out in a literary object whose own "nature" has pre-emptively been reconfigured according to precisely the same influence. To put it another way, the poem enacts and facilitates in and as the literary object it constructs itself to be the modernity towards which it expressly aspires, and in this way establishes—or at least contributes to—an understanding and a practice of literature that are consistent with modernity.[78]

The literary and other ideologies espoused by Ziya Pasha, Ersoy, and others were to become thoroughly mainstream in the years following the Tanzimat and before the founding of the Turkish Republic. This period—which was punctuated by major constitutional reforms in 1876 and 1908, as well as by the rise of the Young Turks—saw a flowering of movements and magazines that called for and attempted to bring about a revolutionization of Turkish literature and culture on the basis, broadly, of a nationalist political credo and West-inspired aesthetic sensibility. In 1891, a "New Literature" ("*Edebiyāt-ı Cedīde*") movement was proclaimed by figures including Tevfik Fikret and Cenab Şehabeddin, who sought in Turkish letters a high art comparable to that of the West. In 1909, a "Dawn of the Future" ("*Fecr-i Ātī*") movement was declared by figures such as Ahmed Haşim and Yakup Kadri Karaosmanoğlu, who—gesturing towards Théophile Gautier—insisted on the autonomy, individuality, and sanctity of art. In 1911, a "National Literature" ("*Millī Edebiyāt*") movement was announced by figures like Ziya Gökalp, Ömer Seyfettin, and Ali Canip Yöntem, who more explicitly than ever before promoted the idea of a native Turkish tradition distinct from both its Eastern roots and its Western models. Gökalp is particularly interesting in this regard. This is because his recommendations for a Turkish national literature—and the language in which this was to be written—came to directly and significantly influence none other than Atatürk and the comprehensive program of political, social, and cultural reform he was to begin instituting after 1923. In a book entitled *The Principles of Turkism* (*Türkçülüğün Esasları*, 1923), he—expanding on ideas earlier put forward by his colleague Seyfettin (in an article on "New Language" ["*Yeni Lisan,*" 1911])— states as his first principle the "creat[ion] [of] our national language," a "Turkish tongue" that would "discard[. . .] the Ottoman language as if it had never been."[79] As he evidently persuaded Atatürk, he continues that this language is to "serve[. . .] as the basis for popular literature."[80]

Everything that I have thus far recounted in this section was to come to a head in 1923, with Atatürk and the founding of the Republic of Turkey. That is, the compulsion to modernize and westernize (not to mention secularize, as I discuss in more detail in Chapter 4) that had underwritten much of the Ottoman Empire's policy and ideology at the highest levels in the preceding century finally arrived at what appears to have always been its in-built telos in that year, a modern nation-state of the European variety. Towards this end, Atatürk—the Republic's first president as well as founder—instituted during its early years, and often personally oversaw, a series of reforms aimed at transforming the fundamental structure of the state. These initiatives included: the abolition of the Sultanate and the Caliphate (1922–4); the abolition of religious schools (*medreseler*) as well as the Ministry of Religious Affairs (1924); the prohibition of religious shrines, dervish orders, the fez, and other religious attire (1925); the adoption of the European clock, the Gregorian calendar, the Swiss civil code, and the Italian penal code (1926); the adoption of Western numerals (1928); and the introduction of a "law of last names" (1932), among many others.[81] Of course, all of these changes—which amounted to the institutionalization of Turkey's new national character in politics, society, and culture—were to feed into and consolidate the continuing process of the modernization of its literature.

In its early years, Republican literature very much followed the example set by the National Literature movement that had so inspired Atatürk earlier in the century. Indeed, it was on the ideological ground first broken by Gökalp and his colleagues that an authentically Turkish novelistic tradition (as well as its poetic and dramatic analogues) might be said to have eventually emerged (as I discuss in more detail below). However, literature during the Republican era—its very idea as well as its practice—was also significantly impacted by another development that was particular to the time, and that was unique to Turkey (at least in the context of the Middle East). In 1928, Atatürk—in line with his other reforms—called for and successfully saw to the elimination of the official modified Arabic script of the Ottoman Empire, and its replacement with a Latinate script derived from those of Turkey's European peers. In addition, he also insisted on the need to substitute the Arabic and Persian loanwords with which Ottoman Turkish was saturated with native Turkish counterparts (for the sake of the distinct national identity and culture that he sought to cultivate). To facilitate these goals, he established an official regulatory body charged with modernizing the language—the Turkish Language Association (Türk Dil Kurumu)—in 1932.[82] While it was certainly dramatic, even spectacular, Atatürk's language reform was far from unprecedented—its groundwork had been laid by nearly a century's worth of Tanzimat- and Constitutional-era reformers, who often advocated for similar and other changes to the language.[83] My interest here, though, is in its realization during the Republican era. This is because beyond the other aspects of the modernization of Turkish literature as hitherto described (its ideologies, forms, and practices), it was at this time that the Ottoman *word* for literature—and thus the sedimented cultural content that it harbored—was directly subjected to the demands of modernity.

As late as 1884, it was still possible to define *edebiyat* (as well as its root) much as it had been defined for centuries. This is how the English diplomat and lexicographer James William Redhouse presents both in his authoritative *A Turkish and English Lexicon* of the same year (this is the base text of the ever-popular *The Redhouse Dictionary*, whose latest edition was published in 2014):

A. ادبيات edebiyat, *s. pl.* The matters pertaining to Arabian philology, the details of grammar, prosody, rhetoric, and logic.[84]

A. أدب edeb, *s., pl.* اداب 1. Discipline of the mind, training, education, learning, accomplishments. 2. Breeding, manners, politeness; respectfulness, modesty. 3. Philological science, especially as applied to the Arabic language and vast literature, prose and verse, sacred and profane. 4. A usually observed mode of action, a rule or custom.[85]

It was *edebiyat* in this, its classical, Arabic-derived sense that seems to have especially irked Nurullah Ataç, one of the architects of the language reform. A poet, a man of letters, and a zealous supporter, even ideologue of "pure Turkish" (*"Öztürkçe"*), Ataç regarded the term—rooted as it was in Arab literary, cultural, and social traditions "sacred" as well as "profane," and in itself referring "especially" to "Arabic language and [. . .] literature"—as incommensurate with the objectives of linguistic and literary modernization in the new national/ist milieu of the Turkish Republic. Among his many other notable contributions to the reform (which were concentrated in the 1940s and 1950s), mainly consisting of the innovation of new, Turkish-derived words to replace this and other foreign loanwords (in this, his only equal was Falih Rıfkı Atay), he thus sought an alternative for *edebiyat*. And finding what he needed in *"yazı,"* Turkish for "writing," he—quite arbitrarily—coined the neologism *"yazın,"* which he intended to refer directly and specifically to the modern, European concept of literature (understood as literary writing in a narrower sense).[86]

Of course, Ataç's efforts here did not gain the traction that he desired. *Edebiyat* remains the primary word used in Turkish to refer to literature, and *yazın*—when deployed—is so more often than not alongside the former (as in the phrase *"edebiyat ve yazın"*), as something akin to a supplementary "belles-lettres" rather than as the out-and-out replacement he envisioned. This, though, is almost beside the point. For by the time Ataç set his sights on *edebiyat* in the 1940s–50s, its meaning and its practice had already so completely deviated from what they had been during the heyday of the Ottoman Empire that it was no longer necessary for anyone but the most hardened linguistic nationalist to worry about the word itself. The fact that he homed in on the Turkish *"yazı"* in particular as a means to express what literature meant in modern Turkey seems to corroborate this. As Ertürk concludes in her excellent study *Grammatology and Literary Modernity in Turkey* (2011), it was in "the breakdown of the Ottoman-Islamic discursive network"—that of *edebiyat*—that literature was "reconstituted and reconfigured [. . .] in a new secularized field of influence," and came to designate, merely, "the practice of [. . .] fiction writing."[87]

Iran

In Iran, the process of literary and cultural modernization followed what is by now the familiar pattern set by Egypt and Turkey. As in these contexts, it can be traced back to the beginning of the nineteenth century. As the widely respected historian of Iran Ervand Abrahamian explains, this period saw "the gradual penetration of the country by the West."[88] Military defeats at the hands of Imperial Russia (during the Russo-Persian Wars of 1804–13 and 1826–8) and Great Britain (during the Anglo-Persian War of 1856–7) not only led to humiliating territorial losses in the north and south of Iran (or Persia, as the country was known to the West since classical antiquity), but also exposed to its ruling Qajar dynasty the technological and other weaknesses of its army. Russia's modernized artillery was regarded with particular awe, given its role in the levelling of Iran's numerically superior forces in the Caucasus region during the first Russo-Persian War. As such, Abbas Mirza—the Qajar Crown Prince during his father Fath'ali's reign as Shah of Iran (1797–1834), and the commander of Iran's army during this war—sought to modernize his forces in preparation for what turned out to be his unsuccessful campaign in the following decade to reconquer the Caucasian territories that had been lost. Once more recalling Muhammad 'Ali's Egypt, he did do by dispatching delegations of Iranian scholars to England in order to study Western military technologies (England was the venue of choice due to its own "Great Game" imperial rivalries with Russia at the time), and by simultaneously bringing in British officers to organize and train his troops. And so began what Abrahamian describes as Iran's "defensive modernization"—a project that though driven by the necessity of military reform, was also to have many more substantial and far-reaching effects on Iranian politics, society, and culture as a whole.[89]

It was under Nasser al-Din, the Qajar Shah from 1848 to 1896, that the majority of reforms comparable to those of the Egyptian *Nahda* and the Ottoman Tanzimat were implemented. His first prime minister, the reform-minded Mirza Taqi Khan Farahani—who served from 1848 to 1851 (shortly thereafter, he was assassinated), and to whom he gave the title "Great Ruler" ("Amir Kabir")—was particularly influential in this regard. During his albeit brief stint in this role, this figure was able to overhaul and streamline Iran's central bureaucracy, tax system, and judiciary, and to at least initiate the expansion of the country's industrial sector, international trade, diplomacy, and military. Among his more prominent cultural achievements in this period were the renovation and expansion of Tehran's famous Grand Bazaar (Bāzār-e Bozorg), and the founding of Iran's first modern university—Dār al-Funūn, later renamed the University of Tehran—in 1851. These changes were met with much hostility among the more conservative elements in Iran's political and religious establishment during the Amir's time (leading directly to his ouster in 1851, and thence his aforementioned assassination). As a result, Nasser al-Din back-pedalled on the idea of reform for a while. However, and due to considerable public pressure, the Shah reverted to the agenda set out by his once-esteemed advisor in the latter years of his reign. Towards the close of the nineteenth century, he introduced important modernizing initiatives in Iran's infrastructure, communications networks, media landscape, and army (including establishing in 1879 the country's Russian-modelled Cossack Brigade [Berīgād-e Qazzāq]), and thus helped pave the way for the modern radical revolution(s) that would take place in the twentieth. Abrahamian sums up the nature and extent of Iran's transformation in the period in question fittingly: "[i]n 1800," he writes, "Iran had been fairly isolated from the world economy. By 1900, it was well on the way to being incorporated into that economy."[90]

Like its Ottoman variant, Iranian literature—*adabiyāt*—had been largely consistent with *adab* up until this point. Moreover, it was and continues to be viewed as an exemplar of the *adab* tradition. After the Sasanian Empire was conquered by the Arab Rashidun Caliphate in 651 and Iran came to be incorporated into the emergent Arabic-Islamic civilization of the region, Iranian *udabā'*—scribes, writers, poets, and bureaucrats—came to be known, even revered for their particular aptitude in this area in the Umayyad and Abbasid courts. At the same time, though, the Persian language (which like Ottoman Turkish utilized a modified version of the Arabic script) retained its status as the literary, cultural, and administrative lingua franca in Iran itself throughout this period and beyond. It experienced a rebirth of sorts with the decline of Arab imperial influence in the country in the eighth to ninth centuries, and emerged in its classical form as Iran was "re-Persianized" under the Samanid (819–999) and Ghaznavid (977–1186) dynasties. Poets now renowned the world over such as Ferdowsi (tenth–eleventh centuries) and Omar Khayyam (eleventh–twelfth centuries) played a crucial role in the establishment and maintenance of classical Persian as Iran's dominant literary language in this period, and their tradition was consolidated by others such as Rumi (thirteenth century), Saʻdi (thirteenth century), and Hafiz (fourteenth century) even as Iran was subject to further invasions—now by the Seljuqs and the Mongols—in the following centuries.

However, despite these especially linguistic specificities in the Iranian context, its *adabiyāt*—a major constituent of the literature of the Islamic Golden Age more generally—very much remained of the Arabic-Islamic world and its ever-expanding network of overlapping, intersecting cultures across the region. A brief recap of the genres of writing that it encompassed helps underline this point. As the Iranian historian, economist, and literary critic Homa Katouzian elaborates, poetry was as central to classical Persian literary culture as it was to that of the Ottoman Empire, and its main forms—the *qaṣīda* (spelled and transliterated identically in Arabic and Persian), the *ghazal* (as above), and the *masnavī* (the Persian version of the Arabic *mathnawī*)—similarly reflected the Arabic influence.[91] So too did its prose, whose genres included the *siyāsatnāme* (as with its Ottoman homonym, this corresponds to the Arabic courtly manual or "mirrors for princes" genre); the *tārīkh* (identical in Arabic and Persian); the *tadhkira* (as above); the *safarnāme* (also in line with what is in this case its Ottoman *near*-homonym, this corresponds to the Arabic *riḥla*); and many others.[92]

In his important recent book *The World of Persian Literary Humanism* (2012), Hamid Dabashi has sought to reinterpret *adab*—which he uses to refer to the Arabic, Turkish, Urdu, *and* Persian literary traditions alike, though his focus is on the latter of these—in terms of a notion of "literary humanism."[93] Understood—or, as he puts it, "translate[d]"—in this way, *adab* serves as the basis for the wider argument he wishes to make about Iranian literature.[94] He argues for a uniquely Persianate literary world that over the course of its 1,400 year history has been undergirded by literary humanism as its "running leitmotif," and that has thereby in itself always been of a worldly and cosmopolitan character.[95] With "Iran as its epicenter" and stretching from Anatolia to Central Asia to South Asia, this world is oriented around the Persian language and the literatures written in it.[96] For this primary reason, it is to be distinguished from its Arabocentric older brother (due to whose hegemony it has been not only marginalized in the literary historiography of the Middle East from the Islamic Golden Age to the present, but also feminized). This is the world, Dabashi concludes, that contemporary Iranian literature—signposted by Iran's Constitutional Revolution of 1906—has inherited, and whose tradition it continues. From "1906 to the present," he writes, "Persian literary humanism reached a fully self-conscious worldly cosmopolitanism outside any royal court and firmly grounded in the public space of its own making, which it calls *vatan* (homeland, nation)."[97]

In order to make his case, Dabashi must pursue several lines of literary critical and historiographical inquiry that are highly pertinent to my own. I address two of these in particular, as his findings in these areas directly contradict my discussion of Iranian literature specifically as well as *adab* more generally. Firstly, Dabashi argues that Persian literary humanism (his rendition of "*adab*") is to be categorically distinguished from the tradition of Islamic scholasticism that arose in tandem with it. Taking issue—quite gracefully—with his teacher George Makdisi's claim that in classical Islam both *adab* and this more religiously oriented scholarship "sprang from concern for a common source: the Sacred Scripture" (as his Arabocentric emphasis led to a neglect of Persian literature), he insists that each in fact "had an entirely different vision of the world."[98] As I have already comprehensively shown (drawing more on Dabashi's colleague at Colombia, Muhsin al-Musawi, than on Makdisi), the critical gesture that Dabashi is here reproducing—that of extricating *adab* from its setting in the life-world of Islam, of decontextualizing and thus *secularizing* it—is a deeply problematic one. It relies on the same belletristic reading of the concept (and Dabashi is explicit about this) that I have demonstrated to be anachronistic, in that it is rooted in European Enlightenment discourses of literature and humanism—of literary humanism—that it then projects onto an altogether incompatible object.[99] The point that the accounts of *adab* provided by Makdisi and others fail to extend to its Persian manifestation seems likewise to miss the mark, given what I have suggested to be *adabiyāt*'s generic continuities with and borrowings from its Arabic sources.

Secondly, he argues that as a conceptual and historiographical category of analysis, "modernity" is "meaningless"—"irrelevant and distorting"— when it comes to "the panorama of the inner logic and historic unfolding of Persian literary humanism."[100] This is because in his view, Iranian literature's "course of development" to the present has been "entirely independent of the European trope of modernity as a defining category," which he takes to be "an altogether colonial construct."[101] As is evident, it is necessary for Dabashi to so strongly dismiss what he casts as an alien critical construct as it by definition marks a radical literary historical break or rupture (however conceived or periodized) that interrupts and thus rends asunder the idée fixe of a *continuous* trajectory of Persian literary humanism that is at the heart of his study. Just as clear—and quite apart from the irony of Dabashi's unreflexive usage of "literary humanism" in the very same sentence as his critique of "modernity"—is the fact that such a break did indeed take place during the period under consideration in this section. It is not a contentious idea that in Iran as in any other peripheral context, literature and culture—like all sectors of society—were very much subject to a process of modernization at this time by which they were disserved from the traditions of their past, and reinvented according to the demands of their present moment. Neither does it seem particularly controversial to say that this process was undertaken under the pressure and influence of modern European, often colonial, forces. The mere existence let alone predominance of "fiction, poetry, and film" in their current forms in Iran— which Dabashi dubiously takes as proof of his trajectory, that it became "fully realized" in the twentieth century—confirms precisely this.[102] A literary history that fails to attend to, or that even systematically misconstrues such phenomena would seem to me questionable, to say the least.

In Iran as in Egypt and Turkey, the modernization of literature and culture and the attendant redefinition of *adabiyāt* were largely prompted by the introduction of the printing press, journalism, and professionalized / institutionalized translation in the late nineteenth century. In 1871–2 (during the reign of Shah Nasser al-Din), the Iranian government—which was then led by Mirza Hosayn Khan, another reform-minded yet short-lived prime minister (his tenure in this role lasted from 1871 to 1873)—established an official Printing House (Dār al-Ṭebā'a), not to mention an official Translation Bureau (Dār al-Tarjama) charged with a similar function as its Egyptian and Ottoman counterparts. Though certainly not the first in Iran (even in the nineteenth century), this press is significant in that it published two government-sponsored newspapers—*The Iran Daily* (*Rūznāma-e Īrān*) and *Information* (*Eṭṭelā'āt*)—both of which were intended to disseminate official views on national and international matters, and both of which contributed to the simplification and standardization of the Persian language (notably, by substituting the Arabic loanwords widespread in classical Persian with native Persian counterparts). Furthermore, it—under the directorship of the highly capable administrator and man of letters Mohammad Hassan Khan, and often in tandem with Dār al-Funūn (which offered instruction in foreign languages, pivotally French, English, and Russian)—published what Abrahamian estimates were more than 160 books by the turn of the century, a substantial number of which were translations of European literary and other classics.[103] Alongside the instructional and technical textbooks, Persian and Arabic literary classics, histories of Iran, and biographies of world historical figures that it produced, there appeared through Dār al-Ṭebā'a the first Persian editions of works by the likes of Descartes, Isaac Newton, Defoe, Dumas, Charles Darwin, and Jules Verne, among others.[104] It was perhaps inevitable that the first novels originally written in Persian—such as those, most famously, of Mirza Abdelrahim Talibi Najjar Tabrizi and Zeyn al-Abedin Maraghei—started to appear during this period, on the back of this press's activities. Apart from this, the central point I wish to convey, Abrahamian directs us towards another important ramification of the press's editorial interests and policies—he suggests that due to its reliance on European-authored historical works, "Iranians began to see their own past as well as world history mainly through Western eyes."[105]

This observation might well be seen to extend to the Iranian *literary* past as well. For at this time of heightened exposure to European literary and other influences, when the country's prevailing political ideology appeared to vacillate from reform to reaction and back again with each new prime minister, the question of Iran's literary and cultural heritage—of literature itself in relation to the dialectical tensions of modernity—was subject to much renewed debate and controversy. Retrospectively speaking, it seems clear that those on the modernizing side of the equation would eventually win the day. In this regard, three major men of letters of the period are particularly noteworthy. The Azerbaijani writer, poet, playwright, linguist, and literary critic Mirza Fath'ali Akhundzade was perhaps the most important of these. One of the key architects of modern Iranian nationalism and a proponent of literary and cultural modernization along these lines, Akhundzade—as Reza Zia-Ebrahimi explains in his detailed reading of his legacy—drew much of his inspiration from the "Aryan race" hypothesis then being propounded by European (read: Orientalist) philologists such as Max Müller and Ernest Renan.[106] As he saw it, Iran in its essentially Aryan fiber and the grandeur of its pre-Islamic past (an age when it was "rule[d]" by "benevolent kings") had been corrupted and contaminated by the invasion of the Arabs—a Semitic race—many centuries ago, and by the imposition of their religion onto its unsuited cultural terrain.[107] As such, Iran had to be cleansed of this inheritance in order to reclaim its true identity and set itself back on its world-historical trajectory towards the modernity of its estranged European kin. In language, this amounted to ridding Persian of the Arabic loanwords by which it continued to be infested (like some of his Ottoman contemporaries, Akhundzade also wanted to replace the Arabic script with a Latinate one). In literature, it comprised abandoning the classical Persian tradition—*adabiyāt*—almost in its entirety (the exception was Ferdowsi, due to his poetic investment in pre-Islamic Iranian history and mythology), and building a new one from the ground up. It was very much on the basis of his internalization of Orientalist philology that Akhundzade developed his views on a modern Iranian literature appropriate to the modern nation-state he sought to bring about.

Akhundzade's vision was further advanced by his disciple, Mirza Aqa Khan Kermani. As Zia-Ebrahimi writes once more, Kermani's contribution to the emergent nationalist discourse of his time was to radicalize his mentor's agenda. In his hands, Akhundzade's historical propositions—which had at least the air of grounded scientific inquiry—turned into anti-Arabist vitriol, and were redirected towards a rhetoric that was as chauvinistic about those whom Kermani regarded as the cause of all Iran's woes over the last millennium as it was effusive and idealizing about the country before Islam. Sentiments such as "I spit on them [Arabs]," "vilest humans, most vicious beasts," "animal-like and even worse than animals" would find their way into Iran's national conversation (via its more far-right voices) in the following century.[108] So too, though, would his likewise sharpened suggestions about the language. Beyond the excision of foreign loanwords and so forth, he called for a halt to the excessive ornamentations and embellishments of classical Persian, which—with everything else he found to be abhorrent in contemporary Iran—he saw as derived from the Arabic influence.[109] While by no means a revolutionary in the vein of Akhundzade and Kermani (he advocated for a more gradual style of reform, based mainly on changes to Iran's legal system), the statesman and journalist Mirza Malkam Khan is considered to be the master of such a simplified and more widely accessible Persian prose style in the late nineteenth century.[110] However, the writings and ideas of all three of these trailblazers of literary and other forms of modernization would only really find their audience in the twentieth.

At the turn of the twentieth century—in 1906, to be precise—Iran instated a new Constitution that would turn out to set the course for the country for the next seventy-three years. Signed into law by Shah Muzaffar al-Din (who having reigned since the death of Nasser al-Din in 1896, himself died shortly thereafter, in 1907), and modelled on the Belgian Constitution, this document established a constitutional monarchy in Iran, with a separation of powers between the executive, legislative, and judicial branches of government. Its Fundamental Laws of 30 December 1906 decreed that while the head of state would retain ultimate authority over the executive branch and armed forces (with the prerogative to appoint ministers, sign bills into law, and declare war on foreign nations), the Iranian people at large would now be represented by a new National Assembly (the Majlis) and Senate (the Majlis-e Sinā, though this was not formed until 1949). This provision was supported by its Electoral Laws of 9 September 1906, which for the first time granted Iranian citizens (with the exception, naturally, of women and a few other groups) the right to elect their political representatives. To these sets of laws were soon added the Supplementary Fundamental Laws of 7 October 1907, which, among other items, formalized Iran's capital, borders, and state symbols; declared Shi'a Islam Iran's official religion; and set up a charter that guaranteed the basic rights of all citizens (to life, property, honor, equality before the law, habeas corpus, free speech, free assembly, and so on).[111]

In practice as well as theory, the Constitution of 1906 established Iran as precisely the modern, European-fashioned nation-state that figures such as Akhundzade, Kermani, and Malkam Khan had earlier demanded. It laid the national groundwork for the sorts of proposals they had forwarded for a modernized Iranian literary and cultural sphere, which could now be more vigorously pursued. It is no coincidence that their literary successors—those who took their ideas most closely to heart, adopting and developing them to suit the needs of their present moment—were often themselves involved in the revolutionary upheavals that surrounded its drafting, whether directly (in their political activities) or indirectly (in their literary writings, journalism, pamphleteering, and so on). Among the most prominent and influential of these was the essayist, journalist, translator, lexicographer, and politician 'Ali Akbar Dehkhoda. Dehkhoda's impassioned pro-Constitutional, even revolutionary stance is reflected in his editorials for the magazine *Trumpet of Israfil* (*Ṣūr-e Isrāfīl*) from 1907 to 1909, its years of operation; his having translated the writings of Montesquieu into Persian; and his election to the Majlis in 1910. However, most significant for my purposes here is his encyclopedic, sixteen-volume Persian dictionary, *Lughatnāme* (1931).[112] This is because this work—the most comprehensive and authoritative dictionary of the language, supported by the Majlis and based out of the Dehkhoda Institute at the University of Tehran since 1945—had the effect of instituting the lexicon of modernity in Persian. In it, as Abrahamian recounts, Dehkhoda and his team of fellow linguists provided for the first time clear definitions of new terms such as "*demokrasi*," "*capitalism*," "*imperialism*," "*sosyalism*," "*aristokrasi*," "*oligarki*," and "*bourzhuazi*," and thus facilitated their relatively undiluted entry into the national discourse.[113] Furthermore, they also redefined a wide range of old, increasingly redundant terms for their times—for example, "*mellat*," formerly "religious community," was rendered "nation"; "*dowlat*" changed in meaning from "patrimonial court" to "national government"; "*adalat*" was changed from "appropriate treatment" to "justice"; and Dabashi's "*vatan*" was changed from "locality" to "homeland."[114] It should come as no surprise that by Dehkhoda's hand, "*adabiyāt*" was inscribed simply and definitively as "literature," with the expanded connotations of " '*ulūm adab, āsār adab*," "literary science, literary works."[115]

In this, its modern sense, *adabiyāt* was brought to fruition by the literary writers of the Constitutional era. Poets such as 'Aref Qazvini, Mohammad Taqi Bahar, and Taqi Rafat—all likewise involved in the political controversies of their time—sought to develop a prosody appropriate to the new national milieu crystallized in and as the Constitution. Bahar—widely regarded as Iran's "Poet Laureate" or "King of Poets" ("*Malik al-Shu'arā'*")—enshrined the prevailing sensibility of his generation of writers in an ode composed shortly after its signing:

> Hope the kingdom will forever flourish
> Upon this auspicious foundation of law.[116]

It seems to me that rather than the supposed "literary humanism" or "worldly cosmopolitanism" of *adabiyāt* in its classical sense, it is precisely this sentiment—which amounts to a literary countersignature of the Constitution of 1906—that contemporary Iranian literature in its many forms has inherited.

* * *

In this section, I have fleshed out my argument about world literature as the worlding of the concept of literature attendant on modernity by detailing the reinscription of *adab* as literature in the Middle East in the nineteenth to the mid-twentieth centuries. This process had the effect of dissociating *adab* from its specifically Arabic-Islamic connotations and manifestations across the region for a millennium and more, and of laying the groundwork for the rise and eventual predominance of modern literary forms there. In this way, it thus both facilitated and enacted the emergence of the modern nation-state—of modernity per se—in the Middle East.

I now further develop this argument with reference to the Middle Eastern novel—its origins, its history, its ascendency—as a paradigmatic form of modernity in the region.

Modern "Literature" and the Origins of the Novel

In the Middle East, the novel arose as a distinct literary form only by virtue of the wider, transregional process of literary and cultural modernization that I have delineated vis-à-vis its key national contexts. In Egypt, Turkey, and Iran, its currency as a mode of literary expression, its very legibility and thus reproducibility, was premised on the internalization of the modern, European concept of literature that took place in each of these countries from the nineteenth to the mid-twentieth centuries, which I have argued is to be regarded as the centerpiece of this process across the region. These observations are supported by much of the major scholarship on the novel in the Arab world and elsewhere in the region. In his *Introduction*, Allen, for instance, argues that in the Arab world, the novel—a "newly imported Western genre[...]"—originated during the *Nahda* (he foregrounds the printing press, journalism, and translation as particularly significant factors in this development), at which point it came to "rapidly supersede[...]" the narrative and other literary traditions of earlier centuries.[117] He expands on this reading in his book *The Arabic Novel: An Historical and Critical Introduction* (1995). Stressing once more the novel's status as an "imported genre" there, he writes that "increasing contacts with Western literatures led to translations of works of European fiction into Arabic, followed by their adaptation and imitation, and culminating in the appearance of an indigenous tradition of modern fiction in Arabic."[118] Badawi and Jayyusi both adopt a similar approach. As noted above, Badawi structures his volume *Modern Arabic Literature* into chapters on what the Western influence rendered as the modern literary forms of the region (including the novel), while Jayyusi opens her anthology *Modern Arabic Fiction* (2005) by explaining that "[t]he process of the establishment of modern Arabic fiction [...] was begun by introducing the new fiction to the Arab audience through translations from Western fiction."[119]

A consideration of the term that is now near-universally used in Arabic for "novel"—"*riwāya*"—helps underline all of the above ("*qiṣṣa ṭawīla*," literally "long story," is sometimes used too, though it is becoming less common). In a short piece on "*Qiṣṣa*" (a term that refers to a specific Arabic narrative genre, but more generally meaning "story" or "narrative"), Kilito has conducted a careful philological analysis of this word. Once signifying "the oral transmission of a poem or a narrative" (that is, in the classical Arabic tradition), "*riwāya*," he demonstrates, was "by general consent" repurposed and universalized as "novel" in the nineteenth- to twentieth-century Arab contexts under discussion.[120] It was so, he continues, under the influence of the very same forces identified by Allen, Badawi, Jayyusi, et al.—as he writes, this "semantic shift [. . .] [was] brought about by the encounter with Western modernity."[121] Thus modernized, *riwāya* came to incorporate into its singular novelistic modality the multitude of distinct narrative genres of classical Arabic—Kilito homes in on "*qiṣṣa*," "*ḥikāya*," "*ḥadīth*," "*maqāma*," and "*riḥla*" in addition to *riwāya* itself in its earlier sense as prominent examples of such genres that, as per Allen, were "superseded" by *riwāya* in its modern sense.[122] Kilito concludes with the provocative suggestion that this process was so successful, so encompassing that "the *riwāya*, the novel" might now be said to be "the true *dīwān* of the Arabs."[123] What Kilito is here describing is perhaps even more vividly evinced in modern Turkish and Persian. For the term that has come to be used for "novel" in both of these languages is a direct and unambiguous borrowing from the same modern European, specifically French sources that precipitated the novelistic traditions in Turkey and Iran in the first place—respectively, "*roman*" (in the Latinate script of modern Turkish) and "*rumān*" (as transliterated from the Persian).

The trajectory of the emergence of the Middle Eastern novel that I have set out is further bolstered by much of the recent scholarship more focused on its specific national contexts. Regarding the early Egyptian and Arabic novel, Wen-chin Ouyang sees it as "aligned [. . .] with the nation, partaking in imagining, building[,] and allegorising the nation, and modernising Arabic culture and literature at the same time."[124] This reading is borne out in the work of its pioneers, notably Jurji Zaydan, Mahmoud

Tahir Haqqi, Haykal, and of course Mahfouz. Turning to the Turkish, Azade Seyhan argues that it "foretells modern Turkey's long and arduous experiment with democracy and the trials of safeguarding the mandates of secularism," and Ertürk relatedly suggests that it only became possible "with the ascendance of modern Turkish linguistic phonocentrism" (as discussed above).[125] Key figures in this tradition include Frashëri, Halide Edib Adıvar, Yakup Kadri Karaosmanoğlu, Reşat Nuri Güntekin, Ahmet Hamdi Tanpınar, and Yaşar Kemal. And with the Iranian (as in the writings of Talibi, Maraghei, Mohammad-Ali Jamalzadeh, Sadegh Hedayat, Ebrahim Golestan, and Houshang Golshiri), Katouzian—foregrounding Jamalzadeh and his influence in particular—notes its comparable critical, secular, and linguistic imperatives.[126]

In his important new volume *The Oxford Handbook of Arab Novelistic Traditions* (2017), Waïl Hassan has sought to dispute what he regards as the "restrictive and outmoded theories" that have undergirded the sort of literary historical scholarship on which I have relied in my account of the Middle Eastern novel.[127] In line with the work of Sheehi, El-Ariss, and Rastegar, he targets the discourse of a unidirectional, Eurocentric modernity that interprets the Arabic novel as having been prompted by the introduction of a foreign genre into the Arab world via translations and adaptations.[128] Against the grain of this "flawed historiography" or "teleology" (which he argues is as prevalent in the Arabic critical tradition as it is in the Anglo-American, as in the canonical work of 'Abd al-Muhsin Taha Badr), he thus proposes "a new theory of the Arabic novel."[129] This theory conceives of its object as "a syncretic merger between Arabic and European forms and techniques," rather than in terms of its "rejection of the former" and "importation of the latter."[130] As Hassan elaborates with reference to Franco Moretti, this approach allows for a more expansive understanding of the Arabic novel, one which sees it as having been informed by "a large, interlocking network of multicultural roots" (including the Arabic, Persian, Indian, African, European, and American narrative traditions).[131]

As might be expected, I find myself unconvinced by Hassan's new framework. In the first few pages of his editorial introduction to the volume, Hassan zooms in on "*riwāya*," and argues that the selection of this particular term—with its rich heritage in classical Arabic as noted above—to designate "novel" "belies the adamant assertions of many critics [. . .] that the novel and the short story bear no relationship whatsoever to older Arabic narrative genres."[132] It seems to me that this attempt towards a philological analysis of *"riwāya"* is not entirely complete. It stops short at the question—indeed, the *history*—of the philological pressures to which the term was subjected and the new functions it was forced to serve in the context of Arab and Middle Eastern modernity (which as a critical, theoretical, and historiographical lens for the novel in the Arab world Hassan also dismisses, as I discuss in more detail forthwith). As Kilito has shown, and as more generally suggested by my account of the reinscription of *adab* in this chapter, *"riwāya"*—like *"adab,"* and in relation to its own—very much underwent a definitional volte-face in that context.[133] The fact that in the Arab world it now refers exclusively and universally to the form of long narrative fiction written in prose that in English we call "the novel," and absolutely *not* to its original object (in Hassan's words, "the oral transmission of pre-Islamic poetry"), confirms this.[134]

More substantial perhaps are what I find to be the issues in Hassan's critique of the notion, broadly, of "modernity" as a horizon for the analysis of the Arabic novel, which propels his own alternative approach. Like Dabashi vis-à-vis the Persian literary tradition, Hassan comprehends "modernity" (along with what it produces as its inverse, "tradition") as an entirely Eurocentric construct, one that was "inherited from Orientalism" and that has "plagu[ed] Arab thought for much of the twentieth century."[135] Its naïve regurgitation among Arab and Anglo-American scholars alike over the last century is responsible for the "Eurocentric teleology" that he considers to have been erroneously projected onto "the Arabic novel and [. . .] Arab modernity in general," and that he wishes to correct.[136]

The issue here (as well as in the other scholarly works I have mentioned) is that Hassan seems to have conflated the critique of "modernity" as a European ideology that was in one way or another imposed on the Arab world (via colonial, imperialism, Orientalism, and so forth) with that of "modernity" as a critical lens for the reading of its novelistic tradition. His argument appears to be that because "modernity" in the first sense *did* historically work in this way (he readily acknowledges that Arab intellectuals, literati, and so on were often themselves enthusiastic modernizers), it—due to its Eurocentric and related implications—is not appropriate in the second, and should no longer be deployed. I'm not sure that this stance is entirely coherent. It results in the misrecognition and mystification of the kinds of concrete historical phenomena that Hassan gestures towards, but falls short of fully addressing—most relevant here, the internalization of the modern, European concepts of literature and the novel that actually transpired in the thought of these modernizers, that set the scene for the rise of the Arabic novel, and that contributed to the displacement of the earlier narratives traditions of the Arab world. As with Dabashi, a literary history that fails to attend to this, the actual, verifiable, and documented legacy of Orientalist philology in the Middle East might be accused of reproducing its ideologies—in this case, the idea of "modernity" and its forms as having been produced in a cross-cultural matrix of overlapping, relatively commensurate influences rather than in the violent conquest of mind and body by external forces. If we want to contest "modernity," we must first fully recognize and attune ourselves to its epochal impact on the world.

And so I return to specters and spectrality. To be fair to Hassan and my other colleagues—all of whose work I hugely value and admire despite possible indications to the contrary—I am sympathetic to the gist of his / their argument(s). For instance, one of Hassan's primary concerns in his volume is to foster renewed critical attention to what he calls the "continuities" between the Arabic novel and distinct Arabic (and other) narrative traditions, which he understands to have been forestalled in the earlier, more limited critical models.[137] He suggests that these links and overlaps are most clearly detected in the Arabic novel after 1967 (when the Arabs experienced a monumental defeat at the Six-Day War with Israel, which Palestinians call the "*Naksa*" ["Setback"]). In that year, the story goes, a sense of crisis rapidly pervaded the Arab world, and Arab novelists started to turn away from the modernizing discourses and ideologies that had led it to that juncture, those of their predecessors. They thus looked back to the past, and began "to reconcile [themselves] to the Arabic narrative tradition, the undercurrent that had fed [the Arabic novel] all along but which was kept hidden or repressed by the advocates of modernity."[138]

My spectral approach to the Arabic novel (and the Middle Eastern novel more generally) allows for a radicalization of this fruitful idea. That is to say, when the novel is clearly and precisely recognized as a form of modernity the effect of whose rise and hegemony was to *supersede* other narrative traditions (in the Middle East, those of *adab* and its forms), to produce them as other to itself and thus obsolete, then according to my account it can also be understood to have *always-already*—from its very inception—been what I have called inf(l)ected by the spectral trace of those traditions and the life-world of which they were the expression. In addition to providing what seems to me a more accurate conception of the novel form per se, this account sidesteps the inevitable pitfalls of periodization (the rigid identification of the Arabic novel before 1967 as an imitation of the European, and after 1967 in terms of its return to Arabic narrative forms). Hassan points towards Mahfouz as an example of this trajectory. He argues that *The Cairo Trilogy* (*Thalāthiyya al-Qāhira*, 1956–7; trans. 1990–2) signposts "the end of a period during which the novelist believed that his task was to imitate European models," and that after 1967, "his own practice and that of other leading novelists changed."[139] As I demonstrate in the following chapter, Mahfouz's novels of even what Rasheed El-Enany describes as his pre-1967, "historical/romantic," "realistic/naturalistic," and "modernist/experimental" phases were *always* infused with Arabic narrative and other traditions, and were so *at the level of form*.[140] If anything, then, 1967 marks not so much the break between periods of literary production that Hassan depicts, but rather an *intensification*, a *coming-to-the-surface* of the spectral logic by which the Arabic and Middle Eastern novel had always been constituted (as is also seen to be the case in my readings of Abdelrahman Munif, Orhan Pamuk, Yasmin Crowther, Marjane Satrapi, and others elsewhere in this book).

Finally, this account—which amounts to a spectral theory of the Middle Eastern novel—offers a framework for reading the Arabic novel alongside the other novelistic traditions of the region, one which is grounded in the solid historical understanding of the overlapping trajectories of (literary and cultural) modernity there that I have sought to develop and relay. Through it, the Middle Eastern novel might—if one were to expand this analysis—be seen as part of something much larger, as metonym and metaphor of what I have called a spectral world literature.

The Comparative Middle East

As I touched on in the Introduction, the term "the Middle East" is a contentious one. As a historical and geographical designator, its coinage in the early twentieth century by the American naval strategist Alfred Thayer Mahan to refer to the Persian Gulf in light of British strategic interests there betrays its underpinnings in a Euro-American imperialist perspective on the world. Derived from the similarly skewed Western categories of "the Orient," "the Near East," and "the Far East," it is through and through a construct of Orientalist epistemology and ontology. It has served and in some respects continues to serve as a conceptual grounds for the homogenization—and thus the rendering politically, militarily, and ideologically manageable—of a vast and diverse region stretching across the Levant, the Gulf, North Africa, Iran, Turkey, and beyond.[141]

The field of study to which this term lends its name is in its very constitution likewise marked by the legacy of Orientalism. As Edward Said and Zachary Lockman have most extensively demonstrated, "Middle East studies" originated in the United States in the immediate post-World War II period, as an offshoot of the new discipline of area studies. At this time of heightened geopolitical tension with the Soviet Union, "the Middle East" pretty much as conceived by Mahan rapidly emerged as an area of vital strategic importance to the US. Under the aegis of the US federal government, and also funded by private (read: corporate) investors such as the Ford and other foundations, the Middle East Institute (MEI) was thus founded in Washington DC in 1946 to promote American interests in the region and provide guidance for policymakers. It published the first journal on the modern Middle East in the country, the *Middle East Journal* (which focused on political, economic, and international relations issues pertinent to the MEI's mission). The MEI was succeeded in 1966 by the Middle East Studies Association (MESA), which formalized and expanded the academic study of the region on the basis of the modernization-oriented model of social science research characteristic of area studies. This emphasis was reflected in its journal, the *International*

Journal of Middle East Studies (which like MESA is still in existence, though also under an entirely revamped scholarly mandate).

Concurrent with these developments was the rise of Middle or Near Eastern Studies departments in US universities, which were also often supported by the federal government as well as other parties. Orientalists to the letter such as H. A. R. Gibb at Harvard University and Bernard Lewis at Princeton University (both of whom were trained at what was then one of Europe's most prestigious centers of Orientalist scholarship, the School of Oriental and African Studies in London) spearheaded the fledgling field. Said eloquently summarizes its inner logic during these early years:

> The parallel between European and American imperial designs on the Orient (Near and Far) is obvious. What is perhaps less obvious is (*a*) the extent to which the European tradition of Orientalist scholarship was, if not taken over, then accommodated, normalized, domesticated, and popularized and fed into the postwar efflorescence of Near Eastern studies in the United States; and (*b*) the extent to which the European tradition has given rise in the United States to a coherent attitude among most scholars, institutions, styles of discourse, and orientations, despite the contemporary appearance of refinement, as well as the use of [. . .] highly sophisticated-appearing social-science techniques.[142]

Lockman explains further:

> [F]rom the 1950s onward concern in elite circles about the dearth of expertise necessary to maintain US global power and the resulting flood of new funding got Middle East studies up and running in the United States. The field took institutional form through a new network of university-based programs and centers, funded by foundations and later by the federal government, charged with fostering language training, interdisciplinary research and teaching on the Middle East, and public education through community outreach and teacher-training programs.[143]

Said's and Lockman's critiques of "Middle East" as both term and field are penetrating. However, the responses they offer to its implications are not particularly revelatory. Towards the end of *Orientalism* (where his discussion of these issues had taken place), Said famously asks (himself, apparently, as much as the reader) whether his book had been "an argument only *against* something, and not *for* something positive"—for, that is, "some alternative to Orientalism."[144] Leaning towards the first of these options, he concludes—appropriately, given the relative novelty of his project at the time—by affirming the inherent value of only "describ[ing] a particular system of ideas."[145] Lockman is even more circumspect. Having worked hard to expose its tainted roots, and despite what he himself regards to be its manifold shortcomings, he seems to resign himself to a state of affairs in which "the Middle East as a designation for this region will be with us for the foreseeable future."[146] He then sets out—and again, this is very much a valid endeavor—to defend Middle East studies in its current, post-*Orientalism* incarnation (as can be seen in MESA and elsewhere, it has since the publication of Said's book largely redefined itself according to his insights), against the sustained assault that has been mounted against it by the sorts of Orientalist or neo-Orientalist scholars who were or would have been protagonists in its earlier, more complicit phase (most prominently, Lewis).[147]

I wish to pursue a more radical approach to "the Middle East." Acknowledging the misgivings of Said, Lockman, and others regarding this term (which would seem to offer sufficient grounds for abandoning it altogether, as has occurred with comparably Orientalist categories such as "the Indian subcontinent" ["South Asia"] and "the Far East" ["East Asia"]), I nevertheless think that there *is* a case to be made for retaining "Middle East" as an analytical lens for the comparison of the literatures and cultures of the countries that have typically—if for mistaken or misguided reasons—been situated within its domain. I take my cue here from the work of Rashid Khalidi. In an essay written in 1998, Khalidi notes the growing scholarly apprehension about the term as per Said and Lockman, and suggests against the way it has traditionally been deployed in area studies the adoption of "a global perspective" whereby comparisons might be conducted both "across *the region* and across *regions*."[148] The advantage of a global framework for addressing the Middle East, he concludes, is that it allows us "to preserve a comprehension of [its] specificities, while being open to the broader trends which are becoming increasingly important in the modern—or postmodern—world in which we live."[149]

In this chapter and in this book as a whole, I have sought to develop just such a framework. I have identified global capitalist modernity as the ultimate horizon of the modernities particular to the countries of the Middle East, and have argued that these modernities have unfolded in closely overlapping and similarly structured ways across the region. Evinced in the region-wide process of the reinscription of *adab* as literature whose genealogy I have traced, the trajectory of modernity in the Middle East precipitated in comparable ways the rise and eventual predominance of modern literary and cultural forms in its individual contexts. On the basis of this, the solid, comprehensive, and reflexive critical framework for the comparison of these forms that I have provided, I thus propose a new, comparative Middle Eastern literary and cultural studies.[150]

Notes

1. This similarity and its historical underpinnings (as I elaborate forthwith) pertain to Urdu as well, where "literature" is designated by "*adbiyāt-i Urdū*." As I do not address the Pakistani or South Asian novel in depth in this book, I have avoided discussing its Urdu variant within the Middle Eastern literary matrix of *adab* that I seek to chart here. For an attempt towards a comparative reading of the Arabic, Turkish, Iranian, *and* Pakistani novel, see Omri (ed.), "The Novelization of Islamic Literatures."
2. See p. 12 in the present volume.
3. Anderson, *Imagined Communities*, p. 25. Emphasis in original.
4. Allen, *An Introduction to Arabic Literature*, p. 134.
5. Ibid. pp. 134, 135.
6. For Allen's excellent overview of these genres, see ibid. pp. 139–67. For my reference to the *maqāma* in the Introduction, see pp. 46–7 in the present volume.
7. Kilpatrick, "*Adab*," p. 54.
8. Ibid. p. 56. Emphasis in original.
9. For a useful summary of the main positions scholars in the field of Arabic literary studies have taken towards *adab* in recent years, see Alshaar, "Introduction," pp. 6–11.
10. This point is further underlined by other important recent contributions on this matter. For instance, in his entry on "*Adab* and the Concept of *Belles-Lettres*" in

the *'Abbasid Belles-Lettres* volume (1990) of *The Cambridge History of Arabic Literature*, the noted classicist S. A. Bonebakker starts with a description of *adab* as "the general term used in modern Arabic for literature or *belles-lettres*" before addressing its complications. Bonebakker, "*Adab* and the Concept of *Belles-Lettres*," p. 16. Likewise, in his edited collection *On Fiction and* Adab *in Medieval Arabic Literature* (2005), Philip Kennedy introduces it simply as "medieval Arabic for '*Belles Lettres*.'" Kennedy, "Preface," p. xi.

11. Home, *Elements of Criticism*, p. 7.
12. Ibid. p. 13.
13. Blair, *Lectures on Rhetoric and Belles Lettres*, pp. 3, 1, 13.
14. al-Musawi, *The Medieval Islamic Republic of Letters*, p. 11.
15. Sacks, *Iterations of Loss*, p. 77.
16. Alshaar, "Introduction," p. 10.
17. Kilito, *Thou Shalt Not Speak My Language*, p. 86.
18. al-Musawi, *The Medieval Islamic Republic of Letters*, p. 1.
19. See Alshaar (ed.), *The Qur'an and* Adab.
20. Indeed, after suggesting that *adab* developed "within the general framework of the Islamic sciences," Allen's references to the religion in his account are mostly to do with its "era," "times," "history," period," and so forth. Allen, *An Introduction to Arabic Literature*, pp. 134, 136, 138, *passim*.
21. Makdisi, *The Rise of Humanism in Classical Islam and the Christian West*, p. 93. Cited in al-Musawi, *The Medieval Islamic Republic of Letters*, p. 181. See also Ibn al-Akfānī, *Kitāb Irshād al-Qāṣid ilā Asnā al-Maqāṣid*.
22. Said, *Orientalism*, p. 42.
23. Ibid. p. 87.
24. Hourani, "Introduction," p. 7.
25. Rogan, *The Arabs*, p. 62.
26. Hourani, *Arabic Thought in the Liberal Age, 1798–1939*, p. iv.
27. Allen, *An Introduction to Arabic Literature*, p. 45.
28. Badawi, "Introduction," p. 1.
29. Ibid. p. 2.
30. Sheehi, *Foundations of Modern Arab Identity*, p. 3.
31. El-Ariss, *Trials of Arab Modernity*, p. 12.
32. Rastegar, *Literary Modernity between the Middle East and Europe*, p. 4.
33. In this usage, I am of course alluding to Dipesh Chakrabarty's injunction (which is explicitly cited and taken up by El-Ariss and Rastegar) to decenter Europe as the axis, as it were, around which the field of postcolonial studies

has revolved, captured by his phrase "provincializing Europe." See Chakrabarty, *Provincializing Europe*.
34. al-Musawi, *The Medieval Islamic Republic of Letters*, p. 182.
35. Sacks, *Iterations of Loss*, p. 78.
36. This text has recently been made available in English translation. See al-Tahtawi, *An Imam in Paris*.
37. See ibid. p. 192 (note 1), *passim*.
38. Ibid. p. 135.
39. Badawi, "Introduction," p. 9.
40. Sacks, *Iterations of Loss*, p. 10.
41. As with al-Tahtawi's *riḥla*, this text has recently been made available in English translation (in fact, in a bilingual, English and Arabic edition). See al-Shidyāq, *Leg over Leg, Volumes One–Four*.
42. al-Shidyāq, *Leg over Leg, Volumes One and Two*, p. 6. The epigraph from al-Shidyāq above is from this edition of the text (see ibid. p. 14).
43. Johnson, "Foreword," pp. x, xxx, xxxvi.
44. Ibid. p. xi.
45. Ibid. p. xxx.
46. al-Shidyāq, *Leg over Leg, Volumes One and Two*, pp. 23, 25, 34. Emphasis in original.
47. Sacks, *Iterations of Loss*, p. 78.
48. Ibid. pp. 92, 93. It should be noted that in making this distinction between the anthropocentric and the theocentric in language, Sacks is citing Nadia al-Baghdadi's work on al-Shidyaq. It should also be noted that while the onus of Sacks's argument here as well as in his readings of al-Bustani and Husayn (to which I refer below) is very much on the reconfiguration of *adab* as European philological concepts and categories were internalized by these highly influential figures during the *Nahda*, he also—as indicated by his turn to the Derridean notion of "iteration" or "iterability"—strongly emphasizes the slippages, contradictions, and aporias in their attempts towards linguistic and literary modernization. Although I have not foregrounded this aspect of *Leg over Leg* or the other texts that I address in this chapter, I of course pursue a comparably Derridean line of analysis in my more in-depth readings of the Middle Eastern novel throughout this book.
49. See Hourani, *Arabic Thought in the Liberal Age, 1798–1939*, pp. 99–102 and Sheehi, *Foundations of Modern Arab Identity*, pp. 15–75.
50. See al-Bustānī, *Khuṭba fī Ādāb al-'Arab*. See also Sheehi, *Foundations of Modern Arab Identity*, p. 19.

51. al-Bustani, "The Culture of the Arabs Today," p. 6 / 15. See also al-Bustānī, *Khuṭba fī Ādāb al-'Arab*, p. 32.
52. Sheehi, *Foundations of Modern Arab Identity*, p. 20. See also al-Bustānī, *Khuṭba fī Ādāb al-'Arab*, pp. 2–3.
53. Sacks, *Iterations of Loss*, p. 80.
54. Ibid. p. 78. See also al-Bustānī, *Kitāb Muḥīṭ al-Muḥīṭ*, p. 14.
55. Hourani, *Arabic Thought in the Liberal Age, 1798–1939*, p. 327.
56. Hussein, *The Future of Culture in Egypt*, p. 15.
57. Ibid. p. 17.
58. Ibid. p. 21.
59. Allan, *In the Shadow of World Literature*, p. 2.
60. Ḥusayn, *Fī al-Shi'r al-Jāhilī*, p. 23. Cited and translated in Sacks, *Iterations of Loss*, p. 117–8.
61. Allan, *In the Shadow of World Literature*, p. 2.
62. Zürcher, *Turkey*, p. 19.
63. Ibid. p. 39.
64. Ibid. p. 2.
65. If one were to transliterate the Ottoman Turkish word "أدبيات" faithfully (according to the guidelines for Ottoman Turkish provided by the *International Journal of Middle East Studies*), then its romanization should read "*adabiyāt*" or "*edebiyāt*." However, I have decided to stick to the modern Turkish orthographic rendering of this term as "*edebiyat*" even when referring to it in its Ottoman sense (as is the case in this paragraph), so as to avoid confusion with the Persian term for literature (which is itself typically reproduced as "*adabiyāt*," a usage I have followed in this book).
66. Halman, *A Millennium of Turkish Literature*, p. 25.
67. See ibid. p. 31.
68. Ibid. p. 34.
69. Ertürk, *Grammatology and Literary Modernity in Turkey*, p. 34.
70. For further detail on this estimate, see Hanioğlu, *A Brief History of the Late Ottoman Empire*, p. 38.
71. Indeed, this policy is explicitly stated by Şinasi, the most important and influential of these early journalists. In his editorial for the first issue of the *Tercüman-ı Aḥvāl*, he claims it as his "bounden duty" to "write this newspaper in a way that will be easily understood by the public at large." Cited and translated in Lewis, *The Turkish Language Reform: A Catastrophic Success*, p. 13.

72. See Ertürk, *Grammatology and Literary Modernity in Turkey*, pp. 35–6.
73. This list is provided by Ertürk. See ibid. p. 36.
74. For more on resistance to modernization in the *'ulemā* establishment, see Heyd, "The Ottoman 'Ulemā and Westernization in the Time of Selīm III and Maḥmūd II." For more on media restrictions during the reign of Abdülhamid II, see Ertürk, *Grammatology and Literary Modernity in Turkey*, pp. 36–7.
75. Ziya Pasha, "*Gazel*," p. 164. Cited in Halman, *A Millennium of Turkish Literature*: p. 65.
76. Ersoy, "*The Secret of Progress*": p. 177. Cited in Halman, *A Millennium of Turkish Literature*, pp. 73–4.
77. Ersoy, "*The Secret of Progress*," p. 177.
78. It should be noted that though this is not particularly evident in "The Secret of Progress" apart from in his glancing reference to "salvation," Ersoy—who wrote the lyrics for the İstiklal Marşı (Independence March), Turkey's national anthem—was quite as committed to his religion as he was to the cause of Turkish nationalism (as can be seen in these lyrics, his nationalism was very much of an Islamic character). What I am in effect arguing here, however, is that in what I have shown to be his reliance on as well as advocacy for Western ideas about literature and the nation-state, he in fact unwittingly contributed to the process of the secularization of both that would find its fullest realization in the Republican era.
79. Gökalp, *Türkçülüğün Esasları*, p. 121. Cited and translated in Lewis, *The Turkish Language Reform*, p. 26. For Seyfettin on language, see ibid. pp. 22–3.
80. Gökalp, *Türkçülüğün Esasları*, p. 121. Cited and translated in Lewis, *The Turkish Language Reform*, p. 26.
81. For a historical overview of early Republican Turkey and Atatürk's policies therein, see Zürcher, *Turkey*, pp. 166–205.
82. For more on the logistics and implementation of the script change in 1928, see Lewis, *The Turkish Language Reform*, pp. 27–39.
83. For more on its prehistory, see ibid. pp. 5–26.
84. Redhouse, *A Turkish and English Lexicon*, p. 49.
85. Ibid. p. 49.
86. For more on Ataç and his many, mostly failed neologisms, see Lewis, *The Turkish Language Reform*, pp. 78–89.
87. Ertürk, *Grammatology and Literary Modernity in Turkey*, p, 45.
88. Abrahamian, *A History of Modern Iran*, p. 35.
89. Ibid. p. 38.

90. Ibid. p. 37.
91. See Katouzian, *Iran*, p. 122. For further detail on these forms in classical Persian literature, their distinctions as well as their borrowings from their Arabic sources, see ibid. pp. 123–34.
92. For an overview of these genres, see ibid. pp. 146–50.
93. Dabashi, *The World of Persian Literary Humanism*, p. ix.
94. Ibid. p. ix.
95. Ibid. p. ix.
96. Ibid. p. viii.
97. Ibid. p. 264. Dabashi's use of the term "*vatan*" to refer to an Iranian public space "of its own making" here is somewhat ironic, given that in Persian, this is a loanword of Arabic origin (*waṭan*). Moreover, and as I discuss in more detail below, the rise of "nation" as a new, unifying focus of political identity and ideology in Iran as in the Arab world during the nineteenth century was precipitated by the same modernity (with all of its European-derived influences) that Dabashi elsewhere dismisses as an interpretive lens, due to what he regards as its Eurocentric, colonial implications.
98. Ibid. p. 11. See also Makdisi, *The Rise of Humanism in Classical Islam and the Christian West*, p. xix.
99. Dabashi states that "[a]*dab* [. . .] categorically relates to literature as *belles-lettres*." Dabashi, *The World of Persian Literary Humanism*, p. ix.
100. Ibid. p. 227.
101. Ibid. pp. 228, 227.
102. Ibid. p. 264.
103. See Abrahamian, *A History of Modern Iran*, p. 40.
104. This list is provided by Abrahamian. See ibid. p. 40.
105. Ibid. p. 40.
106. See Zia-Ebrahimi, *The Emergence of Iranian Nationalism*, pp. 44–53.
107. Ākhundzāde, *Maktūbāt*, pp. 291–2. Cited and translated in Zia-Ebrahimi, *The Emergence of Iranian Nationalism*, p. 48.
108. Kermānī, *Se Maktūb*, p. 130. Cited and translated in Zia-Ebrahimi, *The Emergence of Iranian Nationalism*, p. 57.
109. For more on Kermani, see Zia-Ebrahimi, *The Emergence of Iranian Nationalism*, pp. 53–61.
110. For more on Malkam Khan, see ibid. pp. 26–8.
111. For further detail on the Iranian Constitution of 1906, see Abrahamian, *A History of Modern Iran*, pp. 45–9.

112. For the first published edition of this work, see Dehkhodā, *Lughatnāme*. It should be noted that at the time of his death in 1956, Dehkhoda's dictionary remained incomplete. Gaps in especially its later volumes were filled in during the following years by a team led by Mohammad Moin at the University of Tehran, and like the Oxford English Dictionary it continues to be updated at the Dehkhoda Institute there. The latest version was published online by the University of Tehran Press in 2006.
113. See Abrahamian, *A History of Modern Iran*, p. 36.
114. See ibid. p. 36.
115. "Adabiyāt."
116. Bahār, *Dīvān-e al-Sha'ār-e Shādravān Muḥammad Taqī Bahār, "Malik al-Shu'arā,"* p. 26. Cited and translated in Katouzian, *Iran*, p. 204.
117. Allen, *An Introduction to Arabic Literature*, p. 177. See also ibid. pp. 177–8.
118. Allen, *The Arabic Novel*, pp. 6, 11–2.
119. Jayyusi, "Introduction," p. 14. See also Badawi, "Introduction," p. 1.
120. Kilito, "*Qiṣṣa*," p. 264.
121. Ibid. p. 264.
122. See ibid. p. 262, *passim*.
123. Ibid. p. 268.
124. Ouyang, *Politics of Nostalgia in the Arabic Novel*, pp. v–vi.
125. Seyhan, *Tales of Crossed Destinies*, p. 42; Ertürk, *Grammatology and Literary Modernity in Turkey*, p. x.
126. See Katouzian, *Iran*, pp. 193–200.
127. Hassan, "Toward a Theory of the Arabic Novel," p. 35.
128. See ibid. p. 22.
129. Ibid. pp. 23, 39.
130. Hassan, "Introduction," p. 3.
131. Hassan, "Toward a Theory of the Arabic Novel," p. 39. For my critiques of those of Moretti's ideas on which Hassan bases his theory, see pp. 21–2 (the "law of literary evolution"), pp. 24–6 (the "formal compromise"), and pp. 47–8 (the novel as a "planetary form") in the present volume.
132. Hassan, "Introduction," p. 2.
133. Ironically, Hassan has himself translated one of Kilito's books. See Kilito, *Thou Shalt Not Speak My Language*.
134. Hassan, "Introduction," p. 1.
135. Ibid. p. 3.
136. Hassan, "Toward a Theory of the Arabic Novel," p. 39.

137. See Hassan, "Introduction," p. 3. Hassan titles the first section of the volume "Continuities."
138. Hassan, "Toward a Theory of the Arabic Novel," p. 35.
139. Ibid. p. 35.
140. El-Enany, *Naguib Mahfouz*, p. xi. Hassan subscribes to this periodization of Mahfouz's career. See Hassan, "Toward a Theory of the Arabic Novel," p. 35.
141. See pp. 61–2 in the present volume. For further detail on the origins of the term "Middle East," see Lockman, *Contending Visions of the Middle East*, pp. 97–9.
142. Said, *Orientalism*, pp. 295–6. For Said's full discussion of the early history of Middle East studies in the US, see ibid. pp. 284–328.
143. Lockman, *Contending Visions of the Middle East*, pp. 127–8. For Lockman's discussion of the same, see ibid. pp. 100–48. For his more recent account of the field, one that is more focused on the role of corporate foundations in its emergence, see Lockman, *Field Notes*.
144. Said, *Orientalism*, p. 325. Emphasis in original.
145. Ibid. p. 325.
146. Lockman, *Contending Visions of the Middle East*, p. 99.
147. See ibid. pp. 216–17.
148. Khalidi, "The 'Middle East' as a Framework of Analysis," p. 79. Emphasis added.
149. Ibid. p. 79.
150. Elsewhere, I have with my colleague Anna Ball sought to develop a similar approach to Middle Eastern modernity, but in that case in relation to the field of postcolonial studies and its critical, theoretical, and disciplinary paradigms (hence the idea of "post/colonial modernity" that we forward). See Ball and Mattar, "Dialectics of Post/Colonial Modernity in the Middle East," pp. 8–10.

II

THE MIDDLE EASTERN NOVEL AND THE SPECTRAL LIFE-WORLD OF MODERNITY

3

The Revolution of Form: Naguib Mahfouz from the Suez Crisis to the Arab Spring

> Naguib Mahfouz [. . .] has formed an Arabian narrative art that applies to all mankind.
> "The Nobel Prize in Literature 1988," NobelPrize.org

> The Naguib Mahfouz Medal for Literature is awarded for the best contemporary novel published in Arabic (but not yet in English) [. . .] The award-winning book is subsequently translated and published in an English-language edition by the AUC Press in Cairo, New York, and London.
> "The Naguib Mahfouz Medal for Literature," The American University in Cairo Press

"Naguib Mahfouz"—the very name is saturated with signification. It refers to a local, Cairene writer, one whose literary career and imagination were as firmly anchored in the city of his birth as Charles Dickens's were in London and Honoré de Balzac's were in Paris. *The Cairo Trilogy* (*Thalāthiyya al-Qāhira*, 1956-7; trans. 1990-2), his most celebrated work, still stands as the most profound novelistic monument to this setting. It refers to a national, Egyptian writer, one who has become synonymous with the high literary culture of the country. Indeed, Egypt's most prestigious literary prize—the Naguib Mahfouz Medal for Literature—is named after him. It refers to a regional, Arabic writer, one who in the words of Roger Allen "is widely recognised as the founding father of the Arabic novel."[1] As Allen elsewhere writes, "his career marks the establishment of the genre as a centrally important player in the cultural life of the Arab world."[2] And it refers to a global writer, one whose award of the Nobel Prize in Literature in 1988—the first and thus far only for an Arab writer—had the effect of definitively consecrating the Arabic novel and modern Arabic literature more generally in what Pascale Casanova describes as the space of world literature.[3]

At once signifying local, national, regional, and global literature, what are we to make of the apparent literary overdetermination of "Naguib Mahfouz"? What frame of reference or analytical methodology could possibly be adequate to a name that has been conscripted with equal enthusiasm into a number of distinct, even divergent literary and critical registers? What becomes of literary history when the notion of a stable, unitary context for the situating of a writer and his work has been rendered incongruous, or has at least been reduced to a condition of radical uncertainty (the Cairene novel, or the Egyptian novel, or the Arabic novel, or the global novel, or all of the above)? What becomes of comparison with other writers, texts, and traditions? To begin parsing these difficult questions, it seems to me essential to first and foremost acknowledge and fully attune ourselves to the specific material processes by which "Naguib Mahfouz" has been canonized at each of the levels of literary recognition hitherto noted, to what James English calls "the economy of prestige" as operative across the strata of local to global literary value.[4] Itself the critical act necessitated by our increasingly complex, multiscalar literary and scholarly landscape, deconstructing these processes as they pertain to "Naguib Mahfouz" thus becomes an allegory for reading literature in the world, for reading world literature.

I start by considering how "Naguib Mahfouz" has been framed at the global and, subsequently, national levels of literary recognition and esteem (I explore his regional framing in the next section, below). Naturally, his award of the Nobel in Literature in 1988 is to be regarded as the decisive, definitive symbol of his acclaim on a worldwide scale. The date is significant, for—corresponding to the emergent postcolonial and multicultural ethos of literary and scholarly culture more broadly in this period—the 1980s saw a concerted effort within the Swedish Academy to expand what had hitherto been its overwhelming (though not exclusive) Euro-American emphasis or bias to writers from other parts of the world.[5] And so, in addition to Mahfouz, writers from Latin America, Africa, the

Caribbean, and Asia—not to mention those from within Europe and North America but of previously underrepresented ethnic backgrounds or who work in previously underrepresented languages—came to count for an increasing proportion of Nobel recipients from this time (approximately 38.89 percent of the total from Gabriel García Márquez's award in 1982 to Kazuo Ishiguro's in 2017, in contrast to approximately 8.64 percent beforehand).[6] When it came to Arabic literature, two things helped establish its visibility and familiarity, a sense of its worthiness, among the members of the Academy in the run-up to Mahfouz's award. As Salma Jayyusi reports, the Lund Conference of 1984 brought Swedish and Arab critics and poets together at the University of Lund with the specific intent of attracting the attention of the Academy, and her own Project of Translation from Arabic (PROTA) had been bringing out and promoting a steady stream of English-language translations of Arabic literary texts since it was founded in 1980.[7] Along with the appearance in French of (the first two volumes of) his famous *Trilogy* in 1987 and the tireless scholarly and advocatory activities of Roger Allen as well as Jayyusi herself, all of this was to culminate in the crowning achievement of Mahfouz's career—indeed, of modern Arabic literature—in 1988.[8]

Or so the story goes. As an organization that has designed itself as and that has come to play the role of arbiter of literary value on a worldwide scale, the Swedish Academy—which might be regarded as the institutional face of "World Literature" (its symbolic capital, as it were)—by definition selects and judges the nominees and awardees of its Nobel Prize in Literature according to the broadest possible criteria of "the literary," those of universality. Amounting to the modern, European concept of "literature" discussed in the Introduction to this book, these criteria are pushed to their conceptual limits when it comes to the literatures of the non-Western world, of the peripheries of the world-system. During its expansionist period from the early 1980s, the Academy therefore needed to develop and deploy a number of strategies of what Timothy Brennan calls "containment" in order to accommodate non-Western writers within its prevailing conceptual paradigms.[9] One such strategy is strikingly in evidence in the Academy's citation for Mahfouz upon the announcement of his award. As per the epigraph above, the citation reads as follows:

> Nobel Prize winner in literature, 1988: Naguib Mahfouz, who, through works rich in nuance—now clear-sightedly realistic, now evocatively ambiguous—has formed an Arabian narrative art that applies to all mankind.[10]

In her analysis of this passage, Sarah Lawall has argued that "the Nobel Prize suggests a particular aim and manner of reading, with its committee seeking works of universal scope and essential humanity, no matter how rooted the writer may be in a specific cultural tradition" (qualities that she elsewhere describes as indicative of "the same Eurocentricity" that was supposed to have been overcome with the expansion of the award to non-Western writers).[11] Beyond Lawall, however, it seems to me that the "has" in the Academy's "has formed an Arabian narrative art that applies to all mankind" betrays much more about the Nobel Prize than its principles of selection and judgment. It actively, performatively *frames*, even *constructs* the writer as one who is of and for "all mankind," as one whose works are thus rendered as having always-already been of "universal scope" and "essential humanity" (a point that is further accentuated elsewhere in the citation, with "[h]is work speaks to us all").[12] It's not so much a matter of searching out existing non-Western works that best express or embody these qualities (Lawall's "manner of reading"), but rather one of framing, containing, and, ultimately, domesticating such works according to the standards of literary universality (more a "manner of writing" or "inscribing," so to speak).

Mahfouz's case quite clearly illustrates and bolsters Casanova's demystifying critique of the Nobel Prize as "an ongoing attempt to develop explicit standards of [literary] universality," and English's that it has become "a means of articulating [. . .] a particular category of literature that might be recognized as properly 'global.'"[13] It also demonstrates just how impactful this highest honor of international literary culture can be on a national literary culture, especially in the historically neglected or marginalized national contexts of the non-Western world—the "Nobel Effect," as English puts it.[14] As Hosam Aboul-Ela argues in his excellent article "The Writer Becomes Text: Naguib Mahfouz and State Nationalism in Egypt" (2004), Mahfouz's Nobel win was seen by the Egyptian government under the reign of Hosni Mubarak (President of Egypt from 1981 to 2011) as an opportunity to consolidate the country's reputation and standing in the world. During this period of intensified neoliberalization and integration into the global economy (a process whose groundwork was laid by Mubarak's predecessor Anwar Sadat, President from 1970 to 1981), the state thus made every effort to claim its now globally recognized son as a symbol of Egypt and to project his image as what Aboul-Ela calls its own "benign face."[15] Upon his receipt of the Nobel, it arranged for Mahfouz an elaborate national ceremony presided over by Mubarak himself; it countersigned that international honor by awarding him one of its own important national honors, the Egyptian Medal of Achievement; and in the following years it helped ensure his ubiquitous presence in the Egyptian public sphere—in the media, on billboards, and notably at the Cairo International Book Fair, where Mubarak would host an annual meeting with the country's most prominent writers and intellectuals.[16] In short, it went out of its way to *frame* Mahfouz as "*Adīb Miṣr*"— "Egypt's Writer," the paragon of the country's national literary culture.[17] This construct was institutionalized and persists to this day in the form of the American University in Cairo Press's Naguib Mahfouz Medal for Literature (established in 1996), Egypt's most prestigious literary award. It is perhaps more than mere coincidence that, as per the epigraph above, an AUC Press English-language translation and international publication of each year's prize-winning book is part and parcel of an award given in Mahfouz's name.[18]

While driven by their own, distinct requirements and momentums, the specific material processes by which "Naguib Mahfouz" was framed at, respectively, the global and the national levels of literary recognition and esteem seem to have both had the same effect. They have *inscribed* Mahfouz and his work into their narratives of (literary) modernity, whether at the scale of the global or at that of the national. They have thus obscured: (1) what I regard as the profoundly *local* dimensions of his "narrative art" in favor of an assumed or projected modern literary universality, and (2) his lifelong *critique* of the same modern Egyptian state that adopted his image as its own for its authoritarianism, corruption, and political violence. That is to say, Mahfouz's global / national framing has had the effect of undermining or negating his actual significance for world literature.

In this chapter, I aim to restore this significance. I argue that starting with the *Trilogy*, Mahfouz's novels engage Egyptian political history from the perspective of the margins of Egyptian modernity. They do so, I continue, in form—in Mahfouz, novelistic form is from the outset always-already inf(l)ected in spectral fashion by the others of the national modernity into which he was to be politically conscripted, and thereby by those of the global modernity into which he was to be literarily conscripted. Culminating in the novels of the late, post-1967 phase of Mahfouz's career (which Rasheed El-Enany describes in terms of a return to "indigenous" or "traditional" form), this comprises what I call a "revolution of form."[19] I assess Mahfouz's revolution of form with reference to his late novels *Arabian Nights and Days* (*Layālī Alf Layla*, 1979; trans. 1995) and *Morning and Evening Talk* (*Ḥadīth al-Ṣabāḥ wa al-Masāʾ*, 1987; trans. 2007). In contrast to commentators who identify the cultural outpouring of Tahrir Square and / or what has been termed the "1990's generation" of Egyptian writers as indicative of the Egyptian Revolution of 2011, and overlooked in the scholarship on the Arab Spring (as in Samir Amin, Gilbert Achcar, Hamid Dabashi, and others), I suggest that Mahfouz's engagement with form in these novels enacts a more deeply rooted, organic, and historically conscious *form of revolution* against the abuses of (Egyptian) modernity. My approach to Mahfouz thus provides not only a valuable corrective to his global / national framing to date, but also a powerful new lens for the appreciation of his work in the context of—and, indeed, *as*—world literature.

In the following, I develop this argument in four interrelated sections. First, I offer a literary historical introduction to the four main phases of Mahfouz's novel-writing career, those—as presented by El-Enany—of historical romance, realism, modernism, and, finally, the return to indigenous or traditional form. Following the scholarship of Roger Allen, M. M. Badawi, Salma Jayyusi, Waïl Hassan, El-Enany, and others, I emphasize that Mahfouz's writerly trajectory should indeed be regarded as illustrative of the history of the Arabic novel in general. However, I contest the idea of a radical formal break between each of these phases, between—more broadly—Mahfouz's pre- and post-1967 novels. With reference to the work of Sabry Hafez and Hilary Kilpatrick, I reread the *Trilogy* as an instance of what I call a "spectral Egyptian realism," and demonstrate that despite its shifts, form in Mahfouz is always-already inf(l)ected by the others of Egyptian modernity. Next, I argue that this tendency was to come to its culmination in the novels of Mahfouz's late, indigenous / traditional phase (as most insightfully covered by Wen-chin Ouyang). After introducing Mahfouz's work from this period, I then home in on *Arabian Nights and Days* as an exemplary case study of his wider project at the time. This novel, I show, inverts what David Damrosch and Paulo Horta chart as the Orientalist logic by which the *One Thousand and One Nights* (*Alf Layla wa Layla*, c. ninth–fourteenth centuries) was constructed as a work of world literature, and draws on the frame narrative, folklorish elements, and magical devices of this ur-text of the Arabic popular tradition in order to reinvent the novel as a world literary form. Next, I look into *Morning and Evening Talk*, Mahfouz's last major literary engagement with Egyptian political history. Following in the footsteps of its predecessor, this novel, I show, adopts and adapts the classical Arabic genre of the *ṭabaqāt* in order to reinterpret the 200-year trajectory of modernity in the country (which comes to its crux in the Suez Crisis and its aftermath) from the perspective of its political, social, cultural, and economic margins. Finally, I consider the implications of what the foregoing analyses will have fleshed out as Mahfouz's revolution of form for literary, cultural, and scholarly discourses of the Egyptian Revolution of 2011 and the Arab Spring.

In sum, my intention in this chapter is to make the case that Mahfouz's significance for world literature lies in the formal inf(l)ection of his novels by the others of the modernity by which he, his very name, has been and continues to be worlded—his revolution of form.

Naguib Mahfouz: A Condensed History of the Arabic Novel

In addition to that of Roger Allen, much of the other canonical scholarship on the Arabic novel and on modern Arabic literature more generally—as in the work of M. M. Badawi, Salma Jayyusi, Hilary Kilpatrick, and others—has foregrounded Mahfouz as the "founding father" of the genre, as a figure whose novel-writing career indeed almost single-handedly "established" it in the Arab world.[20] In these and other accounts, Mahfouz's writerly trajectory has served not only as its richest exemplification, but also as an illustration of the history of the Arabic novel per se. Even Waïl Hassan, who otherwise dismisses what he regards as the Eurocentric frameworks on which such histories have typically relied (as discussed in Chapter 2), readily acknowledges Mahfouz's pivotal role in and influence on the development of the genre.[21]

The reason why Mahfouz has been accorded such a privileged position in narratives of the Arabic novel lies not just in the undisputed quality, sophistication, and depth of his literary output, its having uniquely captured in literary form the innermost tensions and contradictions of his native Egypt and its inhabitants—of the Arab world—during the upheavals of the twentieth century. Also, and moreover, it lies in his having, if not by design then certainly in effect, traversed and institutionalized in and for Arabic the aesthetic forms definitive of the modern novel—historical romance, realism, modernism, and the return to indigenous or traditional form—during his career (which spanned seventy years, and generated thirty-four novels as well as innumerable short stories and other literary works). His oeuvre in its various phases, then, has furnished literary historiography with a microcosm or at least a schema—one of continuing value, in my view—of the Arabic novel from its origins through to its maturation and eventual consecration. In the present context, a brief overview of this oeuvre is thus worthwhile as a means to introduce the Arabic novel as well as my approach to it.

Upon embarking on his career as a novelist in the 1930s, Mahfouz had originally envisioned a cycle of thirty historical novels that would chart the history of Egypt from Pharaonic times to the present in the mode of Walter Scott, one of his major European precursors and inspirations. While this ambition was short-lived, it did result in three important and influential novels—*Mockery of the Fates* (*'Abath al-Aqdār*, 1939), *Rhodopis* (*Rādūbīs*, 1943), and *The Struggle of Thebes* (*Kifāḥ Ṭība*, 1944)—that are considered as among the earliest instances of historical romance in Arabic.[22] He soon set his sights on the more immediately pressing political and social concerns of his day, and by the mid-1940s he turned to realism in the style of Dickens and Balzac as the most appropriate novelistic vehicle for the expression of and engagement with the present. Focalized around Cairo, and initiated with the novels *Khan al-Khalili* (*Khān al-Khalīlī*, 1945), *The New Cairo* (*Al-Qāhira al-Jadīda*, 1946), and *Midaq Alley* (*Zuqāq al-Midaq*, 1947), this phase was of course to come to its climax with the appearance of *The Cairo Trilogy* in the mid-1950s.[23] Rigorous psychological investigations and even the use of the interior monologue technique are certainly far from absent in Mahfouz's writing up until this point. However, the extent of Mahfouz's experimentation with modernist aesthetics—featuring a turn to the figure of the alienated individual (often an intellectual) as well as the deployment of additional techniques including stream of consciousness, multiple first-person narration, symbolism, and allegory (à la Fyodor Dostoyevsky, Marcel Proust, James Joyce, Franz Kafka, William Faulkner, and so on)—is not really in evidence until his novels of the following decade. Signposted by the controversial *Children of the Alley* (*Awlād Ḥāritnā*, 1959), and further pursued in *The Thief and the Dogs* (*Al-Liṣ wa al-Kilāb*, 1961), *Chatter on the Nile* (*Tharthara fawq al-Nīl*, 1966), and *Miramar* (*Mīrāmār*, 1967), modernism becomes the driving formal principle of his work from this period.[24] After 1967, as I discuss in more detail in the following sections, Mahfouz increasingly drew on the narrative and other traditions of the Arabic-Islamic past as a means to liberate his writing from what he came to see as his earlier "bondage" to "the European form of the novel."[25]

The scholarship on Mahfouz has tended to assume what El-Enany calls a strict "demarcation line" between each of the phases of his career.[26] As Hassan points out, the notion of a categorical disjunct between Mahfouz's historical romance, realist, modernist, and indigenous / traditional periods is at least partly reinforced by the author himself.[27] In the full flow of his discussion of novelistic form as alluded to above, Mahfouz explains just such a shift in his writing practice (pertaining to his work after 1967):

> When I started writing novels, I used to think that the European form of the novel was sacred. But as you grow older, your outlook changes; you want to free yourself from all that has been imposed on you, albeit in a natural

and spontaneous way, and not just to break rules and be different. You find yourself searching for a [certain] tune deep down, inside yourself. [. . .] As if you were saying to yourself: "Those forms which they [the Europeans] wrote in—were they not artistic moulds that they created? Why can't I create a mould of my own?" [. . .] But I must make clear one important point: imitating the old [i.e. Arabic traditional forms] is no different from imitating the new [i.e. European form]; both are acts of bondage.[28]

In my view, the overreliance on authorial observations and reflections such as this in the scholarship has resulted in the neglect or obfuscation of certain crucial continuities in Mahfouz's novels across his career. I thus follow El-Enany in seeking to restore these continuities to our critical purview. However, whereas for El-Enany they are to be located in the consistent use of *specific* techniques and devices across the periods (including symbolism, internal monologue, heightened prose, the agonized individual subject, and episodic narration), for me they are better and more comprehensively understood in terms of a more general lifelong project on Mahfouz's part.[29] Simply put, the reworking of European form according to local, Egyptian and Arab content, which I interpret in terms of spectral inf(l)ection. As Mahfouz's oeuvre has been read as a benchmark of the history of the Arabic novel per se, this account has the further advantage of expanding on El-Enany's, and offering new purchase on that broader topic. To demonstrate this thesis, I now turn to the *Trilogy* as a case study of Mahfouz's spectral Egyptian realism.

The Cairo Trilogy

Across its three volumes—*Palace Walk* (*Bayn al-Qaṣrayn*, 1956; trans. 1990), *Palace of Desire* (*Qaṣr al-Shawq*, 1957; trans. 1991), and *Sugar Street* (*Al-Sukkariyya*, 1957; trans. 1992), *The Cairo Trilogy* traces the gradually unfolding dialectic of modernity in early to mid-twentieth-century Egypt as focalized through the Cairene patriarch al-Sayyid Ahmad Abd al-Jawad and his family in its various generations. From the outset, the Abd al-Jawad household is presented as the focal point of the narrative—the family home on the first volume's eponymous street in Cairo's al-Jamaliyya district is where much of the action takes place, and al-Sayyid Ahmad, his wife Amina, and their children and grandchildren are the novel's undisputed protagonists across its 1,300 or so pages. Intimately and incisively portrayed, the drama of family life—from its everyday routines, rituals, and relationships to its mounting intergenerational conflicts—suggests much of Cairene society's traditionally conservative attitude towards issues of authority, politics, class, religion, education, gender, marriage, and desire, among others, and the often violent changes to which this society becomes subject with the passing of time. Further, as the members of the family variously make their way into the world, their adventures and encounters open up the city in all of its multilayered, labyrinthine complexity for the reader. The novel thus provides a panorama of a society in transition, and archives for future generations the richness and plenitude of an urban culture otherwise known only to its participants. All this takes place against the backdrop of the major events in Egyptian political history during the period in question. In the wake of World War I, with the Ottoman Empire in full collapse and confronted with the continuing British occupation of their country, the Abd al-Jawad family becomes increasingly impacted by and drawn into the revolutionary nationalism then being pursued by Saad Zaghloul and his Wafd Party. It is not too great a stretch to claim, then, that the *Trilogy* is a novel about a family's—and, by extension, a society's—incorporation into the modern Egyptian nation-state of which it is a reflection and even, as many of the novel's commentators have had it, an allegory.

In light of its subject matter and realist aesthetic, the *Trilogy* appears to cast itself as a family saga in the mode of Thomas Mann and John Galsworthy (whose respective novels *Buddenbrooks* [1901] and *The Forsyte Saga* [1922] were certainly an inspiration for Mahfouz). As Sabry Hafez stresses, however, it is to be distinguished from "many European novels of its ilk" insofar as "it does not take the adventure or education of the individual as its core, but gives the central role to the family and the collective."[30] That is, it reshapes the family saga form so as to encompass something of the lived experience of family in early twentieth-century Egyptian and Arab society, as a unit through which the individual identity is defined rather than a grouping—however restrictive—of more or less independent identities. This presentation has the effect of accentuating the pathos of the Abd al-Jawad family's decline as it is subjected to the growing pressures and demands of modernity through the novel. A brief consideration of the *Trilogy*'s three volumes and, crucially, the structural relationship between them helps underline this point.

Broadly, each of the *Trilogy*'s volumes corresponds to one of the generations of the Abd al-Jawad family. *Palace Walk* is primarily concerned with the generation of al-Sayyid Ahmad and Amina, who represent Cairo's traditionally conservative social and cultural values. Opening in 1917, in the midst of World War I, and closing with the Egyptian Revolution of 1919, it gives flesh to this ethos and the contradictions that undergird it through these two towering figures of modern Arabic literature. Al-Sayyid Ahmad is portrayed as a patriarch, a stern, religiously-minded authoritarian and disciplinarian at home, and as a libertine and even hedonist devoted to the forbidden sensual pleasures of wine, women, and song abroad. Bearing attributes that in their antithetical nature are befitting only of an ancient god, it is no surprise that his family should "revere[. . .]" and "worship" the head of their household as "a man of exemplary piety and resolve," "a higher will," and that there—where his command is tantamount to "God's will"—life in all of its aspects is arranged under "a limitless authority almost like that of religion."[31] Like her children, Amina is entirely subservient to her husband and his autocratic will. Held together by religion, superstition, and custom, her life—confined to the house, or at least to the spaces allotted within it to women and their activities—revolves around him and the young extensions of his self. In its famous opening pages, the novel sees her waking at midnight "to await her husband's return from his evening's entertainment" and then "serv[ing] him until he went to sleep"—one of the "rules of married life."[32] All this, of course, after "invoking the name of God."[33]

Given the symbolic function of these characters as established from the beginning of the novel, the symbolism of al-Sayyid Ahmad's and Amina's deaths many years and several hundred pages later is all the more charged. Al-Sayyid Ahmad dies and the world he represents is destroyed at the hands of what his son Kamal explains are "the most advanced inventions of modern science"—namely, the earth-shattering bombs that descend on al-Jamaliyya during a World War II air-raid, which induce a fatal heart attack.[34] Amina dies, or is at least left paralyzed and comatose due to natural causes, in the very last chapter of the *Trilogy* as a whole—a balanced close to a novel that began with this character awakening from sleep.³⁵ Evoking the world of al-Sayyid Ahmad and Amina, a dead or dying world of entrenched Egyptian and Arab sociocultural traditions, it is fitting that *Palace Walk* adopts an expansive, extravagant, and richly descriptive aesthetic that—as Kilpatrick suggests—more properly belongs to "a medieval tradition of literature" than it does to the modern tradition it nevertheless helps inaugurate in the Arab world.³⁶

Palace of Desire, which is set in the mid-1920s, turns to the generation of al-Sayyid Ahmad and Amina's children, and its central drama is that of their youngest son Kamal's psychological and existential crisis as he becomes increasingly disenchanted with the values of the past. Exposed to Egypt's newly modernized education system and the Western ideas, philosophies, and schools of thought that it had started to curricularize during his adolescence, Kamal is best characterized as a man on the threshold of modernity. Still bound by filial attachments and duties, yet inwardly searching elsewhere for meaning, he seems—as his friend Riyad Qaldas puts in in *Sugar Street*—"an Easterner teetering uncertainly between East and West," one who "goes round and round until he's dizzy."³⁷ His internal struggle is most vividly exemplified by a discussion he has with his father about a newspaper article he had published on Darwinist evolutionary biology—while outwardly professing his continued religious faith, he simultaneously reflects:

> "I've experienced enough torment and deception[. . .]" [. . .] "From now on I won't be taken in by fantasies. Light's light. Our father Adam! He wasn't my father. Let my father be an ape, if that's what truth wants["].³⁸

Further, it sets the scene for and precipitates the pivotal emotional crisis of his life, his unrequited love for Aïda. Unlike his sisters Khadija and Aisha (who had married and moved into their husbands' homes), Aïda—French-educated and from a higher social class—seems to Kamal with her cultured, refined European outlook and, importantly, her secularism thoroughly liberated from the constraints of the past. She is the embodiment of all that he desires but cannot attain. Kamal is thus a transitional figure, and his literal as well as figurative impotence—or at least immobility—makes way for the vigorous and passionate courses of action pursued by his nephews in *Sugar Street*. The third and final volume of the *Trilogy*, which moves forward in time to the 1930s and 1940s, shifts to the third generation of the Abd al-Jawad family. While the women of the family have now attained a degree of autonomy via access to further schooling and the professions, Khadija's sons Abd al-Muni'm and Ahmad respectively commit themselves to the ideologies of the Muslim Brotherhood and of Communism. They stand—somewhat prophetically on Mahfouz's part—for the extremes of Egypt's political spectrum as the nation-state continues to forge its identity and its independence out of the dialectical tensions of modernity. It is appropriate, therefore, that as it has developed, the style of the *Trilogy* should have shifted from the descriptive excess and ornamentation of the first volume to the rigorous psychological and existential interrogations of the second and third, to something more akin to modernism.

Hafez notes that in recent television adaptations of the *Trilogy*, Egyptian and Arab audiences have tended to view al-Sayyid Ahmad—the archetypal patriarch of modern Arab literature—with "melancholy nostalgia and admiration."[39] This response is comprehensible, for in a country that has been and that continues to be shaken to its core by the unresolved antagonisms of modernity, he represents a world that no matter how limited and limiting, is at least anchored in something substantial—history itself and the millennium's worth of meaning and continuity it imparts to the present. In this section, I have argued that Mahfouz doesn't only gesture towards this world in the *Trilogy* via the figure of al-Sayyid Ahmad and others of his generation, he also inscribes it in the very formal texture of his novel, especially its first volume. This is what I mean by what I have referred to as Mahfouz's "spectral Egyptian realism." The realist aesthetic of the *Trilogy* is from its outset mediated by the representational requirements of a world that novelistic realism cannot—by virtue of its imbrication with modern notions of the literary, with modernity—encompass, and that it has contributed to ousting. Like al-Sayyid Ahmad himself in contemporary Egyptian and Arab culture, Mahfouz's inf(l)ection of novelistic form starting in the *Trilogy* has cast a long shadow indeed. As I proceed to show in the following sections, this tendency—brought to its crux in the novels of the post-1967 phase of his career—is the undercurrent of all Mahfouz's writing.

1,001 Nights—and Days—of World Literature

Mahfouz's experimentation with classical to medieval Arabic-Islamic narrative and other forms might be traced back to *Children of the Alley*, which—first published in 1959—features elements of the historiographical, biographical, and allegorical genres associated with *adab* (as covered in Chapter 2). However, he only fully dedicated himself to this tradition and what amounts to its novelistic revival after 1967. In addition to *Arabian Nights and Days* and *Morning and Evening Talk*, the novels that contributed most significantly to this project in this period include *The Harafish* (*Malḥamat al-Ḥarāfīsh*, 1977) and *The Journey of Ibn Fattouma* (*Riḥlat Ibn Faṭṭūma*, 1983). As indicated by their original titles, the first of these taps into the mode of Arabic folk or popular epic known as the *sīra al-shaʿbiyya* ("*malḥamat*" translates as "epic"), while the second draws on that of the *riḥla* as made famous by Ibn Battuta, its eponymous protagonist's model and inspiration. In her discussion of Mahfouz's engagement with pre-modern forms in these texts, Wen-chin Ouyang has argued that his primary concern was to "fashion [. . .] from Arab cultural and literary heritage national allegories that interrogate the presence of the past in the contemporary structure of political authority"—that it was with the "past-present collusion" and its continuing role in the shaping of the modern Egyptian and Arab nation-state.[40] With this important insight in mind, and aiming to build upon it, I now turn to *Arabian Nights and Days* as a case study of Mahfouz's project during this phase of his career.

Arabian Nights and Days picks up where its source- or intertext, the *One Thousand and One Nights*, leaves off. Set in the same unnamed, medieval / mythical Arab city as its source, it opens with Shahriyar—having become enchanted by the "white magic" of her tales—deciding to spare Shahrzad's life and fathering a child with her.[41] This outcome, however, is anything but happy. Having worked through what had hitherto been the all-embracing trauma of his morbid jealousy, the Sultan, now stripped of his identity-defining delusion, is left exposed to the possibility of the absurd, and he suffers another, deeper break—"[e]xistence itself," he reflects, "is the most inscrutable thing in existence."⁴² Meanwhile, his wife is racked by guilt at the blood that had been shed before her, and deeply concerned about the fate of a kingdom that had been erected on such murderous foundations. And so begins the one thousand and second night, so to speak. In the seventeen episodic chapters that follow, we encounter many characters from the original *Nights* (in addition to Shahriyar and Shahrzad, these include Dandan, Dunyazad, Aladdin, Sindbad, Qut al-Quloub, and others) as well as several more of Mahfouz's own invention in new stories of power, authority, corruption, violence, revolution, faith, transcendence, madness, love, desire, fate, and—indeed—storytelling itself. Throughout, the world of the novel is—as with its source—imbued with magic, with the fantastic. Djinn (or "genies," as the English translation has it), the supernatural beings of Arabic-Islamic mythology, intrude upon the lives of the flesh and blood characters, and—accentuating their inherent proclivities—prompt them to good or evil deeds at their whim. As Ouyang puts it, "[t]he fantastic [thus] comes to cohabit with realism in the world of the novel."⁴³ Given its subject matter and formal devices, it is not difficult to see why Ouyang should so vigorously assert that *Arabian Nights and Days* be read as a "contemporary political allegory," and more specifically as one that "depicts and problematises the process through which the 'past' developed into the 'present' as well as both the 'past' and the 'present.'"⁴⁴

Although complex and multilayered, Mahfouz's engagement with the contemporary in this novel is undeniable. In it, the stories he recounts of political revolutionaries corrupted by power and redeemed by the will of the people; of religious leaders and their followers surrendering their agency, their selves, and their lives entirely to the Almighty; and of the often brutal restrictions imposed upon women in an inequitable social structure bear the unmistakable mark of Egyptian and Arab political history in the twentieth century (or at least of Mahfouz's perspective on this). For instance, the parallel narratives of Fadil Sanaan and Ma'rouf the Cobbler, as El-Enany notes, bring quite sharply to mind the distinct approaches to matters of appropriate revolutionary strategy, political leadership, and legitimacy pursued by, respectively, Gamal Abdel Nasser and Saad Zaghloul.⁴⁵ While Fadil is seduced by the malicious djinni Sakhrabout's offer of unlimited power and ends up an autocrat who betrays the revolution that he had instigated, Ma'rouf refuses the devil's pact put forward by another djinni at the risk of his life and is consequently appointed his district's Governor due to the intervention of the urban poor he had faithfully served earlier on.[46] That of Sheikh Abdullah al-Balkhi suggests that no matter how pure a religious leader's intentions may be in his devotion to the Path of salvation for himself and his disciples, a life detached from their own and from society's present, material needs is nothing but mere self-indulgence. As Fadil puts it before his fall, "[a]s for the people of obliteration of self, they are dedicated to themselves, and as for the people of holy war, they dedicate themselves to God's servants."[47] And that of Dunyazad implies that the pursuit of love and desire beyond the bounds of a patriarchal and religious society's strictures—i.e. marriage arranged and sanctioned by a male authority figure—is akin to "ruin" for women, and that it would contribute to its already rather "low opinion of [their] sex" and perhaps even result in a version of honor killing.[48]

Drawing on this sort of textual evidence, Ouyang concludes of *Arabian Nights and Days* that it portrays "the attempt at establishing a sovereign, free, secular, [and] democratic state as the perceived outdated, traditional, divinely ordained, [and] hierarchical dynastic systems fall apart."[49] More generally, she elsewhere writes, it comprises a thoroughgoing critique of "the presence of the past in [. . .] present practices of power," of "the burden of the past" in Egyptian and Arab modernity.[50] In developing this argument, Ouyang is certainly attentive to what she calls the "dialectic [. . .] of form[. . .]" operative in the novel and the "ideological statements" that it is making.[51] However, it seems to me that its form is making a rather different statement than the one she articulates. This is because the rise of the European-modelled novel form in Egypt and the Arab world is imbricated with that of the European-modelled state there, and is therefore complicit with the characteristic political and other ruptures of peripheral modernity that Mahfouz indeed allegorizes in the text. By seeking, in his own words, to "free [him]self" from his earlier "bondage" to that form—in this case, by reconfiguring it on the basis of the frame narrative, folklorish elements, and magical devices of the ur-text of the Arabic popular tradition, the *One Thousand and One Nights*—Mahfouz is in fact involved in a project of *reintegrating* aspects of the "past" into the modernity and the modern forms from which that past had been forcibly, violently, and traumatically dissevered. If there is a critical statement being made here, it is one that is directed against not "the presence," but rather—and precisely—the *absence* of "the past in [the] present."

In the novel, this dialectic is most explicitly played out through the character Gamasa al-Bulti, a figure of spectrality who hovers at the interstices of the other characters' lives and narratives and who often plays a decisive role in bringing them to their climax. When we first encounter him, Gamasa is Chief of Police under the corrupt Governor Khalil al-Hamadhani. Entirely subservient to his benefactor and the hierarchical order that he represents, Gamasa—"the sword of state"—willingly carries out the political arrests, persecutions, and violence that the Governor demands.[52] When challenged, he explains that "[m]y duty is to carry out orders."[53] Into this state of affairs the virtuous though playful djinni Singam soon intervenes. Showing Gamasa the error of his ways and reminding him of Allah, Singam inspires him to assassinate the Governor for the good of the kingdom, upon which Shahriyar sentences the unrepentant murderer to death. Now—and this is where things become interesting—at the moment of his execution, Singam replaces Gamasa's body with a likeness or double, and gives the original the shape of another, known as Abdullah the Porter. Gamasa—now "both Abdullah the living and Gamasa the dead," a "strange experience never before known to man"—is thus rendered in the world of the novel a specter à la lettre.[54] Inhabiting the worlds of both the dead and the living, of, indeed, the past and the present, yet belonging fully to neither, this specter comes to haunt that of the latter, striving beyond comprehension or reason to inf(l)ect it with the mad, prophetic wisdom—the trace—of the former. Further, it is with the words of this specter that the novel ends. At this point, we return to Shahriyar—the figurehead of its political order and allegorical embodiment of the state—and find him at the denouement of his existential quest. Gamasa / Abdullah or Gamasa-as-Abdullah offers him the following guidance:

> I give you the words of a man of experience, who said: "It is an indication of truth's jealousy that it has not made for anyone a path to it, and that it has not deprived anyone of the hope of attaining it, and it has left people

running in the deserts of perplexity and drowning in the seas of doubt; and he who thinks that he has attained it, it dissociates itself from, and he who thinks that he has dissociated itself from it has lost his way. Thus there is no attaining it and no avoiding it—it is inescapable."[55]

And so *Arabian Nights and Days* concludes with what is quite literally a statement of what had been its driving formal and thematic principle all along, the fundamentally ambiguous—non-essential, non-binary, liminal—"truth" of one of its ghosts uttered to the novel's representative of the contemporary world.

The critical implications of *Arabian Nights and Days*—or at least of my approach to it—are consolidated and expanded when taking into account the history of its source text's constitution as a work of world literature. As has been widely discussed, the classic we today refer to as the *One Thousand and One Nights*, *The Thousand and One Nights*, or *The Arabian Nights* is through and through an invention, even a fantasy of the European Orientalist imagination of the eighteenth and nineteenth centuries. It was through the translatorial mediation—involving arrangement, selection, abridgement, bowdlerization, plagiarism, flights of fancy, and sometimes sheer fabrication—of Orientalists such as Antoine Galland (1704–17), Edward William Lane (1840, 1859), and Richard Francis Burton (1885) that the "original" Arabic text (a composite work based on Indian and Persian sources and gradually assembled over the course of the ninth to the fourteenth centuries) was rendered amenable to a European reading public and thus disseminated in the world.[56] Referring to the Galland translation (the first in Europe), David Damrosch suggests that this "most orientalist of texts," a "translational mirage" set the precedent for later European and world versions by "exclud[ing] [the] localized stories" of the original and "emphasiz[ing] [the] 'universal'" ones.[57] In his recent book-length study *Marvellous Thieves: Secret Authors of the Arabian Nights* (2017), Paulo Horta pushes this line of inquiry further. Looking closely into the backgrounds of all three of the Galland, Lane, and Burton translations (as well as others of the period), he details quite extensively how they—and consequently the *Nights*'s entry into world literature—were shaped by the "asymmetrical" contexts of imperial conflict at the time and thus by "Orientalism as a framework for understanding the Middle East."⁵⁸ On the basis of the evidence provided by these and other scholars, it seems fair to say that the *Nights*—a popular collection which had little or nothing to do with classical to medieval Arabic-Islamic *adab*, and which was generally considered base or lowbrow in Arabic-Islamic literary culture—emerged on the back of these translations as the Oriental Renaissance's paradigm of the Arabic literary heritage.

Taking into account its paratextual apparatus (not to mention its modified title), the English translation of *Arabian Nights and Days* appears to reproduce and perpetuate the Orientalist sensibility that undergirded the construction of its source. Its ornate and colorful cover design as well as blurbs that highlight the novel's "magical" features—its "fantasy," its "entertaining arabesque of intrigue [. . .]," and so forth—tap into what the publishers evidently take as its global audience's long-established image of the *One Thousand and One Nights* and the part of the world from which it came.⁵⁹ As my foregoing discussion has demonstrated, however, Mahfouz's project in the novel proper is exactly the opposite of that implied by this marketing strategy. In it, Mahfouz *inverts* the Orientalist logic by which the *One Thousand and One Nights* was constructed and the Arabic literary heritage thus forged in and for the world. He does so by *reinventing* the novel form—the ultimate form of world literature—according to the narrative and other devices of his source. That is to say, he deconstructs the worlding of the Arabic literary tradition by reconstructing world literature and its forms from the perspective of that tradition.

Certainly, Mahfouz is not the first or only Arab or Middle Eastern—let alone world—writer to have substantially engaged with the *One Thousand and One Nights* in his novels. As Richard van Leeuwen has argued, the *Nights* has been so pivotal to the novelistic imaginations and practices of so many Arab writers since the beginning of the twentieth century that it can be said to have "deeply influenced the development of the novel as a literary genre" per se in the Arab world.⁶⁰ In roughly chronological order, these writers range from Taha Husayn, Tawfiq al-Hakim, and Fathy Ghanem from the beginning to middle of this period to Tayeb Salih, Emile Habibi, Mostafa Nissabouri, Hani al-Rahib, Rachid Boudjedra, Elias Khoury, Leïla Sebbar, Assia Djebar, Ahmed Fagih, Waciny Laredj, and Hanan al-Shaykh closer to the end.⁶¹ The special significance of Mahfouz's contribution, though, lies in the depth, rigour, and expansiveness of his project of introducing not just that of the *Nights*, but also other Arabic literary forms to the novel, and of course the truly global reach he attained for his work via his Nobel Prize fame. In its broadest dimensions, this is what the late phase of his career represents.

A Counter-History of Crisis: Mahfouz at the Margins of Egyptian Modernity, Nasser to Mubarak

The project that Mahfouz so compellingly articulates in and as *Arabian Nights and Days* is expanded upon even further in *Morning and Evening Talk*, his last major literary engagement with Egyptian political history. In this novel, Mahfouz deploys the mode of formal experimentation that defines its predecessor to chart the impact of the pivotal political and other events in the country from the time of the French Campaign in Egypt and Syria (1798–1801) to the 1980s on the lives and indeed deaths of the members of a sprawling, multi-branched Cairene family over five generations. Its subject matter is nothing less than Egyptian modernity itself, and the sweeping political, social, cultural, and economic transformations that it has wrought over the *longue durée*—as El-Enany puts it, the novel is "an account of the evolution of Egypt from medievalism to modernity."⁶² As such, it might also be considered an end-of-career sequel of sorts or countersignature to *The Cairo Trilogy*. However, whereas the *Trilogy* zooms in on some twenty years of this history in 1,300 pages, *Morning and Evening Talk* covers 200 years in 200. It manages what for a shorter novel is its extraordinarily broad scope and concerns by turning to the classical to medieval Arabic genre of biographical dictionary known as the *ṭabaqāt*, and—in characteristic Mahfouzian fashion—adopting and adapting its form in light of the demands of contemporary novelistic representation.

Like much of Mahfouz's novelistic output, *Morning and Evening Talk* is focalized entirely around Cairo and its inhabitants. Assuming the form of its classical-medieval precedent, it is comprised of sixty-seven alphabetically ordered character sketches of Cairene men and women from successive generations of the interrelated al-Misri, al-Murakibi, and al-Qalyubi families (each of which is traced back to its early nineteenth-century patriarch, respectively Yazid, Ata, and Muʻawiya). Each entry reads like a condensed biographical notice, or even obituary—eschewing any hint of artistic embellishment, the basic facts of its subject's birth, lineage, marriage(s), children, and death are related in a plain and simple manner. Each also foregrounds how its subject's life intersected with the defining national events of his or her day. From the Napoleonic invasion, these include the reign of Muhammad ʻAli (1805–48), the ʻUrabi Revolt (1879–82), the Egyptian Revolution (1919), the Free Officers Revolution (1952), the Nasser Presidency / "pan-Arabist" period (1956–70), the Suez Crisis (1956), the Six-Day War (1967), the Sadat Presidency / "*Infitah*" period (1970–81), and so on through the 1980s. Through these entries, then, a vision of the arc of modern Egyptian history as "the awakening of a nation into the universal consciousness of modernity" (in Timothy Mitchell's words) cumulatively emerges.[63] More resoundingly, though, they—by virtue of their biographical anchoring—serve to evoke a sense of the intimate and often tragic, the profoundly human consequences of this history for the individuals, families, and thus society caught within its inexorable logic.

Traditionally, the *ṭabaqāt* genre is oriented around the lives of notable historical figures (i.e. men) such as the Prophet and his companions; other political, military, and religious leaders; theologians; scholars; poets; and so forth—those who made a significant contribution to the shaping of Arabic-Islamic history.[64] In *Morning and Evening Talk*, Mahfouz—even while drawing on it as part of his late-phase project—deviates from his model in a number of ways so as to make through his engagement with form a similar sort of "statement" as discussed above. Firstly, he turns away from the world-makers and luminaries who in the *ṭabaqāt* were presented as synonymous with the Arabic-Islamic heritage per se, and towards ordinary, everyday Egyptians from a variety of walks of life, backgrounds, and statuses. This shift suggests Mahfouz's prioritization of social history or history from below in the making and very character of a nation, his understanding of the nation as constituted in the mutual imbrication of the public and private spheres (as also seen elsewhere in his work). Secondly, he includes as many women as he does men among his character sketches, which—again as seen elsewhere—signals his disavowal of the *ṭabaqāt*'s predisposition towards the "great men" of history. And thirdly, he attends to what Ouyang summarizes as "stories" (such as those of love, marriage, etc.), "forms of knowledge" (such as magic, home economy, management, etc.), and "types of activities" (such as political participation, etc.) rarely touched on in the *ṭabaqāt* in his entries, which provides for a wider-ranging panorama of the nation as it is lived and experienced by its populace.[65]

Given these modifications, Mahfouz's statement in the novel might be taken as one that seeks solely to critique or dismantle the past represented by the *ṭabaqāt* (and Ouyang does appear to take this stance on it).[66] As in *Arabian Nights and Days*, though, form in *Morning and Evening Talk* tells an altogether more interesting and complicated story. The very use of the *ṭabaqāt*—with its disjointed biographical entries and alphabetical rather than linear or chronological ordering—in the context of a form that typically relies on character focalization and narrative progression says something about Mahfouz's perspective on the modernity that comprises the subject matter of his novel. As also reflected in the thematic content of these entries, it expresses what Christina Phillips calls the "fragmentation" of "traditional Arab society [. . .] and the family nucleus in particular" under the conditions imposed by history.[67] While certainly adapted for the present, Mahfouz's turn to the *ṭabaqāt* is, then, an attempt to restore a principle or even ideal of order, cohesion, and unity from the past to a nation-state and a form that had so violently spiralled away from their roots.

All of this is vividly illustrated by Mahfouz's references to the Suez Crisis and delineation of its traumatic human repercussions in the novel. Mahfouz's take on this event in particular is important for my argument, insofar as Suez signalled a crucial turning point in the history of the modern Egyptian state and laid the foundations for certain authoritarian, corrupt tendencies therein that would persist until the Egyptian Revolution of 2011, and beyond. It consolidated or even made Gamal Abdel Nasser's reputation as a figurehead of Egyptian nationalism and—not unrelatedly—pan-Arabism, while at the same time masking forms of political violence directed against those on the political, social, cultural, and economic margins of the Egyptian modernity that it helped establish. Mahfouz addresses Suez from the perspective of these margins, and thus draws attention to those excluded from and the sociocultural fabric rent asunder by modernity. Furthermore, Suez was a key moment in the construction of new global as well as national images of Egypt for the twentieth century, as projected by the various global and national participants in the conflict. As per my wider argument in this chapter, Mahfouz evades all these framings (in this case as pertaining to a historical episode rather than his own writing), and instead strives relentlessly to bring a local, subnational viewpoint into the mix. In so doing, he develops a rigorous critique of a state whose mutation into a repressive military dictatorship under Hosni Mubarak he was witnessing at the time of writing, while sidestepping the readily available temptation of political universalism.

The history of the Suez Crisis—referred to in the Arab world as the Tripartite Aggression—is a familiar one. On 26 July 1956, Nasser announced the nationalization of the British-controlled Suez Canal Company, which had operated the geostrategically vital waterway on behalf of the United Kingdom and its interests—imperial administration, international trade, Middle Eastern oil, and so forth—since 1882. "Today," he told his Alexandrian audience at the climax of his two-and-a-half-hour speech, "the Suez Canal is an Egyptian company."[68] In response, the United Kingdom, France, and Israel (as decided in a secret meeting held in Sèvres from 22 to 24 October) invaded Egypt on 29 October in the same year, with the aim of not just regaining control over the canal, but also ousting Nasser himself and what Robert Rhodes James—a British historian and former Conservative Member of Parliament—characterized as the "grievous," "intolerable" threat that he posed to the "West[. . .]."[69] The offensive was short-lived. Facing mounting diplomatic pressure from the United Nations as well as financial pressure from the United States (whose President Dwight D. Eisenhower had opposed the invasion from the outset), the joint British-French-Israeli forces were obliged to withdraw on 6 November. The upshot of this fiasco was the elevation of Nasser's status to that of national, regional, and Third-Worldist hero (despite his having been soundly militarily defeated); the evisceration of the United Kingdom's remnant imperial ambitions and standing in the world; the resignation of British Prime Minister Anthony Eden; and, indirectly, the Six-Day War of 1967.[70]

Suez also resulted in the reconfiguration of Egypt's political image on a global as well as a national scale. The major historiographies of Suez from the last several decades serve as a useful index of contemporaneous political discourses of the country and its place in the world. On the one hand, histories—such as those of Keith Kyle (2002) and William Roger Louis (2006)—that have sought to explore the Crisis from the perspective of the British Empire and its decline have tended to emphasize the restrictive anglocentric notion of Egypt as a thorn in the side of empire.[71] While of course critical of the imperial assumptions that lay behind the action itself, these studies somewhat downplay the rich history and internal dynamics of Egyptian popular resistance to the British presence since the nineteenth century, clearly essential for understanding the Egyptian take on Suez. They thus unconsciously echo the sorts of British newspaper, newsreel, and radio accounts of the country in wide circulation at the time.[72] On the other hand, those—such as by William Roger Louis and Roger Owen (1989), Laura James (2006), and Simon Smith (2008)—that have pursued what Smith calls "the Egyptian perspective" in revisionist fashion have overwhelmingly focused on Nasser and his international relations.[73] Taking Nasser and his policy decisions as representative of Egypt and indeed the Arab world per se (according to James, he "changed the political face of the region and defined a common Arab identity"), these texts obscure the plurality of Egyptian responses to the Crisis.[74] They thus suggest something of what Nasser's self-cultivated nationalist populism was intended to achieve in the country during the event.

As reflected in the recent historiography, what is lost to the official image of Egypt crystallized in both the United Kingdom and Egypt itself during Suez is a sense of the deep political, social, cultural, and economic fissures that lay behind the transcendent symbolism of the moment. Nasser and his policies were always highly contentious in Egypt, not least because the Free Officers Revolution that brought him into power and that laid the ideological groundwork for the nationalization policy in 1956 disenfranchised numerous segments of the Egyptian public sphere. Among the groups that were deprived—sometimes via measures including mass political imprisonment and execution—of their role in the political life of the country were the British-installed King Farouk's circle of comprador royals, ministers, and civil servants; the landowning aristocracy; the previously ascendant nationalist Wafd Party; the more radical Egyptian Communist Party; and the Muslim Brotherhood.[75] The idea of Egypt as unified behind, even defined by Nasser's leadership reduces such complexity and deep-seated division to a widespread visual from the British media during the Crisis—that of Nasser's handsome, charismatic face hovering over and giving direction to the captivated Egyptian demos-as-crowd, whether intended to indicate a 1930s-styled fascist demagogue (as in Britain) or an icon of national liberation (as in Egypt).[76] In other words, it strips the Egyptian political subject of any sort of localized individual or group identity, of difference, and of subjectivity itself.

In *Morning and Evening Talk*, Mahfouz redirects our attention towards precisely these occlusions inherent to the global and national framings of Suez, towards the margins of the modern Egyptian state articulated on the back of the Crisis. Always referring to it as either the "war of 1956" or the "Tripartite Aggression," he narrates Suez—the moment of Egypt's and the Third World's heroic stand against imperial domination—in entirely negative terms.[77] In his insistence on its human costs (including numerous deaths, the breaking up of families, and thus wider societal fragmentation), he provides a local perspective that counters official history's homogenized image of an Egypt united behind Nasser.

For instance, Mahfouz relates the deaths of Surur al-Aswani and Muhammad Ibrahim during Suez within biographical entries reserved for their parents, respectively Gamila Surur Aziz and Shazli Muhammad Ibrahim. This strategy not only reminds us of the sorts of stories of individual tragedy forgotten to the history of Suez, but also subtly gestures towards its impact on an Egyptian family structure traditionally dependent on lineage and continuity. In one of the rare moments of poetic licence in the novel, he concludes Gamila's entry by evoking the pathos of her stunted lineage after the loss of her son and other family members: "Gamila was delivered from her loneliness and sadness in 1970, dying of stomach cancer at the age of sixty-three. At the time of her death she resembled a branch without shoots on a family tree."[78] The representation of familial collapse gives way to that of wider sociopolitical antagonism in the entries for Hazim Surur Aziz and Halim Abd al-Azim Dawud. Given their status as members of Egypt's landowning upper-middle class elite whose interests are directly threatened by Nasser's nationalization policy, it is understandable that Hazim's wife Samiha and Halim should both be "delighted" at the news of the Western invasion of their country.[79] Samiha goes so far as to "lock [...] herself in her room and [...] dance" when hearing of this turn of events, and later disturb even her husband by the zealousness with which she celebrates Nasser's death.[80] Here, Suez lends Mahfouz the opportunity to explore the depth and hold of class affiliations in Egyptian society, affiliations which he reveals have come to supersede any sense of national or communal belonging in times of crisis. Finally, questions of class identification and status give way to those of the individual in the entry for Nadir Arif al-Minyawi near the close of the book. With "the Tripartite Aggression and the impounding of British companies," Nadir loses his job at the English metal company for which he had been working.[81] Rather than experiencing this event as a defeat (as do Samiha, Halim, and others), however, Suez ends up making the cynical, self-serving, and opportunistic young man's career. He marries into the family of one of the Revolutionaries (thus distancing himself from his own family, class, and background), upon which he is able to considerably advance his professional position and amass a great fortune. Likewise, he is blown along the winds of Sadat's *Infitah* in the 1970s, by which time his lack of any firm conviction in anyone or anything beyond himself had precipitated his divorce and left him utterly—yet unrepentantly—isolated.

In the context of a novel that has sought to chart some 200 years of Egyptian history, it is somewhat telling that Mahfouz should choose to present one of his chronologically (as well as structurally) latter characters in this way. For according to Mahfouz, this history is one which has seen the eclipse of a society once held together by the values—however imperfect—of a shared and continuous Arabic-Islamic heritage, and the rise of a debased modern substitute grounded in nothing but the ideology of mercenary self-interest as embodied and in fact explicitly stated by Nadir. "[F]ortune," he explains at the end of his entry, "is for the strong, morality for the weak."[82] It is also fitting that Mahfouz should pinpoint Suez as the crisis, classically speaking, of Nadir's personal narrative. While in the broad sweep of the novel it is only one of many turning points in Egypt's long trajectory towards modernity, the role that Suez plays in Nadir's life suggests that Mahfouz viewed it as something like a point of origin for the state and the society within which he was living during the composition of *Morning and Evening Talk*. He was, after all, a lifelong proponent of the Wafd Party and its version of nationalism as gradual reform, and vigorously objected to the sort of abrupt Nasserite revolution that had led Egypt—with a few twists and turns along the way—to the Mubarak era.[83]

In 1996, well into Mubarak's reign, Mohamed Fadel's film *Nasser 56* was released in Egyptian cinemas to massive popular acclaim. A meticulously researched historical drama centered on Nasser (played by one of Egypt's leading actors Ahmed Zaki) and the events that transpired in the country forty years previously, its opening scene—which features the lowering of the Union Jack against the backdrop of an undesignated Egyptian cityscape—sets the tone of the film as one of nationalistic, patriotic pride.[84] As Joel Gordon discusses, it proceeds to portray Nasser from the nationalization announcement to the withdrawal of the foreign troops as a "populist hero," a "man of the people."[85] While initially ambiguous about it, officials in the Mubarak state media apparatus that had the final say over all such projects quickly latched onto the film and associated themselves—their regime—with its success. As they saw it, Gordon reports, "to script Nasser at Suez" on the forty-year anniversary of the Crisis, "to depict such a powerful moment of national unity" served for them as a means "to counter social trends that [were] nationally divisive, even 'un-Egyptian.'"[86] In other words, the film functioned for the Mubarak regime as a means to identify itself with Nasser's revolution and its ideological sway in the country, while veiling or occluding the political, social, cultural, and economic antagonisms that—traced back to the earlier period and projected forward to 2011—had only been exacerbated in the intervening years.[87]

As I have argued in this section, it is precisely this logic of nationalism-as-ideological-mystification that Mahfouz deconstructs in *Morning and Evening Talk*. Written at the height of the Mubarak era, reflecting on the deep history of the modernity that had led Egypt to that juncture, and hinging on Suez as an axis around which the modern Egyptian state turned, the novel is nothing if not a critique of Mahfouz's contemporary moment. That Mahfouz should have deployed the form of the *ṭabaqāt* in the novel suggests what I have called his "revolution of form" as the most appropriate vehicle for the expression of that critique. In this sense, *Morning and Evening Talk* might well be regarded as the true novel of the Egyptian Revolution of 2011.

Prophecies of Revolution: Mahfouz and the "1990's Generation" in Tahrir Square

In the wide-ranging body of work on the literary and cultural dimensions of the Egyptian Revolution of 2011 that has been generated since that fateful year, scholarly attention has fallen chiefly on Tahrir Square and what has been called the "1990's generation" of Egyptian writers. The focal point and symbolic epicenter of the Revolution, Tahrir—located in the heart of downtown Cairo—saw the assemblage of hundreds of thousands of young men and women from multiple sectors of Egyptian society in a demonstration against the Mubarak regime that ran from 25 January up until the President's resignation on 11 February (an event that was intermittently repeated through 2013, when the Egyptian army ousted the newly elected President Mohamed Morsi in a coup d'état and imposed military control over that highly charged public space).[88] Scholars such as Jeannie Sowers and Chris Toensing, Ayman El-Desouky, Walid El Hamamsy and Mounira Soliman, Mona Baker, Samia Mehrez, and Linda Herrera, among many others, have homed in on Tahrir as a site not just of revolution proper, but also of the emergence of a new, revolutionary popular culture, a people's language and even poetics of revolution comprised of the slogans, chants, songs, satire, banners, street art, graffiti, and digital media of those assembled there.[89] In their accounts, it was via this cultural as well as corporal reclamation of Tahrir as a genuinely public space that the Egyptian demos became for the "first time" involved in "creating a political community" (in Sowers's words), and that a "radical transformation" was initiated in "the relationship between people, their bodies, and space" (in Mehrez's words).[90] This sense of Tahrir as the locus of an enactment and embodiment of collective democratic agency is immaculately captured in Jehane Noujaim's first-hand documentary of the Revolution, *The Square* (*Al-Mīdān*, 2013). While in hindsight it was perhaps always doomed to political failure, the enduring image of the Revolution that comes across in this film is one of Tahrir's aspirational and steadfast youth, liberal intelligentsia, women, and Muslim Brothers coming together in open dialogue about their country's future.[91]

I would like to dwell for a moment on El-Desouky's account of the Revolution in particular. This is because in distinction to the majority of other scholarly approaches (which tend to contextualize the events of 2011 in relation only to Mubarak's thirty-year reign), El-Desouky takes a longer historical view that resonates well with my argument in this chapter. In his book *The Intellectual and the People in Egyptian Literature and Culture:* Amāra *and the 2011 Revolution* (2014), he argues that in its broadest implications, Tahrir signifies the spontaneous expression of the Egyptian demos as the repressed other not just of the Mubarak-era sociopolitical order, but also of the project of Egyptian modernity per se stretching back to the *Nahda*. In a categorization that persisted in Egyptian intellectual culture until 2011, *Nahdawi* intellectuals such as Rifa'a al-Tahtawi, Khayr al-Din al-Tunisi, Butrus al-Bustani, Salim al-Bustani, 'Abdallah al-Nadim, 'Abd al-Rahman al-Kawakibi, and others widely dismissed "the people" as "peasant[s]" (*fallāḥīn*), as remnants of the pre-modern past that Egypt was striving to transcend.[92] In 2011, all this changed. In their "*amāra*"—an Egyptian term that El-Desouky uses to refer to the "verbal and visual expressions, as well as body gestures and movements" of those gathered in Tahrir, their unmediated *parole*—"the people" interrupted this narrative and forged for the first time their own culture from below.[93] I will return to El-Desouky shortly. For now, it is important to underline a general idea from his work that I very much share—the Revolution as a response to the unresolved antagonisms of modernity.

Turning now to the "1990's generation," this term has been used to refer to the Egyptian writers of the period who abandoned the realist and modernist forms predominant among their older colleagues, and deployed instead what Sabry Hafez calls an "aesthetics of fragmentation" that reflects their experience of Egypt's increasingly fragmented social reality at the time.⁹⁴ In his canonical treatment of their work, "The New Egyptian Novel: Urban Transformation and Narrative Form" (2010), Hafez suggests that these writers were responding to a "triple crisis"—"socio-economic, cultural[,] and political"—that they and their generation faced.⁹⁵ He lists Samir Gharib 'Ali, Mahmud Hamid, Wa'il Rajab, Ahmad Gharib, Muntasir al-Qaffash, Atif Sulayman, May al-Tilmisani, Yasser Shaaban, Mustafa Zikri, Nura Amin, Mahmud Hamid, and Somaya Ramadan as among the most prominent of them (to whom one might add Ahmed Alaidy, Hamdi Abu Golayyel, Muhammad al-Fakharani, and others), and summarizes their output vis-à-vis this "unpropitious context" as follows:

> Their work constitutes a radical departure from established norms and offers a series of sharp insights into Arab culture and society. Formally, the texts are marked by an intense self-questioning, and by a narrative and linguistic fragmentation that serves to reflect an irrational, duplicitous reality, in which everything has been debased. The works are short, rarely more than 150 pages, and tend to focus on isolated individuals, in place of the generation-spanning sagas that characterized the realist Egyptian novel. Their narratives are imbued with a sense of crisis, though the world they depict is often treated with derision. The protagonists are trapped in the present, powerless to effect any change.⁹⁶

Writing on the cusp of the Revolution, it is not difficult to see both Hafez's essay itself as well as its subject matter as prophetic of the revolutionary desires and energies that would come to a head in 2011. Indeed, Noha Radwan has made this very same point in her post-Revolution contribution to this analysis, "One Hundred Years of Egyptian Realism" (2016). Taking a similar approach to the 1990's generation writers, she identifies them as a "[r]evolutionary [c]lass" which in its opposition to Egypt's prevailing conditions of political, social, and economic oppression participated in and was continuous with that constituted at Tahrir.⁹⁷

Mahfouz has not generally been considered in or alongside the matrix of revolutionary literature and culture that I have outlined, let alone as belonging to it. As my foregoing discussion has suggested, and as I proceed to detail, this is a major oversight. The one exception I have come across is El-Desouky. In line with what has been said about the 1990's generation, he suggests in an earlier essay on "Heterologies of revolutionary action: On historical consciousness and the sacred in Mahfouz's *Children of the Alley*" (2011) that Mahfouz—specifically, the Mahfouz of that controversial 1959 novel—"anticipates" in many ways the revolutionary outpouring of 2011.[98] *Children of the Alley*, he argues, "represents one of the very first attempts in aesthetically approaching popular consciousness in high literary form."[99] As he elaborates in *The Intellectual and the People in Egyptian Literature and Culture*, it transcribes in literary form the "*amāra*" or "popular imaginary of the people" that was to find its literal, collective expression in Tahrir.[100]

I wish to make a more radical claim about Mahfouz. In especially his late novels, he—beyond prophecy, anticipation, or aesthetic treatment—literally *enacts* an alternative to the Egyptian modernity that had precipitated the Revolution. He does so in his revolution of form. In this sense, he doesn't just represent or foreshadow something of the *amāra* of 2011; rather, he produces his very own *amāra*, one distinctively rooted in and taking its contours from the Arabic-Islamic literary and cultural heritage as crystallized in its forms. In this way, he is directly and actively engaged in what I call a *form of revolution* against the conditions—which are as much *cultural* as they political and so forth—that had driven Egyptian modernity; that had brought about the successive Nasser, Sadat, and Mubarak military dictatorships; and that had prompted the Revolution of 2011. Along these lines, and beyond the specifically Egyptian context that I have addressed in this section, Mahfouz's late work also imparts a crucial lesson for our continuing critical interrogation of the Arab Spring per se in light of what must now be acknowledged as its (near-) universal failure.

The most thoughtful scholarly responses to the Arab Spring have sought to contextualize the revolutionary fervour that unfolded across Tunisia, Libya, Egypt, Yemen, Syria, Bahrain, and further afield from 2010 in relation to longer regional and global histories than, naturally, were ever apparent in the mainstream news media or elsewhere. Samir Amin, for instance, interprets it vis-à-vis "the long evolution of the place of the Arab world in the world systems of yesterday and today," and homes in on the *Nahda* as a "miscarriage" and "abortion" that had precipitated the particularly skewed, contradictory version of Arab modernity responsible for the mass regional disaffection behind the events of 2010 and after.[101] Gilbert Achcar looks beyond "[d]espotism" and other such familiar explanations, and towards the "deep roots" and "underlying socioeconomic factors" of the uprising—in his account, neoliberalism and its endemic crises in the Arab world are the most significant among these.[102] And Hamid Dabashi sees it in terms of a "retrieval of a cosmopolitan worldliness" that in the Arab world (as in Iran, as discussed in Chapter 2) was repressed under the dual pressure of the postcolonial nation-state or "domestic tyranny" on the one hand, and neoimperialism or "globalized imperialism" on the other.[103]

Clearly, this work cumulatively represents an invaluable historicizing corrective to popular and other discourses of the Arab Spring, one by which not just a regional, but also a genuinely *global* revolutionary praxis responsive to the deep history of modernity might be envisioned moving forwards. Across it, however, there seems to be a missing element, namely that of *culture*. As per my discussion of the incorporation process in the Introduction to this book, the sort of world-systems approach that Amin for one relies on in his reading of the Arab Spring has typically overlooked the centrality of cultural transformation in the incorporation and modernization of the periphery.[104] Persisting not just in his, but also in the other accounts of the Arab Spring that I have mentioned, this oversight has led to the neglect of one of the key dimensions of the modernity that had propelled the Arab world to that juncture.[105]

It is precisely this that Mahfouz's late novels not only direct our attention towards, but also critically engage. Taking their aesthetic and political bearings from the history of Arab modernity *as culture*, they—especially *Morning and Evening Talk*—enact in the revolution of form that they attempt a rooted, organic, and historically conscious form of revolution against this history. Overlooked in the literary, cultural, and scholarly discourses of the Arab Spring, this form of revolution comprises Mahfouz's most profound, posthumous lesson for us as we continue to imagine revolutionary alternatives to the conflicts, crises, and contradictions of the day.

Notes

1. Allen, *An Introduction to Arabic Literature*, p. 186.
2. Allen, *The Arabic Novel*, p. 111.
3. See Casanova, *The World Republic of Letters*, pp. 82–125, *passim*.
4. See English, *The Economy of Prestige*.
5. During the eighty-one years of its existence up until 1982 (when the Columbian Gabriel García Márquez won it), only seven writers not from Europe or North America had been awarded the Literature Nobel—Rabindranath Tagore (India, 1913); Gabriela Mistral (Chile, 1945); Shmuel Yosef Agnon (Israel, 1966); Miguel Ángel Asturias (Guatemala, 1967); Yasunari Kawabata (Japan, 1968); Pablo Neruda (Chile, 1971); and Patrick White (Australia, 1973). Of these, only two wrote primarily in a non-European language (Agnon and Kawabata).
6. These writers include García Márquez (Columbia, 1982); Wole Soyinka (Nigeria, 1986); Octavio Paz (Mexico, 1990); Nadine Gordimer (South Africa, 1991); Derek Walcott (Saint Lucia, 1992); Toni Morrison (United States, 1993); Kenzaburō Ōe (Japan, 1994); Gao Xingjian (China, 2000); V. S. Naipaul (United Kingdom, 2001); J. M. Coetzee (South Africa, 2003); Orhan Pamuk (Turkey, 2006); Mario Vargas Llosa (Peru, 2010); Mo Yan (China, 2012); and Kazuo Ishiguro (United Kingdom, 2017).
7. See Jayyusi, "The Arab Laureate and the Road to Nobel," pp. 17–18.
8. See ibid. pp. 18–19.
9. Brennan, *At Home in the World*, p. 200. Brennan draws on the examples of Walcott's award in 1992 and Morrison's in 1993 to underline this point. See ibid. pp. 200–1.
10. "The Nobel Prize in Literature 1988."
11. Lawall, "Naguib Mahfouz and the Nobel Prize: Reciprocal Expectations," p. 23.
12. "The Nobel Prize in Literature 1988."
13. Casanova, *The World Republic of Letters*, p. 148; English, *The Economy of Prestige*, p. 304.
14. English, *The Economy of Prestige*, p. 302.
15. Aboul-Ela, "The Writer Becomes Text," p. 343.
16. See ibid. p. 343.
17. See ibid. p. 344.
18. See "The Naguib Mahfouz Medal for Literature."

19. El-Enany, *Naguib Mahfouz*, p. xi.
20. See, for example, Badawi, "Introduction," p. 21; Jayyusi, "Introduction," p. 21; and Kilpatrick, "The Egyptian Novel from *Zaynab* to 1980," p. 239.
21. See Hassan, "Toward a Theory of the Arabic Novel," p. 35.
22. These novels have recently been translated into English and made available in a single volume. See Mahfouz, *Three Novels of Ancient Egypt*.
23. Likewise, all of these novels are now available in English translation.
24. Again, all these texts have now been translated into English.
25. al-Ghīṭānī, *Najīb Maḥfūẓ Yatadhakkar*, p. 109, 108. Cited and translated in El-Enany, *Naguib Mahfouz*, p. 130.
26. El-Enany, *Naguib Mahfouz*, p. xii. El-Enany proceeds to complicate what he regards as the artificiality of such a rigid chronological approach by foregrounding formal and aesthetic parallels between works usually seen as belonging to different phases. See ibid. pp. xi–xii.
27. See Hassan, "Toward a Theory of the Arabic Novel," p. 35.
28. al-Ghīṭānī, *Najīb Maḥfūẓ Yatadhakkar*, pp. 108–9 / El-Enany, *Naguib Mahfouz*, p. 130.
29. See El-Enany, *Naguib Mahfouz*: p. xii.
30. Hafez, "Introduction," p. xiii.
31. Mahfouz, *The Cairo Trilogy*, pp. 41, 55, 291, 254, 788.
32. Ibid. p. 5.
33. Ibid. p. 5.
34. Ibid. p. 1203. For al-Sayyid Ahmad's death, see ibid. pp. 1198–208. Amina's encounter with modernity and its inventions is likewise traumatic—in a rare departure from her life of quiet domesticity, she decides to visit the local mosque, only to be struck and left severely injured by one of Cairo's early automobiles. See ibid. pp. 175–85.
35. See ibid. pp. 1306–13.
36. Kilpatrick, "The Egyptian Novel from *Zaynab* to 1980," pp. 245–6.
37. Mahfouz, *The Cairo Trilogy*, p. 1170.
38. Ibid., p. 893.
39. Hafez, "Introduction," p. xxii.
40. Ouyang, *Politics of Nostalgia in the Arabic Novel*, pp. 166, 167.
41. Mahfouz, *Arabian Nights and Days*, p. 2.
42. Ibid. p. 2.
43. Ouyang, *Poetics of Love in the Arabic Novel*, p. 129.
44. Ibid. p. 129.

45. See El-Enany, *Naguib Mahfouz*, p. 166.
46. For Fadil Sanaan's and Ma'rouf the Cobbler's respective stories, see Mahfouz, *Arabian Nights and Days*, pp. 179–93 and 194–206.
47. Ibid. p. 165. For the Sheikh's story, see ibid. pp. 157–71.
48. Ibid. pp. 81, 83. For Dunyazad's story, see ibid. pp. 77–105.
49. Ouyang, *Poetics of Love in the Arabic Novel*, p. 133.
50. Ouyang, *Politics of Nostalgia in the Arabic Novel*, p. 166.
51. Ouyang, *Poetics of Love in the Arabic Novel*, p. 128.
52. Mahfouz, *Arabian Nights and Days*, p. 43.
53. Ibid. p. 34.
54. Ibid. p.53.
55. Ibid. p.227.
56. For a useful historical overview of the composition of the "original," see Irwin, *The Arabian Nights*, p. 48.
57. Damrosch, *What is World Literature?*, pp. 44, 137.
58. Horta, *Marvellous Thieves*, pp. 16, 3.
59. Mahfouz, *Arabian Nights and Days*, front cover, back cover.
60. Van Leeuwen, "*A Thousand and One Nights* and the Novel," p. 114.
61. This list is derived from that provided by van Leeuwen. See ibid. pp. 103–14.
62. El-Enany, *Naguib Mahfouz*, p. 136.
63. Mitchell, *Rule of Experts*, p. 13.
64. For a useful overview of this genre, see al-Qāḍī, "Biography, medieval."
65. Ouyang, *Politics of Nostalgia in the Arabic Novel*, p. 192.
66. See ibid. pp. 192–3.
67. Phillips, "Translator's Note," p. 210.
68. Cited and translated in Rogan, *The Arabs*, p. 300. For the full text of Nasser's speech, see "The speech given by President Gamal Abdel Nasser in Alexandria."
69. Rhodes James, *Anthony Eden*, p. 457.
70. For a succinct overview of the Suez Crisis, see Rogan, *The Arabs*, pp. 298–304.
71. See Kyle, *Suez* and Louis, *The Ends of British Imperialism*.
72. For British media discourses of the Suez Crisis, see Shaw, *Eden, Suez and the Mass Media*.
73. Smith, "Introduction," p. 11. See also Louis and Owen, *Suez 1956*; James, *Nasser at War*; and Smith (ed.), *Reassessing Suez 1956*.
74. James, *Nasser at War*, p. ix.

75. For a detailed discussion of the repression and disenfranchisement of these groups (especially the Communists and the Muslim Brotherhood) under Nasser, see Roussillon, "Republican Egypt interpreted," pp. 340–2.
76. See Shaw, *Eden, Suez and the Mass Media*: pp. 23–39, *passim*.
77. Mahfouz, *Morning and Evening Talk*, pp. 35, 41, *passim*.
78. Ibid. p. 35. For Muhammad Ibrahim's death, which is recounted in a more matter-of-fact way, see ibid. p. 107.
79. Ibid. p. 41. For Halim's "delight," see ibid. p. 61.
80. Ibid. p. 41.
81. Ibid. p. 194.
82. Ibid. p. 196.
83. See El-Enany, *Naguib Mahfouz*, pp. 3–4, 22–8.
84. See Fadel (dir.), *Nasser 56*.
85. Gordon, "Nasser 56 / Cairo 96," p. 600.
86. Ibid. p. 605.
87. For an excellent discussion of the continuities in the Egyptian state structure from Nasser and Sadat through to Mubarak, see Roussillon, "Republican Egypt interpreted."
88. Estimates as to the extent of the 2011 demonstration range from the 200,000 reported by Stratfor to the 1,000,000 reported by Al Jazeera. See, respectively, "Gauging the Size of the Egyptian Protests" and "Protesters flood Egypt streets."
89. See Sowers and Toensing (eds), *The Journey to Tahrir*; El-Desouky, *The Intellectual and the People in Egyptian Literature and Culture*; El Hamamsy and Soliman (eds), *Popular Culture in the Middle East and North Africa*; Baker (ed.), *Translating Dissent*; Mehrez (ed.), *Translating Egypt's Revolution*; and Herrera, *Revolution in the Age of Social Media*.
90. Sowers, "Egypt in Transformation," p. 6; Mehrez, "Translation Revolution," p. 14.
91. See Noujaim (dir.), *The Square*.
92. El-Desouky, *The Intellectual and the People in Egyptian Literature and Culture*, pp. 10, 11.
93. Ibid. p. x.
94. Hafez, "The New Egyptian Novel," p. 56.
95. Ibid. p. 48.
96. Ibid. p. 49.
97. Radwan, "One Hundred Years of Egyptian Realism," p. 268. Emphasis in original.

98. El-Desouky, "Heterologies of revolutionary action," p. 428.
99. Ibid. p. 436.
100. El-Desouky, *The Intellectual and the People in Egyptian Literature and Culture*, p. 78.
101. Amin, *The Reawakening of the Arab World*, pp. 18, 128, 129.
102. Achcar, *The People Want*, pp. 5, 6.
103. Dabashi, *The Arab Spring*, p. 11. Emphasis in original removed.
104. See pp. 17–18 in the present volume.
105. It should be noted that uniquely among these scholars, Dabashi predicts that in the long run, the Arab Spring "will not leave a stone unturned in the [. . .] above all cultural" as well as political, social, and economic "disposition of these societies." Dabashi, *The Arab Spring*, p. 6. The problem with Dabashi's account of an imminent cultural shift here is that it—apart from having failed to transpire—is premised on what in Chapter 2 I demonstrated to be his mistranslation of the literary culture to which he is calling for a return, and his misreading of the history that saw its supersession in the first place. See pp. 149–51 in the present volume.

4

Islam and the Limits of Translation: Orhan Pamuk and the Ottoman Revival

Everything is translatable.

                                        Emily Apter, *The Translation Zone*

Nothing is translatable.

                                        Emily Apter, *The Translation Zone*

I'm not mourning the Ottoman Empire. I'm a Westernizer. I'm pleased that the Westernization process took place. I'm just criticizing the limited way in which the ruling elite—meaning both the bureaucracy and the new rich—had conceived of Westernization. They lacked the confidence necessary to create a national culture rich in its own symbols and rituals. They did not strive to create an Istanbul culture that would be an organic combination of East and West; they just put Western and Eastern things together. There was, of course, a strong local Ottoman culture, but that was fading away little by little. What they had to do, and could not possibly do enough, was invent a strong local culture, which would be a combination—not an imitation—of the Eastern past and the Western present. I try to do the same kind of thing in my books.

                               Orhan Pamuk, Interview with *The Paris Review*

Orhan Pamuk is widely regarded as a paragon of the contemporary global writer. The recipient of the Nobel Prize in Literature in 2006 as well as a host of other international honors and awards, his novels have sold over 13 million copies worldwide, have been translated into sixty-three languages, and have been met with universal critical acclaim. It is what has been accentuated as Pamuk's cosmopolitan, secular-liberal literary stance on themes including the East / West encounter, the history of the Ottoman Empire, the cultural politics of Islam in Turkey up to the present day, authoritarianism and repression there, the figure of the writer or artist, the social value of literature and the arts, and so forth that the global literary industry has chosen most consistently to celebrate in its framing of the author and his work. This impression of Pamuk is reinforced by what has been taken as the characteristic style in which his novels are written. Writing for the *London Review of Books*, Adam Shatz characterizes this as "the Esperanto of international literary fiction," a "playful postmodernism" that mixes genres and pays homage to Western models like Fyodor Dostoyevsky, Thomas Mann, Marcel Proust, James Joyce, William Faulkner, and Jorge Luis Borges.[1] Not to mention by the international outcry that surrounded the lawsuit that was brought against him in Turkey in 2005 due to comments he had made on the Armenian Genocide and the mass killings of Kurds in the country.[2] At the time, he became something of an icon of artistic freedom and the freedom of speech in the domain of world literature, with PEN America, numerous celebrity authors, and various other groups speaking out in his support. Currently, Pamuk spends about half of his time in that most cosmopolitan of cities, New York, as Robert Yik-Fong Tam Professor in the Humanities at Columbia University.

The carefully cultivated image of Pamuk as a worldly, cosmopolitan, and secular-liberal writer—one to which the author himself has certainly contributed—is best encapsulated by the "born translated" paradigm of world literature recently forwarded by Rebecca Walkowitz. In her 2015 book by that title, Walkowitz identifies the contemporary novel that is from the outset "written for translation"—and thus self-consciously attuned to and embedded within our increasingly globalized circuits of literary production, translation, circulation, and consumption—as an important new critical lens for understanding the landscape of world literature today.[3] Through readings of works by J. M. Coetzee, Kazuo Ishiguro, David Mitchell, Caryl Phillips, Amy Waldman, Mohsin Hamid, Jamaica Kincaid, and others, she develops a model of world literature that locates the translatability and transnational migrations of literary texts at its heart. Significantly for my purposes, Walkowitz includes Pamuk in her canon of "born translated" writers (most of whom work in English), and even draws on his later novel *Snow* (*Kar*, 2002; trans. 2004) as an introductory illustration of her central thesis. Channelling the general critical consensus noted above, she argues that this as well as others of Pamuk's writings "solicit translation by emphasizing international lineage, postmodern devices, and 'Istanbul cosmopolitanism'" while also "reflect[ing] on global circulation," that they "engage directly with the phenomenon of world literature."[4] Inevitably perhaps, this sort of approach leads to the echoing of outdated assumptions about Pamuk's native city and his take on it, that it is an inter- or third space "between Europe and Asia."[5]

Exemplified by Walkowitz, the image of Pamuk as a global writer has come to define the aesthetics and politics, the ethos, of his novels as these have made their way into the world. It has functioned to undermine the nature and extent of his engagement with the local, especially his native city, Istanbul, and its Ottoman, Islamic heritage. By extension, it has obscured the specific ways in which such engagement is reflected in his reconfiguration and reinvention of novelistic form. As per my argument about Naguib Mahfouz in Chapter 3, it has—in short—negated what I regard as his actual significance for world literature.

As in the previous, I aim in this chapter to restore this significance. I do so via a sustained focus on *The Black Book* (*Kara Kitap*, 1990; trans. 1994, 2006), Pamuk's opus of 1990, as this novel has been translated and read in Britain and the United States. Concerning an Istanbul lawyer, Galip, and his search for his missing wife Rüya through the semiotic labyrinth of Istanbul and its aborted Ottoman, Islamic past, *The Black Book* is exemplary in terms of its embeddedness in the local, its formal and linguistic complexity and innovation, and the almost willful misinterpretation it has provoked. I start with a detailed critical introduction to the novel in relation to the history of the Turkish modernity that serves as its ultimate horizon, and with reference to important recent scholarship on Pamuk (as in the work of Azade Seyhan and Erdağ Göknar, among others). Next, I inquire into its English translations. Offsetting Güneli Gün's (1994) and Maureen Freely's (2006) respectively foreignizing and domesticating translation strategies against my own literal translations of select passages, and drawing on the translation theory of Lawrence Venuti, I show that both are by definition unable to capture the logic and significance of

Pamuk's culturally specific use of language. This, I argue, is comprised of his attempt to reintegrate the Arabic and Persian loanwords of Ottoman Turkish into the modern Turkish that had excised them. This translational limitation, I suggest, has strongly influenced the novel's Anglo-American reception, which has tended to emphasize its worldly postmodernism at the expense of its rich and nuanced investment in the local.

In the counter-reading I then pursue, I argue that anything but a postmodernist deconstruction of the myths of national and religious identity, *The Black Book* in fact comprises an evocation of Istanbul's (and Turkey's) Ottoman, Islamic heritage in the face of a Turkish secular modernity by which this heritage has been and continues to be repressed. I detail this argument through close attention to Pamuk's treatment of Islam, especially Sufism and its mystical Hurufi order, as this is indicated by the imagery of the mannequin, the face, and the writer that saturates and even structures the novel. I conclude that *The Black Book*, while certainly deploying postmodernist elements, systematically revises these and reshapes novelistic form according to this content, which amounts to the repressed other of Turkish secular modernity. Cumulatively, it thereby inscribes what I call "cultural neo-Ottomanism" as form. I end the chapter by considering the implications of Pamuk's cultural neo-Ottomanism for questions of the Islamic Revival in the Middle East and the postsecularism / secularism debate (represented, in my analysis, by Talal Asad, Jürgen Habermas, Charles Taylor, and Joseph Massad on the one hand, and by Aamir Mufti on the other).

In sum, my intention in this chapter is to contest the "born translated" idea, and demonstrate that Pamuk and his work are better understood as *untranslatable* in the many senses proposed by Emily Apter.[6] More compellingly than in the standard narratives about Pamuk and his place in it, this is what he signifies both for and about world literature.

Orhan Pamuk, *The Black Book*, and the Dialectics of Turkish Modernity

Pamuk is naturally and inescapably heir to the heritage of the Turkish novel as discussed in Chapter 2.[7] However, he doesn't merely assume the mantle of that already established tradition. Following in the footsteps of his great literary and spiritual predecessor Ahmet Hamdi Tanpınar, he rather adopts a deeply reflexive, critical stance on it.[8] For Pamuk, novelistic writing and the novel form itself are imbricated with and indeed inseparable from the dialectics of past and present, tradition and modernity, and religion and secularism that came to define the Turkish state and Turkish literature alike over the course of the twentieth century. The imaginative locus of all of his work, this dialectic feeds into every aspect of his writing—from his storylines, modes of characterization, and thematic emphases to his structuring devices, formal innovations, and use of language to his geographical and historical settings. It imbues all with the distinct and often melancholy light of deep historical consciousness.

The remit of Pamuk's lifelong writerly project is evident as early as his very first novel, *Cevdet Bey and His Sons* (*Cevdet Bey ve Oğulları*, 1982). Reminiscent of Mahfouz, this novel charts in social realist fashion the political, social, and cultural upheavals of Turkey in the transitional years of the early twentieth century as witnessed and experienced by a multigenerational Istanbul family. Likewise set in or around Istanbul, *Silent House* (*Sessiz Ev*, 1983; trans. 2012), *The Black Book*, *The New Life* (*Yeni Hayat*, 1994; trans. 1997), *A Strangeness in My Mind* (*Kafamda Bir Tuhaflık*, 2014; trans. 2015), and *The Red-Haired Woman* (*Kırmızı Saçlı Kadın*, 2016; trans. 2017) all turn to the latter part of the twentieth century, and traverse in their various ways the topographies of a self-divided and self-alienated contemporary city whose inhabitants have become lost to themselves in the labyrinth of modernity and must therefore seek new meaning by excavating—sometimes literally—their own and their city's past. *The White Castle* (*Beyaz Kale*, 1985; trans. 1990) and *My Name is Red* (*Benim Adım Kırmızı*, 1998; trans. 2001) turn back the clock and recreate Ottoman Istanbul in the sixteenth to seventeenth centuries in all of its civilizational grandeur, minutely tracing along the way the discourses and intrigues of empire, statecraft, religion, art, and desire in that time and place for their inverse revelations of the present. *Snow* comprises Pamuk's most direct interrogation of the role of religion in contemporary Turkey to date, and brings his acute historical awareness to bear on the question of the Islamic Revival's impact on the country in recent years. And finally, *The Museum of Innocence* (*Masumiyet Müzesi*, 2008; trans. 2009)—both a novel and an actual museum that Pamuk established in Istanbul's Beyoğlu district in 2012—archives the social history of the city in the 1970s to 1980s, a history defined not by the nation and its monuments, but rather by the individual and his / her personal artifacts as these indicate the otherwise forgotten lived experience of a society in transition. Currently, Pamuk is working on another Ottoman-themed novel, this time set in the early nineteenth century (a period that he hasn't previously covered).

This is a rich oeuvre indeed, one which is far from exhausted by the brief thematic survey I have attempted. Within it, I focus on *The Black Book*. Pamuk's breakthrough novel, *The Black Book* rapidly became one of the fastest selling and most controversial books in Turkish literary history upon its original publication in 1990 (it sold over 70,000 copies within its first few weeks on the shelves), and furthermore precipitated the author's international reputation and celebrity when it appeared in English shortly thereafter. As noted above, my particular interest in it lies in the depth of its engagement with the dialectics of modernity, religion, and secularism in Turkey; its formal and linguistic sophistication; and the revealing nuances of its translation history and its subsequent global circulation and reception. For these reasons, *The Black Book* offers special insight not only into the scope and essence of Pamuk's project as a whole, but also into some of the key questions of world literature today. However, it is a complex, multilayered novel that resists the sort of brief summarization that would typically preface a close reading. Instead, I start by providing a more detailed critical introduction to it—its plot, characters, and themes; its formal features; its geographical setting; and its historical setting—in relation to Pamuk's other work as well as the wider contexts of Turkish modernity, and with reference to the recent scholarship on the author. In the following and throughout this chapter, I use Freely's 2006 translation for textual citations from the novel due to its relative clarity and precision (an issue I discuss at length in the next section).

Plot, Characters, Themes

The Black Book is a novel ostensibly about Galip (whose name means "victor" in Turkish), a westernized lawyer living in Istanbul, and his search for his mysteriously disappeared wife and first cousin Rüya ("dream") through the backstreets and alleyways of the city. Left with only a cryptic, nineteen-word goodbye letter by his wife, Galip sets out to find her in a quest that takes him from dilapidated family apartments, private archives of left-wing political manifestos, and the poorer quarters of the city to Istanbul's public squares, markets, mosques, newspapers offices, nightclubs, ateliers, and brothels. He soon realizes that Rüya has likely taken up with his cousin and her half-brother Celâl (whose name alludes to the given name of Rumi, the thirteenth-century Persian Sufi mystic and poet), a columnist for the daily newspaper *Milliyet*. His search for his wife thus also becomes a search for Celâl. So Galip reads through the thirty-year archive of Celâl's columns, seeking clues as to their whereabouts.

These columns have a pronounced impact on Galip. They delve in highly literate, imaginative, and self-conscious ways into Istanbul's and Turkey's cultural history, their archaeologies, architectures, arts, media, politics, philosophies, religions, and fashions. They include florid speculations on the dead civilizations exposed by the imaginary drying up of the Bosphorus; ironic accounts of Istanbul's consumption patterns as registered in Alâaddin's shop; melancholy assessments of the loss of authentic Istanbullu gestures nevertheless preserved by a lonely craftsman's mannequins; verbatim reproductions of conversations between the master polemicists of the Turkish press; metaphysical reflections on Turkish identity; and extensive improvisations on the history of Islam in Turkey, especially on Rumi, Sufism, and Hurufism. They initially have the effect of forcing Galip to question his (constructed) westernized identity, leading to a profound psychological break. Then, through the mystical Sufi doctrine of Hurufism to which they expose him, they prompt him to develop a new hermeneutical paradigm that allows him for the first time to properly decipher the signs of his city as well as his own historically mediated place within it, his identity.

Galip's search for his wife thus takes an inwards turn, and becomes a search for himself. The search, and the novel, concludes with Galip's discovery of the murder of both Rüya and Celâl—of his "dream" of a fulfilled westernized identity in Turkey—most likely at the hands of F. M. Üçüncü, an Islamic Revivalist and fanatical reader of Celâl's columns. This discovery is simultaneous with that of his vocation as a writer very much in the mode of his (absent) mentor Celâl—indeed, he becomes Celâl's, and Pamuk's, double. It turns out, then, that the novel's apparently simple thematic premise was all along a device for exploring Turkish cultural identity, the traumas resultant from the Kemalist repression of the Ottoman, Islamic heritage during the Republican era of modernization and secularization in the 1920s to 1930s, and the formation of new identity positions that revive or memorialize that past culturally rather than politically.

Structure, Style, Form, Genre

The Black Book consists of thirty-six chapters divided into two parts. Each chapter is prefaced by an epigraph borrowed from a wide range of classic Western and Eastern literary, religious, and other historical sources. Broadly, Part One, culminating in Chapter Nineteen ("Signs of the City"), traces the collapse of Galip's westernized identity, whereas Part Two sees Galip, under the influence of Celâl's meditations on Sufism and Hurufism, develop a new identity as a writer attuned to Istanbul's repressed Ottoman and Islamic past. Throughout, the chapters alternate between the third- and first-person modes. The third-person chapters are focused on Galip as he searches for his wife across Istanbul and through the annals of Turkish cultural history. The first-person chapters reproduce verbatim Celâl's newspaper columns for *Milliyet* in all their imaginative and speculative glory. Despite the highly literate and literary qualities of the more immediately striking "Celâl" chapters (which for all of their idiosyncrasies retain the standard subject-object-verb word order of Turkish), the "Galip" chapters are formally more complex. Their limited third-person form is riddled with free indirect discourse, stream of consciousness, analepses, fantasy scenarios in the subjunctive, metadiegetic narratives, and other narrative devices. Indeed, as only fully manifest in the original Turkish despite the efforts of the novel's translators, Pamuk's writing style in the "Galip" chapters becomes increasingly more convoluted, his sentences longer and more ornate, as Galip's quest intensifies and he himself becomes more frenzied in the run-up to his break from his habituated identity.

The "Galip" and "Celâl" chapters are dialectically intertwined in a number of ways. Most straightforwardly, each of the "Celâl" chapters presents the text of the newspaper column that Galip had read in the immediately preceding third-person chapter for clues as to his cousin's and therefore his wife's whereabouts. As the columns direct Galip's search and thus the action of the subsequent third-person chapter, the relationship between the third- and first-person chapters determines the shape of the narrative, the novel, as it unfolds. On a broader thematic level, the "Galip" and "Celâl" chapters represent, respectively, the individual's search for meaning and identity in the conflicted cultural and historical terrain of Istanbul, and that terrain itself (or at least Celâl's melancholy reflections on it). As Galip reads through the columns, they and the material they contain have the effect of forcing him to question his identity, and eventually to reintegrate himself into the urban culture he is newly able to interpret. The central thematic of the novel is thus formally manifest in the relationship between the "Galip" and "Celâl" chapters. Finally, Galip's process of reintegration is only complete as he comes to write Celâl's column for himself in Part Two of the novel (specifically, Chapter Twenty-Nine is the first of the "Galip" columns). Galip's adoption of the role of the writer suggests a synthesis between the hitherto separate "Galip" and "Celâl" strands, and a resolution—signified in form—of the novel's central conflict. In taking up the column and the novelistic space allotted it, Galip newly emerges as a first person with authority over and thus the right to author his own identity. Indicative of Galip's new identity position, the act of writing itself as well as its content also come to suggest the cultural project of *The Black Book* as a whole.

Since its first appearance in English translation in 1994, *The Black Book* has nigh-universally been deemed by the Anglo-American scholarly, critical, and journalistic establishment a "postmodernist" novel of one sort or another. From *Edebiyât* to *New Literary History* to the *London Review of Books*, and beyond, it has been branded a "postmodern meta-narrative," a "postmodern speculation[. . .]," a "Post-Modern detective novel," a "metaphysical thriller," a "Borgesian labyrinth," and so on.[9] Within this spectrum of overlapping generic designations, its categorization as a "postmodern detective novel" or "thriller" requires particular attention. Commentators have often pointed out that by stopping short of explicitly revealing the identity of Rüya's and Celâl's murderer, Pamuk—taking his cue from the likes of Jorge Luis Borges, Italo Calvino, and Umberto Eco, among others—is drawing on familiar postmodernist techniques in order to destabilize the norms of the classic detective novel (a decipherable world of clues, an orderly resolution, closure, etc.). Certainly, Pamuk himself invites these sorts of comparisons. He makes Rüya a reader and translator of detective fiction, and even directly references what many have taken as his own narrative strategy early on in the text: "Galip once told Rüya," Pamuk writes, "that the only detective book he'd ever wanted to read would be the one in which not even the author knew the murderer's identity."[10] However, this sort of reading fails to account for the logic of *cross*-cultural generic play behind Pamuk's indeed overt engagement with the detective novel, the local and specific reasons why he seeks to upend the genre and its norms, and the alternate system of interpreting clues that Galip—a model for the reader now, as well as the writer—develops in Part Two of the novel. In other words, it falls into an interpretive trap quite intentionally laid by Pamuk.

Towards the end of Part One, in the pivotal Chapter Nineteen, Pamuk makes it clear that for Galip it is specifically *Istanbul's* semiotic richness that exceeds the classic detective-hero's interpretive capabilities and thus the detective novel's—a genre that had been "conceived abroad"—interpretive norms.[11] On the verge of his urban revelation, Galip reflects "[h]ow different [are the signs of the city] from the cosy world of Rüya's detective novels, where authors never vexed a hero with more signs than he needed."[12] It is the Western detective paradigm that fails here, and not what Pamuk's postmodernist critics have as interpretation per se. This should be unsurprising in a novel so much about the cultural failings brought about by external cultural influences. And so Galip is compelled to *re*interpret Istanbul's signs through the lens of what might be regarded as an alternate, "Eastern" hermeneutic, one that is anchored in local rather than global cultural and historical content: "[i]t was perhaps possible to look into the faces of his fellow citizens and see in them the city's long history—its misfortunes, its lost magnificence, its melancholy and pain—but these were not carefully arranged clues pointing to a secret world" (as in a detective novel); rather, "they came from a shared defeat, a shared history, a shared shame."[13] As I have noted, this hermeneutic is only fully developed in Part Two, by way of Galip's study of Hurufi doctrine. However, his incipient perceptual and intellectual transformation is clearly indicated in this same chapter, when he sees and reads Taksim Square—an important Kemalist landmark—anew: "[a]ll at once he was stepping into a poor, forgotten country he had never seen before, beholding the brash modern square at its centre."[14] As Galip's emerging interpretive abilities feed into his discovery of writing as vocation, *The Black Book* might more accurately be read as a *Künstlerroman* than as a postmodernist novel in any of that genre's shadings or variations.[15]

To my knowledge, no other critics have described *The Black Book* as a *Künstlerroman*. Azade Seyhan has come closest, though, by approaching it as "a quest," "a bildungsroman about rebuilding or a new *Bildung* ('education or formation')."[16] The novel, she argues, stages a three-tiered process of *Bildung*: first, "the mourning of a culture lost to a mismanaged modernity"; second, "the quest for re-presenting that culture as a corrective endeavour (*Bildung* as rebuilding a lost cultural legacy through remembrance)"; and third, "turning the city into an encyclopedic site of a new pedagogy."[17] This reading occurs within a wider-ranging chapter on "Istanbul: City as Trope and Topos of Crossed Destinies" in Seyhan's book about the Turkish novel, and as such is naturally and quite perceptively focused on questions of urban hermeneutics. As a result, however, it somewhat downplays that of writing as a vocation of "re-presenting" and "remembrance."

In *The Black Book*, as I have suggested, it is only through Galip's discovery of writing as vocation that a public, expressive form adequate to the task of mourning and re-presenting a lost culture is forged. As in classic *Künstlerromane* by Johann Wolfgang von Goethe, Marcel Proust, James Joyce, and others, Galip's turn to writing is spurred by a rejection of and a metaphorical or psychological exile from bourgeois values— here, the values of the Turkish secular modernity by which he had been socially and culturally indoctrinated from his earliest youth. While, as I have also noted, this turn is prompted by Galip's study of Sufi and Hurufi doctrine, it would be misguided to jump from this premise to Sooyong Kim's and Bernt Brendemoen's respective conclusions about the novel, that it is "Sufi allegory" or "sufi tale."[18] Just as it not only adopts, but also adapts postmodernist formal devices for its own ends, the novel—less drastically—rather only draws on and incorporates Sufi material in order to register Galip's development of what I have called an "Eastern" hermeneutic within the wider arc of the *Künstlerroman* form. Sufism, in other words, provides Galip with the inspiration and interpretive capabilities necessary for the ulterior project of writing. As he himself states in the last words of the novel, when he is finally in a position to narrate his story in the first-person, "writing [. . .] writing [. . .] writing" is "the only consolation" for the losses wrought by history, for the losses of Rüya—his dream—and Celâl.[19] As Erdağ Göknar has clarified, the novel is therefore to be regarded as an instance of "secular-sacred Turkish literary modernity," one that reflexively engages with and infl(l)ects—but still operates within—the secular field of Republican literature.[20]

Geographical Setting

The Black Book is set entirely in Istanbul, which has often been referred to as the novel's "central character." Like a character in a novel by, say, Honoré de Balzac or Leo Tolstoy, Istanbul's multifaceted "psychological" traits—most significantly, the sense of what he calls *"hüzün"* (loosely, "melancholy") that pervades the city—are drawn by Pamuk as meticulously as are its physical traits, ranging from its topography and landmarks to the faces and gestures of its inhabitants. No mere backdrop to the narrative that takes place within it, the novel is perhaps primarily about how to read the city. As Galip scours it in search of his wife, the veil of accustomed perceptions woven by his Western lifestyle begins to drop, and Istanbul transforms into a repository of signs to be deciphered for their hidden meanings. As in Walter Benjamin's work on urban modernity, the signs of the city—its faces, streets, monuments, and artifacts—become for Galip material expressions or embodiments of the contradictions of in this case Turkish secular modernity.[21] In Chapter Nineteen, he begins his initiation into what is earlier described as the "mystery" of Istanbul (its "misfortunes," its "lost magnificence," its "melancholy and pain," as in the passage cited above), central to which is his growing sensitivity to the *hüzün* with which its signs are cryptically saturated.²² In order to properly understand Galip's trajectory and thus *The Black Book* as a whole (not to mention Pamuk's other writings), then, it is necessary to get to better grips with this concept of "*hüzün*." To do so, I now turn to Pamuk's exquisite memoir / impressionistic cultural history *Istanbul: Memories and the City* (*İstanbul: Hatıralar ve Şehir*, 2003; trans. 2005), where he discusses it at length.

From the outset of this text, Pamuk makes is clear that his relationship with Istanbul is mediated by *hüzün*: "[f]or me," he writes, Istanbul "has always been a city of ruins and end-of-empire melancholy. I've spent my life either battling with this melancholy, or (like all Istanbullus) making it my own."²³ As with his novels, the act of writing *Istanbul* appears to have been a gesture in this direction on Pamuk's part. Throughout the memoir, he identifies instances of *hüzün* in the declining stature of his family; in Istanbul's Ottoman ruins and hastily modernized architecture; in the writings of the city's poets, novelists, columnists, and encyclopedists; and elsewhere. In Chapter Ten, he interrupts these reflections with an abstract, philological account of the term. In its original Arabic (حزن) and Qur'ānic usage, he notes, it at first conveyed "a feeling of deep spiritual loss."²⁴ However, it soon became bifurcated, and "two very different *hüzüns*" started to emerge in classical Arabic-Islamic culture.²⁵ The first signifies the melancholy attendant on material or worldly losses, and originates from an (un-Islamic) overinvestment in the transitory world. The second, derived from Sufi mysticism, signifies "the spiritual anguish we feel because we cannot be close enough to Allah," the anguish of metaphysical dualism and the void it opens up between the material and the spiritual realms.²⁶ Due to its association with religious devotion, it is *hüzün* in this second modality that has been particularly resonant in the history of Islamic culture, and that has dominated the mood of Turkish poetry and music since the beginning of the nineteenth century. However, and this is the key point that Pamuk wants to put across, the honor accorded to *hüzün* in the Sufi tradition is not sufficient to explain just how central and pervasive the concept has become in specifically *Istanbullu* culture in the twentieth century. In Istanbul, *hüzün*—a communal mood of "worldly failure, listlessness[,] and spiritual suffering" that is "unique" to the city—is rather to be understood as derived from "the history of the city following the destruction of the Ottoman Empire."[27]

Istanbul's *hüzün* is, then, the anguish and unfulfilled longing caused by what might be considered a *historical* dualism, by the void that *history* has opened up between an (idealized) past held together by Turkey's Ottoman and Islamic heritage and a present divorced from that past under the Kemalist process of modernization and secularization. This is precisely the *hüzün* that pervades *The Black Book* and indeed all of Pamuk's Istanbul novels. While throughout his work Pamuk develops a variety of distinct literary strategies for negotiating it, *The Black Book* represents perhaps the most penetrating and comprehensive of these through what I have discussed as Galip's writerly *Bildung*.

Historical Setting

The Black Book is set in the days before the 1980 Turkish military coup d'état, the Republic of Turkey's third up to that point, orchestrated by General Kenan Evren against the government of President Süleyman Demirel. Foreshadowing his own murder some 400 pages further into the novel, Celâl writes near the beginning of the first of his columns (Chapter Two) that this was an era when Istanbul's streets were riddled by a "frenzied killing spree."[28] He is referring here to the spate of political assassinations carried out in the 1970s by militant right- and left-wing splinter groups such as the infamous proto-fascist militia The Idealist Youth (Ülkücü Gençlik, also known as the "Grey Wolves"). Such violence left over 5,000 members of these factions as well as public figures including high ranking officials and union leaders dead on the streets of Istanbul and elsewhere. It had a pronounced effect on Turkish public and political life, disrupting civil order and exacerbating already deadlocked relations between Turkey's two leading parties, Demirel's conservative Justice Party (Adalet Partisi) and Bülent Ecevit's social-democratic Republican People's Party (Cumhuriyet Halk Partisi). Alongside Turkey's economic and financial crisis, the pressure increasingly mounted by Kurdish separatists, and the "threat" of Islamic fundamentalism, it was a major contributing factor to the military's takeover of power in 1980—the Turkish military had, after all, been constitutionally tasked with upholding Kemalist and Republican ideals from 1923.[29] Culminating in Celâl's murder, its history and effects are marked everywhere in *The Black Book*.

While *The Black Book* is most immediately framed in relation to Turkish political history in the 1970s, its more substantial context is the longer history of Turkey's modernization and secularization in the twentieth century, the horizon of all Pamuk's work.[30] For Pamuk, Turkey in the 1970s (and thereafter) can in fact only be understood with reference to this background. I'll illustrate this point by turning to Part Two of the novel. As noted above, Galip gradually assumes Celâl's role and identity through this section. Impersonating his absent mentor, he receives a string of disturbing phone calls from one of Celâl's fanatical readers and likely his eventual murderer. Identifying himself only as "Mehmet," a careful reading suggests that this figure's real identity is actually that of F. M. Üçüncü, a character briefly mentioned elsewhere in the novel.

In 1962, Üçüncü had published a Hurufi-inspired tract—*The Mystery of the Letters and the Loss of Mystery*—that described the unbridgeable historical and metaphysical schism between East and West, and called for Turkey's return to its pure Eastern heritage via its rediscovery of Hurufi mystery.[31] Thus positioned as an Islamic Revivalist of a mystical, prophetic bent, a clear link is established between Üçüncü and the name "Mehmet," the Turkish name for the Prophet. In his conversations with Galip (who he believes is Celâl), Mehmet / Üçüncü harangues his interlocutor for his address in order—as he eventually confesses—to kill him. His grievances are serious and long-standing—Celâl not only seduced his wife some twenty years earlier, but also betrayed a failed Messianic coup of the early 1960s that he believes might have gotten the country out of "the shameful shadow of Europe" and "back on its feet."[32] The underlying impetus of Mehmet / Üçüncü's murderous desire, though, is that Celâl had "deceived us all, deceived the entire nation with [his] bold lies, scandalous dreams, paranoid obsessions, insinuating refinements, elegant turns of phrase, and endearing antics."[33] For the caller, Celâl's deception amounts to his having undermined the Revivalist vision of a return to a pure, authentic Turkish identity—"[b]ecause of you," Mehmet / Üçüncü tells Celâl / Galip, "I've never had the chance to be myself," to be the self he would have been if Celâl's columns hadn't spuriously posited Turkish identity as a combination of its Islamic past with its modern, secular present.[34] Rather than any specific political act like informing on his peers, it was in the writing of his columns that Celâl had betrayed the coup that would have reversed the process of Turkish secular modernity.

Dominating much of Part Two, this extended episode underlines the depth of Pamuk's historical awareness, his understanding of the short history of coups, political violence, and Islamic Revivalism as mediated by a longer history of modernization and secularization. Even more significantly, it also articulates a distinction between two modes of recovering the losses wrought by history and coming to terms with its *hüzün*. The first, what I call "political neo-Ottomanism," is exemplified by Mehmet / Üçüncü and aimed at restoring a glorious past through a violence that ultimately reproduces that of Kemalist reform. The second, "cultural neo-Ottomanism," is exemplified by Celâl / Galip and aimed at reintegrating the past into the present by way of literary and cultural acts that revive or memorialize the Ottoman, Islamic heritage. As the narrative unfolds and Galip takes up Celâl's column, it becomes clear with which mode Pamuk aligns himself. If there is any doubt, one might refer to Pamuk's historical novels (most notably *My Name is Red*), which literally recreate in and for contemporary Turkish culture Ottoman Istanbul in all of its magnificence and complexity.

Beyond its setting, *The Black Book* must be historically contextualized in another sense too. It was written between 1985 and 1990, when the long-term effects of the 1980 coup were beginning to become apparent. In 1983, Evren's military junta ceded power to a democratically elected government. The political transition was in essence a rapid one (even if fraught with tensions and restrictions); however, the coup was to have a more enduring impact on the Turkish economy. Under Evren, the neoliberal-minded statesman Turgut Özal (later Prime Minister and then President of Turkey) was appointed State Minister and then Deputy Prime Minister in charge of economic affairs. Under Özal's guidance, the Turkish economy was to be integrated into the global economy—his extensive program of liberalization included lending Turkish support to the International Monetary Fund, the reduction of import and export tariffs, the floating of the exchange rate, the expansion of foreign direct investment, and the privatization of previously state-run industries.³⁵ As Turkish cultural historians such as Nurdan Gürbilek and Esra Özyürek have noted, these policies had the paradoxical effect of liberalizing the culture industries during one of the most politically repressive eras of Turkey's modern history.

Gürbilek summarizes what she calls the "new cultural climate" that arose in Turkey in the 1980s in terms of a "[r]eturn of the [r]epressed."³⁶ In her account, it was specifically "the provocative strategies of the market" that allowed groups that were "unable to express themselves within the founding Republican ideology" and that had "no place in the Kemalist modernizing design"—namely, "Kurds, 'minorities,' [and] Islamists"—to find for the first time their voice in Turkey's cultural landscape.³⁷ Variously reshaped by political, ethnic, religious, commercial, and other interested claims, the past itself thus became a site of increasingly pointed cultural struggle and contestation during this period. For Özyürek, Turks began to lose their faith in the future-oriented Kemalist agenda in the 1980s, and—like Galip—instead turned back to "their past" for "clues [. . .] to help them understand or control the present."³⁸ It was at this time that the "administered amnesia" of the Kemalist era started to be challenged, and that Turkey's repressed historical traumas—pivotally, the Armenian Genocide of 1915, the Turkish-Greek population exchange of 1923, and the Kurdish massacres ongoing since the 1920s—emerged as sites of public memory.³⁹ As Özyürek for one indicates by opening her edited volume on these matters with a reference to the novel, *The Black Book* is very much a product of what both she and Gürbilek posit as the collective Turkish cultural rediscovery of the past that was taking place at the very moment when Pamuk was writing.⁴⁰ As I hope to have shown, it also models and exemplifies just such a project of rediscovery, and makes an original and compelling case for its future directions well beyond anything thus far seen from Turkey's political establishment.

Translating the Untranslatable: Languages of Domestication and Foreignization

The Black Book has been translated into English twice, by Güneli Gün in 1994 and by Maureen Freely in 2006. These translations—especially the first—have from their first appearance to the present day very much served as the basis of the novel's circulation and reception in Britain and the United States, and thereby in the wider world. As the primary means by which the novel has been carried beyond that of its origin and into a global cultural landscape, they have quite literally worlded it, or facilitated its entry into the domain of world literature. Along the way, they have strongly influenced the ways in which it has been read and discussed in that context. As such, the stakes of the respective translatorial strategies they have employed for rendering globally legible the formal, linguistic, and cultural content of the original text are particularly high.

To illustrate the mediating role of these translations vis-à-vis world literature, I start by looking into their respective approaches to *The Black Book*'s first sentence. This analysis offers insight into what following Lawrence Venuti I identify as Gün's foreignizing and Freely's domesticating translatorial strategies, the differences between them, and—crucially—their shared and inevitable failure to capture the logic and significance of Pamuk's experimental engagement with language.

In its original Turkish, the first sentence of *Kara Kitap* reads as follows:

> Yatağin başindan ucuna kadar uzanan mavi damali yorganin engebeleri, gölgeli vadileri ve mavi yumuşak tepeleriyle örtülü tatli ve ilik karanlikta Rüya yüzükoyun uzanmiş uyuyordu.[41]

To highlight important features of the Turkish, I've broken the sentence into its constituent parts and attempted a translation as faithful as possible to the original word order:

> Yatağin başindan ucuna kadar uzanan
> mavi damali yorganin
> engebeleri, gölgeli vadileri ve mavi yumuşak tepeleriyle
> örtülü
> tatli ve ilik karanlikta
> Rüya yüzükoyun uzanmiş uyuyordu.

> The bed from its beginning to its end
> the blue checkered quilt

its mountains, shady valleys and soft blue hills
covered with
in the sweet and warm darkness of
Rüya facedown outstretched slept.

The grammatically correct form of a Turkish sentence that, like this one, comprises a definite subject ("Rüya"); a verb, in this case intransitive ("uyuyordu," "slept"); and an object ("yatağin," "the bed")—along with one or more prepositional phrases ("tatli ve ilik karanlikta," "in the sweet and warm darkness of")—is subject-object-verb. So the sentence should read "Rüya yatağin tatli ve ilik karanlikta uyuyordu"—literally, "Rüya the bed in the sweet and warm darkness of slept." Here, however, Pamuk has rearranged the word order, and deferred the subject to the end of the sentence, alongside the verb. While this would be appropriate for an *in*definite subject, in this case Pamuk has produced what is known as a "*devrik cümle*" ("inverse sentence"), now a high-literary embellishment among contemporary Turkish writers. As Freely explains in her essay "A Translator's Tale" (2006), this device allows the writer to "offer up a string of allusive images that float[. . .] about unanchored and haiku-like until the last word pin[s] them down."[42] The use of such an usual sentence structure has special resonance in a novel like *Kara Kitap*. Not only do what Pamuk himself describes as the "long and dizzying baroque sentences" that result reflect Galip's increasingly frenetic quest through Istanbul; they also originate from what he continues is "the chaos, history, present richness, indeterminacy[,] and energy of the city."[43] Pamuk's use of language is thus intimately bound up with his narrative and its setting. As a translation can by definition only ever approximate the original (to greater or lesser degrees of accuracy depending on the strategy pursued), the linguistic distances opened by translation therefore become spatial distances from Istanbul.

In her version, Gün renders the sentence as:

Rüya slept on her stomach in the sweet and warm darkness under the blue-checkered quilt which covered the entire bed with its undulating, shadowy valleys and soft blue hills.[44]

As can be seen, Gün has shifted the word order here, notably moving the subject and verb to their natural English positions. However, I hold that she leans towards a foreignizing translatorial strategy as per Venuti. For Venuti, foreignizing translation seeks to resist and counteract what he calls "the violence of translation," "the reconstitution of the foreign text in accordance with values, beliefs[,] and representations that pre-exist it in the target language."[45] As both "a theory" and a "practice" of translation, it does so by striving to signify "the linguistic and cultural difference of the foreign text."[46] Gün's sentence seems to do just that, specifically by attempting to replicate the sensual flow of the original. It maintains the original's accumulation of overlapping, endlessly modified prepositional phrases, and its lack of secondary boundary marks as well as its adjectival insistence leave the anglophone reader breathless, with a sense of Leavisite exasperation. As with Gün's translation as a whole (I look into her other translatorial choices below), it is a far cry from the "fluen[cy]" and "transparency" that for Venuti mark a more domesticating approach, and draws attention to the English in defamiliarizing and potentially subversive ways.[47]

As Freely has it:

Rüya was lying facedown on the bed, lost to the sweet warm darkness beneath the billowing folds of the blue-checked quilt.[48]

From the perspective of the grammatical and syntactic norms of standard English, this is clearly a cleaner, more eloquent sentence than Gün's (even though the latter is not, strictly speaking, incorrect). Indeed, in contrast to the latter, its defining qualities are precisely the "fluency" and "transparency" that characterize domesticating translation. As Venuti also says of this approach to translation, its effect is "to bring back a cultural other as the same" by means of language.[49] In this case, the cultural content lost to or domesticated by way of translation is what Azade Seyhan calls in her critique of the Freely rendition "the spirit of Pamuk's idiom."[50] For Freely, this is an acceptable price to pay when weighed against the alternative provided by Gün. As she explains in her "Translator's Afterword" (2006) to her version of the novel, Gün's attempt at what might be regarded as stylistic or idiomatic fidelity results in a text that is "somewhat opaque," one where:

> All too often, the grand, allusive flourishes are lost on readers accustomed to the simpler and more straightforward logic of English. The passive voice becomes cumbersome and even obfuscating. [...] Mesmerizing lists of verbal nouns (the doing of... the seeing of... the having been done unto of) begin to grate on the nerves. The tenses are robbed of their nuances, and the graceful unfolding of cascading clauses becomes an ungainly procession of non sequiturs. The verb that should have been the twist in the tail appears so early it robs the long sentence of its suspense, so that, instead of gaining momentum, each sentence seems to double back on itself. It's not just the meaning that gets muffled, it's the music.[51]

Against Gün's stylistic / idiomatic fidelity, Freely's approach might be described in terms of something like "musical fidelity." It is comprised of a faithfulness to the inner music of the original, one whose challenge is to "reorder the various parts of the sentence in a way that allow[s] it to unfold and reveal its heart."[52] Given that Pamuk minutely oversaw and edited all of Freely's work, this approach and the elegant, well-wrought English that ensued from it appear to be those to which the author himself ultimately gave his sanction.

When judged according to the English-language products that came from them, Gün's and Freely's respective translatorial strategies both have their merits and their flaws. Gün's led to a text whose language more closely resembled that of the original, though at the expense of the now customary clarity and accessibility of English-language literary fiction. Freely's led to one which provided that clarity and access, though at the expense of the deliberate linguistic intricacy of the original. However, these approaches and indeed foreignizing and domesticating translation per se are much more closely aligned with one another than would seem to be the case from the foregoing analysis. They are so in one crucial respect—their shared and constitutive inability to capture the Turkey-specific project of cultural reinscription and revision that Pamuk pursues as much through his use of language in *Kara Kitap* as he does through other narrative and formal means. In the novel, Pamuk—in what is in this case a *linguistic* correlative to Galip's identity quest as the novel's protagonist digs deeper into his and his city's cultural history—increasingly re/turns in his use of language to the very Arabic and Persian loanwords of Ottoman Turkish that had been supplanted by modern Turkish equivalents via the comprehensive program of language reform undertaken during the early years of the Republic.[53] Exhuming these buried and forgotten remnants of Turkish cultural history, he thus layers his text with a subtle commentary on and intervention into the linguistic dimensions of Turkish secular modernity via his use of language. Self-evidently, it is not possible to carry this usage and its broader cultural-historical significance across in translation, no matter the translatorial strategy employed. As I shall expand upon shortly, it is properly *untranslatable*, and in more senses than one.

Gün does, though, give it a go. As Klaus Gommlich and Esim Erdim on the one hand and Sevinç Türkkan on the other detail in their studies of her translation, she does so through a variety of foreignizing mechanisms. Notably, and in addition to her replication of Pamuk's unusual sentence constructs as discussed above, she attempts literal renditions of his idiomatic Turkish expressions (e.g. "You've vacated your face again") and draws on English words rooted in Greek, Latin, and German rather than in Anglo-Saxon as a means of approximating his reference to the Arabic and Persian loanwords of Ottoman Turkish (e.g. "Whenever I cast a restorative gaze on the past, I seem to perceive a throng perambulating in the dark").[54] Along the lines advocated by Venuti, this approach might well be said to upset norms and values encoded in English, the target language. The issue here, though, is that it—like any other approach to translation—cannot by definition articulate the cultural work being carried out in the original *on the source language itself*, the entire point and significance of Pamuk's linguistic experimentation in the first place. For this reason, foreignization—no matter how destabilizing its effects might be in the host culture—seems in the final analysis doomed to domesticate precisely those elements of the source culture that it claims to evoke. In contrast to Gün, and attuned to this as well as other problems inherent to foreignization, Freely abandons any attempt at mirroring Pamuk's use of language in her domesticating approach. Opting instead for a more standardized form of English, she directs her translation towards a clearer illumination of his narrative and thematic material (as complex as this is in itself) than that afforded by her peer's unnatural, obscurantist English. She thus facilitates access to the foreign *content* of his work. Just as foreignization appears to some degree to domesticate, domestication seems in this way to foreignize—or at least to keep-foreign—the source text and the culture whence it came.[55]

As the Pamuk example has demonstrated, there remains in all translation whatever the strategy employed a hard kernel of language—the very foreignness of the foreign tongue in which the original text is written—that resists what it itself necessitates and prompts, the attempt to render the text legible in the language of the target culture. In other words, to draw on the work of Emily Apter, the logic of translation is at its core defined by untranslatability as both its condition of possibility and its necessary, structural limitation. As it is only by way of this logic that a text like *Kara Kitap* can reach beyond its culture of origin and enter into the world (as *The Black Book*), one might well conclude with Apter that it is not only "translation" (as Walkowitz would have it), but also and moreover "untranslatability" that is "constitutive of world forms of literature."[56] To build on this account, if untranslatability (which amounts to the loss of meaning, sense, and connotation attendant on the transfer of a text from one linguistic register to another, and thus of its cultural specificity as embodied in language) mediates the text's given mode of appearance in the world, then it also determines and sets a limit on how it is read—which is to say, *mis*read—in the world. In the case of *The Black Book*, the untranslatability of Pamuk's engagement with the Turkish language has set a significant bar on interpretations of the novel in Anglo-American literary culture, and has thereby contributed to the dissemination of an image of the author and his work that is amenable to that context.

As Apter further develops it in *Against World Literature: On the Politics of Untranslatability* (2013), the notion of untranslatability has a number of other important implications for our understanding of *The Black Book* as well as of Turkish and Middle Eastern literatures more generally in global context. Beyond its immediate function of identifying a feature of language, Apter also uses this concept to refer to the other limitations by which any act or project of translation is necessarily—and increasingly—beset. Namely, what might be considered the "hard" barriers of state sovereignty, ethno-linguistic nationalism, and the military-linguistic checkpoint, and the "soft" barriers of cultural difference and incommensurability.[57] Under this expanded comprehension, untranslatability helps explain why an author like Ahmet Günbay Yıldız—the second highest-selling in contemporary Turkish literature, who writes Islamic salvation novels—has never been translated into English, and why other comparably prominent figures such as Yakup Kadri Karaosmanoğlu, Ahmet Hamdi Tanpınar, Sabahattin Ali, Yusuf Atılgan, and Oğuz Atay only occasionally so. Saliha Paker attributes the scarcity of Turkish to English literary translations—amounting to what Melike Yılmaz Baştuğ estimates is a total of 138 volumes between 1880 and 2004—to a persistent "Orientalist" prejudice that has confined Anglo-American interest in Turkish literature from the Ottoman period to the present to academics and specialists.[58] A similar explanation might be—and indeed has been—put forward for the dearth of literature from the Arabic-Islamic world more broadly in English translation. Discussing this issue, Edward Said suggested in 1994 that "one reason for this odd state of affairs is the longstanding prejudice against Arabs and Islam that remains entrenched in Western, and especially American, culture."[59] The more recent scholarship has only confirmed and reinforced this analysis.[60] What *The Black Book* suggests is that even when a text from this or any other part of the world is translated and thus permitted to pass through the hard and soft borders of state, nation, ethnicity, culture, language, and so forth, it remains in a fundamental way untranslated.

The Mannequin, the Face, the Writer: Cultural Neo-Ottomanism as Form

As noted above, and as mediated by what I have now shown to be the limits of its translation(s), *The Black Book* has generally been read in terms of its purported postmodernism—"the Esperanto of international literary fiction"—in Britain and the United States since its appearance in English.[61] No doubt, the novel employs postmodernist elements, and thus invites such readings. However, Pamuk's postmodernism is directed towards a set of Turkey-specific literary and cultural ends that have gone under the radar of the majority of the Anglo-American scholars, critics, and reviewers I have mentioned. Pamuk's own comments on this genre of fiction and the writers with whom he has most often been compared helps clarify this distinction. As he explains in his famous 2005 interview with *The Paris Review*, "Borges and Calvino liberated [him]" upon his rediscovery of their work in 1985 (the year he embarked on *Kara Kitap*).[62] But they liberated him from a very specific object, from the constraints of a traditional Islamic literary tradition that—"so reactionary, so political, and used by conservatives in such old-fashioned and foolish ways"—he had not previously considered workable material.[63] Guided by these models, he began to distinguish between "the religious and literary connotations of Islamic literature" at that juncture, and thereby to start "appropriat[ing] its wealth of games, gimmicks, and parables."[64] That is to say, the postmodernism Pamuk deploys in *Kara Kitap* is worlds away from the internationalist version that a reviewer like Adam Shatz attributes to him, embedded—as it is—in a more local literary and cultural tradition than has hitherto been assumed. Certainly, there are exceptions to what I have suggested is the rule of the Anglo-American literary establishment's emphasis on *The Black Book*'s playful metafictionality and overall deconstructive drive (I have already referred to Seyhan's and Göknar's excellent readings). This, though, seems to me very much the mainstream of the Anglo-American attitude towards the novel.

To retrieve Pamuk from his worldly appropriation to date and to highlight the actual significance of *The Black Book* in and for world literature, I now pursue a counter-reading of the novel. Building on my earlier thematic, formal, and contextual introduction, I do so through a close reading of what many if not most other critics have in my view either under- or misrepresented—Pamuk's treatment of Turkey's Ottoman and Islamic heritage. Hinging on the narrative and formal as well as thematic role of Sufism and Hurufism therein, this treatment is fleshed out through the imagery of the mannequin, the face, and the writer that saturates and structures the novel, and inscribes in novelistic form a recovery of the repressed other of Turkish secular modernity. It is not only the modern Turkish novel that is inf(l)ected by what amounts to Pamuk's inscription of cultural neo-Ottomanism as form in *The Black Book*, but also the postmodernist novel itself as understood and practiced in the realm of world literature.

The Mannequin

We first encounter the mannequin in Celâl's column of Chapter Six ("Bedii Usta's Children"), where he describes his discovery of "the fearsome secret history of Turkey's mannequins."[65] As Celâl narrates, one day a middle-aged man—evidently enthralled by Celâl's speculations on Turkish cultural history and identity—came "huffing and puffing" to his office at *Milliyet* proclaiming that "the special thing that makes us what we are" was to be found in these "strange and dusty creatures."[66] It is soon revealed that this man is the son of one Bedii Usta, an actual historical figure and the "first undisputed master, the patron saint" of Turkey's mannequins.[67] And so to relate his "secret history," Celâl excavates that of Bedii Usta. Bedii Usta, he finds out, was commissioned by the late-Ottoman Sultan Abdülhamid II to supply models for the Istanbul Naval Museum upon its establishment in 1897. Although Pamuk doesn't really explore the background of this museum in the novel, it should be noted as an instance of the substantial investment made by Ottoman and Republican elites from the late nineteenth to the mid-twentieth centuries in what Benedict Anderson calls "political museumizing."[68] As the Ottoman historian Wendy Shaw explains, this practice is best understood as a response to the steady erosion of the Ottoman Empire's political, territorial, and military reach through the nineteenth century until the end of World War I.[69] Increasingly needing to redefine the sprawling, multi-ethnic, and multi-confessional Ottoman state on the basis of narrower nationalist lines suited to the eventuality of a nation-state in the Anatolian heartland (that is, the nation-state that came to fruition in 1923 as the Republic of Turkey), Ottoman administrators and technocrats of the period such as Osman Hamdi Bey drew inspiration from European ideas of the museum, archaeology, and history. In them and their associated technologies of excavation, collection, organization, and display, these figures would find the means to represent "new communal identities" and stage "developing modes of Ottoman nationalism" in the public sphere.[70] It was to serve this project of publicly codifying, mythifying, and institutionalizing a new national identity that Bedii Usta's talents were first enlisted. Indeed, the mannequins that resulted—his "first marvels"—were of "valiant youths who had sunk so many a Spanish and Italian vessel in the Mediterranean three centuries earlier standing in their full glory among the royal launches and the galleons."[71]

Unfortunately for Bedii Usta, his offerings were so lifelike that, before long, they came up against the Ottoman Sheikh al-Islam's aniconistic prohibition on representations of the human form.[72] "To replicate," Celâl narrates, "God's creations so perfectly was to compete with the Almighty, so the mannequins were swiftly removed from view."[73] Bedii Usta and his mannequins were thus driven underground both literally and figuratively, to a basement atelier in his house in Istanbul's Galata district. There, they soon came to represent for the craftsman—and this is what so intrigues Celâl about them—an embodied authenticity of Turkish gesture, mannerism, and dress that was to be lost to Turkish history in the twentieth century.

"Twenty arduous years later," Celâl continues, "in the great westernizing wave of the early years of the Republic," mannequins began to appear in Istanbul's display windows, and provided consumers eager to throw aside "their fezzes to don panama hats" and discard "their scarves in favour of low-slung heels" with models of European elegance to emulate.[74] It is not just the clothing seductively draped around the mannequins that was being imitated here, though. The very form of the mannequin—considered a cypher of consumerist modernity since at least Walter Benjamin and the nineteenth-century Parisian writers he cites in, among others, Convolutes B, G, and Z of *The Arcades Project*—suggests the importation and replication of European technologies of advertising that objectify the body for consumption and thereby aggravate the ever-increasing artificiality and commodification of social relations during the period.[75]

According to historian Mark Sandberg, the mannequin—as consumer spectacle made flesh—enjoyed a popular high point in Western Europe from 1880 to 1910, when it "proliferated throughout many of the visual-cultural venues of European urban life" and "could be found increasingly in storefront windows, at international exhibitions, and in several interrelated forms of popular museum display."[76] In Istanbul, though, the commercial mannequin only started to appear during the Republican era of the 1920s. As in the Scandinavian contexts that Sandberg primarily addresses, its belatedness there relative to the Western European contexts where it first arose has important consequences for its phenomenology. For rather than manifesting in the modality of the archetypal Parisian display mannequin, as what Jean Baudrillard calls a "second-order simulacrum" (a mass-produced object designed to copy and replace an original), the Istanbul mannequin appears as a "third-order simulacrum"—a copy of a copy, or a copy lacking an original.[77] In other words, while the Parisian mannequin is modelled on and models the fashion-conscious European urbanite, the Istanbul mannequin—modelled only on its already prevalent European counterpart—lacks a point of origin in a concrete (if partially imagined) signified. It thus metonymically figures the wider early Republican culture by way of which it came to prominence. In Benjamin's terms, this was a culture defined by a fundamentally phantasmagoric relation to its European other, one that aspired to a fantastic image of the Occident as generated by the consumer products, fashions, films, books, magazines, schools of thought, and everything else brought into the country by (commercially minded) Kemalists at that time.[78] As one shopkeeper to whom Bedii Usta unsuccessfully tried to sell his wares puts it (per Celâl), the purpose of the mannequins was to sell not dresses, "but dreams," "the dream of becoming 'the others' who'd worn that dress."[79]

If Istanbul's mannequins sought to measure up to their European variants, Bedii Usta's went the opposite direction. They remained faithful to their "original," Bedii Usta's Istanbullu compatriots and their features down to their finest detail—the way they "laughed, wiped [their] noses, walked, looked askance, washed [their] hands, [and] opened bottles."[80] It is unsurprising, then, that they should have been rejected by Istanbul's commercial culture. Per Celâl once more, the mannequins "did not look like the European models to which we were meant to aspire; they looked like us."[81] Despairing of this culture, Bedii Usta consequently "went back to realizing his own dreams, his real dreams, in his own dark atelier," and spent the last fifteen years of his life "giving these terrible homespun images the semblance of flesh and blood, producing more than a hundred and fifty new mannequins, each one a work of art."[82]

Thus buried in the underworld of Bedii Usta's atelier, his mannequins, his works of art come—much like his own column on Bedii Usta and, indeed, *The Black Book* itself—to fulfill for Celâl a revivifying or memorializing function within the wider context of Turkish secular modernity. For it was not just Istanbul's fashions and other features of its material culture that were affected by the vicissitudes of history, but also—as Bedii Usta and his son came to notice—its inhabitants' native modes of bodily self-expression. As the son explains to Celâl, "the gestures our people used in the street began to lose their innocence" due to "those damn films [. . .] brought in from the West canister by canister to play in our theatres for hours on end"—"each and every thing they did," Celâl expands, "was an imitation."[83] In his artistic commitment to the authentic Istanbullu gesture, then, Bedii Usta—whose mannequins thus bring to mind the Brechtian *Gestus*, embodying and holding static as they do the lost truth of their time and place against a profane, postlapsarian backdrop of dis/simulation—was able to preserve something of Istanbul's cultural history for future generations. And upon visiting the atelier and seeing the mannequins for himself, Celâl discovers that the "essence" or "mystery" they harbour is precisely that of his own "true identity."[84] What follows from Celâl is a highly charged elegy to that which had been vanquished by history:

> They were deities mourning their lost innocence, they were ascetics in torment, longing but failing to be someone else, hapless lovers who'd never made love, never shared a bed, who'd ended up killing each other instead. They, like me, like all of us, had, once upon a time, in a past so far away it seemed like heaven, caught by chance a glimpse of an inner essence, only to forget what it was. It was this lost memory that pained us, reduced us to ruins, though we still struggled to be ourselves.[85]

In one of the most striking instances of overlap or entanglement between the "Galip" and "Celâl" strands of the novel, Galip visits the atelier earlier described by Celâl in Chapter Seventeen ("Do You Remember Me?"). A step on the long road of his writerly *Bildung*, this visit—whereby he witnesses and experiences first hand the otherwise mostly abstract content of Celâl's column—indicates Galip's gradual internalization of his cousin's perspectives on Turkish cultural history and foreshadows his later adoption of Celâl's identity and vocation. Thus literalizing the narrative conceit of tracing Celâl's steps, of walking in his shoes, Galip finds just what he had earlier read about, an "underground city" of mannequins that acted as a last refuge of history in amnesiac times.[86] As his guide, Bedii Usta's grandson explains, each incarnation of Istanbul—"Byzantium, Vizant, Nova Roma, Anthusa, Tsargrad, Miklagrad, Constantinople, Cospoli, Istin-Polin"—"had beneath it the underground passages in which the previous civilization had taken refuge," leading to "an extraordinary sort of double city [. . .] with the underground city ultimately wreaking revenge on the overground city that had supplanted it."[87] Suspecting, the guide continues, that "our history could only survive underground," his father and grandfather used the "underground roads strewn with skeletons" surrounding their house to "create citizens who carried their histories, their meanings, on their faces," to "etch meanings onto the faces of [their] mannequins that were no longer to be seen in our streets, our homes, or anywhere in society."[88] And as he absorbs his guide's lecture and gazes on these petrified remnants of history (including a mannequin Celâl already lost to Istanbul's underworld), Galip comes to a momentous, Celâl-esque epiphany about his country, its past, its people, and its anguish—his own—that will turn out to direct the remainder of his trajectory towards selfhood:

> Once upon a time, they had all lived together, and their lives had had meaning, but then, for some unknown reason, they had lost that meaning, just as they'd also lost their memories. Every time they tried to recover that meaning, every time they ventured into that spider-infested labyrinth of memory, they got lost; as they wandered about the blind alleys of their minds, searching in vain for a way back, the key to their new life fell into the bottomless well of their memories; knowing it was lost to them forever, they felt the helpless pain known only by those who have lost their homes, their countries, their past, their history. The pain they felt at being lost and far from home was so intense, and so hard to bear, that their only hope was to stop trying to remember the secret, the lost meaning they'd come here to seek, and, instead, hand themselves over to God, to wait in patient silence for the hour of eternity.[89]

The Face

I now turn to Part Two of the novel to continue tracing Galip's *Bildung* and discovery of vocation with reference to the imagery of the face as anticipated in the passages cited above. Reflecting on his discussions of various Turkish historical figures in his columns, Celâl rhetorically asks his readers early on in Part Two, "Have you seen all these faces? Have you noticed that, in some strange way, they all look alike?"[90] He then announces a new focus for his investigations into Turkish cultural history: "[f]rom now on I shall devote myself utterly to the hidden poetry of our faces, the terrifying secret that lurks inside our human gaze."[91] In the immediately following "Galip" chapter, Chapter Twenty-Four ("Riddles in Faces"), Galip—now living in Celâl's abandoned apartment in Istanbul's Nişantaşi district—takes this cue and starts attempting to decipher the faces in Celâl's vast, thirty-year collection of yearbooks, photograph albums, and newspaper clippings. Although unsuccessful at first, he soon finds the guidance he needs in Celâl's archive, specifically in his cousin's "books, treatises, and clippings on Hurufism."[92] This is because Hurufism, an obscure Sufi sect whose central doctrine of "the mystery of letters" Galip had earlier encountered in passing, promises significant new insight into "the meanings in faces."[93]

As Galip learns, the Hurufi sect was founded by one Fazlallah of Astarabad (or Fażlu l-Lāh Astar-Ābādī), a fourteenth century Persian mystic. After a late-adolescent spiritual awakening instigated by a nomadic dervish's recitation of Rumi, Fazlallah abandoned his duties as a judge, his family, and his hometown to follow the Sufi path as an itinerant religious seeker. He made Haj to Mecca twice before temporarily settling in Isfahan in central Iran, and during his travels he experienced a series of richly symbolic and prophetic dreams about figures like Solomon, Jesus, and Muhammad. In one of these dreams—which Pamuk makes sure to mention—he was visited by a dervish who later actually appears, claiming that he had dreamt of Fazlallah too. During the actual visit, Fazlallah and the dervish sat together leafing through a book and "saw their faces in the letters," then, on looking up, "saw the letters of the book in each other's faces."[94] Proclaiming himself a prophet, a messiah, Fazlallah accumulated a following of seven disciples in Isfahan, and set out to preach that—in Pamuk's words—"the world [...] was awash with secrets and that the only way to penetrate these secrets was to penetrate the mystery of the letters."[95]

For Fazlallah, as the historian of Islam H. T. Norris explains, "the key to open the seven[th] sealed book, the Koran, is a cabalistic system of letters that is expounded, by him, or by others, in the *Hidāyat-nāma*, the *Jāwidān*, and in the *Mahram-nāma*"—the canonical texts of the Hurufi tradition.[96] The face of Allah—immutable, imperishable—is, Norris continues, manifest in man, "the best of forms—*zuhūr kibriyā*," and is exactly replicated in the face of Adam.[97] Further, the twenty-eight letters of the Arabic alphabet (the language revealed to Muhammad) and the thirty-two letters of the Persian alphabet (that revealed to Fazlallah, thus requiring him to account for four extra letters) are hidden in the face of man. Our two brow lines, four eyelash lines, and one hairline make up seven letters which are then doubled at the onset of puberty, when—in Pamuk's gloss—our "late-arriving" nose divides the face in two.[98] Taking into consideration several other "real and imaginary lines," this number is doubled once more, providing for the twenty-eight letters which correspond exactly and not coincidentally to Muhammad's twenty-eight Arabic letters as well as to the number of Allah's attributes as revealed in the Qur'ān. Thus divine truth—or Allah—can, in a sort of hyper-literalization of Emmanuel Levinas, be witnessed through the proper, esoteric interpretation of the letters in the face. For Fazlallah, the divine light shines through the face of man in the form of letters, and this comprises their mystery.[99]

As one might expect given his worship of "letters, people, and idols instead of God" as well as his self-identification as the new Messiah, Fazlallah was imprisoned, sentenced, and executed for heresy at the behest of the Miran Shah in Alinja—a town in what is now Azerbaijan—circa 1394 / 1395.[100] Under the new leadership of the poet Nesimi (or Alī 'Imādu d-Dīn Nasīmī), his increasingly persecuted followers emigrated to the momentarily less hostile climate of Anatolia, where their ideas took root and began to spread throughout the villages and towns of the Ottoman heartland. Their most significant influence was on the Bektaşi Order, a Shi'a Alevi Sufi order founded in the thirteenth century. Already widespread in

Anatolia and the Balkans, this sect continued to prosper among Ottoman elites and peasantry alike until it was banned by Sultan Mahmud II in 1826 due to the objections of Sunni and more orthodox Sufi religious leaders. Although the Bektaşis enjoyed a brief public and popular resurgence during the Ottoman Empire's Tanzimat period in the mid-nineteenth century, they—like the Hurufis and the larger and more prestigious Nakşibendi and Mevlevi orders—were dealt a final blow soon after the founding of the Republic of Turkey in 1923. After an initial attempt to incorporate the Sufi orders into the Republic by placing them under the administration of the newly established Ministry of Religious Affairs (which ensured their continued social and legal status while stripping them of genuine political participation—a form of laicism), the Kemalists—taken aback by the Sheikh Said rebellion of February 1925—were forced to take more drastic measures and formally abolished the orders later in the same year. The Sufi orders were thus driven underground, where for much of the twentieth century many maintained a sizeable following and continued to operate in a "public secret" fashion. Recently, they have begun to experience something of a resurgence of public presence under the revivalist or accommodationist policies of President Recep Tayyip Erdoğan and his Justice and Development Party (Adalet ve Kalkınma Partisi).[101]

To round off his readings of Celâl's materials on the Hurufis, Galip comes across the Üçüncü treatise on *The Mystery of the Letters* that I mentioned above. In it, Üçüncü—to expand on my earlier note on this text—provides an account of Fazlallah and goes on to describe how "the world was divided into two opposing halves."[102] "[T]he East and the West," he declares, "were as different from each other as good and evil, white and black, the angels and the devils."[103] As substantiated by great historical events such as Alexander's cutting of the Gordian knot, the Crusades, Hannibal's passage across the Alps, the Islamic conquest of al-Andalus, and Mehmet the Conqueror's triumphant entry into Constantinople, "the winning side" in any historical period "was the one that succeeded in seeing the world as a mysterious place awash with secret and double meanings."[104] Given that Hurufism—which provided the means of entry into that mystery—had "vanished from the earth" at the onset of Turkey's Republican era, "the world had lost its mystery, just as our faces had lost their letters."[105] Üçüncü thus calls for a revival of Hurufism in Turkey so as to redress the woeful historical defeat of the East:

> [I]t was on Turkish soil that the Messiah who would become the saviour of all the East would make His appearance, and it therefore followed that, in preparation for that day, if they were to recover the lost mystery, His future followers should begin by establishing correspondences between faces and the new Latin alphabet that Turkey adopted in 1928.[106]

After the twenty-eight Arabic letters of the Qur'ān had been modified by Fazlallah to suit the needs of his 32-lettered Persian alphabet, this further adjustment of "the mystery of the letters" for the twenty-six letters of the post-language reform Latinate Turkish alphabet as required for a modern Turkish Hurufism seems—to put it mildly—a *reductio ad absurdum* on the author's part.

The Writer

Üçüncü's reading of Turkish secular modernity leads him to demand what is in effect an Islamic revolution based on the revival of Hurufi mystery—a form of what I have called political neo-Ottomanism. On the other hand, Galip's reading of the history and theories of Hurufism provides him with the hermeneutical apparatus necessary for deciphering "the letters in his face," and thus his own hitherto repressed cultural identity.[107] This development is simultaneous with and comprises the foundation of his discovery of writing as vocation. It is upon seeing "his face" as "a sheet of paper covered in writing, an inscription riddled with secret signs" that he, for the first time, "wrote."[108] Channelling Celâl, he writes the first of a series of columns which is then published in *Milliyet* under his cousin's name, and which continues and expands Celâl's project (this column is reproduced verbatim in the following chapter of the novel). He begins the column with the words, "I gazed into the mirror and read my face."[109] This opening marks Galip's adoption of Hurufism not just as a means of reading his identity, but also—as with Pamuk—as a content to be inscribed in the form of writing (as opposed to that of direct political engagement). This content and the entirety of the Ottoman, Islamic heritage that it metonymizes is thus culturally revived or memorialized within the amnesiac context of Turkish secular modernity. Thus coterminous with *The Black Book* itself, Galip's act of writing—in both the material it contains and the sublation it performs between the "Galip" and "Celâl" strands of the novel—signifies what I have designated as Pamuk's inscription of cultural neo-Ottomanism as form.

* * *

In *The Black Book*, Pamuk's cultural neo-Ottomanism amounts to an inf(l)-ection of novelistic form from the standpoint of the repressed other of Turkish secular modernity. As a framework for understanding not just this novel, but also—by extension—his lifelong writerly project, it more faithfully encompasses Pamuk's reflexive literary negotiation of the dialectics of modernity, religion, and secularism in Turkey than the majority of other interpretive models put forward in the global literary establishment. It identifies precisely the nature and extent of Pamuk's contribution to the Turkish novel per se. Firmly situated within the secular field of Republican literature, the Turkish novel has—as critics such as Seyhan, Göknar, and others have underlined—been implicitly or explicitly premised on and complicit with the defining ideologies of the Republican state for much of the twentieth century.[110] It is these ideologies; their long-term political, social, and cultural consequences; and their literary—especially novelistic—incarnations that Pamuk is addressing, challenging, and to some extent overturning via his cultural neo-Ottomanism. Furthermore, he is also adapting the postmodernist techniques and devices of the global writers with whom he has most often been compared for a specifically Turkish cultural-historical endeavor through it. Properly untranslatable and unreadable beyond his culture of origin, Pamuk's cultural neo-Ottomanism is what cannot—but also what by the same token *must*—be recognized as his contribution to world literature.

Pamuk, the Islamic Revival, and the Postsecularism / Secularism Debate

Beyond its many literary implications both in Turkey itself and further afield, Pamuk's cultural neo-Ottomanism also teaches us a valuable lesson as we continue to grapple with the phenomenon of the Islamic Revival in the Middle East as well as the postsecularism / secularism debate that it has in no small measure spurred, or at least accented. Broadly, the term "Islamic Revival" (in Arabic, "*tajdīd*") is a collective designation for the range of Islamic political, social, and cultural movements that have newly come to prominence across the region—most dramatically, in Iran, Afghanistan, Pakistan, Palestine, Lebanon, Egypt, and the Islamic State in addition to Erdoğan's Turkey—since the 1970s. It also refers to the associated rise of public, institutionalized expressions and other forms of faith among Muslim communities in other parts of the world—notably Western Europe and North America—in the same period. The Revival has generally been interpreted as a backlash against the (perceived) failure of the modern, secular Middle Eastern nation-state to deliver on its promises of emancipation, inclusivity, and growth, as brought to a head in the Arab defeat at the Six-Day War of 1967 and the subsequent collapse of pan-Arabism as a unifying regional ideology. In its various manifestations and in a number of different ways, it has called—in many cases successfully—for a return to some sort of authentic Islamic tradition and identity as the basis of national and regional life against the degradations imposed by westernization, neoliberalism, and authoritarianism.

It is in response to the Revival and the wider global trend of religious resurgence—which pertains to the other major faiths too, monotheistic and otherwise—of which it has been seen as a part that the notion of a "postsecular" society, age, or time was forwarded and the relevant theoretical, historiographical, and political recalibrations ventured. Jürgen Habermas is often credited with coining or at least popularizing the term in an article entitled "Notes on Post-Secular Society," first published in *New Perspectives Quarterly* in 2008. Indeed, it entered into the mainstream of the humanities and social sciences lexicon at around that time. However, we find the most fully fledged and rigorous articulation of the postsecular quite a bit earlier, in Talal Asad's writings on the genealogical origins of the modern secularism / religiosity binary stretching back to the early 1990s and culminating in his book *Formations of the Secular: Christianity, Islam, Modernity* (2003). In this body of work, Asad established precisely the interpretive framework on which many of the later and more familiar approaches have implicitly or explicitly relied.

To put it crudely, Asad's major intervention was to dismiss the idea that secularism is merely the separation of religion from politics. Instead, he posits "the secular" and "the religious" as mutually imbricated categories that were constituted alongside one another within what he calls the "project" of modernity and its most complete realization, the modern nation-state.[111] That is to say, as modernity—via the nation-state—institutionalized the principles of "constitutionalism, moral autonomy, democracy, human rights, civil equality, industry, consumerism, freedom of the market[,] and secularism," it contrived the very distinction between secularism and religiosity that it and its ideologues then projected as one of its *conditions* rather than *by-products*.[112] The imperative to secularize at the heart of modernization in both theory and practice is, in turn, derived from this genealogy. Under this reading, the postsecular—which Asad describes in terms of the "resurgence of religion"—can be interpreted as a function of the unresolved antagonisms of modernity, as the return of that which the modern world had cast as other, inferior, and inadequate to itself.[113]

It seems to me that this is very much the general theoretical and historical outlook on which Habermas's observations about postsecular society are based. When he calls for "mutual recognition" and "shared citizenship" between those in or who identify with the "secular" and "religious" camps of this society, he does so with an eye towards fostering "civil" social relations in the context of the "firmly entrenched nation state[. . .]" and its increasingly apparent "plurality of cultures and religious worldviews."[114] Likewise, Charles Taylor—in his equally influential book *A Secular Age* (2007)—conceives of the postsecular "age" or "time" (as pertaining primarily to the North Atlantic world) as one in which "the hegemony of the mainstream master narrative of secularization will be more and more challenged," and where "many forms of belief and unbelief jostle [. . .] and hence fragilize each other."[115] For modern democracy to maintain its "cohesion" under such conditions of plurality, he continues, its faith and non-faith communities alike must subscribe and commit themselves to what he capitalizes as its "Modern Moral Order" (its political ethic, democratic and inclusive ideals, concern with human rights, and so on).[116] Regarding Islam and its Revival in particular, Joseph Massad directly takes his cue from Asad in his book *Islam in Liberalism* (2015), the most comprehensive thus far attempted on this topic. Reframing secularism in the terms of European, Enlightenment liberalism, he—citing Asad—argues that "the liberal mission is to have the Islamic tradition 'remade in the image of liberal Protestant Christianity'" and its values of "freedom, liberty, equality, the right-bearing individual, democratic citizenship, women's rights, sexual rights, freedom of belief, secularism, [and] rationality."[117] The Revival, then, is to be understood as in part a rejection of the imperial assumptions and Orientalist prejudices behind secularism-as-liberalism's construct of Islam as its non-modern—which is to say, non-European—other.

As both a theoretical model and a purported description of the contemporary world, the postsecular and what Aamir Mufti sees as its "growing influence [. . .] across the humanistic disciplines" have faced a mounting challenge from especially avowed or self-described secular critics of the Saidian variety.[118] In an important special issue of *boundary 2* on "Antinomies of the Postsecular" (2013), Mufti compiled a range of responses from such critics, including Melinda Cooper, Stathis Gourgouris, Bruce Robbins, Vassilis Lambropoulos, and others as well as himself. I focus here on Mufti's own intervention, as I find this to be the most penetrating and certainly the most relevant of these. His critique of the postsecular comes down to three main points. First, the "internal[. . .] incohern[ce]" of the concept.[119] "Does the *post* in *postsecular*," Mufti rhetorically asks, "mark a transition in the world at large, in intellectual practices concerned with understanding the world, or some combination of both?"[120] Second, its implied political affiliation with or even support for the processes it claims to objectively assess. Mufti indicts what he calls "the new ethnography of Islam" in general and Saba Mahmood's work in particular for their "*active* agreement with Islamism itself"—by which he means contemporary political Islam—"when the latter thinks of itself in revivalist terms as a return to the true tradition of Islam."[121] And third, its obfuscation of the historical conditions of colonialism and imperialism by which the sociopolitical role and very definition of "religion"—with Islam again serving as Mufti's primary example—were reconfigured in the non-Western world. Scholars such as Mahmood (to whom one might add Massad) foreclose "the dialectical perception that revivalist claims of religious authenticity are undeniable products of the very cultural logics"— those of colonial modernity—"they disavow and disown."[122] All this leads Mufti to reaffirm his commitment to Saidian secular criticism, as developed over the course of his career.[123]

Pamuk's cultural neo-Ottomanism in *The Black Book* and elsewhere suggests a fruitful mediation between what I have outlined as the postsecularist and secularist positions. Situated on the broadly postsecularist side of the equation, it does so by reframing what has thus far been a *politically* oriented debate on the grounds of *culture*. Anticipating and pre-empting Mufti's as well as other qualms, it works through and just as vigorously rejects the *political* claims of Islamic Revivalism (as dramatized in Part Two of *The Black Book*), while fully acknowledging and forging a coherent *cultural* response to the historical conditions—namely, Kemalism as its variant of "colonial" modernity—by which Islam and all of the other features of the Ottoman past were eclipsed in Turkey. And as form, it not only stakes out, but also puts into practice and enacts in national culture a postsecularism that compellingly and in my view definitively answers the questions posed by postsecularism's naysayers. Would that Turkey's and the Middle East's politicians read *The Black Book* and take up the lesson it carries for us all!

Notes

1. Shatz, "Wanting to Be Something Else," p. 15.
2. For the interview in which Pamuk made these comments, see Teuwsen, "Der meistgehasste Türke."
3. Walkowitz, *Born Translated*, p. 4. Emphasis in original removed.
4. Ibid. p. 16.
5. Ibid. p. 17.
6. As per the epigraphs above, Apter introduces the notion of the "untranslatable" in her book *The Translation Zone: A New Comparative Literature* (2006). For the epigraphs, see Apter, *The Translation Zone*, pp. xii, xi. However, when I return to this topic later in the chapter, I draw principally on her more detailed later work on it.

7. See pp. 136–46 and 158–9 in the present volume.
8. Tanpınar was a mid-twentieth-century Turkish novelist whose literary reflections on the cultural losses wrought by enforced modernization and secularization in Turkey were a pivotal influence on Pamuk and his writing. He is particularly noted for *A Mind at Peace* (*Huzur*, 1949; trans. 2008) and *The Time Regulation Institute* (*Saatleri Ayarlama Enstitüsü*, 1961; trans. 2013). For Pamuk on Tanpınar's influence, see Pamuk, *Istanbul*, pp. 97–104, 221–38.
9. Andrews, "The Black Book and Black Boxes," p. 105; Almond, "Islam, Melancholy, and Sad, Concrete Minarets," p. 77; Parrinder, "Mannequin-Maker," p. 22; Marx, "Two worlds," Innes, "Istanbul Expressed," p. 247.
10. Pamuk, *The Black Book* (2006), p. 50. Beyond *The Black Book*, Pamuk returns to and similarly plays with the detective novel genre in *The New Life*, *My Name is Red*, and *The Red-Haired Woman*, all of whose plots revolve around an unsolved (and potentially unsolvable) murder.
11. Pamuk, *The Black Book* (2006), p. 225.
12. Ibid. p. 216.
13. Ibid. p. 218.
14. Ibid. p. 223.
15. In making this distinction, I am quite aware that "*Künstlerroman*" is as much a Western aesthetic category as "postmodernism." However, my use of this term vis-à-vis *The Black Book* does not carry with it the domesticating implications that I am arguing "postmodernism" carries. Under the "postmodernism" label, the novel abandons such archaic concepts as stable identity, historical truth, and religious truth in favor of an endless play of indeterminate and free-floating signifiers, and is forced into place as an example of a global aesthetic suited for European and American cultural terrains. Its deeper engagement with Turkish culture and history is thus largely—and ironically—forgotten. Under the "*Künstlerroman*" label, this engagement is by necessity brought to the fore—it is precisely by assessing Galip's growth into a writer that Pamuk's take on the cultural losses brought about by Kemalism and his unique resolution to the conflicts and contradictions of Turkish modernity might be gleaned. "*Künstlerroman*," then, is not only a more accurate description of *The Black Book*, but also provides criticism with a lens through which the thematic and formal content lost to the "postmodernism" category and those who employ it might be retrieved.
16. Seyhan, *Tales of Crossed Destinies*, p. 150.
17. Ibid. p. 151.

18. Kim, "Mürşid ile Mürid," p. 235; Brendemoen, "Orhan Pamuk and his 'Black Book.'"
19. Pamuk, *The Black Book* (2006), p. 461.
20. Göknar, *Orhan Pamuk, Secularism and Blasphemy*, p. 219.
21. To my knowledge, there has been no extended critical work on Pamuk and Benjamin. A Benjaminian reading of *The Black Book* and indeed of Pamuk's entire oeuvre would be fascinating, as would a comparative analysis of any of their shared predilections (which range from urban modernity, urban archaeology, architecture, and history to melancholy, the aesthetics of perception, the fragment, the refuse / detritus of civilization, Proust, translation, libraries, and messianism). Pamuk himself invites this comparison in his "Preface" to his collection of essays *Other Colours* (*Öteki Renkler*, 1999; trans. 2007). There, after stating his admiration for Benjamin ("I am hardly alone in being a great admirer of the German writer-philosopher Walter Benjamin"), he goes on to suggest that like *The Arcades Project* (1972; trans. 1999), *Other Colours* is also "a book made only from fragments." Pamuk, *Other Colours*, pp. x, xi.
22. Pamuk, *The Black Book* (2006), p. 64.
23. Pamuk, *Istanbul*, p. 6.
24. Ibid. p. 81.
25. Ibid. p. 81.
26. Ibid. p. 81.
27. Ibid. pp. 82, 83.
28. Pamuk, *The Black Book* (2006), p. 16.
29. For a useful historical overview of this troubled period, see Zürcher, *Turkey*, pp. 241–77.
30. See pp. 136–46 in the present volume for an overview of the relevant historical background.
31. See Pamuk, *The Black Book* (2006), pp. 302–6.
32. Ibid. pp. 331, 381.
33. Ibid. p. 382.
34. Ibid. p. 387.
35. For an overview of this period, see Zürcher, *Turkey*, pp. 278–91.
36. Gürbilek, *The New Cultural Climate in Turkey*, p. 78.
37. Ibid. p. 9.
38. Özyürek, "Introduction," p. 2.
39. Ibid. p. 3.

40. See ibid. p. 1.
41. Orhan Pamuk, *Kara Kitap*, p. 11.
42. Freely, "A Translator's Tale," p. 31.
43. Pamuk, *Other Colours*, p. 138.
44. Pamuk, *The Black Book* (1994), p. 3.
45. Venuti, *The Translator's Invisibility*, p. 18.
46. Ibid. p. 23.
47. Ibid. p. 1.
48. Pamuk, *The Black Book* (2006), p. 3.
49. Venuti, *The Translator's Invisibility*, p. 18.
50. Seyhan, *Tales of Crossed Destinies*, p. 213.
51. Freely, "Translator's Afterword," p. 464.
52. Ibid. p. 464.
53. See pp. 144–6 in the present volume for an overview of the language reform.
54. Pamuk, *The Black Book* (1994), pp. 49, 161. These examples are borrowed from the studies mentioned above. See Gommlich and Erdim, "Evolving Imagery in the Translation of Orhan Pamuk's *Kara Kitap*," p. 242 and Servinc Turkkhan, "Orhan Pamuk's *Kara Kitap*," p. 53 (NB "Servinc Turkkhan" is a misspelling of "Sevinç Türkkan" on the part of the journal).
55. Along these lines, Maria Tymoczko has provided the most thoroughgoing critique of Venuti's conceptual apparatus. In what is in effect a generalization of the above, she suggests that domestication / foreignization is in fact a false dichotomy, and that the "ambiguity and inconsistency" inherent to any act of translation renders "polarities such as *literal* and *free*, or *formal equivalence* and *dynamic equivalence*, or *domesticating* and *foreignizing*, or *fluent* and *resistant*" both formally and functionally incoherent when we try to apply them. Tymoczko, *Translation in a Postcolonial Context*, p. 56. Emphasis in original. See also ibid. pp. 41–61.
56. Apter, *Against World Literature*, p. 16.
57. See ibid. pp. 2–4, *passim*.
58. Paker, "Turkish," p. 619. Culminating in the figure cited above, Baştuğ provides a useful decade-by-decade breakdown of this translation history. See Baştuğ, *A Translational Journey*: pp. 10–46.
59. Said, "Embargoed Literature," p. 98.
60. For book-length studies of Arabic to English translation, both of which generally conform to Said's view, see Altoma, *Modern Arabic Literature in Translation* and Faiq (ed.), *Cultural Encounters in Translation from Arabic*.

61. As might be expected, the initial response to the novel in Turkey itself was more politicized. As Pamuk recounts in an interview with *Publishers Weekly* conducted upon its first English translation, it was subject to "huge media attacks" from those on both the religious right (who claimed that it mocked the Sufi material it references) and the secularist left (who thought that it undermined the legacy of Kemalism). Stone, "Orhan Pamuk," p. 36. For a range of early scholarly readings in Turkey, see Esen (ed.), *Kara Kitap Üzerine Yazılar* (1992) and Esen (ed.), *Kara Kitap Üzerine Yazılar* (1996).
62. Gurría-Quintana, "Orhan Pamuk, The Art of Fiction No. 187," p. 130. The epigraph above is from this interview. For the epigraph, see ibid. p. 132.
63. Ibid. p. 130.
64. Ibid. p. 130.
65. Pamuk, *The Black Book* (2006), p. 59.
66. Ibid. pp. 59, 61.
67. Ibid. p. 59.
68. Anderson, *Imagined Communities*, p. 183. Pamuk has, of course, substantially engaged with the idea of the museum in Turkey elsewhere. His novel *The Museum of Innocence* and actual "The Museum of Innocence" (whose collections are comprised of the everyday objects and artifacts that fill the pages of the novel) both suggest a unique, individualized slant on this highly visible feature of Istanbul's cultural topography, and might be read as anti-museums positioned against those of the nation and its official history.
69. By 1918, the Empire's former territories in the Balkans, North Africa, and the Levant had been almost entirely lost to European imperial powers or independently liberated.
70. Shaw, *Possessors and Possessed*, p. 18. For the relevant historical background, see ibid. pp. 1–30.
71. Pamuk, *The Black Book* (2006), p. 60.
72. Unnamed in the novel, the Ottoman Empire's Sheikh al-Islam at the time that Bedii Usta was active was Mehmet Cemaleddin Efendi.
73. Pamuk, *The Black Book* (2006), p. 60. Pamuk deals extensively with the aesthetic dimensions of representation under Islamic law in *My Name is Red*.
74. Ibid. p. 60.
75. See especially his "Convolute Z," in Benjamin, *The Arcades Project*, pp. 693–7.
76. Sandberg, *Living Pictures, Missing Persons*, p. 4.

77. For his main presentation of these concepts, see Baudrillard, *Simulacra and Simulation*, pp. 1–42.
78. For Benjamin on phantasmagoria, see pp. 38–9 in the present volume.
79. Pamuk, *The Black Book* (2006), p. 61.
80. Ibid. p. 63.
81. Ibid. p. 61.
82. Ibid. p. 61.
83. Ibid. p. 63.
84. Ibid. p. 64.
85. Ibid. p. 64.
86. Ibid. p. 189.
87. Ibid. p. 191.
88. Ibid. p. 191.
89. Ibid. p. 194.
90. Ibid. p. 269.
91. Ibid. p. 269.
92. Ibid. pp. 293, 294.
93. Ibid. p. 293.
94. Ibid. p. 297.
95. Ibid. p. 298. For more detail on the life of Fazlallah, see Bashir, *Fazlallah Astarabadi and the Hurufis*, pp. 1–44.
96. Norris, "The Ḥurūfi Legacy of Faḍlullāh of Astarābad," p. 92.
97. Ibid. p. 92.
98. Pamuk, *The Black Book* (2006), p. 297.
99. For more detail on Hurufi doctrine as pertaining to the mystery of the letters, see Bashir, *Fazlallah Astarabadi and the Hurufis*, pp. 61–84.
100. Pamuk, *The Black Book* (2006), p. 298.
101. For more detail on Sufism and the Sufi orders in Turkey in the twentieth century, see Yükleyen, "Sufism and Islamic groups in Contemporary Turkey" and Silverstein, "Sufism and Modernity in Turkey."
102. Pamuk, *The Black Book* (2006), pp. 303–4.
103. Ibid. p. 304.
104. Ibid. p. 304.
105. Ibid. p. 305.
106. Ibid. p. 317.
107. Ibid. p. 321.
108. Ibid. pp. 322, 325.

109. Ibid. pp. 326, 334. Emphasis in original removed.
110. While making this point, these critics have also posited a counter-tradition of sorts that is signposted by earlier twentieth-century novelists such as Halide Edib and Ahmet Hamdi Tanpınar. For both, this counter-tradition culminates with Pamuk. See Seyhan, *Tales of Crossed Destinies* and Göknar, *Orhan Pamuk, Secularism and Blasphemy*.
111. Asad, *Formations of the Secular*, pp. 14, 13. Emphasis in original removed.
112. Ibid. p. 13.
113. Ibid. p. 1.
114. Habermas, "Notes on Post-Secular Society," p. 29, 21.
115. Taylor, *A Secular Age*, pp. 534, 531.
116. Ibid. p. 532.
117. Massad, *Islam in Liberalism*, p. 3.
118. Mufti, "Introduction," p. 1.
119. Mufti, "Why I Am Not a Postsecularist," p. 9.
120. Ibid. p. 9. Emphasis in original. As I do not return to this point below, I will devote a few words to it here. Basically, the concept does not seem to me incoherent in the way that Mufti is suggesting it is. Asad, for instance, opens *Formations of the Secular* by clearly and unambiguously identifying the "resurgence of religion" as an increasingly prominent feature of the contemporary world. As this resurgence casts doubt on the long-held tenet in modernization theory that modernity leads to secularism, a transition—in Mufti's terms—in intellectual practices becomes necessary, which Asad proceeds to provide via his genealogical account of the emergence of the categories of "the secular" and "the religious" in modernity. In other words, the "post" in "postsecular" marks a *specific* combination of worldly and intellectual change, wherein the former has demanded and prompted the latter.
121. Ibid. p. 12. Emphasis in original.
122. Ibid. p. 12.
123. See ibid. pp. 17–19.

5

Women in the Literary Marketplace: The Anglophone Iranian Novel and the Feminist Subject

[...] English will certainly take its place in history as the world's *first* genuinely global language.
                David Crystal, "Diversity? We ain't seen nothing yet!"

What seems to me to be happening is that those peoples who were once colonized by the language are now rapidly remaking it, domesticating it, becoming more and more relaxed about the way they use it—assisted by the English language's enormous flexibility and size, they are carving out large territories for themselves within its frontiers.
                Salman Rushdie, *Imaginary Homelands*

In the last several decades, the anglophone Arab or Middle Eastern novel has emerged as its own distinct branch of multicultural writing in Britain and the United States, alongside other comparably "cosmopolitan" or "exotic" variants of this literary trend. Since the 1980s, English-language literary fiction by immigrant, exilic, second- or third-generation, mixed heritage, or otherwise diasporic writers of Arab or other Middle Eastern descent and now living in these countries has been steadily on the rise in terms of its quantity, commercial success, popular and critical appreciation, recognition in international award culture, presence in school and university curricula, and so forth. The most prominent of the authors associated with this trend include: Leila Aboulela, Diana Abu-Jaber, Susan

Abulhawa, Etel Adnan, Rabih Alameddine, Anita Amirrezvani, Nadeem Aslam, Fadia Faqir, Nuruddin Farah, Rawi Hage, Laila Halaby, Mohsin Hamid, Mohammed Hanif, Khaled Hosseini, Randa Jarrar, Porochista Khakpour, Hanif Kureishi, Laila Lalami, Hisham Matar, Claire Messud, Farnoosh Moshiri, Elif Shafak, Kamila Shamsie, Dalia Sofer, and Ahdaf Soueif, among others.

In itself, what I will broadly refer to as the genre of the "anglophone Middle Eastern novel" might be and indeed has been traced back to the early twentieth century and the pioneering writings of especially Ameen Rihani and Khalil Gibran (both of whom were Lebanese-American).[1] However, it was only from the 1980s that it really came into its own in the sorts of ways mentioned above. This is due to the same political, social, and cultural developments as those discussed in the Introduction to explain the rise of the Middle Eastern novel in general to worldly prominence at the time, as well as other influences specific to the case.[2] These include: the increasing rate of immigration from the Middle East to Britain and America from the 1960s (not least on the back of the region's various conflicts and crises); the education of second- and third-generation immigrants in those countries; their corresponding attunement to English as a literary language; their (literary) coming of age from the 1980s; and, most pivotally, the massive upsurge of public, media, and thus commercial interest in Middle East-themed literary fiction there in the wake of 9/11 and the "War on Terror."[3] Having accumulated something like a critical mass on the basis of these and other contributing factors, the anglophone Middle Eastern novel today is to be considered a key site of and mechanism for the discursive and representational worlding of the region.

Thus far, the majority of scholarly attention in this area has fallen on the anglophone *Arab* novel. Major monographs have been written and edited collections produced on this topic by Layla Al Maleh, Waïl Hassan, Nouri Gana, Carol Fadda-Conrey, and Steven Salaita, among others.[4] In this chapter, I focus on the anglophone *Iranian* novel as an important but often neglected strand of the larger tapestry of the anglophone Middle Eastern novel. I do so in light of the "comparative Middle East" framework that I have set out in this book, in an analysis that might—as suggested by the list of writers I have provided above—be extended to anglophone

Turkish, Somali, Afghanistani, Pakistani, and other literary fiction as well. That is to say, I read the anglophone Iranian novel as a specifically diasporic Iranian literary response to and engagement with Iran's iteration of the Middle Eastern modernity whose wider trajectory I have outlined. As such, it might be productively addressed alongside anglophone novels that are rooted in and take their bearings from other parts of the region, given their comparable and apparently ubiquitous narrative emphasis on the modern histories of the countries from which they and their authors originated. Along these lines, the anglophone Middle Eastern novel per se might be defined according to its commitment to the region's modern history and its portrayal in international context.

Specifically, my interest here is in the English language as a medium for the worlding of Iran. In addition to the role of English as today's predominant global language and de facto common denominator of global literary fiction (as suggested by the epigraphs above), it is also important to take into account in an analysis such as mine its more localized resonances when it comes to questions of Iran and its representation.[5] It is not only that Britain and America were the major destinations for Iranians who chose or were forced to flee the country after the Iranian Revolution of 1979 and the subsequent installation of a radical Islamic theocracy there, and that much if not most of the diasporic fiction (as well as other literature) that has been written since then has been in English. Also, the geopolitical tensions between these two countries and Iran have been especially pronounced throughout this period, as most spectacularly manifest in the Iran hostage crisis of 1979 to 1981 through to the as-yet-unresolved diplomatic stand-off regarding Iran's purported nuclear weapons program. In turn, a pervasive sense of antagonism has come to infuse political and media discourses and representations of Iran in the English-speaking world (and "the West" more generally), with a number of significant consequences for the anglophone Iranian novel in the political and material contexts of its production, circulation, and reception. Crucially, as I elaborate below, what might be conceived of as the anglo-Iranian imaginary (the combined political, media, and literary language of Iran in the English-speaking world) has been saturated with questions and concerns about gender—especially women's rights—in Iran throughout this period. Given all of the above, the anglophone Iranian novel seems to me a particularly valuable case study for the possibilities afforded and limitations imposed by the model of "global anglophone literature"—which amounts to the English studies version of "world literature"—as this has come to the fore within the disciplinary nexus of English in recent years.

In a recent article, Nasia Anam has sought to provide some background on this relatively new notion of the "global anglophone." Looking into statistical data on academic hiring patterns and scholarly trends gleaned from sources such as the Modern Language Association and WorldCat, she argues that the term—which can now be seen to have near-universally supplanted "postcolonial" in new US English department job searches in non-British or American literatures—"does not come from scholarship" (it has only very rarely been used in the titles of published articles and monographs over the last decade).[6] On this basis, she goes on to suggest that its continued deployment among scholars and departments alike is therefore nothing but "capitulation" to "the neoliberal [. . .] market forces" that prompted its rise to institutional prominence, and that against it, our task is to restore postcolonialism and its critical project of "resist[ing] hegemony."[7]

While I do not necessarily disagree with Anam's conclusions, I find her reading of "global anglophone" deeply flawed. It entirely neglects the two decades'-worth of serious disciplinary conversations about what a *PMLA* "Special Topic" from 2001 has as "Globalizing Literary Studies," which I see as having very much laid the groundwork for the "global anglophone" formulation itself as well as its eventual consecration. Edited by Giles Gunn, and featuring contributions by Paul Jay, Stephen Greenblatt, Edward Said, Rey Chow, and others, that *PMLA* issue was itself a milestone not only in conceptualizing the relationship between "globalization" and "literature," but also—as Gunn writes—in thinking through "how best to engage it critically."[8] In his entry, Jay focuses on the "globalizing" of English studies in particular. Positing the "globalization of English"—the language itself as well as the literatures produced in it—as "a simple fact of contemporary history," he calls for "a transnational approach [. . .] that avoids simply colonizing the literature of the 'other.'"[9] And the designations he comes up with for this new disciplinary turn include everything but "global anglophone" per se—"transnational literatures in English," "world literatures in English," "global literatures in English," "English literatures written in diasporic conditions," and simply "Literatures in English."[10] Similarly, Susie O'Brien and Imre Szeman stress the need for a global reconfiguration of literary studies—especially English—in a special issue of *The South Atlantic Quarterly* that was also published in 2001. In distinction to Jay and the other *PMLA* contributors, though, they do home in on "anglophone," and make a detailed case for its "advantages" over "postcolonial" due to what they regard as the political, historical, literary, and institutional shortcomings of the latter.[11] Whether or not we buy into these sorts of arguments for it or associated terms, neither the current ascendency of "global anglophone" nor its pros and cons relative to "postcolonial" can be understood without tapping into the long-standing disciplinary debate about globalization in literary studies.

In its broadest remit, this chapter examines the disciplinary questions and issues raised by the "global anglophone" model through the lens of the anglophone Iranian novel. I start with a historical overview of the field of diasporic Iranian literature after the Revolution, and critically contextualize its landmark texts with reference to the scholarship on this topic (as in recent books by Sanaz Fotouhi and Nima Naghibi). I pay particular attention to autobiographies / memoirs and novels written by women in this period, given what I have suggested is the gendered tenor of the anglo-Iranian imaginary. Drawing on the work of Max Saunders, I forward the notion of "autobiografiction" as critical lens through which these most prominent of anglophone Iranian literary genres might be read alongside one another. Next, I assess how the US discourse of Iran as a "rogue state" has deployed the (Islamophobic, "Clash of Civilizations") rhetoric of gender repression there in order to further US geopolitical interests in the region. This discourse, I suggest, has come to define the Anglo-American publishing industry's approach to Iranian literature.

Having thus established the political and material contexts of the anglophone Iranian novel, I then delve more deeply into its representations of gender. Following Hamid Dabashi and others, I argue that the massive popular and critical acclaim by which Azar Nafisi's memoir (or, in my terms, autobiografiction) *Reading Lolita in Tehran: A Memoir in Books* (2003) was met was based on its conformity to and reproduction of the "rogue state" idea of Iran, and its related disavowal of any form of feminism—especially Islamic feminism—other than the secular-liberal or universal. I also note that it was precisely this sort of rejection of religious sentiment or affiliation in Iranian secular modernity that (partially) precipitated its return during and after the Revolution. Yasmin Crowther's and Marjane Satrapi's likewise autobiografictional (graphic) novels *The Saffron Kitchen* (2006) and *Persepolis* (2000–3; trans. 2003, 2004), I continue, work against the cosmopolitan literary and political ideals to which Nafisi's text subscribes, and instead plot trajectories of feminist agency in Iran rooted in and taking their contours from a sense of *multiple belonging* in nation, religion, family, and profession. Individually and together, they thus remap what Timothy Brennan and Graham Huggan critique as the cosmopolitan novel's characteristic narrative of flight (from an inherently violent and repressive "Third World") as what following Elleke Boehmer I identify as a narrative of return to and active participation in the world. In so doing, they, I conclude, articulate new and compelling visions of Iranian modernity for their global audiences, and bring important Iranian perspectives to bear on the contemporary discussion of Islamic feminism in literature and culture (as in the work of Lila Abu-Lughod, Margot Badran, miriam cooke, Saba Mahmood, and others).

The Crowther and Satrapi texts serve as valuable objects for global anglophone literature as this framework continues to implicate itself in English studies. More resoundingly, though, they also emerge in my analysis as *models* for the sort of critical, decolonizing methodology attentive to the politics of literary and cultural globalization that the framework must adopt if it is to meet the charge of complicity put forward by its critics.

Anglophone Iranian Literature: Language, Genre, and Gender in the Diaspora

According to some estimates, more than five million Iranians have emigrated from their country of origin since the Revolution of 1979 (mainly to countries in Western Europe and North America, though Turkey contains a sizable Iranian diasporic community too).¹² Consequently, a diasporic Iranian literary culture predominantly in English and largely focalized around themes of exile, emigration, first- and second-generation immigrant experiences, cultural and linguistic difference, identity and belonging, memory, nostalgia, trauma, gender, "writing back" to the Islamic Republic, and so on has emerged in this period.¹³ Characterized by Sanaz Fotouhi as "a new category of writing in world literatures in English," anglophone Iranian literature has been dominated by autobiographies / memoirs and novels written—more often than not—by women.¹⁴ She counts the total number of such texts to have been produced as of 2015 at "well over 200."¹⁵ While several notable examples appeared in the late 1990s, it was really after 9/11 that British and American publishers keen to tap into the commercial appeal of the Middle East and its related literatures started to bring them out en masse. At the time, texts such as Nafisi's *Reading Lolita in Tehran* were catapulted to the forefront of the popular Anglo-American imagination of the region, and started to regularly crop up on bestseller lists, among reviewers and award-granting committees, in curricula, and in reading groups. In a formulation that I shall return to momentarily, Fotouhi summarizes the general sensibility of this material well:

> Diasporic Iranian literature in English occupies an ambivalent discursive space, constructed at the junctions of Iranian history and literatures and Western literatures and philosophies, and reflects the complexities and multiplicities of Iranian migratory experiences. Often written against the grain of history, [. . .] it is a *hybrid form* that defies classification.¹⁶

Regarding the autobiographies / memoirs, notable instances in addition to *Reading Lolita* include Gelareh Asayesh's *Saffron Sky: A Life between Iran and America* (1999), Tara Bahrampour's *To See and See Again: A Life in Iran and America* (1999), and Azadeh Moaveni's *Lipstick Jihad: A Memoir of Growing up Iranian in America* (2005). Drawing on the work of Suzette Henke, Fotouhi reads these texts and the genre of diasporic Iranian life-writing per se in terms of "scriptotherapy," whereby the process of writing about traumatic personal experiences—in this case, those of the Revolution and the forms of displacement attendant on it in particular—is understood as a therapeutic tool.[17] Nima Naghibi productively expands on this line of analysis. Aiming to explain the politics of the autobiographies / memoirs as well as their sudden surfacing in the late 1990s, and delving more deeply into psychoanalytic theory, she notes that their authors were mostly at a formative stage of their childhood or adolescence when the Revolution took place. As she continues, they experienced it and the personal and familial upheavals—including their unhoming—that resulted as "interrupt[ion]," "rupture," and "trauma."[18] Having been unable to assimilate it at the time, the Revolutionary crisis then returned for this generation of writers as they came to maturity some twenty years later as a haunting psychic kernel to be worked through in the specific form of the autobiographical narrative. In their writings, "nostalgia for a lost childhood"—which Naghibi sees as the predominant tone of their work—is thus intimately bound up with "nostalgia for a lost (prerevolutionary) nation / home."[19]

For Naghibi, the autobiographies / memoirs belong to Graham Huggan's category of the "ethnic autobiography" as developed in his book *The Postcolonial Exotic: Marketing the Margins* (2001).[20] As Huggan describes it, this term refers to a commodified genre of primarily anglophone life-writing from non-majoritarian internal or external cultural contexts that is produced and packaged to meet the growing popular demand for "cultural authenticity" in Britain, America, and other English-speaking countries.[21] While offering "indirect access to 'exotic' cultures," it—as commodity—re/presents those cultures according to the values and needs of the "mainstream reading public" there, and thus renders the ethnic other "amenable" to (which is to say, salable in) the Anglo-American market.[22] When it comes to Iranian women's autobiographies / memoirs, it might be said that the demand for authenticity is heightened, made all the more acute, due to the prevailing preconception of Iranian women as veiled, and of their stories as undisclosed, silenced, or repressed. Indeed, publishers have often played on Orientalist desires to unveil what Naghibi characterizes as "the simultaneously eroticized and abject Muslim woman" in their marketing strategies, most immediately by featuring images of veiled women on book covers and juxtaposing these with subtitles promising intimate revelations about their lives.[23]

Naghibi's analysis of the autobiographies / memoirs might well be extended to the novels. After all, their authors belong to the same generation as Nafisi et al; they began publishing their work within the same general timeframe as their peers; and their experiences of the Revolution, displacement, and so forth mostly occurred at a similar stage of their development. Moreover, many if not most of their writings reflect precisely the same implicitly or explicitly "nostalgic" political orientation as that which Naghibi attributes to the autobiographies. Even a cursory thematic survey of some of the most prominent and widely acclaimed of their novels reveals an overwhelming emphasis on issues of Revolutionary trauma (or, the-Revolution-as-trauma); exile, emigration, and cultural dislocation; and the abuses and violence attendant on Iran's post-Revolution Islamic regime (especially those visited upon women in the country).[24]

Farnoosh Moshiri is probably the best known of the diasporic Iranian novelists. A political exile living in Texas since 1986 (when she was granted asylum by the United States government), her novels *At the Wall of the Almighty* (1999) and *The Bathhouse* (2001) both deal with political imprisonment in the early days of the Revolution. The latter is especially provocative, given Moshiri's treatment of her young female protagonist—a captive both literally and figuratively—and her increasing psychological and emotional subservience to her prison guard and the autocratic, patriarchal state that he represents.[25] Another exile living in the US, the Jewish-Iranian writer Dalia Sofer also addresses political imprisonment in her semi-autobiographical novel *The Septembers of Shiraz* (2007). There, in an allegory of the fate of the Jewish-Iranian community per se in the wake of the Revolution, she charts a Jewish-Iranian family's flight from the country after its patriarch is accused of being a Zionist spy and then arrested, imprisoned, and tortured. The Iranian-American writer Anita Amirrezvani turns to historical parallelism to suggest contemporary Iranian women's oppression in her novel *The Blood of Flowers* (2007). Set in the Oriental lushness of seventeenth-century Isfahan, this text hinges on the trope of woman-as-commodity as its fourteen-year-old heroine is forced into laboring for her uncle and then into a loveless marriage after her father dies.[26] And finally, Porochista Khakpour—likewise Iranian-American—takes a more nuanced, reflexive stance on anglo-Iranian representation in her novel *Sons and Other Flammable Objects* (2007). Set in Los Angeles and New York in the aftermath of 9/11, it follows its first- and second-generation Iranian immigrant characters as they attempt to navigate the dilemmas of identity, heritage, and cultural stereotyping in a palpably hostile American culture.[27]

From the foregoing overview, one might say that these and other diasporic Iranian novels work towards depersonalizing and sublimating the Revolutionary traumas experienced first-hand by autobiographers like Asayesh, Bahrampour, and others for literary ends, that they crystallize them in the form of archetypal narrative figures and images that aim to capture the tyrannical heart of Iran's Islamic regime. Like the autobiographies / memoirs, they elicit a strong affective response on the part of the reader, and forcefully convey a particular impression of Iran to their international audiences. Although they do so in a weaker way than their correlates in the field of life-writing—paratextually rather than textually, as it were—the novels even appeal to market demands for authenticity. Publishers have been especially keen to play up their authors' biographical credentials—their Iranian origins, experiences of the Revolution, exilic or emigratory trajectories, and so on—on book jackets, while the writers themselves have usually been more than willing to volunteer such information about their backgrounds in interviews.[28] As such, and on the basis of their thematic, political, and material parallels with the latter, they very much belong to the same sphere of anglo-Iranian representation as the autobiographies / memoirs.

In addition to those that I have outlined, another, less obvious parallel between the dominant genres of anglophone Iranian literature might be identified. Recalling Fotouhi's description of anglophone Iranian literature in general in terms of its "hybrid form," the nature of this overlap is for me more accurately pinpointed by the notion of "autobiografiction" as forwarded by Max Saunders in his recent work. Derived from a 1906 essay by Stephen Reynolds, and developed with reference to European modernist writers such as Marcel Proust, James Joyce, and Virginia Woolf, this term in Saunders's account designates a complex, interstitial space between autobiography and fiction wherein the "generic boundary-lines" of both are "blurred," "deconstructed."[29] It is meant to indicate—and Saunders demonstrates this through his literary readings—that "all autobiography has fictional tendencies" and "all fiction [. . .] has an autobiographical dimension."[30] I would like to suggest that Saunders's thesis can fruitfully be extended to anglophone Iranian literature, and that "autobiografiction" serves as a powerful lens for reading its autobiographies / memoirs and novels in relation to one another. As I proceed to show, generic boundary-lines in exemplars of both of these genres are constitutively unstable, and—crucially—their autobiografictional elements mediate their representations of women in a number of significant ways.

The "Rogue State" and the Geopolitics of Gender

In the previous section, I provided a brief critical introduction to anglophone Iranian literature. I now contextualize this category of writing and establish the political and material conditions of its production, circulation, and reception in the English-speaking world with reference to the prevailing political and media discourses and representations of Iran there—especially the United States—since the Revolution. I start with President George W. Bush's infamous State of the Union Address of 29 January 2002, where he in effect laid the ideological foundations of US foreign policy for a generation. From its beginning to its end, Bush's Address was framed in relation to the events of the previous September, America's "hour of shock and suffering."[31] The "two great objectives" he proceeded to outline for the nation moving forwards were very much presented in light of 9/11 and its continuing emotive resonances for his audience, the nation at large.[32] "First," he said, "we will shut down terrorist camps, disrupt terrorist plans, and bring terrorists to justice," and "second," "we must prevent the *terrorists and regimes* who seek chemical, biological[,] or nuclear weapons from threatening the United States and the world."[33] Generally unremarked until the onset of the Iraq War in 2003, it seems to me that Bush's deft deployment of a rhetoric of American "suffering" and his allusions to a "sorrow [. . .] and pain that will never completely go away" was from the outset designed to pave the way for the sleight of hand by which he was to conflate "terrorists" and "regimes" in this passage.[34] It was intended to overwhelm the sorts of critical faculties that might take issue with what he continued was the implication of the North Korean, Iranian, and Iraqi "regimes" in that "suffering," and to inflame national sentiments against the threat that they purportedly posed (their seeking after "weapons of mass destruction" that "could [be] provide[d] [. . .] to terrorists").[35] Indeed, as history has proven, the great irony of the Address as a whole is that although it was rhetorically anchored in 9/11, its overall momentum was in fact away from "terrorism" per se and towards those states. To the boisterous approbation of Congress, Bush concluded simply and definitively that it was *they* who comprised the epoch's real "axis of evil."[36]

In regard to North Korea, Iran, and Iraq, the designation "axis of evil" was new at the time of Bush's Address in 2002. However, the geopolitical thinking and ambitions behind it were anything but. These states had been high on the US foreign policy hit list for decades, and policymakers had been attempting to formulate links between them from at least as early as 1979. In that year, the US State Department launched its list of what it called "State Sponsors of Terrorism," which—regularly updated—was eventually to include all three as well as Libya, South Yemen, Syria, Cuba, and Sudan. In turn, this list served as the basis for the so-called "Rogue States" doctrine, which established the most comprehensive and unified foreign policy framework to date for identifying and responding to the global threat posed by these states. Developed over the course of the George H. W. Bush and Bill Clinton administrations, and amounting to a political, diplomatic, and military call to arms, Anthony Lake—one of President Clinton's National Security Advisors—compiled and published what became the defining statement on rogue states in an article for *Foreign Affairs* that first appeared in 1994. For Lake, such states—taken together—had emerged by the time of writing (that is, after the collapse of the Soviet Union and the end of the Cold War) as the single greatest peril to the "global" (that is, US-led) "democratic order."[37] With "ties between them" growing and mutually seeking to "thwart" the "global trend," they shared a number of "common characteristics": as he saw it, they "are ruled by cliques that control power through coercion," "suppress basic human rights," "promote radical ideologies," "are embarked on ambitious and costly military programs—especially in weapons of mass destruction," and "sponsor [. . .] terrorism and assassination worldwide."³⁸ "[T]he United States," Lake concluded, "has a special responsibility for developing a strategy to neutralize, contain[,] and [. . .] perhaps eventually transform these backlash states into constructive members of the international community."³⁹

Seeing as the "Rogue States" doctrine was itself in part devised vis-à-vis that country and its developments since 1979, it is hardly a surprise that Iran should seem to fit the bill so perfectly.⁴⁰ Per Lake's defining characteristics of rogue states in the order that he presents them:

- Since the Revolution, Iran—officially renamed the "Islamic Republic of Iran" in 1979—has been ruled by a "clique" of fundamentalist Twelver Shi'a clerics and theocrats. Led by the Ayatollahs Khomeini (1979–89) and Khamenei (1989–present), these circles, closed, have controlled and very much continue to control power in the country (indeed, the state's entire political structure) through "coercion." Specifically, they have done so by means of the Sharia and its rigid enforcement in all areas of public and private life by the state's Islamic religious police.
- In this period, Iran's "human rights" record—when weighed against the appropriate international norms and standards such as those enshrined in the Universal Declaration of Human Rights (1948)—has been truly dire.⁴¹ At the level of state, most forms of political freedom have been severely curtailed, and elsewhere, journalist, publishing, and religious freedoms have been restricted; personal (dress, marriage, travel, etc.), sexual (homosexuality, adultery, etc.), and other freedoms have been criminalized and are subject to punishment by law (including by public execution and stoning); women have been reduced to an inferior legal and social status to that of men in most areas of civil life (with the compulsory hijab acting for many as a symbol of their immiseration); and police brutality and repression when it comes to violations of the above has been rampant. The state's adoption of near-emergency measures to contain, subdue, and decimate the "Green Revolution" of 2009–10—including instituting mass surveillance over the digital media, shutting down communications throughout the country, arresting protestors on a

mass scale, turning a blind eye to rape and torture under imprisonment, backing militia violence, and unabashedly executing its enemies—serves as only a particularly egregious reminder of its long-standing stance towards its citizenry.
- Iran's fundamentalist—or "radical"—version of Shi'a Islam is not just the law of the land, as per the above. The state—specifically, its Islamic Revolutionary Guard Corps—has with varying degrees of success also sought to "promote" its ideology, or at least its regional standing, by supporting or developing affiliations with other comparably "radical" regional organizations or governments throughout this period. Most notably, Hamas in Palestine, Hezbollah in Lebanon, the al-Assad dynasty in Syria, and the Shi'a political parties in Iraq. Throughout, Iran's leaders have maintained a sharply hostile attitude towards the US, Israel, and Saudi Arabia in particular.
- Since the 2000s, Iran has reputedly been embarked on a program to develop nuclear weapons—or "WMD"—technology and capabilities. This has led to a tense and as-yet-unresolved diplomatic stand-off with the international community, especially the US.
- Finally, Iran has been accused of "sponsoring terrorism" abroad via subsidiaries like Hamas and Hezbollah, which are considered by the US to be terrorist organizations. The most spectacular act broadly of this sort that has taken place on home soil was of course the hostage crisis.[42]

Given the above—mostly verified facts about Iran since 1979 (it has always insisted that its nuclear program is intended for civilian energy production)—why should the term "rogue state" seem in itself to be so self-evidently objectionable when applied to the country, not to mention to others? Why has the international community roundly rejected it (in addition to the US, only the UK and Ukraine have employed it in their official foreign policy discourses)? And why have political theorists from across the political spectrum near-unanimously sought to discredit it as a foreign policy tool or viewpoint?

Political theorists on the right have generally accepted the official premise that "rogue state" accurately describes states such as Iran in their internal and especially external policies, yet have taken issue with the term's effectiveness in what they therefore take to be the justified foreign policy objectives of containment and deterrence. As Robert Litwak puts it, "the designation is rooted in tangible external behavior of concern," which is to say "behavior" that is considered objectively unlawful in the context of international law as defined by the United Nations Charter.[43] The overriding problem they have detected is that the term implies a homogeneity or unified set of goals across disparate states. Litwak states the case most clearly: "[p]olicies," he argues, "should be fashioned to address the particular circumstances in each country rather than grouping countries under generic categories such as 'rogue state.'"[44] James Lebovic expands on this point by detailing what he calls the "unexamined assumptions" that follow from this and other categories, including privileging an aggressive course of action (pre-emptive strikes, coercion, sanctions, etc.); overstating the threat; and planning only for the short-term.[45] Derek Smith likewise pushes for a more balanced consideration of the threats posed by rogue states, one that emphasizes diplomacy and coordination with the international community over the sorts of unilateralist strategies that have hitherto been pursued (and that Litwak and Lebovic also criticize).[46] Of course, this set of approaches is itself structured around its own "unexamined assumptions" of objectivity and of what Lake calls the "special responsibility" of the United States in dealing with, or at least leading the way on, international matters.

Political theorists on the left have looked more deeply into "rogue state," its historical emergence, and its deployment by the US political establishment as an ideological weapon in the battle for global hegemony. In so doing, they have developed critical, decolonizing readings of the term as a reification of specifically US military and geostrategic interests. Michael Klare has provided the most substantial and influential account of the "Rogue States" doctrine. He argues that confronted with the prospect of potentially disastrous cutbacks on US military funding at the end of the Cold War, senior officials including Generals Colin Powell (who became Chairman of the Joint Chiefs of Staff in 1989) and George Butler (who was promoted to the Office's Director of Strategic Plans and Policy in the same year) reacted "by seeking to invent a new *raison d'être* for the military establishment [. . .] based on non-Soviet threats to US security."[47] As only minor threats existed at the time, the Pentagon was compelled to elevate them into "major adversaries" that posed "a clear and present danger to American security interests."[48] This was achieved via what Klare calls a "New Demonology," a method—as per Lake—of foregrounding their anti-Western orientation, proliferation activities, sponsoring of terrorism, violent and immoral intentions, and so on.[49] Thus, the "Rogue States" doctrine was born in the early 1990s, and fostered through the foreign policy discourses of successive administrations.

Building on Klare's work, Noam Chomsky and Jacques Derrida have sought to uncover the performative contradictions of "rogue state" as it has filtered into and reshaped the very language of global politics. Chomsky distinguishes between literal and ideological versions of the term. In its literal usage, he argues, it refers to a state "that defies international laws and conventions" and "does not consider itself bound by [them]"; however, in its prevailing ideological use, it merely consolidates and amplifies whatever is presented about that state "by those who have the power to control discourse, propaganda, framework of discussion, and so on."[50] Providing a catalogue of US military and other atrocities from the last fifty years (such as in Vietnam, Central American, Sudan, and elsewhere) and highlighting the non-designation of US allies that fulfill the literal definition (such as Indonesia under Suharto, Israel, and others), he then suggests that "the leading 'rogue state' in the world is the United States."[51] As he writes in one of his full-length books on the topic, "a 'rogue state,'" then, "is not simply a criminal state, but one that defies the orders of the powerful—who are, of course, exempt."[52] In his book on it, *Rogues: Two Essays on Reason* (2003; trans. 2005), Derrida expands on this notion of "exemption," or more precisely "exception" (à la Carl Schmitt, Walter Benjamin, and Giorgio Agamben). The idea here is that the very act of naming or branding a state "rogue" and thereby of declaring its exception from the international community itself constitutes an assumption of sovereignty over that community, and thus a roguishness logically prior to that of the state identified as "rogue" (as it undermines and even flouts the basic tenets on which the UN was founded, the democracy and equality of states). As he expounds:

> [T]hose states that are able or in a state to denounce or accuse some "rogue state" of violating the law, of failing to live up to the law, of being guilty of some perversion or deviation, those states that claim to uphold international law and that take the initiative of war, of police or peacekeeping operations because they have the force to do so, these states, namely the United States and its allied states in these actions, are themselves, as sovereign, the first rogue states.[53]

Chomsky's and Derrida's readings bring home the fallacies of objectivity and American exceptionalism in critical thinking about the "Rogue States" doctrine. I would like to extend their insights towards what the US policymakers who developed the doctrine cite as one of their main points of contention with the states they target, their "suppression"—in Lake's words—of "basic human rights." Specifically, I wish to look into how US political and media discourses of women and women's rights in rogue states feed into the wider geopolitical objectives and sense of antagonism that the doctrine articulates, and help lay the ideological foundations for military and other interventions. As in the run-up to the US-led invasion of Afghanistan in 2001, the question of gender has been at the forefront of public debates and popular representations of Iran ever since the erection of the "Islamic Republic" in 1979—evidently, it has been inflated into a geopolitical one in this period. Further, this question is inextricably intertwined with that of religion in the country. While Lake dismisses the suggestion that the "American quarrel" with Iran is based on a "clash of civilizations" or on "opposition to Iran as a theocratic state," the sorts of gendered images of the country that have arisen during this decades-long stand-off demonstrate that its castigation as a "rogue" has everything to do with the archetypal Islamophobic notion of Islam as the West's "civilizational" other.[54] With—as William Beeman writes—"the bearded, scowling visage of Ayatollah Ruhollah Khomeini serv[ing] [. . .] as a visual trope for the negative, devilish view of Iran in the United States," it is unequivocally the case that US discourses of gender in the country are undergirded by hostility towards the particularly *Islamic* form of its political, social, and cultural reinvention since the Revolution.⁵⁵ For example, a quick survey of Iran-related coverage from mainstream American news media outlets ranging from *The New York Times* to *Fox News* over the last thirty to forty years will reveal a preponderance of stories on women's repression under the Islamic Republic and its theocratic regime (in addition to those on its nuclear program). A similar emphasis might also be found in much of the scholarly literature. For instance, in *Women and Politics in Iran: Veiling, Unveiling, Reveiling* (2007)—often cited as the authoritative work on this topic—Hamideh Sedghi writes of a monolithic regime that implements Sharia-derived biopolitical mechanisms including "concealing women's bodies, gender segregation[,] and inequality" merely, and cynically, in order to "consolidate its [. . .] 'Islamic' posture and identity," its "power."⁵⁶

In response to these accounts, I follow Arshin Adib-Moghaddam in his call for a "critical Iranian studies," one in which "our understanding of post-revolutionary Iran" is *"pluralize[d]."*⁵⁷ Regarding questions of gender there (which Adib-Moghaddam doesn't address in detail), the wide-ranging scholarly discourse on Islamic feminism that has come to prominence (not to mention controversy) in recent years serves as a useful means towards such pluralization. I take my cue here from Lila Abu-Lughod, Margot Badran, Saba Mahmood, and miriam cooke, who have all in their various ways sought to contest the sorts of assumptions about gender in the Islamic world that I have noted vis-à-vis Iran. For example, the issue of the veil—a stand-in for that of women's repression in general under Islam—is naturally central to their work, and each has complicated standard narratives about it and its significance by providing rich, empirically grounded analyses of what has often (but of course not always) been its willing deployment by Muslim women throughout the region as a sign of their political, social, and / or cultural identity.⁵⁸ The "feminist *hijab*," in Badran's words.⁵⁹ In Iran during the initial phases of the Revolution, cooke writes, "nationalist women [. . .] supported the clerics in their resistance against the westernized shah" and "adopted the veil [. . .] to demonstrate their anti-West nationalist convictions."⁶⁰ In what seems to me a gesture of neoimperialist silencing or dismissal, these women and their stories—more generally, what cooke elsewhere describes as the "multiple belongings" of women in Iran and elsewhere in the region—have been altogether occluded in the political and media discourse of gender in that "rogue state."[61] And as Iran-oriented Islamic feminist scholars such as Arzoo Osanloo, Roksana Bahramitash, Eric Hooglund, and Mehri Honarbin-Holliday have shown, their voices, claims, and struggles for representation have only become more pronounced since the Revolution.[62]

Azar Nafisi: Secular vs Islamic Feminisms in Post-Revolutionary Iran

The discourse of Iran as a "rogue state" and everything associated with it has through and through defined the Anglo-American publishing industry's approach to Iranian literature. It has acted as a baseline assumption in publishers' policies regarding the selection of Iranian texts to put their weight behind, whether in English or in translation; their editorial handling; their promotion and marketing; their worthiness for submission to relevant awards; and so on. Correspondingly, the kinds of texts from or about Iran that have been made available to and that have been pushed on audiences in the English-speaking world have by and large served to reinforce the political and media prejudices about the country that have arisen since the Revolution. They are consistent with and contribute to the overall anglo-Iranian imaginary that has been forged in this period, and suggest that when what David Damrosch describes as the "values and needs" of a host culture regarding a source are so pervasively shaped by a political concept like "rogue state," it is difficult for such a text—for world literature—to exist except as a politicized refraction of that culture and its interests.[63]

Azar Nafisi's *Reading Lolita in Tehran*, to which I now turn, provides a clear illustration of this thesis as it pertains to representations of gender in post-Revolutionary Iran. While this text is of course formally known as a memoir, I show that its autobiographical depiction of women's experiences in the Islamic Republic is in many important respects *fictionalized*, not to mention shaped and structured according to the influence of the (Western) works of literary fiction which Nafisi deploys as points of reference throughout. That is to say, the text is better understood as an *autobiografictional* one, as per the Saunders formulation set out above.

Furthermore, Nafisi's widely celebrated, cosmopolitan take on gender, "secular" and "Islamic" feminisms, and related matters in the country provides a useful point of contrast with the novels and graphic novels proper that I address in the following section. In their countervailing narratives of women's lives and trajectories of (Islamic) feminist agency there, these texts, in turn, help us to think beyond the "rogue state" caricature of Iran on which Nafisi's story as well as its success are based.

In *Reading Lolita*, Nafisi recounts her personal and professional experiences as a woman and a teacher of English literature in Iran in the 1990s, and the mounting restrictions and degradations imposed upon herself, her students, her colleagues, her family, and her classroom under the country's newly empowered Islamic regime. Throughout, her narrative is imaginatively anchored in the Western literary canon, especially the novels of Vladimir Nabokov, F. Scott Fitzgerald, Henry James, and Jane Austen. In addition to drawing general ethical and political inspiration from these figures, she organizes the text around them and their works (her four chapters are titled "Lolita," "Gatsby," "James," and "Austen"); pursues extended literary readings that seek to reveal through classics like Nabokov's *Lolita* (1955) the shortcomings and outright abuses of the Islamic regime; and tells of her attempts to teach them both at the University of Tehran (until 1995, when she was ousted from her faculty position for refusing to veil), and thereafter in a private book club that she sets up for a group of her female students. Much of Nafisi's time is spent constructing parallels between, say, Nabokov's villains and Austen's heroines and comparable Iranian "characters," whom her students and—by extension—her readers are consequently invited to "read" through the lens of fiction. For example, she explicitly compares Iran's ruling clerics to Nabokov's Humbert Humbert, of course one of the most infamous characters in Western literature—suggesting that like the latter their modus operandi is in effect one of "grooming" Iran's citizenry for their own illicit ends, "the Ayatollah[s]," she explains, aim ultimately "to shape others according to their [. . .] dreams and desires."[64] Although the weight of the narrative lies more on the subversive *acts* of reading and teaching themselves, the texts to which Nafisi refers and her take on them thus establish the interpretive parameters of her story of life—especially as endured by women—under theocracy. Special narrative attention is paid to instances of women's oppression and gendered violence in that context, as carried out by—among others—brothers overzealous to control and delimit their siblings' activities, "Morality Squads" which inspect women's attire and behavior at every turn, and prison guards who rape and murder their captives. What *Reading Lolita* offers, in sum, is an idiosyncratic, stylized, and gendered account of post-Revolutionary Iran that, masquerading as factual, is through and through mediated by fiction.

Reading Lolita won the Book Sense Book of the Year Award and hit *The New York Times*'s bestseller list upon its initial publication in 2003. Since then, the book has become a mainstay of the popular anglo-Iranian imaginary, and to this day is still commonly cited and read as an essential introduction to Iran in classrooms, reading groups, reviews, blogs, and elsewhere. It is probably fair to say that due largely to the efforts of the publishing industry, it has become the best-known work of contemporary Iranian literature in Britain and the United States.

The book has not, though, been without its share of controversy. The backlash against it stems from an article by Hamid Dabashi on "Native informers and the making of the American empire," which first appeared in the Egyptian newspaper *Al-Ahram Weekly* in 2006 and shortly prompted a rigorous and heated debate. In this piece, a polemic really, Dabashi explodes the text as "a kaffeeklatsch version of English literature as the ideological foregrounding of American empire," as a contemporary heir of "the most pestiferous colonial projects of the British in India."[65] He does the same with its author and her reputation—in a series of ad hominems, he exposes Nafisi's lack of "scholarly credential[s]" and "credib[ility]," her "recruit[ment]" by stock figures of American neoconservatism and Islamophobia such as Paul Wolfowitz and Bernard Lewis, and her having come to personify in American public life the role of "native informer and colonial agent."[66] As might be expected, many took issue with the overall tone and tenor of Dabashi's prose, incendiary as this is. However, it seems to me that the article's impact was based more on what at the time was its fresh and conspicuous attempt towards an ideology critique of Nafisi's representation of Iran. What appeared to resonate—both positively and negatively—with the many scholars and critics who responded to it almost as soon as it came out was its demystification and denaturalization (as warmongering neoimperial propaganda) of what up to that point had been appreciated by readers as a perfectly honest and straightforward narrative about that rogue state.

Since the Dabashi article, the critical debate on *Reading Lolita* has been sharply polarized. Commentators such as Gideon Lewis-Kraus, Robert Fulford, and Firoozeh Papin-Matin have spoken out in Nafisi's defence, and have respectively taken Dabashi to task for his "strategic misreading," his cultural "Stalinis[m]," and his neglect of "the extreme social and political conditions that forced Nafisi underground."[67] Others have doubled down on the critical insights behind his prose, generally with more balanced attention to Nafisi's text itself. Seyed Mohammad Marandi scours the text for "misrepresentations of Iranian society and Islam"; Roksana Bahramitash reads it as an instance of post-9/11 "Orientalist feminism"; Mitra Rastegar situates it in the context of a longer, gendered "Orientalist tradition" of literary representation; John Carlos Rowe identifies it as "an excellent example of how neoliberal rhetoric is now being deployed by neoconservatives"; and Amy DePaul acknowledges that it "voices neoconservative sentiments" even while attempting to redeem certain aspects of its portrayal of Iran.[68] The US-based Iranian émigré writer and academic Fatemeh Keshavarz has gone so far as to write an entire book-length counter-autobiography with the explicit intent of dispelling myths about a joyless Iran spread by *Reading Lolita* and other contributions to what she calls the "New Orientalist narrative."[69]

Rather than attempt to untangle the many strands of this discussion, I wish in my reading of *Reading Lolita* to follow a line of inquiry set out by Rowe. Considering the success of Nafisi's book in "Idaho," he emphasizes that this was largely based on its appeal to "Western readers with feminist commitments, especially the feminist universalism that ignores the different historical and cultural situations of women around the world"—which is to say, second-wave feminism.[70] As with Dabashi's more general critique of the text's neoimperialist agenda, this point is intended to defamiliarize Nafisi's representation of women and gender in Iran, and to indicate that her narrative is premised on principles that—inscribed therein as self-evident and universal—are in fact local, particular, and "Western." Thus gesturing towards a third-wave rereading of the text, it lays the critical groundwork for alternative narratives of women's experiences in Iran and elsewhere in the Middle East of the sort that Islamic feminists (among others) have started to pursue.

Nafisi's brand of feminism is elucidated through an analysis of her portrayal of post-Revolutionary Iranian women's identities and subjectivities. Her treatment of women is marked first and foremost by omission. As noted above, many Iranian women willingly adopted the veil as a visual, bodily indicator of their political, social, and / or cultural empowerment during the Revolutionary years of the late 1970s. Nowhere in *Reading Lolita* does Nafisi even acknowledge their existence, let alone attempt to engage with their stories, perspectives, or interiority. Rather, she presents Iranian women as uniformly subject to and victims of the Sharia, a patriarchal construct that she stresses is responsible for the innumerable illustrations of gendered violence, brutality, and humiliation she makes sure to scatter across each of her pages.[71] She goes further, and hints at women's masochistic, death-driven internalization of Islamic law in her description of Sanaz, one of her students, and her feelings of "satisfaction" and "compensation" upon being arbitrarily flogged.[72] Later, towards the end of the book, Nafisi brings the sexual undertone of this thought to the surface. "Living in the Islamic Republic," she writes, "is like having sex with a man you loathe"—as she elaborates, "you make your mind blank" and "pretend to be somewhere else, [. . .] forget your body, [. . .] hate your body."[73] By this account, the Islamic Republic and, by extension, Islamic society in toto amounts to a male ideological formation driven by a psychosexual need—sublimated as statecraft—to control and dominate, to master, women's bodies. And as women, it follows, succumb to and internalize the less-than-meagre role into which they are cast by the state, any hope or even inkling of resistance they might once have held on to fades. Their situation thus becomes inexorable and permanent.

A faint glimmer of light does, though, emerge in the narrative, specifically in the private, interior space of Nafisi's living room. It is there that the weekly meetings of her book club are held, and that what Nafisi describes as the socio-economically as well as religiously "mixed" group of her female students—a "deceptive synecdoche" of Iranian women, in Rowe's estimation—are assembled.[74] There, as each of these women "shed[s] [her] mandatory veils and robes," she acquires "an outline and a shape," and so metamorphoses into "her own inimitable self."[75] It is clear that for the author, it is only by discarding the veil and the weight of Islamic law it carries that a woman in Iran can become a unique individual, a subject. Elsewhere in the text, Nafisi makes this point—which amounts to a disavowal of the possibility of any sort of coherent and fulfilled female identity or subjectivity under Islam—explicit. Responding to the questions that it has posed, she writes that "Islamic feminism"—which she defines as an attempt "to reconcile the concept of women's rights with the tenets of Islam"—is a "myth," a "contradictory notion," one which by her reckoning was promulgated by "the rulers" as a means of keeping "us modern men and women [. . .] in our place."[76] In so doing, she unambiguously positions herself as precisely the secular-liberal, universalizing, and "Western" feminist to whom Rowe alludes, and her book as an "ethnic autobiography" (à la Graham Huggan) or—to bring home its fictitiousness—a "cosmopolitan fiction" (à la Timothy Brennan).[77]

Reading Lolita's critics have underlined the book's implication in contemporary neoimperialist, neo-Orientalist, and roguish discourses and representations of Iran well. However, it seems to me that in what I will refer to as the text's broadly cosmopolitan literary and political stance towards the country and especially issues of women's rights, gender, and feminism there, it is involved in and it contributes to an even more substantial, *historical* obfuscation, one whose effect has been to further perpetuate the deep-seated political, social, and cultural antagonisms from which the present moment in all of its violence is derived. That is to say, the text's cosmopolitanism—in this case, its autobiografictional presentation of the "universal" ideals of secularism, liberalism, and modernity (as evident in Nafisi's treatment of Iranian women)—inscribes in and as literary form precisely the same rejection of religious sentiment or affiliation that had in part facilitated the project of Iranian secular modernity, and that had thereby in part precipitated its return during and after the Revolution of 1979.

As Ervand Abrahamian explains, Iran under the Pahlavi dynasty was subject to a wide-ranging program of modernizing and secularizing reforms as promised by the Constitution of 1906 (which the previously ascendant Qajar dynasty was unable to fully deliver).[78] Reza Shah—in power from 1925 to 1941, and in Abrahamian's words the "great 'reformer,' 'modernizer,' and [. . .] 'secularizer'"—sought throughout his reign to delink religion from public and political life in the country.[79] Most relevant for my purposes here, he implemented a new dress code that eventually prohibited women from wearing either the hijab or the chador in public places.[80] Mohammad Reza Shah—in power from 1941 to 1979—"continued [. . .] where his father had been forced to leave off."[81] Significantly, his White Revolution involved the further de-Islamization of laws pertaining to women's issues, rights, and social status.[82] With Islam thus effectively driven underground or othered in Iranian modernity via these and many other mechanisms, it is quite comprehensible that Abrahamian should conclude that "[t]he White Revolution [. . .] paved the way for an Islamic Revolution."[83] Moreover, it is only with this background in mind that the realities of women's lived experience in contemporary Iran—specifically, what in many cases has been their choice to reveil as a sign of what for much of the twentieth century was their repressed political, social, and / or cultural identity—can be fully understood.

In counterpoint to *Reading Lolita* and its intentional cosmopolitan fabrication of Iranian women's experiences, I have found the recent scholarly work on Islamic feminism instructive for getting to better grips with these sorts of realities, and thus with the actual forms of feminist engagement and activism that have been taking place in the country in recent years. Margot Badran provides a useful point of entry into this material in her book *Feminism in Islam: Secular and Religious Convergences* (2009). Acknowledging that many—like Nafisi—find the "'feminism and Islam'" conjunction to be an "oxymoron," she counters that "the new radical feminism in Muslim societies [. . .] will be 'Islamic feminism.'"[84] She bases this prediction on the following factors: the region-wide and indeed global consolidation of the Islamic Revival by the time of writing in the 2000s; the expanding educational opportunities Muslim women have been afforded in these societies, which have led to "gender-progressive readings of Islamic sacred scripture"; the potential of a specifically "Islamic" feminism to reach across class and other social divides there; the growth of Muslim diasporic communities around the world and their accompanying exposure to feminist thought; and the globalized media, which have helped Muslim women in various contexts to connect with one another.[85] Saba Mahmood considers the "conceptual challenges" that these sorts of developments pose to "feminist theory"—by which she means the tradition of second-wave feminism—in her book, *Politics of Piety: The Islamic Revival and the Feminist Subject* (2005).[86] Homing in on the Egyptian women's piety movement as an extended ethnographic case study, she argues that traditional feminist approaches to questions of agency, resistance, and liberation must be revised vis-à-vis Islamic contexts where "women's active support for socioreligious movements that sustain principles of female subordination" has set the stage for "their enhanced public role in religious and political life."[87]

Since its initial publication, Mahmood's book in particular has come to serve as something of a lightning rod for the vigorous and often heated debate that the issue of Islamic feminism has prompted. In addition to Aamir Mufti, a number of other scholars have taken *Politics of Piety* to task on empirical as well as ideological grounds.[88] The major point of contention in the scholarly responses to this work is that in it, Mahmood fails to provide sufficient ethnographic evidence to support the claims she makes about women's changing status in Egyptian public life and the implications of this shift for feminist thinking.[89] Nevertheless, I find her theoretical articulations highly suggestive, and, moreover, supported in the Iranian context when one takes into account the empirically rich writings of Iran-focused Islamic feminist scholars such as those mentioned above. In *The Politics of Women's Rights in Iran* (2009), Arzoo Osanloo, for instance, details how Iranian women have since the Revolution been renegotiating their rights as women *and* Muslims in a multitude of what she calls "dialogic sites"— including Quranic reading groups, Tehran's Family Court, and law offices—that they themselves have been involved in (re)fashioning.[90] It seems to me that Badran, Mahmood, Osanloo, and others provide an exemplary framework for understanding the repressed other of Nafisi's text, Iranian women who are committed to both rights and religion in their country.

Yasmin Crowther and Marjane Satrapi: "Multiple Belonging" in Women's Narratives of Return

Yasmin Crowther's *The Saffron Kitchen* and Marjane Satrapi's *Persepolis* complicate the cosmopolitan literary and political ideals to which Nafisi's text subscribes. Likewise written and published in the context of the anglo-Iranian imaginary (though the latter originally appeared in French), and also heavily autobiografictional (though both are weighted more towards the "fiction" side of the equation), they plot trajectories of feminist agency in Iran rooted in and taking their contours from a sense of what following miriam cooke I call Iranian women's "multiple belongings" in nation, religion, family, and profession. In her book *Women Claim Islam: Creating Islamic Feminism Through Literature* (2000), cooke deploys this phrase to refer to the many ways in which Arab women writers such as Assia Djebar, Nawal El Saadawi, Fatima Mernissi, and Zaynab al-Ghazali have negotiated their often conflicting gender and faith commitments.[91] Responding as women to the various demands of global politics, national politics, religious community, the extended family circle, and work, these and other writers, she continues, develop in their work an Islamic feminism that is conceived not in terms of "a fixed identity," but rather in those of "a new, contingent subject position."[92] Extrapolating from cooke for Iranian women writers, the same might very much be said about Crowther and Satrapi. That is, Crowther and Satrapi provide in their novels rare literary expressions of an *Iranian* Islamic feminism, and thus suggest an important rejoinder to the discursive and representational limits of the anglo-Iranian imaginary to date.

Individually and together, the Crowther and Satrapi texts remap what Brennan and Huggan variously critique as the cosmopolitan novel's characteristic narrative of flight from an inherently violent and repressive "Third World." In what following Elleke Boehmer I identify as "the audacious crossing of different perspectives" in which they are engaged, they offer what Boehmer elsewhere writes is a "critical comparative—and also *postcolonial*—purchase on globalised realities."[93] Specifically, in their narratives of women returning to and actively participating in the Iranian contexts where strong feminist subject positions are most urgent, they forge new, critical perspectives on the global reality of neoimperialism and the ways in which the issues of women's rights, gender, and feminism in Iran have been conscripted for its ends. In so doing, they articulate new and compelling visions of Iranian modernity for their global audiences.

Crowther's *The Saffron Kitchen*

The Saffron Kitchen is a novel of migration. Partially autobiographical, it tells the stories of Sara, a British-Iranian woman living in West London, and Maryam, Sara's mother and a first-generation Iranian immigrant to Britain.[94] Its narrative unfolds in the interstices between mother and daughter, first- and second-generation immigrants, and Britain and Iran. It opens with Sara suffering a miscarriage, which prompts a series of reflections on motherhood and her relationship with her own mother. Meanwhile, Maryam abandons her alienating adoptive home in Britain, and returns to Mashhad and Mazareh, the Iranian towns of her youth. Sara thus arranges a trip to Iran in order to attempt the bridge the chasm that had been opened up between herself and her mother, and there, she learns of Maryam's juvenile love for Ali, a domestic servant; her rebellion against the strict code of feminine behavior that had been imposed on her (etiquette, arranged marriage, housewife status, etc.); and her rape at the hands of soldiers under her father's—a general in Mohammad Reza Shah's army—command. During her travels, Sara witnesses first-hand the abuse and subjugation of women in contemporary Iran. More resoundingly, though, she also comes to understand that her mother's exilic non-belonging is another form of constraint, and that Iranian women have access to many more opportunities for redemptive self-fulfilment and self-realization than she had been led to believe at home. Anchored in the author's own experiences, the topos of migration as pursued by Crowther in *The Saffron Kitchen* thus provides the narrative grounds for—to recall the Boehmer formulations—the crossing of different political, social, and cultural perspectives, and thereby a critical comparative take on especially gender-related matters in Britain and Iran. In other words, migration serves in the novel as a literary device directed towards an open, cross-cultural dialogue of the sort that has all too often been derailed by (gendered) preconceptions and prejudices about these countries (especially of course one of them).

The Saffron Kitchen is explicitly and perhaps a little self-consciously framed against what Crowther recognizes to be her anglophone audience's prevailing sense of Iran as other, as rogue. For instance, she has Maryam reply to a Mazareh villager's questions about British views on the country with: "[i]n London, I'm surrounded by people who know [it] only through their news, a cartoon of Iran."[95] As part of her own response to such caricatures, Crowther endeavors to rehistoricize contemporary Iranian politics and to dramatize the personal as well as geopolitical ramifications of the country's negative portrayal in the media and elsewhere. She sets Maryam's childhood in 1953, and in so doing carves out a narrative space for characters to witness and discuss the ousting of Mohammad Mosaddegh—Iran's prime minister from 1951 to 1953, who had of course sought to nationalize the British-controlled oil industry there—in the infamous Shah-backed and UK- and US-orchestrated coup d'état of that year. Alarmed by the mounting violence in Mashhad between pro-Shah militias and citizens loyal to their prime minister, Maryam turns to her powerful and well-connected aunt Soroya for answers. Naturally, given that she belongs to an upper-middle-class family which also includes a general, Soroya explains to her naïve young niece that "Mossadeq [sic]" is "a sick old man whom the world mocks" and that "[w]e need a strong leader to make strong alliances and secure our place in this world."[96] Although no other interpretation of these events is provided in the narrative proper, Crowther's depiction of Maryam's father makes for an implicit counterpoint to Soroya's account—with the General's links to the Shah, his abuse of power in his household appears to allegorize that of "strong" leadership at a national level. Similarly, Crowther also attends to Western media projections of the 1979 Revolution. When her character is exposed to contemporaneous television images of "lopsided bodies hanged, dangling and dead, from towering cranes in Mashhad" and of "men beating themselves with chains," she has Maryam—now in England—respond "[t]hat's not my Iran."[97] In so doing, she suggests a disconnect between representation and reality in addition to the more literal one between pre- and post-Revolutionary times in the country. And to amplify this sentiment, apparently her own, she has Dr. Ahlavi—a likewise emigrant family friend—declare "I am proud of my country" in the face of those who would write it off as part of "'the axis of evil,' [. . .] the scourge of the earth."[98]

In the novel, Crowther is particularly concerned with the representation / reality gap as it pertains to Iranian women, and she traverses it by way of the migrations of her characters. Maryam's arrival in England in the early 1960s provides her with an immigrant's perspective on the country in its post-imperial years of social and demographic transformation. Although Maryam attempts to assimilate (chiefly by marrying an Englishman, Edward), she retains her outsider's sense of non-belonging in a climate still rife with fears and anxieties about non-natives. Her mother-in-law's hesitation when confronted with the idea of a foreigner in the family brings all this home for her.[99] Required by this representative of the British social order to live up to yet another ideal—this time "Western"—of femininity, Maryam eventually realizes that just like her old, her new "world" imposes its own "traditions," "habits," and norms regarding "how to appear just so" on her in her always-already inevitably gendered being.[100] Recoiling from this world, and spiralling into isolation and alienation (as further aggravated by the collapse of her marriage), she thus returns to Iran. And it is only when back in her country of origin that she is able to recognize that "there are many types of freedom and each has its price: freedom to love, to travel, to belong," and that "[f]or each freedom we choose, we must give up another."[101] In a paradigmatic inversion of "there" to "here" (read: "East" to "West") trajectory of the cosmopolitan novel, the experience of migration thus enables Maryam to weigh her youthful aspirations against their "price," belonging, and to choose the latter as she returns to Iran, to Ali, and reconstructs her life.

Crowther narrates Maryam's return to post-Revolutionary Iran largely from Sara's estranged but increasingly sensitive perspective as a non-native Iranian. A stand-in for both the author and the reader, Sara travels to the country in an attempt to track down her mother. There, she certainly witnesses something of the gender inequality that the media landscape at home had led her to expect. For instance, when she meets Hassan, an old family friend, he refuses any physical contact as he believes that "touching [her] will make him unclean."[102] Nevertheless, the brunt of her narrative is on the redemptive possibilities available to Iranian women, which she—cutting through the gendered assumptions and stereotypes with which she had hitherto been inundated—comes to understand through the immediacy and affective resonances of her migratory experience. Sara meets a series of strong, independent Iranian women during her journey, most notably Shirin, who exercises a domestic authority that in the context of the novel as a whole symbolically upends the patriarchal authority to which Maryam had been subject in her father's household.[103] Pivotally, Sara's Iranian *Bildung* is facilitated by her evolving relationship with her mother while in the country. Indeed, she herself undergoes—by proxy—the passions and deprivations of her mother's past there. When he refuses to touch her hand, she feels as if "Hassan had slapped her or seen her naked," an echo of what Maryam had felt under the soldiers' hands.[104] Further, her indignation at the injustice of Shirin's behavior when she bars Ali from her home bears a trace of Maryam's frustration at her conservative father's expectations.[105] This unconscious but felt identification with the contexts of her mother's past prepares Sara to hear for the first time the story of Maryam's rape. The defining event of her mother's life, Sara can only comprehend this story and take on the burden of historical as well as familial memory that it carries through her own return to and encounter with Iran.

It is by crossing the gendered borders separating "us" from "them" and reflexively navigating the unfamiliar terrain of Iran's modern political, social, and cultural history, of Iran's modernity, that Crowther prepares her readers—like Sara—for Maryam's story. Lying behind the discourses and representations of the anglo-Iranian imaginary, Crowther thus teaches, are lives and histories, multiple forms of belonging and identity that the anglophone Iranian novel—when inf(l)ected by a consciousness of the repressed other of Iranian modernity—can direct us towards.

Satrapi's *Persepolis*

Also based on autobiographical experience, *Persepolis* is a graphic novel that tells the story of Marji—a fictionalized version of the author—and her childhood in Iran during the early years of the Islamic Republic, her emigration to Austria during her adolescence, and her eventual return to her country of origin. As Satrapi explains in her author's "Introduction" to the work, it was intended as a corrective to what she calls the "image" of "fundamentalism, fanaticism, and terrorism" that has come to be associated with the country.[106] To this end, the graphic novel medium serves a number of important functions. Its stylized, black and white, and often expressionistic comic book panels visually indicate something of the cartoonish quality by which Iran and its inhabitants are typically represented, and to which Satrapi is responding. Further, they provide a particularly apt means of expressing Satrapi's protagonist's child's-eye perspective on the world around her and her maturation under political, social, and cultural circumstances that are often larger than life. Indeed, as Marji witnesses or otherwise learns about Iran's history, the Revolution of 1979, the dress codes and other laws imposed by the Islamic regime, the Iran-Iraq War (1980–8), the excesses and abundance of the West (as represented by Austria), and so forth, the panels take on extravagant, even fantastical proportions. And finally, as suggested by the massive popular and critical acclaim by which the work was met (it has now sold over two million copies around the world), its almost instantaneous appearance in English and other languages after its original French publication, and its adaptation into an award-winning animated film in 2007, the panels have proved particularly accessible and amenable to international audiences seeking an alternative point of entry into Iran.[107]

Persepolis opens in the midst of the post-Revolutionary overturning of Iranian society. Signifying what will be a wider set of concerns on Satrapi's part throughout the narrative, the first chapter of Book I—"The Story of a Childhood"—is entitled "The Veil." At ten years old, Marji's experience of the new dress code as it is imposed upon herself, her family, and her friends in 1980 foreshadows her more mature rebellion against it and all that it metonymizes as the narrative proceeds. Against the backdrop of panels featuring rows upon rows of identically clad and thus indistinguishable girls and women, and influenced by her mother's involvement in the public demonstrations that women were still spearheading as late as 1980, she and her girlfriends at school—neither liking nor comprehending it—instinctively adopt a mischievous, playful attitude towards this symbol of their religiously mediated socialization and gendering.[108] From the outset, Satrapi makes sure to frame her protagonist's sense of the state in which she is living in relation to Iran's longer history. Guided by her secular, liberal, and to a degree Marxism-inclined Tehrani family, Marji comes to understand the Islamic Republic as but the latest incarnation of the "2500 years of tyranny and submission" to which the country had hitherto been subject (a history that stretches from the Persian Empire and the Arab invasion through to the age of modern imperialism).[109] And so by both nature and nurture Marji is pretty much fated to chafe against the regime and its restrictions.

Absorbing the politics of micro-resistance exemplified by her parents and their illegal, alcohol-fuelled parties, Marji's youthful rebellion is a westward-looking one. She searches out the latest offerings from icons of Euro-American pop culture such as Michael Jackson, Kim Wilde, and Iron Maiden—of course banned in Iran as "decadent"—in Tehran's black market; decks herself out with fashions styled after them, including a denim jacket and Nikes; and allows a few desultory strands of hair to peek out from under her veil (which, as Satrapi explains, is a means of "show[ing] your opposition to the regime").[110] Her own, teenage form of "lipstick jihad," to borrow the title of the Moaveni memoir. Naturally, she soon comes up against the Women's Branch of the Guardians of the Revolution (the Islamic religious police), which was formed in 1982 to deter against the threat of improper veiling and more general immodesty among women. Calling her a "little whore," they violently pull down her headscarf and threaten to take her to "the Committee" (where secret detention and torture were the norm), all of which leads to a minor breakdown on Marji's part.[111] Increasingly worried about her state of mind as well as physical well-being under these circumstances, and with the Iraqi armed forces now encroaching on Tehran itself, Marji's parents decide that a change of scenery would be in their daughter's best interests and thus send her off to Austria to complete her schooling.

Book II, "The Story of a Return," starts off in Vienna, with its well-stocked supermarkets, rich urban culture, and parties. At first, this supposedly liberal foreign city seems to offer Marji the sense of freedom and possibility that was not available to her at home. However, recalling Maryam in *The Saffron Kitchen*, her experience of it soon takes a turn for the worse. Coming into her adolescence, and increasingly subject to racial abuse based on deep-seated European prejudices about her culture of origin (including from the nuns with whom she had been boarding as well as Vienna's newly prominent skinheads), she begins to feel as out of place there as she did in Tehran.[112] She attempts to assimilate by befriending a group of fellow outcasts and reinventing herself as a punk, but this leaves her with the impression that she was "distancing [her]self from [her] culture" and "betraying [her] parents and [her] origins."[113] And so, again like Maryam, she returns to Tehran and her family. While she finds that all of the old restrictions—and more—still apply in her now visibly war-ravaged native city, she also sees that a resistance movement led by women and based on the sorts of acts towards which she had been unconsciously inclined in her youth had flourished during her absence. Conceived within the Islamic parameters of the state, and articulating new forms of feminist agency and empowerment, the women's struggle in Iran—a "discreet" one, directed towards liberation *from within*—provides Marji with the rooted and fulfilling sense of identity, vocation, and belonging that she had lacked abroad.[114] It is only through her return to her country and participation in its politics, then, that she can complete her *Bildung* and become what Nafisi—referring to something completely different—describes as "her own inimitable self."

As with Crowther, Satrapi thus brings the repressed other of Nafisi's text to the surface of the anglo-Iranian imaginary. In so doing, she expresses something of the reality of Iranian women's experiences and forms of agency in the context of the longer history of modernity in the country. Precisely, that is, the reality that the Nafisi text and others of its kind obscure.

* * *

In *The Saffron Kitchen* and *Persepolis*, the form of the cosmopolitan novel is inf(l)ected by the others of Iranian modernity. In the trajectories of return that they chart, these novels open within the domain of the anglo-Iranian imaginary a space for alternative notions of feminist identity, agency, and belonging in Iran based on a deeper engagement with Iranian history than has been evident elsewhere in the dominant political, media, and literary language of the country. In so doing, they help pluralize our understanding of it. They thus serve not only as objects for a global anglophone literature attuned to material from the Middle East, but also as models for what seems destined to become an ineluctably politicized field.

Notes

1. For a discussion of the origins of the anglophone *Arab* novel in particular, see Hassan, *Immigrant Narratives*, pp. 38–77.
2. See pp. 53–4 in the present volume.
3. Hassan provides a rich discussion of, again, specifically *Arab* immigration to Britain and America in its political, social, and cultural contexts during this period. See Hassan, *Immigrant Narratives*, pp. 14–28. I look into Iranian immigration in more detail below.
4. See Al Maleh (ed.), *Arab Voices in Diaspora*; Hassan, *Immigrant Narratives*; Gana (ed.), *The Edinburgh Companion to the Arab Novel in English*; Fadda-Conrey, *Contemporary Arab-American Literature*; and Salaita, *Modern Arab American Fiction*.
5. For the epigraphs, see Crystal, "Diversity?" and Rushdie, *Imaginary Homelands*, p. 64. Crystal has written the canonical text on this topic. See Crystal, *English as a Global Language*.
6. Anam, "Introduction." Emphasis in original removed.
7. Ibid. Emphasis in original removed.
8. Gunn, "Introduction," p. 21.
9. Jay, "Beyond Discipline?," pp. 33, 34.
10. Ibid. pp. 43, 44. Since his article in the *PMLA* issue, Jay has written a full-length monograph on this topic. Expanding on his earlier work, he develops there a fully fledged program for the "global reframing of the origins, production, and concerns of what we have called 'English' literature" vis-à-vis globalization and its epochal impact on English-language literary and cultural production. Jay, *Global Matters*, p. 5.
11. O'Brien and Szeman, "Introduction," p. 611.
12. See "Iran Population 2019."
13. For a useful overview of twentieth-century Iranian literary production prior to the Revolution, see Katouzian, *Iran*, pp. 180–201.
14. Fotouhi, *The Literature of the Iranian Diaspora*, p. 2.

15. Ibid. p. 4.
16. Ibid. p. 7. Emphasis added.
17. Ibid. p. 98.
18. Naghibi, *Women Write Iran*, p. 128.
19. Ibid. p. 128.
20. See ibid. p. 131.
21. Huggan, *The Postcolonial Exotic*, p. 157. Emphasis in original removed.
22. Ibid. p. 155. Huggan notes that some ethnic autobiographies can also work against their commodification and cooptation by "'playing the market' to their own ideological ends." Ibid. p. 176.
23. Naghibi, *Women Write Iran*, p. 131. Fotouhi offers a representative sampling of such book covers and a discussion of the various paratextual devices publishers have used in marketing these texts. See Fotouhi, *The Literature of the Iranian Diaspora*, pp. 122–37. I return to the issue of the veil vis-à-vis Iran and anglophone Iranian literature in more detail below.
24. In addition to the anglophone Iranian novels on which I primarily focus here and throughout this chapter, one might detect a similar emphasis in the few contemporary Persian-language Iranian novels that have been selected for translation into English to date. Noteworthy examples include Shahrnush Parsipur's *Women Without Men* (*Zanān Bidūn-i Mardān*, 1989; trans. 1998) and Shahriar Mandanipour's *Censoring an Iranian Love Story* (unpublished in Persian; trans. 2009). See pp. 237–8 in the present volume for a discussion of the politics of translation vis-à-vis material from the Middle East.
25. Moshiri's two other novels—*Against Gravity* (2006) and *The Drum Tower* (2014)—both expand on this sort of sentiment, and respectively attend to the traumas of exile and civil strife as precipitated by the Revolution.
26. Amirrezvani's second novel—*Equal of the Sun* (2012)—is also a historical one, and engages with questions of gender in Iran's royal courts in the sixteenth century.
27. Khakpour's second novel—*The Last Illusion* (2016)—similarly explores Iranian-American identity after 9/11.
28. Once more, see Fotouhi, *The Literature of the Iranian Diaspora*, pp. 122–37 for further information about the paratextual framing of anglophone Iranian literary texts.
29. Saunders, "Autobiografiction," pp. 1056, 1055.
30. Ibid. p. 1056. See also Saunders, *Self Impression*.
31. "President Delivers State of the Union Address."

32. Ibid.
33. Ibid. Emphasis added.
34. Ibid.
35. Ibid.
36. Ibid.
37. Lake, "Confronting Backlash States," p. 45.
38. Ibid. pp. 45, 46, 52.
39. Ibid. pp. 46.
40. For Lake on Iran as a rogue state, see ibid. pp. 52–3, *passim*.
41. See "Universal Declaration of Human Rights."
42. For a detailed historical overview of the Iranian Revolution, the establishment of the Islamic Republic, and the wholesale restructuring of Iranian politics, society, and culture since then, see Abrahamian, *A History of Modern Iran*, pp. 155–95.
43. Litwak, *Rogue States and U.S. Foreign Policy*, p. 7.
44. Ibid. p. xiv.
45. Lebovic, *Deterring International Terrorism and Rogue States*, p. 2. See also ibid. pp. 2–6.
46. See Smith, *Deterring America*, pp. 3–14.
47. Klare, *Rogue States and Nuclear Outlaws*, p. 10.
48. Ibid. pp. 14, 25.
49. Ibid. p. 24. See also ibid. pp. 24–6.
50. "Rogue States Draw the Usual Line: Noam Chomsky interviewed by Christopher Gunness."
51. Ibid.
52. Chomsky, *Rogue States*, p. 30.
53. Derrida, *Rogues*, p. 102.
54. Lake, "Confronting Backlash States," p. 52. At the time that Lake and others were developing the "Rogue States" doctrine, it was of course Bernard Lewis and Samuel Huntingdon who were responsible for the re-popularization of the "clash of civilizations" thesis. See Lewis, "The Roots of Muslim Rage" and Huntingdon, "A Clash of Civilizations?"
55. Beeman, *The "Great Satan" vs. the "Mad Mullahs,"* p. 10.
56. Sedghi, *Women and Politics in Iran*, pp. 201, 7–8.
57. Adib-Moghaddam, *Iran in World Politics*, p. vii. Emphasis added.
58. See Abu-Lughod, "Introduction," pp. 14–5; Badran, *Feminism in Islam*, pp. 230–1; Mahmood, *Politics of Piety*, p. 3; and cooke, *Women Claim Islam*, pp. xi–xii.

59. Badran, *Feminism in Islam*, p. 231.
60. cooke, *Women Claim Islam*, p. xi.
61. Ibid. p. 59.
62. See Osanloo, *The Politics of Women's Rights in Iran*; Bahramitash and Hooglund (eds), *Gender in Contemporary Iran*; and Honarbin-Holliday, *Becoming Visible in Iran*. I return to this scholarship in more detail below.
63. Damrosch, *What is World Literature?*, p. 283.
64. Nafisi, *Reading Lolita in Tehran*, p. 33.
65. Dabashi, "Native informers and the making of the American empire."
66. Ibid.
67. Lewis-Kraus, "Pawn of the Neocons?"; Fulford, "Reading Lolita at Columbia"; Papin-Matin, "Reading & Misreading Lolita in Tehran."
68. Mohammad Marandi, "Reading Azar Nafisi in Tehran," p. 179; Bahramitash, "The War on Terror, Feminist Orientalism and Orientalist Feminism," p. 223; Rastegar, "Reading Nafisi in the West," p. 108; Rowe, "Reading Reading Lolita in Tehran in Idaho," p. 253; DePaul, "Rereading Reading Lolita in Tehran," p. 77.
69. Keshavarz, *Jasmine and Stars*, p. 2.
70. Rowe, "Reading Reading Lolita in Tehran in Idaho," pp. 258–9.
71. Including forced veiling, public dress inspections, delimited career prospects, seclusion in public and private life, prohibited contact with men, biased marriage laws, virginity tests, and physical abuse.
72. Nafisi, *Reading Lolita in Tehran*, p. 73.
73. Ibid. p. 329.
74. Ibid: p. 11; Rowe, "Reading Reading Lolita in Tehran in Idaho," p. 260. Rowe points out that as per Nafisi's text, each of these women is sufficiently privileged and educated to have attended university, and each subscribes to the general value-system that Nafisi had espoused when she was their professor.
75. Nafisi, *Reading Lolita in Tehran*, pp. 5, 6.
76. Ibid. p. 262.
77. Brennan, *At Home in the World*, p. 42. For Brennan, non-Western literary texts are accepted for publication in London and New York only if they subscribe to what he calls a "cosmopolitan" political aesthetic that can appeal and be sold to a wide domestic readership. See ibid. pp. 36–44.
78. See pp. 154–6 in the present volume for further details on the Constitution of 1906.
79. Abrahamian, *A History of Modern Iran*, p. 72.

80. See ibid. pp. 83–4, 93–5, *passim*.
81. Ibid. p. 123.
82. See ibid. p. 134.
83. Ibid. p. 140.
84. Badran, *Feminism in Islam*, pp. 1, 219.
85. Ibid. p. 219.
86. Mahmood, *Politics of Piety*, p. 2.
87. Ibid. pp. 5, 6.
88. See pp. 252–3 in the present volume for Mufti's critique of Mahmood.
89. See, for example, Klassen, "Agency, Embodiment, and Scrupulous Women"; Moghadam, "*Between Warrior Brother and Veiled Sister*"; Bangstad, "Saba Mahmood, *Politics of Piety*"; and Van der Veer, "Embodiment, Materiality, and Power."
90. Osanloo, *The Politics of Women's Rights in Iran*, p. 11.
91. See cooke, *Women Claim Islam*, pp. 59–60.
92. Ibid. p. 60. Emphasis in original removed.
93. Boehmer, *Colonial and Postcolonial Literature*, p. 236; Boehmer, "Global and Textual Webs in an Age of Transnational Capitalism," p. 14. Emphasis in original.
94. Crowther has discussed the autobiographical dimensions of the novel as well as her research trips to Iran in an interview. See "An interview with Yasmin Crowther."
95. Crowther, *The Saffron Kitchen*, p. 132.
96. Ibid. pp. 68, 68–9.
97. Ibid. pp. 114, 115.
98. Ibid. p. 137.
99. See ibid. pp. 156–8.
100. Ibid. p. 222.
101. Ibid. p. 133.
102. Ibid. p. 203.
103. See ibid. pp. 254–5.
104. Ibid. p. 203.
105. See ibid. pp. 254–5.
106. Satrapi, *The Complete Persepolis*, p. 2.
107. For the film adaptation, see Satrapi and Paronnaud (dirs), *Persepolis*.
108. For panels that foreground the homogenizing effects of the veil, see Satrapi, *The Complete Persepolis*, pp. 3, 75, 95, 307, *passim*. For Marji's mother's protests, see ibid. p. 4. For Marji's instinctive childhood rebellion, see ibid. p. 3.

109. Ibid. p. 11.
110. Ibid. pp. 131–2, 75.
111. Ibid. p. 133.
112. For instances of hostility towards Marji based on her background, see ibid. pp. 179, 229.
113. Ibid. p. 195.
114. Ibid. p. 304.

Conclusion: Futures of Spectrality

"Does spectrality have a future?" This question was asked of me by a colleague during an English department conference on "Literature and Environment" at the University of Colorado at Boulder in 2016, at which I presented my Munif material. Knowing my colleague, I at the time took it as an objection to and opportunity to reflect on my reliance on Derrida in light of the declining currency of high theory in the Continental tradition in literary studies. In a somewhat inadequate effort to suggest the opposite, I replied by listing the names of a number of contemporary Derridean literary scholars and discussing some of the ways in which they have been continuing to bring Derridean thought to bear on key issues in world literature, comparative literature, and postcolonial studies in recent years. In this Conclusion, I return to my colleague's question and the implicit repudiation of theory that it marks in a more detailed and systematic way. Such a response, it seems to me, has become all the more urgent in the years since the conference. In this period, a growing momentum appears to have accumulated behind the idea of a "postcritical" turn in literary studies, as articulated and developed by Rita Felski and a few other scholars. Comprising the most comprehensive and potentially revolutionary challenge that theory has faced in the literary academy since its wholesale adoption and institutionalization in the 1980s and 1990s, Felski's call for a sea change in how we do, think about, and teach criticism needs to be addressed in an unrepentantly theory-oriented project such as mine. By engaging with it and the intervention that it attempts here, I lay out some of the wider critical, theoretical, and disciplinary implications of this book.

Felski's book of 2015—*The Limits of Critique*—represents perhaps the defining statement of what might now be identified as the "postcritique" or "postcritical" school of literary studies.[1] Tapping into anxieties that have previously been voiced by scholars such as Eve Kosofsky Sedgwick, Stephen Best and Sharon Marcus, Lisa Ruddick, and others (in terms of "paranoid reading," "symptomatic reading," and so forth), Felski opens with the observation that "critique"—in her view the "dominant metalanguage" of literary studies—is and has always been undergirded by a "hermeneutics of suspicion."[2] As a "style of thinking" that has infused and guided the prevailing theoretical frameworks of the discipline over the last forty years (Marxism, psychoanalysis, poststructuralism, deconstruction, the new historicism, postcolonial studies, feminism, gender studies, critical race theory, and so on), it, she continues, is structured around the following constants:

> [A] spirit of skeptical questioning or outright condemnation, an emphasis on its precarious position vis-à-vis overbearing and oppressive social forces, the claim to be engaged in some kind of radical intellectual and / or political work, and the assumption that whatever is *not* critical must therefore be *un*critical.[3]

Under this paradigm, the literary text is from the outset lost to its social and political contexts, and the acts of reading and interpretation are reduced to stale, joyless, and predictable exercises of "interrogat[ing], unmask[ing], expos[ing], subvert[ing], unravel[ing], demystify[ing], destabiliz[ing], tak[ing] issue, and tak[ing] umbrage."[4] Critique, in short, effaces the singularity of the text and the affective, experiential, and creative—the positive—possibilities that it elicits. In so doing, it forecloses "alternative forms of intellectual life."[5]

For Felski and her colleagues, a reimagining of critique and a retrieval of these "alternative forms" of thought are necessary today more than ever given the crisis of the humanities in general and of literary studies in particular. As Felski writes, her book "is motivated by a desire to articulate a positive vision for humanistic thought in the face of growing skepticism about its value."[6] While I do not believe that this puts into question the sincerity of her more internal misgivings about literary studies, it is thus with an eye towards what might be considered the extra-disciplinary (or at least extra-critical) concerns of the corporatization of the university, the assault on the humanities, the job market, enrollments, and all the rest that she develops her "vision" of what she calls "postcritical reading."[7] Intending with this designation to indicate a working-through rather than a working-against in relation to the critique tradition, and directing it as much to pedagogy as to scholarship, she defines the postcritical in terms of a "greater receptivity" to the text and what it "unfurls, calls forth, [and] makes possible."[8] Under this model, one which is strongly influenced by Bruno Latour and actor-network theory, the text—"incandescent, extraordinary, sublime, utterly special"—is conceptualized not as a passive receptacle of underlying social and political content, but rather as a "coactor" in reading and interpretation that "makes a difference" and "makes things happen."[9] Postcritique, in sum, is a practice of "coproduction between actors rather than an unravelling of manifest meaning, a form of making rather than unmaking."[10]

If the *PMLA* is any indication (and in such matters it generally is), the response to Felski's work among literary scholars has, by and large, been positive. The "Theories and Methodologies" section of a 2017 issue of the journal was devoted to *The Limits of Critique*, and of the eight reviews of the book contained therein, seven—those of Sarah Beckwith, Stephen Best, Susan Stanford Friedman, Diana Fuss, Patrick Jagoda, Heather Love, and James Simpson—are more than effusive in their approbation. In these entries, the substantial critical inquiry usually expected from "Theories and Methodologies" mostly amounts to an occasional prodding—quite gentle—of Felski's premises and an expansion of her insights for the specificities of fields such as medieval studies and the digital humanities, among others. The only real note of dissent comes from Bruce Robbins. In addition to what in an interview with *The Chronicle of Higher Education* he notes is Felski's mischaracterization of the tenor of contemporary literary scholarship, Robbins in his *PMLA* review dismisses her project as "a corporate restructuring" of literary studies and castigates her deployment of actor-network theory for its "suppression" of questions of power and systemic injustice.[11] Scathing, the tone of Robbins's review unfortunately lent itself to an all-too-easy rebuttal on Felski's part. In her "Response" to her *PMLA* interlocutors, she accuses him, in turn, of targeting only "figments of his imagination," of being "scattershot" in his remarks, of not having a proper "grasp" of actor-network theory, and ultimately of being "more than offensive" in his comments on the neglect of power and injustice in her work.[12] Despite Felski's evident pique, the points that Robbins makes about her work are—rhetoric aside—substantial, and demand more careful and thorough consideration. I now turn to these in detail, with more balanced attention to Felski's text itself.

First, the point about "corporate restructuring." By this, I think that Robbins is suggesting that what he takes to be the categorical rejection of critique designated by Felski's notion of "postcritique" helps render literary studies amenable to the neoliberal agenda of contemporary university administrators, boards of trustees, and legislators. That is, by blunting its radical edge and attempting to move it towards what Felski sees as more positive values, postcritique contributes to or indeed comprises the discipline's capitulation to precisely the same oppressive social and political forces that it had over the last forty or so years dedicated itself to "interrogating, unmasking, [and] exposing." I'm not sure that this is an accurate representation of Felski's project. Throughout the book, she goes out of her way to clarify that her intention is one not of abandoning critique altogether, but rather of loosening its hold over the literary academy so that other critical and interpretive possibilities might also be imagined. Further, while she is certainly conscious of the exigency and expedience of a new justification for literary studies as such in today's climate, her proposals are very much guided by her sense of the discipline's intrinsic shortcomings rather than by its need to explain itself to hostile outsiders, as it were. She is a genuine, committed, and concerned literary intellectual, and her credentials beyond the book confirm this.

However, it seems to me that there *is* a case to be made against postcritique along these lines, one which Robbins gestures towards but which runs much deeper than anything presented in his *PMLA* article.

The implications of postcritique for literary studies vis-à-vis today's world and our understanding of it are brought to the surface if we interrogate what Felski actually says about the term in the book more closely. Towards the end of *The Limits of Critique*, Felski offers a summary of all that she aims to retrieve through it and the approach to literary texts that it facilitates—"aesthetic pleasure, increased self-understanding, moral reflection, perceptual reinvigoration, ecstatic self-loss, emotional consolation, [and] heightened sensation."[13] In general, and as more fully elaborated in her earlier book *Uses of Literature* (2008), it is "aesthetic experience" that she wants us to remember and re-attune ourselves to in our scholarship and pedagogy.[14]

The conceptual vocabulary that Felski employs in this passage is telling. For what can this language amount to except a return to an essentially Romantic understanding of the literary object and the liberal humanist values of the European Englightenment tradition which it inscribes and embodies? Over the forty or so years of its predominance in the literary academy, critique as defined by Felski herself has in no small measure endeavored to unmask what Terry Eagleton calls "the ideology of the aesthetic" for its imbrications with the various forms and discourses of political, social, cultural, and economic hegemony attendant on European modernity at the time of its ascendance.[15] Evidently reproduced in and by her notion of postcritique, it is *this* ideology and the outdated assumptions about literature that it harbors to which Felski's project capitulates. Having *already* been comprehensively demystified and destabilized by Marxism, psychoanalysis, poststructuralism, postcolonialism, feminism, and the rest, a return to these ideas can only be seen as regressive and even reactionary at our contemporary juncture. The very fact that Felski has been able to gain considerable traction for her proposals suggests, if anything, that the project of critique is as yet incomplete.

Second, the point about actor-network theory. This is not the place to go into the intricacies of Latour and his work. What can be addressed, though, is Felski's appropriation of this work as a grounding for her notion of postcritique. As alluded to above, the basic ontology and epistemology on which Felski's project depends is one which sees the literary text as a co-actor in reading and interpretation that exists only in a vast and endlessly proliferating network of attachments and entanglements with other actors, human and non-human alike. Such actors include "[s]peed bumps, microbes, mugs, baboons, newspapers, unreliable narrators, soap, silk dresses, strawberries, floor plans, telescopes, lists, paintings, [and] can openers."[16] Under this worldview (and it is a worldview), there is no social totality or context that precedes the text; rather, the social is a product of the attachments and entanglements within which the text is always-already embedded. Informed by actor-network theory, the task of the critic—or should I say postcritic?—then becomes one of "direct[ing] [. . .] attention to the many actors with which literature is entangled and the specifics of their interaction."[17] Reading is thus conceived as a lived, participatory, and creative practice, even experience of tracing connections and making meaning across rather than beyond the surface of the network.

The problems with this approach to reading as well as the worldview on which it is based seem to me self-evident. As shorthand for scholarship and pedagogy per se, it, in a word, flattens out depth; obscures hierarchy and mediation in political, social, cultural, and economic life; and—to return to Robbins—"suppresses" questions of power and inequality. Starkly two-dimensional, it is premised on the assumption that all actors within a network exist on the same plane of influence and connectivity as each other. This is a distortion of basic, common-sense reality, let alone the sorts of more sophisticated worldviews proffered by critique in its various colors and shadings.

To take the example of Arundhati Roy's novel *The God of Small Things* (1997), which Felski draws upon to illustrate the valences of her postcritical teaching methodology.[18] While her students' enthusiasm about the question of "[h]ow [. . .] works of art move us, and why" as elicited by this and other texts might be all good and well in an undergraduate course, what is lost to this inquiry is the far more pressing one of why *The God of Small Things* and not another novel is being read in that context in the first place.[19] This cannot be understood or grappled with without looking beyond the reader-text dyad of aesthetic experience, beyond the surface of the network and into the ulterior contexts of literary studies in its shifting trends, the global publishing industry, global award culture, the globalization of English, British imperial history in South Asia, Orientalism, and so forth—the contexts, that is, that mediated this particular anglophone Indian novel's international success in the late twentieth century and thus determined its canonization as an exemplar of postcolonial or world literature in the contemporary American undergraduate literature classroom. It is critique and only critique as Felski defines it that can direct our attention beyond the dissimulating surface of things, and towards the depths—violent and blood-soaked as these might be—of their actual historical and material being.

In this book, I have sought to contribute to and expand the project of critique for the world literature debate. I have argued that from its origins to the present day, world literature has been premised on precisely the same concept of "literature" to which Felski wants us to uncritically return. Drawing on a Derridean logic of spectrality, I have shown that the effect of this concept as it has historically spread around the world has been to facilitate and enact the incorporation of its others into the logic and parameters of global capitalist modernity. I have pursued this argument with reference to the Middle Eastern novel in its historical development as well as its contemporary worldly manifestations, and have demonstrated the systematic haunting of form therein by the alternative forms of political, social, cultural, and economic life in the region designated and expressed by the classical Arabic-Islamic concept of *adab*. Through this analysis, I have attempted to reorient world literature around the paradigmatic critical figure of the specter. It is only by adopting a critical stance towards "literature" and all that it signifies that the reality of its existence in the world might be gleaned.

Moving forwards, our task and indeed responsibility is one of expanding this analysis to the world in endless critique. To recall Derrida once more, it is to the ghosts of those not yet born as well as already dead that we are beholden.

Notes

1. Felski, with Elizabeth Anker, has also brought out a co-edited volume on this topic, which in addition to the editors includes contributions by Toril Moi, Heather Love, Simon During, Jennifer Fleissner, Ellen Rooney, C. Namwali Serpell, Christopher Castiglia, Russ Castronovo, John Michael, and Eric Hayot. See Anker and Felski (eds), *Critique and Postcritique*.

2. Felski, *The Limits of Critique*, p. 1, 5. Emphasis in original removed. For the earlier scholarly work in this direction, see Sedgwick, *Touching Feeling*, pp. 123–51; Best and Marcus, "Surface Reading"; and Ruddick, "When Nothing is Cool."
3. Felski, *The Limits of Critique*, p. 2. Emphasis in original.
4. Ibid. p. 5.
5. Ibid. p. 10.
6. Ibid. p. 186.
7. Ibid. p. 12.
8. Ibid. p. 12.
9. Ibid. pp. 11, 12.
10. Ibid. p. 12.
11. Robbins, "Not So Well Attached," pp. 372, 375. For the interview in which Robbins claims that Felski is "not paying attention to the many varied and extremely interesting ways in which people's positive appreciation is part of their critical practice," see Parry, "What's Wrong With Literary Studies?"
12. Felski, "Response," pp. 387, 388.
13. Felski, *The Limits of Critique*, p. 188.
14. Ibid. p. 188. See also Felski, *Uses of Literature*.
15. For further discussion of Eagleton and the ideology of the aesthetic, see pp. 7–10 in the present volume.
16. Felski, *the Limits of Critique*, p. 163.
17. Ibid. p. 189.
18. See ibid. pp. 180–1.
19. Ibid. p. 181.

Bibliography

Aboul-Ela, Hosam, "The Writer Becomes Text: Naguib Mahfouz and State Nationalism in Egypt," *Biography*, 27:2 (2004), pp. 339–56.

Abrahamian, Ervand, *A History of Modern Iran* (Cambridge and New York: Cambridge University Press, 2008).

Abrams, M. H., *The Mirror and the Lamp: Romantic Theory and the Critical Tradition* (London, Oxford, and New York: Oxford University Press, 1953).

Abu-Lughod, Janet L., *Before European Hegemony: The World System A.D. 1250–1350* (Oxford and New York: Oxford University Press, 1989).

Abu-Lughod, Lila, "Introduction: Feminist Longings and Postcolonial Conditions," in Lila Abu-Lughod (ed.), *Remaking Women: Feminism and Modernity in the Middle East* (Princeton and Oxford: Princeton University Press, 1998), pp. 3–31.

—, *Veiled Sentiments: Honor and Poetry in a Bedouin Society* (Berkeley, Los Angeles, and London: University of California Press, 2000).

Achcar, Gilbert, *The People Want: A Radical Exploration of the Arab Uprising*, trans. G. M. Goshgarian (Berkeley, Los Angeles, and London: University of California Press, 2013).

"Adabiyāt," Dehkhoda Dictionary, 2017, <http://dictionary.abadis.ir/?LnType=dehkhoda,fatofa,moeen,amid&Word=ادبیات> (last accessed 30 November 2019).

Adib-Moghaddam, Arshin, *Iran in World Politics: The Question of the Islamic Republic* (London: Hurst Publishers Ltd, 2007).

Adorno, Theodor W., *Aesthetic Theory*, trans. Robert Hullot-Kentor (London and New York: Continuum, 2002).

—, *Against Epistemology: A Metacritique; Studies in Husserl and the Phenomenological Antinomies*, trans. Willis Domingo (Cambridge and London: The MIT Press, 1982).

Ahmed, Siraj, *Archaeology of Babel: The Colonial Foundation of the Humanities* (Stanford: Stanford University Press, 2017).

—, "Notes from Babel: Toward a Colonial History of Comparative Literature," *Critical Inquiry*, 39:2 (2013), pp. 296–326.

"'Ain Dar rig sets new course," Saudi Aramco, 22 February 2017, <https://www.saudiaramco.com/en/news-media/news/2017/ain-dar-rig-sets-a-new-course> (last accessed 4 December 2019).

Ākhundzāde, Fatḥ'alī, *Maktūbāt: Nāmehā-e Shāhzāde Kamāl al-Dawle bi Shāhzāde Jalāl al-Dawle* (Frankfurt am Main: Alborz Verlag, 2006).

Ali, Tariq, "A Patriarch of Arab Literature," *Counterpunch*, 1 February 2004, <http://www.counterpunch.org/2004/02/01/a-patriarch-of-arab-literature> (last accessed 30 November 2019).

Allan, Michael, *In the Shadow of World Literature: Sites of Reading in Colonial Egypt* (Princeton and Oxford: Princeton University Press, 2016).

Allen, Chadwick, *Trans-Indigenous: Methodologies for Global Native Literary Studies* (Minneapolis and London: University of Minnesota Press, 2012).

Allen, Roger, *An Introduction to Arabic Literature* (Cambridge and New York: Cambridge University Press, 2000).

—, *The Arabic Novel: An Historical and Critical Introduction* (Syracuse: Syracuse University Press, 1995).

Almond, Ian, "Islam, Melancholy, and Sad, Concrete Minarets: The Futility of Narratives in Orhan Pamuk's *The Black Book*," *New Literary History*, 34:1 (2003), pp. 75–90.

Alshaar, Nuha, "Introduction: The Relation of *Adab* to the Qur'an: Conceptual and Historical Framework," in Nuha Alshaar (ed.), *The Qur'an and* Adab*: The Shaping of Literary Traditions in Classical Islam* (Oxford and New York: Oxford University Press, 2017), pp. 1–58.

—, (ed.), *The Qur'an and* Adab*: The Shaping of Literary Traditions in Classical Islam* (Oxford and New York: Oxford University Press, 2017).

Altoma, Salih J., *Modern Arabic Literature in Translation: A Companion* (London: Saqi Books, 2005).

Amara, Ahmad, "The Negev Land Question: Between Denial and Recognition," *Journal of Palestine Studies*, 42:4 (2013), pp. 27–47.

Amin, Samir, *The Reawakening of the Arab World: Challenge and Change in the Aftermath of the Arab Spring* (New York: Monthly Review Press, 2016).

—, *Unequal Development: An Essay on Social Formations of Peripheral Capitalism*, trans. Brian Pearce (Sussex: The Harvester Press, 1976).

"An interview with Yasmin Crowther," BookBrowse, 2006, <https://www.bookbrowse.com/author_interviews/full/index.cfm/author_number/1408/Yasmin-Crowther?> (last accessed 30 November 2019).

Anam, Nasia, "Introduction: Forms of the Global Anglophone," *Post45*, 22 February 2019, <http://post45.research.yale.edu/2019/02/introduction-forms-of-the-global-anglophone> (last accessed 30 November 2019).

Anderson, Benedict, *Imagined Communities: Reflections on the Origin and Spread of Nationalism* (London and New York: Verso, 2016).

Andrews, Walter G., "The Black Book and Black Boxes: Orhan Pamuk's *Kara Kitap*," *Edebiyât: The Journal of Middle Eastern Literatures*, 11:1 (2000), pp. 105–29.

Anker, Elizabeth S. and Rita Felski (eds), *Critique and Postcritique* (Durham and London: Duke University Press, 2017).

Apter, Emily, *Against World Literature: On the Politics of Untranslatability* (London and New York: Verso, 2013).

—, *The Translation Zone: A New Comparative Literature* (Princeton and Oxford: Princeton University Press, 2006).

Arberry, A. J., *The Seven Odes: The First Chapter in Arabic Literature* (London: George Allen & Unwin, 1957).

El-Ariss, Tarek, *Trials of Arab Modernity: Literary Affects and the New Political* (New York: Fordham University Press, 2013).

Arrighi, Giovanni, *The Long Twentieth Century: Money, Power, and the Origins of Our Time* (London and New York: Verso, 2010).

Asad, Talal, *Formations of the Secular: Christianity, Islam, Modernity* (Stanford: Stanford University Press, 2003).

Badawi, M. M., "Introduction: I. The background," in M. M. Badawi (ed.), *Modern Arabic Literature* (Cambridge and New York: Cambridge University Press, 1992), pp. 1–23.

Badran, Margot, *Feminism in Islam: Secular and Religious Convergences* (Oxford: Oneworld Publications, 2009).

Bahār, Muḥammad Taqī, *Dīvān-e al-Shaʿār-e Shādravān Muḥammad Taqī Bahār, "Malik al-Shuʿarā'."* Vol. *I* (Tehrān: Amīr Kabīr, 1965).

Bahramitash, Roksana, "The War on Terror, Feminist Orientalism and Orientalist Feminism: Case Studies of Two North American Bestsellers," *Critique: Critical Middle Eastern Studies*, 14:2 (2005), pp. 223–37.

Bahramitash, Roksana and Eric Hooglund (eds), *Gender in Contemporary Iran: Pushing the Boundaries* (London and New York: Routledge, 2011).

Baker, Mona (ed.), *Translating Dissent: Voices from and with the Egyptian revolution* (London and New York: Routledge, 2016).

Ball, Anna and Karim Mattar, "Dialectics of Post/Colonial Modernity in the Middle East: A Critical, Theoretical, and Disciplinary Overview," in Anna Ball and Karim Mattar (eds), *The Edinburgh Companion to the Postcolonial Middle East* (Edinburgh: Edinburgh University Press, 2019), pp. 3–22.

Bangstad, Sindre, "Saba Mahmood, *Politics of Piety: The Islamic Revival and the Feminist Subject*," *Feminist Theory*, 11:2 (2010), pp. 216–8.

Barakat, Halim, *The Arab World: Society, Culture, and State* (Berkeley, Los Angeles, and London: University of California Press, 1994).

Barrett, Ross and Daniel Worden (eds), *Oil Culture* (Minneapolis and London: University of Minnesota Press, 2014).

Bashir, Shahzad, *Fazlallah Astarabadi and the Hurufis* (Oxford: Oneworld Publications, 2005).

Baştuğ, Melike Yılmaz, *A Translational Journey: Orhan Pamuk in English* (Saarbrücken: VDM Verlag Dr. Müller, 2009).

Baudrillard, Jean, *Simulacra and Simulation*, trans. Sheila Faria Glaser (Ann Arbor: The University of Michigan Press, 1994).

Beeman, William O., *The "Great Satan" vs. the "Mad Mullahs": How the United States and Iran Demonize Each Other* (Santa Barbara: The Greenwood Press, 2005).

Benjamin, Walter, *The Arcades Project*, trans. Howard Eiland and Kevin McLaughlin (Cambridge and London: Harvard University Press, 1999).

Berman, Marshall, *All That Is Solid Melts Into Air: The Experience of Modernity* (London and New York: Penguin Books, 1988).

Best, Stephen and Sharon Marcus, "Surface Reading: An Introduction," *Representations*, 108:1 (2009), pp. 1–21.

Blair, Hugh, *Lectures on Rhetoric and Belles Lettres. In Three Volumes. Vol. I* (Dublin: Whitestone, Colles, Burnet, Moncrieffe, Gilbert, Walker, Exshaw, White, Beatty, Burton, Byrne, Parker, & Cash, 1783).

Blanco, María del Pilar and Esther Peeren, "Introduction: Conceptualizing Spectralities," in María del Pilar Blanco and Esther Peeren (eds), *The Spectralities Reader: Ghosts and Haunting in Contemporary Cultural Theory* (London: Bloomsbury, 2013), pp. 1–27.

Bloom, Harold, *The Western Canon: The Books and School of the Ages* (New York: Harcourt Brace & Company, 1994).

Boehmer, Elleke, *Colonial and Postcolonial Literature: Migrant Metaphors* (Oxford and New York: Oxford University Press, 2005).

—, "Global and Textual Webs in an Age of Transnational Capitalism; or, What Isn't New About Empire," *Postcolonial Studies*, 7:1 (2004), pp. 11–26.

Bonebakker, S.A., "*Adab* and the Concept of *Belles-Lettres*," in Julia Ashtiany, T. M. Johnstone, J.D. Latham, R.B. Serjeant, and G. Rex Smith (eds), *The Cambridge History of Arabic Literature: 'Abbasid Belles-Lettres* (Cambridge and New York: Cambridge University Press, 1990), pp. 16–30.

Boullata, Issa J., "Social Change in Munīf's *Cities of Salt*," *Edebiyât: The Journal of Middle Eastern Literatures*, 8:2 (1998), pp. 191–216.

Brendemoen, Bernt, "Orhan Pamuk and his 'Black Book,'" Orhan Pamuk Site, n.d., <https://www.orhanpamuk.net/popuppage.aspx?id=75&lng=eng> (last accessed 30 November 2019).

Brennan, Timothy, *At Home in the World: Cosmopolitanism Now* (Cambridge and London: Harvard University Press, 1997).

Buck-Morss, Susan, *The Dialectics of Seeing: Walter Benjamin and the Arcades Project* (Cambridge and London: The MIT Press, 1989).

al-Bustani, Butrus, "The Culture of the Arabs Today," trans. Stephen Sheehi, in Tarek El-Ariss (ed.), *The Arab Renaissance: A Bilingual Anthology of the Nahda* (New York: The Modern Language Association of America, 2018), pp. 5–19.

al-Bustānī, Buṭrus, *Khuṭba fī Ādāb al-'Arab* (Bayrūt: s.n., 1859).

—, *Kitāb Muḥīṭ al-Muḥīṭ, ay, Qāmūs Muṭawwal li-Lughat al-'Arabiyya* (Bayrūt: s.n., 1867).

"Cabinet Approves Plan to Provide for the Bedouin Sector in the Negev," Prime Minister's Office, 11 September 2011, <https://mfa.gov.il/MFA/PressRoom/2011/Pages/Cabinet_approves_plan_Bedouins_Negev_11-Sep-2011.aspx> (last accessed 30 November 2019).

Casanova, Pascale, *The World Republic of Letters*, trans. M. B. DeBevoise (Cambridge and London: Harvard University Press, 2004).

Cervantes, Miguel de, *Don Quixote*, trans. Edith Grossman (New York: HarperCollins, 2003).

Chakrabarty, Dipesh, *Provincializing Europe: Postcolonial Thought and Historical Difference* (Princeton and Oxford: Princeton University Press, 2007).

Chatty, Dawn, *From Camel to Truck: The Bedouin in the Modern World* (Cambridge: The White Horse Press, 2013).

Cheah, Pheng, *Spectral Nationality: Passages of Freedom from Kant to Postcolonial Literatures of Liberation* (New York and Chichester: Columbia University Press, 2003).

—, *What is a World?: On Postcolonial Literature as World Literature* (Durham and London: Duke University Press, 2016).

Chomsky, Noam, *Rogue States: The Rule of Force in World Affairs* (London: Pluto Press, 2000).

Cohen, Margaret, "Walter Benjamin's Phantasmagoria," *New German Critique*, 48 (1989), pp. 87–107.

Cohen, Walter, *A History of European Literature: The West and the World from Antiquity to the Present* (Oxford and New York: Oxford University Press, 2017).

cooke, miriam, *Tribal Modern: Branding New Nations in the Arab Gulf* (Berkeley, Los Angeles, and London: University of California Press, 2014).

—, *Women Claim Islam: Creating Islamic Feminism Through Literature* (London and New York: Routledge, 2000).

Cooppan, Vilashini, "Ghosts in the Disciplinary Machine: The Uncanny Life of World Literature," *Comparative Literature Studies*, 41:1 (2004), pp. 10–36.

Crowther, Yasmin, *The Saffron Kitchen* (London: Abacus, 2006).

Crystal, David, "Diversity? We ain't seen nothing yet!," David Crystal: linguist, writer, editor, lecturer, broadcaster, 16 June 2006, <www.davidcrystal.com/?fileid=-4854> (last accessed 30 November 2019).

—, *English as a Global Language* (Cambridge and New York: Cambridge University Press, 2003).

Dabashi, Hamid, "Native informers and the making of the American empire," *Al-Ahram Weekly*, 1–7 June 2006, <https://web.archive.org/web/20060603021934/http://weekly.ahram.org.eg/2006/797/special.htm> (last accessed 30 November 2019).

—, *The Arab Spring: The End of Postcolonialism* (London and New York: Zed Books, 2012).

—, *The World of Persian Literary Humanism* (Cambridge and London: Harvard University Press, 2012).

Damrosch, David, *What is World Literature?* (Princeton and Oxford: Princeton University Press, 2003).

Dehkhodā, 'Alī Akbar, *Lughatnāme* (Tehrān: Dāneshgā-e Tehrān, 1931).
Deleuze, Gilles and Félix Guattari, *Nomadology: The War Machine*, trans. Brian Massumi (Seattle: Wormwood Distribution, 2010).
DePaul, Amy, "Rereading Reading Lolita in Tehran," *MELUS: Multi-Ethnic Literature of the United States*, 33:2 (2008), pp. 73–92.
Derrida, Jacques, *Margins of Philosophy*, trans. Alan Bass (Chicago: The University of Chicago Press, 1982).
—, *Of Grammatology*, trans. Gayatri Chakravorty Spivak (Baltimore and London: Johns Hopkins University Press, 1976).
—, *Rogues: Two Essays on Reason*, trans. Pascale-Anne Brault and Michael Nass (Stanford: Stanford University Press, 2005).
—, *Specters of Marx: The State of the Debt, the Work of Mourning, and the New International*, trans. Peggy Kamuf (London and New York: Routledge, 1994).
El-Desouky, Ayman A., "Heterologies of revolutionary action: On historical consciousness and the sacred in Mahfouz's *Children of the Alley*," *Journal of Postcolonial Writing*, 47:4 (2011), pp. 428–39.
—, *The Intellectual and the People in Egyptian Literature and Culture: Amāra and the 2011 Revolution* (Basingstoke and New York: Palgrave Macmillan, 2014).
Eagleton, Terry, *Literary Theory: An Introduction* (Minneapolis and London: University of Minnesota Press, 1996).
—, *The Ideology of the Aesthetic* (Oxford: Blackwell Publishers, 1990).
El-Enany, Rasheed, *Naguib Mahfouz: The Pursuit of Meaning* (London and New York: Routledge, 1993).
English, James F., *The Economy of Prestige: Prizes, Awards, and the Circulation of Cultural Value* (Cambridge and London: Harvard University Press, 2005).
Ersoy, Mehmet Âkif, "*The Secret of Progress*," trans. Nermin Menemencioğlu, in Nermin Menemencioğlu and Fahir İz (eds), *The Penguin Book of Turkish Verse* (Harmondsworth: Penguin Books, 1978), p. 177.
Ertürk, Nergis, *Grammatology and Literary Modernity in Turkey* (Oxford and New York: Oxford University Press, 2011).
Esen, Nüket (ed.), *Kara Kitap Üzerine Yazılar* (İstanbul: Can Yayınları, 1992).
—, (ed.), *Kara Kitap Üzerine Yazılar* (İstanbul: Can Yayınları, 1996).
"Ethnic Cleansing," United Nations Office on Genocide Prevention and the Responsibility to Protect, n.d., <https://www.un.org/en/genocideprevention/ethnic-cleansing.shtml> (last accessed 30 November 2019).

Fadda-Conrey, Carol, *Contemporary Arab-American Literature: Transnational Reconfigurations of Citizenship and Belonging* (New York and London: New York University Press, 2014).

Fadel, Mohamed (dir.), *Nasser 56* (Egyptian Radio and Television Union, 1996).

Faiq, Said (ed.), *Cultural Encounters in Translation from Arabic* (Clevedon, Buffalo, and Toronto: Multilingual Matters Ltd, 2004).

Felski, Rita, "Response," *Publications of the Modern Language Association*, 132:2 (2017), pp. 384–91.

—, *The Limits of Critique* (Chicago and London: The University of Chicago Press, 2015).

—, *Uses of Literature* (Malden and Oxford: Blackwell Publishing, 2008).

Fotouhi, Sanaz, *The Literature of the Iranian Diaspora: Meaning and Identity since the Islamic Revolution* (London: I. B. Tauris, 2015).

Foucault, Michel, *The Order of Things: An Archaeology of the Human Sciences*, trans. Tavistock / Routledge (London and New York: Routledge, 2002).

—, "What is an Author?," in James D. Faubion (ed.), *Michel Foucault: Aesthetics, Method, and Epistemology, Essential Works of Foucault, 1954–1984: Volume Two*, trans. Josué V. Harari (London and New York: Penguin Books, 2000), pp. 205–22.

Freely, Maureen, "A Translator's Tale," *World Literature Today*, 80:6 (2006), pp. 30–3.

—, "Translator's Afterword," in Orhan Pamuk, *The Black Book*, trans. Maureen Freely (New York: Vintage International, 2006), pp. 463–6.

"Frequently Asked Questions: What countries are the top producers and consumers of oil?," U.S. Energy Information Administration, 9 April 2018, <https://www.eia.gov/tools/faqs/faq.php?id=709&t=6> (last accessed 30 November 2019).

Fukuyama, Francis, *The End of History and the Last Man* (New York: The Free Press, 1992).

Fulford, Robert, "Reading Lolita at Columbia," *National Post*, 6 November 2006, <https://www.meforum.org/campus-watch/10620/reading-lolita-at-columbia-on-hamid-dabashi> (last accessed 30 November 2019).

Gana, Nouri (ed.), *The Edinburgh Companion to the Arab Novel in English: The Politics of Anglo Arab and Arab American Literature and Culture* (Edinburgh: Edinburgh University Press, 2013).

"Gauging the Size of the Egyptian Protests," Stratfor, 31 January 2011, <https://worldview.stratfor.com/article/gauging-size-egyptian-protests> (last accessed 30 November 2019).

Genette, Gérard, *Métalepse. De la figure à la fiction* (Paris: Éditions du Seuil, 2004).
al-Ghīṭānī, Jamāl, *Najīb Maḥfūẓ Yatadhakkar* (al-Qāhira: Akhbār al-Yawm, 1987).
Ghosh, Amitav, *Incendiary Circumstances: A Chronicle of the Turmoil of Our Times* (New York: Houghton Mifflin, 2006).
Goethe, Johann Wolfgang von, *Conversations of Goethe with Johann Peter Eckermann*, trans. John Oxenford (New York: Da Capo Press, 1998).
—, "Conversations with Eckermann on *Weltliteratur* (1827)," in David Damrosch (ed.), *World Literature in Theory* (Chichester: Wiley Blackwell, 2017), pp. 15–21.
—, *West-East Divan: The Poems, with "Notes and Essays": Goethe's Intercultural Dialogues*, trans. Martin Bidney and Peter Anton von Arnim (Albany: State University of New York Press, 2010).
Gökalp, Ziya, *Türkçülüğün Esasları* (Ankara: Matbuat ve İstihbarat Matbaası, 1923).
Göknar, Erdağ, *Orhan Pamuk, Secularism and Blasphemy: The Politics of the Turkish Novel* (London and New York: Routledge, 2013).
Gommlich, Klaus and Esim Erdim, "Evolving Imagery in the Translation of Orhan Pamuk's *Kara Kitap*," *Across Languages and Cultures*, 2:2 (2001), pp. 237–49.
Gordon, Joel, "Nasser 56 / Cairo 96: Reimaging Egypt's Lost Community," in Albert Hourani, Philip Khoury, and Mary C. Wilson (eds), *The Modern Middle East: A Reader* (London and New York: I. B. Tauris, 2004), pp. 597–613.
Graff, Gerald, *Professing Literature: An Institutional History* (Chicago and London: The University of Chicago Press, 2007).
Gunn, Giles, "Introduction: Globalizing Literary Studies," *Publications of the Modern Language Association*, 116:1 (2001), pp. 16–31.
Gürbilek, Nurdan, *The New Cultural Climate in Turkey: Living in a Shop Window*, trans. Victoria Holbrook (London and New York: Zed Books, 2011).
Gurría-Quintana, Ángel, "Orhan Pamuk, The Art of Fiction No. 187," *The Paris Review*, 47:175 (2005), pp. 115–41.
Habermas, Jürgen, "Notes on Post-Secular Society," *New Perspectives Quarterly*, 25:4 (2008), pp. 17–29.
—, *The Theory of Communicative Action, Volume 2: Lifeworld and System: A Critique of Functionalist Reason*, trans. Thomas McCarthy (Boston: Beacon Press, 1987).

Hafez, Sabry, "An Arabian Master," *New Left Review*, 37 (2006), pp. 39–66.

—, "Introduction," in Naguib Mahfouz, *The Cairo Trilogy: Palace Walk, Palace of Desire, Sugar Street*, trans. William Maynard Hutchins, Olive E. Kenny, Lorne M. Kenny, and Angele Botros Samaan (New York, London, and Toronto: Everyman's Library, 2001), pp. vii–xxiii.

—, "The New Egyptian Novel: Urban Transformation and Narrative Form," *New Left Review*, 64 (2010), pp. 47–62.

Halman, Talat S., *A Millennium of Turkish Literature: A Concise History* (Syracuse: Syracuse University Press, 2011).

El Hamamsy, Walid and Mounira Soliman (eds), *Popular Culture in the Middle East and North Africa: A Postcolonial Outlook* (London and New York: Routledge, 2013).

Hanioğlu, M. Şükrü, *A Brief History of the Late Ottoman Empire* (Princeton and Oxford: Princeton University Press, 2008).

Hassan, Waïl S., *Immigrant Narratives: Orientalism and Cultural Translation in Arab American and Arab British Literature* (Oxford and New York: Oxford University Press, 2011).

—, "Introduction," in Waïl S. Hassan (ed.), *The Oxford Handbook of Arab Novelistic Traditions* (Oxford and New York: Oxford University Press, 2017), pp. 1–16.

—, "Toward a Theory of the Arabic Novel," in Waïl S. Hassan (ed.), *The Oxford Handbook of Arab Novelistic Traditions* (Oxford and New York: Oxford University Press, 2017), pp. 19–47.

Hayot, Eric, *On Literary Worlds* (Oxford and New York: Oxford University Press, 2012).

Hermes, Nizar F., "Why You Can/'t Believe the Arabian Historian Cide Hamete Benengeli: Islam and the Arabian Cultural Heritage in *Don Quixote*," *The Comparatist*, 38 (2014), pp. 206–26.

Herrera, Linda, *Revolution in the Age of Social Media: The Egyptian Popular Insurrection and the Internet* (London and New York: Verso, 2014).

Hervey, Mary F. S., *Holbein's "Ambassadors": The Picture and the Men* (London: G. Bell & Sons, 1900).

Heyd, Uriel, "The Ottoman 'Ulemā and Westernization in the Time of Selīm III and Maḥmūd II," in Albert Hourani, Philip Khoury, and Mary C. Wilson (eds), *The Modern Middle East: A Reader* (London and New York: I. B. Tauris, 2004), pp. 29–59.

Hitchcock, Peter, "Oil in an American Imaginary," *New Formations*, 69 (2010), pp. 81–97.

Home, Henry, Lord Kames, *Elements of Criticism. In Three Volumes. Volume I* (Edinburgh: A. Millar and A. Kincaid & J. Bell, 1762).

Honarbin-Holliday, Mehri, *Becoming Visible in Iran: Women in Contemporary Iranian Society* (London and New York: I. B. Tauris, 2008).

Hopkins, Terence K. and Immanuel Wallerstein, "Capitalism and the Incorporation of New Zones into the World-Economy," *Review (Fernand Braudel Center)*, 10:5/6 (1987), pp. 763–80.

Horta, Paulo Lemos, *Marvellous Thieves: Secret Authors of the Arabian Nights* (Cambridge and London: Harvard University Press, 2017).

Hourani, Albert, *Arabic Thought in the Liberal Age, 1798–1939* (Cambridge and New York: Cambridge University Press, 1983).

—, "Introduction," in Albert Hourani, Philip Khoury, and Mary C. Wilson (eds), *The Modern Middle East: A Reader* (London and New York: I. B. Tauris, 2004), pp. 1–20.

Huggan, Graham, *The Postcolonial Exotic: Marketing the Margins* (London and New York: Routledge, 2001).

Huntingdon, Samuel P., "A Clash of Civilizations?," *Foreign Affairs*, 72:3 (1993), pp. 22–49.

Ḥusayn, Ṭāhā, *Fī al-Shi'r al-Jāhilī* (Sūsa: Dār al-Ma'ārif, 1998).

Hussein, Taha, *The Future of Culture in Egypt*, trans. Sidney Glazer (Cairo: Palm Press, 1998).

Husserl, Edmund, *The Crisis of European Sciences and Transcendental Phenomenology: An Introduction to Phenomenological Philosophy*, trans. David Carr (Evanston: Northwestern University Press, 1970).

Ibn al-Akfānī, Muḥammad ibn Ibrāhīm, *Kitāb Irshād al-Qāṣid ilā Asnā al-Maqāṣid: Mawsū'a Mūjaza fī al-'Ulūm al-'Arabiyya al-Islāmiyya wa Muṣannafātihā* (Bayrūt: Maktabat Lubnān Nāshirūn, 1998).

Ibn Khaldûn, *The Muqaddimah: An Introduction to History*, trans. Franz Rosenthal (Princeton and Oxford: Princeton University Press, 2005).

Innes, Charlotte, "Istanbul Expressed," *The Nation*, 260:12 (1995), pp. 245–8.

"Iran Population 2019," World Population Review, 2019, <http://worldpopulationreview.com/countries/iran-population> (last accessed 30 November 2019).

Irwin, Robert, *The Arabian Nights: A Companion* (London and New York: Tauris Parke Paperbacks, 2004).

Jabbur, Jibrail S., *The Bedouins and the Desert: Aspects of Nomadic Life in the Arab East*, trans. Lawrence I. Conrad (Albany: State University of New York Press, 1995).

James, Laura, *Nasser at War: Arab Images of the Enemy* (Basingstoke and New York: Palgrave Macmillan, 2006).

Jameson, Fredric, *A Singular Modernity: Essay on the Ontology of the Present* (London and New York: Verso, 2002).

—, *Marxism and Form: Twentieth-Century Dialectical Theories of Literature* (Princeton and Oxford: Princeton University Press, 1974).

—, *The Political Unconscious: Narrative as a Socially Symbolic Act* (London and New York: Routledge, 2002).

Jay, Paul, "Beyond Discipline? Globalization and the Future of English," *Publications of the Modern Language Association*, 116:1 (2001), pp. 32–47.

—, *Global Matters: The Transnational Turn in Literary Studies* (Ithaca and London: Cornell University Press, 2010).

Jayyusi, Salma Khadra, "Introduction," in Salma Khadra Jayyusi (ed.), *Modern Arabic Fiction: An Anthology* (New York and Chichester: Columbia University Press, 2005), pp. 1–70.

—, "The Arab Laureate and the Road to Nobel," in Michael Beard and Adnan Haydar (eds), *Naguib Mahfouz: From Regional Fame to Global Recognition* (Syracuse: Syracuse University Press, 1993), pp. 10–20.

Johnson, Rebecca C., "Foreword," in Aḥmad Fāris al-Shidyāq, *Leg over Leg, Volumes One and Two*, trans. Humphrey Davies (New York and London: New York University Press, 2015), pp. ix–xxxvi.

Jones, Sir William, *Poems Consisting Chiefly of Translations from the Asiatick Languages. To which are added Two Essays, I. On the Poetry of the Eastern nations. II. On the Arts, commonly called Imitative* (Oxford: Clarendon Press, 1772).

—, *The Moallakát, or Seven Arabian Poems, which were Suspended on the Temple at Mecca; with a Translation, a Preliminary Discourse, and Notes Critical, Philological, Explanatory* (London: J. Nichols, 1782).

Kadir, Djelal, "To World, To Globalize: Comparative Literature's Crossroads," *Comparative Literature Studies*, 41:1 (2004), pp. 1–9.

Katouzian, Homa, *Iran: Politics, History and Literature* (London and New York: Routledge, 2013).

Kennedy, Philip F., "Preface," in Philip F. Kennedy (ed.), *On Fiction and Adab in Medieval Arabic Literature* (Wiesbaden: Harrassowitz Verlag, 2005), pp. xi–xxii.

Kermānī, Mīrzā Āqā Khān, *Se Maktūb* (Frankfurt am Main: Alborz Verlag, 2005).

Keshavarz, Fatemeh, *Jasmine and Stars: Reading More than Lolita in Tehran* (Chapel Hill: The University of North Carolina Press, 2007).

"Key World Energy Statistics, 2017," International Energy Agency, 19 September 2017, <https://webstore.iea.org/key-world-energy-statistics-2017> (last accessed 30 November 2019).

Khalidi, Rashid, "The 'Middle East' as a Framework of Analysis: Re-Mapping a Region in the Era of Globalization," *Comparative Studies of South Asia, Africa and the Middle East*, 18:1 (1998), pp. 74–80.

Kilito, Abdelfattah, "*Qiṣṣa*," in Franco Moretti (ed.), *The Novel, Volume 1: History, Geography, and Culture* (Princeton and Oxford: Princeton University Press, 2006), pp. 262–8.

—, *Thou Shalt Not Speak My Language*, trans. Waïl S. Hassan (Syracuse: Syracuse University Press, 2008).

Kilpatrick, Hilary, "*Adab*," in Julie Scott Meisami and Paul Starkey (eds), *The Routledge Encyclopedia of Arabic Literature* (London and New York: Routledge, 2010), pp. 54–6.

—, "The Egyptian Novel from *Zaynab* to 1980," in M. M. Badawi (ed.), *Modern Arabic Literature* (Cambridge and New York: Cambridge University Press, 1992), pp. 223–69.

Kim, Sooyong, "Mürşid ile Mürid: *Kara Kitap*'i Bir Yorumlama Çerçevesi Olarak Tasavvuf," in Nüket Esen (ed.), *Kara Kitap Üzerine Yazılar* (İstanbul: Can Yayınları, 1996): pp. 233–55.

Klare, Michael, *Rogue States and Nuclear Outlaws: America's Search for a New Foreign Policy* (New York: Hill and Wang, 1995).

Klassen, Pamela E., "Agency, Embodiment, and Scrupulous Women," *The Journal of Religion*, 84:4 (2004), pp. 592–603.

Kyle, Keith, *Suez: Britain's End of Empire in the Middle East* (London: I. B. Tauris, 2002).

Lacan, Jacques, *The Seminar of Jacques Lacan, Book XI: The Four Fundamental Concepts of Psychoanalysis*, trans. Alan Sheridan (New York and London: W. W. Norton & Company, 1998).

Lake, Anthony, "Confronting Backlash States," *Foreign Affairs*, 73:2 (1994), pp. 45–55.

Lawall, Sarah, "Naguib Mahfouz and the Nobel Prize: Reciprocal Expectations," in Michael Beard and Adnan Haydar (eds), *Naguib Mahfouz: From Regional Fame to Global Recognition* (Syracuse: Syracuse University Press, 1993), pp. 21–7.

Lazarus, Neil, "Cosmopolitanism and the Specificity of the Local in World Literature," *The Journal of Commonwealth Literature*, 46:1 (2011), pp. 119–37.

Lebovic, James H., *Deterring International Terrorism and Rogue States* (London and New York: Routledge, 2006).

LeMenager, Stephanie, *Living Oil: Petroleum Culture in the American Century* (Oxford and New York: Oxford University Press, 2014).

Lewis, Bernard, "The Roots of Muslim Rage," *The Atlantic*, 266:3 (1990), pp. 47–60.

Lewis, Geoffrey, *The Turkish Language Reform: A Catastrophic Success* (Oxford and New York: Oxford University Press, 1999).

Lewis-Kraus, Gideon, "Pawn of the Neocons?: The debate Over Reading Lolita in Tehran," *Slate*, 30 November 2006, <https://slate.com/culture/2006/11/the-attack-on-reading-lolita-in-tehran.html> (last accessed 30 November 2019).

Litwak, Robert S., *Rogue States and U.S. Foreign Policy: Containment after the Cold War* (Washington DC: Woodrow Wilson Center Press, 2000).

Lockman, Zachary, *Contending Visions of the Middle East: The History and Politics of Orientalism* (Cambridge and New York: Cambridge University Press, 2010).

—, *Field Notes: The Making of Middle East Studies in the United States* (Stanford: Stanford University Press, 2016).

Louis, William Roger, *The Ends of British Imperialism: The Scramble for Empire, Suez, and Decolonization* (London: I. B. Tauris, 2006).

Louis, William Roger and Roger Owen, *Suez 1956: The Crisis and its Consequences* (Oxford: Clarendon Press, 1989).

Lukács, Georg, *History and Class Consciousness: Studies in Marxist Dialectics*, trans. Rodney Livingstone (London: The Merlin Press, 1971).

—, *The Theory of the Novel: A historico-philosophical essay on the forms of great epic literature*, trans. Anna Bostock (London: The Merlin Press, 1971).

Mahan, Alfred, "The Persian Gulf and International Relations," *The National Review*, XL (1902), pp. 27–45.

Mahfouz, Naguib, *Arabian Nights and Days*, trans. Denys Johnson-Davies (New York: Anchor Books, 1995).

—, *Morning and Evening Talk*, trans. Christina Phillips (Cairo and New York: The American University in Cairo Press, 2007).

—, *The Cairo Trilogy: Palace Walk, Palace of Desire, Sugar Street*, trans. William Maynard Hutchins, Olive E. Kenny, Lorne M. Kenny, and Angele Botros Samaan (New York, London, and Toronto: Everyman's Library, 2001).

—, *Three Novels of Ancient Egypt: Khufu's Wisdom, Rhadopis of Nubia, Thebes at War*, trans. Raymond Stock, Anthony Calderbank, and Humphrey Davies (New York, London, and Toronto: Everyman's Library, 2007).

Mahmood, Saba, *Politics of Piety: The Islamic Revival and the Feminist Subject* (Princeton and Oxford: Princeton University Press, 2005).

Makdisi, George, *The Rise of Humanism in Classical Islam and the Christian West with Special Reference to Scholasticism* (Edinburgh: Edinburgh University Press, 1990).

Al Maleh, Layla (ed.), *Arab Voices in Diaspora: Critical Perspectives on Anglophone Arab Literature* (Amsterdam and New York: Editions Rodopi, 2009).

Mangan, Katherine, "2 Women Say Stanford Professors Raped Them Years Ago," *The Chronicle of Higher Education*, 11 November 2017, <https://www.chronicle.com/article/2-Women-Say- Stanford/241749> (last accessed 30 November 2019).

Mardrus, J. C., *The Book of the Thousand Nights and One Night, Volume III*, trans. Powys Mathers (London and New York: Routledge, 1986).

Marx, Bill, "Two worlds: Turkey's East-West tensions spin out narrative arabesques," *The Boston Phoenix*, 20 March 1994, <https://www.orhanpamuk.net/popuppage.aspx?id=74&lng=eng> (last accessed 30 November 2019).

Marx, Karl, *Capital: A Critique of Political Economy, Volume I*, trans. Ben Fowkes (London and New York: Penguin Books, 1990).

—, *Grundrisse: Foundations of the Critique of Political Economy*, trans. Martin Nicolaus (London and New York: Penguin Books, 1993).

—, "The Communist Manifesto," in David McLellan (ed.), *Karl Marx: Selected Writings* (Oxford and New York: Oxford University Press, 1977), pp. 221–47.

Massad, Joseph A., *Islam in Liberalism* (Chicago and London: The University of Chicago Press, 2015).

Meeker, Michael E., *Literature and Violence in North Arabia* (Cambridge and New York: Cambridge University Press, 1979).

Mehrez, Samia, "Translation Revolution: An Open Text," in Samia Mehrez (ed.), *Translating Egypt's Revolution: The Language of Tahrir* (Cairo and New York: The American University in Cairo Press, 2012), pp. 1–23.

—, (ed.), *Translating Egypt's Revolution: The Language of Tahrir* (Cairo and New York: The American University in Cairo Press, 2012).

Meyer, Stefan, *The Experimental Arabic Novel: Postcolonial Literary Modernism in the Levant* (Albany: State University of New York Press, 2000).

Mitchell, Timothy, *Carbon Democracy: Political Power in the Age of Oil* (London and New York: Verso, 2011).
—, *Rule of Experts: Egypt, Techno-Politics, Modernity* (Berkeley, Los Angeles, and London: University of California Press, 2002).
Moghadam, Valentine M., "Between Warrior Brother and Veiled Sister: Islamic Fundamentalism and the Politics of Patriarchy in Iran. By Minoo Moallem. Politics of Piety: The Islamic Revival and the Feminist Subject. By Saba Mahmood," *Signs: Journal of Women in Culture and Society*, 32:1 (2006), pp. 275–8.
Mohammad Marandi, Seyed, "Reading Azar Nafisi in Tehran," *Comparative American Studies*, 6:2 (2008), pp. 179–89.
Moretti, Franco, "Conjectures on World Literature," *New Left Review*, 1 (2000), pp. 54–68.
—, *Distant Reading* (London and New York: Verso, 2013).
—, "On *The Novel*," in Franco Moretti (ed.), *The Novel, Volume 1: History, Geography, and Culture* (Princeton and Oxford: Princeton University Press, 2006), pp. ix–x.
—, (ed.), *The Novel, Volume 1: History, Geography, and Culture* (Princeton and Oxford: Princeton University Press, 2006).
—, (ed.), *The Novel, Volume 2: Forms and Themes* (Princeton and Oxford: Princeton University Press, 2006).
Mufti, Aamir R., *Forget English!: Orientalisms and World Literatures* (Cambridge and London: Harvard University Press, 2016).
—, "Introduction," *boundary 2*, 40:1 (2013), pp. 1–4.
—, "Orientalism and the Institution of World Literatures," *Critical Inquiry*, 36:3 (2010), pp. 458–93.
—, "Why I Am Not a Postsecularist," *boundary 2*, 40:1 (2013), pp. 7–19.
Munif, Abdelrahman, *Cities of Salt*, trans. Peter Theroux (New York: Vintage International, 1987).
—, *The Trench*, trans. Peter Theroux (New York: Vintage International, 1991).
—, *Variations on Day and Night*, trans. Peter Theroux (New York: Vintage International, 1993).
Munīf, 'Abd al-Raḥman, *Mabda' al-Mushāraka wa al-Ta'mīm al-Bitrūl al-'Arabi* (Bayrūt: s.n., 1972).
—, *Mudun al-Milḥ: Al-Tīh* (Bayrūt: Al-Mu'assasa al-'Arabiyya lil-Dirasāt wa al-Nashr, 1984).
al-Musawi, Muhsin J., *The Medieval Islamic Republic of Letters: Arabic Knowledge Construction* (Notre Dame: University of Notre Dame Press, 2015).

Nafisi, Azar, *Reading Lolita in Tehran: A Memoir in Books* (New York: Random House, 2003).
Naghibi, Nima, *Women Write Iran: Nostalgia and Human Rights from the Diaspora* (Minneapolis and London: University of Minnesota Press, 2016).
Nixon, Rob, *Slow Violence and the Environmentalism of the Poor* (Cambridge and London: Harvard University Press, 2011).
Norris, H. T., "The Ḥurūfī Legacy of Faḍlullāh of Astarābad," in Leonard Lewisohn (ed.), *The Heritage of Sufism, Volume II: The Legacy of Medieval Persian Sufism (1150–1500)* (Oxford: Oneworld Publications, 1999).
Noujaim, Jehane (dir.), *The Square* (Noujaim Films, 2013).
O'Brien, Susie and Imre Szeman, "Introduction: The Globalization of Fiction / the Fiction of Globalization," *The South Atlantic Quarterly*, 100.3 (2001), pp. 603–26.
Omri, Mohamed-Salah (ed.), "The Novelization of Islamic Literatures," *Comparative Critical Studies*, 4:3 (2007), pp. 317–453.
Osanloo, Arzoo, *The Politics of Women's Rights in Iran* (Princeton and Oxford: Princeton University Press, 2009).
Ouyang, Wen-chin, *Poetics of Love in the Arabic Novel: Nation-State, Modernity and Tradition* (Edinburgh: Edinburgh University Press, 2012).
—, *Politics of Nostalgia in the Arabic Novel: Nation-State, Modernity and Tradition* (Edinburgh: Edinburgh University Press, 2013).
Özyürek, Esra, "Introduction: The Politics of Public Memory in Turkey," in Esra Özyürek (ed.), *The Politics of Public Memory in Turkey* (Syracuse: Syracuse University Press, 2007), pp. 1–15.
Paker, Saliha, "Turkish," in Peter France (ed.), *The Oxford Guide to Literature in English Translation* (Oxford and New York: Oxford University Press, 2001), pp. 619–24.
Palumbo-Liu, David, Bruce Robbins, and Nirvana Tanoukhi, "Introduction: The Most Important Thing Happening," in David Palumbo-Liu, Bruce Robbins, and Nirvana Tanoukhi (eds), *Immanuel Wallerstein and the Problem of the World: System, Scale, Culture* (Durham and London: Duke University Press, 2011), pp. 1–23.
Pamuk, Orhan, *Istanbul: Memories and the City*, trans. Maureen Freely (London: Faber and Faber, 2005).
—, *Kara Kitap* (İstanbul: Can Yayınları, 1990).
—, *Other Colours: Essays and a Story*, trans. Maureen Freely (London: Faber and Faber, 2007).

—, *The Black Book*, trans. Güneli Gün (New York: Harcourt Brace & Company, 1994).
—, *The Black Book*, trans. Maureen Freely (New York: Vintage International, 2006).
Papin-Matin, Firoozeh, "Reading & Misreading Lolita in Tehran: A Propaganda Tool?," Islam Online Archive, October 2007, <https://archive.islamonline.net/?p=703> (last accessed 30 November 2019).
Parrinder, Patrick, "Mannequin-Maker," *London Review of Books*, 17:19 (1995), p. 22.
Parry, Marc, "What's Wrong With Literary Studies?: Some scholars think the field has become cynical and paranoid," *The Chronicle of Higher Education*, 27 November 2016, <https://www.chronicle.com/article/Whats-Wrong-With-Literary/238480> (last accessed 30 November 2019).
Phillips, Christina, "Translator's Note," in Naguib Mahfouz, *Morning and Evening Talk*, trans. Christina Phillips (Cairo and New York: The American University in Cairo Press, 2007), pp. 209–11.
Pizer, John, *The Idea of World Literature: History and Pedagogical Practice* (Baton Rouge: Louisiana State University Press, 2006).
Prawer, S. S., *Karl Marx and World Literature* (London and New York: Verso, 2011).
"President Delivers State of the Union Address," The White House: President George W. Bush, 29 January 2002, <https://georgewbush-whitehouse.archives.gov/news/releases/2002/01/20020129-11.html> (last accessed 30 November 2019).
"Protesters flood Egypt streets," *Al Jazeera*, 1 February 2011, <https://www.aljazeera.com/news/middleeast/2011/02/2011215827193882.html> (last accessed 30 November 2019).
Puchner, Martin, *Poetry of the Revolution: Marx, Manifestos, and the Avant-Gardes* (Princeton and Oxford: Princeton University Press, 2006).
al-Qāḍī, Wadād, "Biography, medieval," in Julie Scott Meisami and Paul Starkey (eds), *The Routledge Encyclopedia of Arabic Literature* (London and New York: Routledge, 2010), pp. 150–2.
Rabaté, Jean-Michel, *The Ghosts of Modernity* (Gainesville: University Press of Florida, 1996).
Radwan, Noha, "One Hundred Years of Egyptian Realism," *Novel: A Forum on Fiction*, 49:2 (2016), pp. 262–77.
Rastegar, Kamran, *Literary Modernity between the Middle East and Europe: Textual transactions in nineteenth-century Arabic, English, and Persian literatures* (London and New York: Routledge, 2007).

Rastegar, Mitra, "Reading Nafisi in the West: Authenticity, Orientalism, and 'Liberating' Iranian Women," *WSQ: Women's Studies Quarterly*, 34:1&2 (2006), pp. 108–28.

Redhouse, J. W., *A Turkish and English Lexicon. Shewing in English the Significations of the Turkish Terms. Part I* (Constantinople: A. H. Boyajian, 1884).

Rhodes James, Robert, *Anthony Eden* (London: Weidenfeld & Nicolson, 1986).

Robbins, Bruce, "Not So Well Attached," *Publications of the Modern Language Association*, 132:2 (2017), pp. 371–6.

Rogan, Eugene, *The Arabs: A History* (London and New York: Allen Lane, 2009).

"Rogue States Draw the Usual Line: Noam Chomsky interviewed by Christopher Gunness," *Agenda*, May 2001, <https://chomsky.info/200105> (last accessed 30 November 2019).

Roussillon, Alain, "Republican Egypt interpreted: revolution and beyond," in M. W. Daly (ed.), *The Cambridge History of Egypt, Volume 2: Modern Egypt, from 1517 to the End of the Twentieth Century* (Cambridge and New York: Cambridge University Press, 1998), pp. 334–93.

Rowe, John Carlos, "Reading Reading Lolita in Tehran in Idaho," *American Quarterly*, 59:2 (2007), pp. 253–75.

Ruddick, Lisa, "When Nothing is Cool," *The Point Magazine*, 2015, <https://thepointmag.com/2015/criticism/when-nothing-is-cool> (last accessed 30 November 2019).

Rushdie, Salman, *Imaginary Homelands: Essays and Criticism 1981–1991* (London: Granta Books, 1992).

Sacks, Jeffrey, *Iterations of Loss: Mutilation and Aesthetic Form, al-Shidyaq to Darwish* (New York: Fordham University Press, 2015).

Said, Edward W., "Embargoed Literature," in Anuragha Dingwaney and Carol Maier (eds), *Between Languages and Cultures: Translation and Cross-Cultural Texts* (Pittsburgh: University of Pittsburgh Press, 1994), pp. 97–102.

—, *Orientalism* (New York: Vintage Books, 1979).

—, *The Politics of Dispossession: The Struggle for Palestinian Self-Determination 1969–1994* (London: Vintage, 1995).

Salaita, Steven, *Modern Arab American Fiction: A Reader's Guide* (Syracuse: Syracuse University Press, 2011).

Sandberg, Mark, *Living Pictures, Missing Persons: Mannequins, Museums, and Modernity* (Princeton and Oxford: Princeton University Press, 2002).

Satrapi, Marjane, *The Complete Persepolis* (London: Vintage Books, 2008).
Satrapi, Marjane and Vincent Paronnaud (dirs), *Persepolis* (2.4.7. Films & France 3 Cinéma, 2007).
Saunders, Max, "Autobiografiction: Experimental Life-Writing from the Turn of the Century to Modernism," *Literature Compass*, 6:5 (2009), pp. 1041–59.
—, *Self Impression: Life-Writing, Autobiografiction, and the Forms of Modern Literature* (Oxford and New York: Oxford University Press, 2010).
Schmidt, Rachel, *Forms of Modernity:* Don Quixote *and Modern Theories of the Novel* (Toronto, Buffalo, and London: University of Toronto Press, 2011).
Schwab, Raymond, *The Oriental Renaissance: Europe's Rediscovery of India and the East, 1680–1880* (New York and Chichester: Columbia University Press, 1984).
Sedghi, Hamideh, *Women and Politics in Iran: Veiling, Unveiling, Reveiling* (Cambridge and New York: Cambridge University Press, 2007).
Sedgwick, Eve Kosofsky, *Touching Feeling: Affect, Pedagogy, Performativity* (Durham and London: Duke University Press, 2003).
Seyhan, Azade, *Tales of Crossed Destinies: The Modern Turkish Novel in a Comparative Context* (New York: The Modern Language Association of America, 2008).
Shatz, Adam, "Wanting to Be Something Else," *London Review of Books*, 32:1 (2010), pp. 15–7.
Shaw, Tony, *Eden, Suez and the Mass Media: Propaganda and Persuasion During the Suez Crisis* (London: I. B. Tauris, 2009).
Shaw, Wendy, *Possessors and Possessed: Museums, Archaeology and the Visualization of History in the Late Ottoman Empire* (Berkeley, Los Angeles, and London: University of California Press, 2003).
Sheehi, Stephen, *Foundations of Modern Arab Identity* (Gainesville: University Press of Florida, 2004).
al-Shidyāq, Aḥmad Fāris, *Leg over Leg, Volumes One and Two*, trans. Humphrey Davies (New York and London: New York University Press, 2015).
—, *Leg over Leg, Volumes One–Four*, trans. Humphrey Davies (New York and London: New York University Press, 2013–4).
Silverstein, Brian, "Sufism and Modernity in Turkey: From the authenticity of experience to the practice of discipline," in Martin van Bruinessen and Julia Day Howell (eds), *Sufism and the 'Modern' in Islam* (London: I. B. Tauris, 2007), pp. 39–60.

Smith, Derek D., *Deterring America: Rogue States and the Proliferation of Weapons of Mass Destruction* (Cambridge and New York: Cambridge University Press, 2006).

Smith, Simon C., "Introduction," in Simon C. Smith (ed.), *Reassessing Suez 1956: New Perspectives on the Crisis and its Aftermath* (Farnham: Ashgate Publishing, 2008), pp. 1–12.

—, (ed.), *Reassessing Suez 1956: New Perspectives on the Crisis and its Aftermath* (Farnham: Ashgate Publishing, 2008).

Sowers, Jeannie, "Egypt in Transformation," in Jeannie Sowers and Chris Toensing (eds), *The Journey to Tahrir: Revolution, Protest, and Social Change in Egypt* (London and New York: Verso, 2012), pp. 1–17.

Sowers, Jeannie and Chris Toensing (eds), *The Journey to Tahrir: Revolution, Protest, and Social Change in Egypt* (London and New York: Verso, 2012).

Spivak, Gayatri Chakravorty, *Death of a Discipline* (New York and Chichester: Columbia University Press, 2003).

—, "Translator's Preface," in Jacques Derrida, *Of Grammatology*, trans. Gayatri Chakravorty Spivak (Baltimore and London: Johns Hopkins University Press, 1976), pp. ix–lxxxvii.

Sprinker, Michael (ed.), *Ghostly Demarcations: A Symposium on Jacques Derrida's Specters of Marx* (London and New York: Verso, 1999).

Stone, Judy, "Orhan Pamuk: 'Enigma is Sovereign,'" *Publishers Weekly*, 241:51 (1994), p. 36–7.

Szeman, Imre, "Literature and Energy Futures," *Publications of the Modern Language Association*, 126:2 (2011), pp. 323–5.

Szeman, Imre and Dominic Boyer, "Introduction: On the Energy Humanities," in Imre Szeman and Dominic Boyer (eds), *Energy Humanities: An Anthology* (Baltimore and London: Johns Hopkins University Press, 2017), pp. 1–14.

—, (eds), *Energy Humanities: An Anthology* (Baltimore and London: Johns Hopkins University Press, 2017).

al-Tahtawi, Rifa'a Rafi', *An Imam in Paris: Account of a Stay in France by an Egyptian Cleric (1826–1831)*, trans. Daniel L. Newman (London: Saqi Books, 2004).

Tanoukhi, Nirvana, "The Scale of World Literature," *New Literary History*, 39 (2008), pp. 599–617.

Taylor, Charles, *A Secular Age* (Cambridge and London: The Belknap Press, 2007).

Teuwsen, Peer, "Der meistgehasste Türke," *Das Magazin*, 5 February 2005, <http://archive.is/7FCD> (last accessed 4 December 2019).

"The Arab Bedouin and the Prawer Plan: Ongoing Displacement in the Naqab," Adalah—The Legal Center for Arab Minority Rights in Israel, 2012, <http://www.scribd.com/doc/122424008/The-Arab-Bedouin-and-the-Prawer-Plan-Ongoing-Displacement-in-the-Naqab> (last accessed 30 November 2019).

"The Naguib Mahfouz Medal for Literature," The American University in Cairo Press, n.d., <https://aucpress.com/about-us/naguib-mahfouz-medal> (last accessed 30 November 2019).

"The Nobel Prize in Literature 1988," NobelPrize.org, 13 October 1988, <https://www.nobelprize.org/prizes/literature/1988/summary> (last accessed 30 November 2019).

"The speech given by President Gamal Abdel Nasser in Alexandria on the 4th anniversary of the Revolution 'Nationalizing the Suez Canal,'" President Gamal Abd El Nasser, 26 July 1956, <http://nasser.bibalex.org/Speeches/browser.aspx?SID=495&lang=en> (last accessed 30 November 2019).

Theroux, Peter, "Abdelrahman Munif and the Uses of Oil," *Words Without Borders*, October 2012, <https://www.wordswithoutborders.org/article/abdelrahman-munif-and-the-uses-of-oil> (last accessed 30 November 2019).

Thomsen, Mads Rosendahl, *Mapping World Literature: International Canonization and Transnational Literatures* (London and New York: Continuum, 2008).

Turkkhan, Servinc, "Orhan Pamuk's *Kara Kitap*: (British) Reception vs. (American) Translation," *Making Connections: Interdisciplinary Approaches to Cultural Diversity*, 11:2 (2010), pp. 39–58.

Tymoczko, Maria, *Translation in a Postcolonial Context: Early Irish Literature in English Translation* (Manchester: St. Jerome Publishing, 1999).

"UN rights chief urges Israel to reconsider bill that would displace thousands of Bedouins," UN News, 25 July 2013, <http://www.un.org/apps/news/story.asp?NewsID=45495#.U0AW5_ldU01> (last accessed 30 November 2019).

"Universal Declaration of Human Rights," United Nations, 2015, <https://www.un.org/en/udhrbook/pdf/udhr_booklet_en_web.pdf> (last accessed 30 November 2019).

Updike, John, *Odd Jobs: Essays and Criticism* (New York: Random House, 2012).

Van der Veer, Peter, "Embodiment, Materiality, and Power," *Comparative Studies in Society and History*, 50:3 (2008), pp. 809–18.

Van Leeuwen, Richard, "*A Thousand and One Nights* and the Novel," in Waïl S. Hassan (ed.), *The Oxford Handbook of Arab Novelistic Traditions* (Oxford and New York: Oxford University Press, 2017), pp. 103–17.

Venuti, Lawrence, *The Translator's Invisibility: A History of Translation* (London and New York: Routledge, 1995).

Vitalis, Robert, *America's Kingdom: Mythmaking on the Saudi Oil Frontier* (London and New York: Verso, 2009).

Walkowitz, Rebecca L., *Born Translated: The Contemporary Novel in an Age of World Literature* (New York and Chichester: Columbia University Press, 2015).

Wallerstein, Immanuel, *The Modern World-System I: Capitalist Agriculture and the Origins of the European World-Economy in the Sixteenth Century* (Berkeley, Los Angeles, and London: University of California Press, 2011).

—, *World-Systems Analysis: An Introduction* (Durham and London: Duke University Press, 2004).

Watt, Ian, *Conrad in the Nineteenth Century* (Berkeley, Los Angeles, and London: University of California Press, 1979).

—, *Myths of Modern Individualism: Faust, Don Quixote, Don Juan, Robinson Crusoe* (Cambridge and New York: Cambridge University Press, 1996).

—, *The Rise of the Novel: Studies in Defoe, Richardson and Fielding* (Berkeley, Los Angeles, and London: University of California Press, 2001).

White, Ben, "Israel: Ethnic cleansing in the Negev," *Al Jazeera*, 22 October 2012, <http://www.aljazeera.com/indepth/opinion/2012/10/2012102114393741506.html> (last accessed 30 November 2019).

Williams, Raymond, *Marxism and Literature* (Oxford and New York: Oxford University Press, 1977).

Wilson, Sheena, Adam Carlson, and Imre Szeman (eds), *Petrocultures: Oil, Politics, Culture* (Montreal and Kingston: McGill-Queen's University Press, 2017).

Xinos, Ilana, "Petro-Capitalism, Petrofiction, and Islamic Discourse: The Formation of an Imagined Community in *Cities of Salt*," *Arab Studies Quarterly*, 28:1 (2006), pp. 1–12.

Yaeger, Patricia, "Editor's Column: Literature in the Ages of Wood, Tallow, Coal, Whale Oil, Gasoline, Atomic Power, and Other Energy Sources," *Publications of the Modern Language Association*, 126:2 (2011), pp. 305–26.

Young, Robert J. C., *Colonial Desire: Hybridity in Theory, Culture and Race* (London and New York: Routledge, 1995).

Yükleyen, Ahmet, "Sufism and Islamic groups in Contemporary Turkey," in Reşat Kasaba (ed.), *The Cambridge History of Turkey, Volume 4: Turkey in the Modern World* (Cambridge and New York: Cambridge University Press, 2008), pp. 381–7.

Zia-Ebrahimi, Reza, *The Emergence of Iranian Nationalism: Race and the Politics of Dislocation* (New York and Chichester: Columbia University Press, 2016).

Ziya Pasha, "*Gazel*," trans. Nermin Menemencioğlu, in Nermin Menemencioğlu and Fahir İz (eds), *The Penguin Book of Turkish Verse* (Harmondsworth: Penguin Books, 1978), p. 164.

Zürcher, Erik J., *Turkey: A Modern History* (London: I. B. Tauris, 2004).

Index

Aboul-Ela, Hosam, 180–1
Abrahamian, Ervand, 147, 152, 283–4
Abrams, M. H., 8–9
Abu-Lughod, Lila, 277
Achcar, Gilbert, 209
actor-network theory, 302, 303, 304–5
adab
   as belles-lettres, 114, 116–18, 119
   al-Bustani's treatment of, 132
   classical Arabic-Islamic concept of, xi, 25–6, 50, 110, 111, 114
   defined, 114–16
   genres of, 25–6, 114–16, 120
   Islam as the episteme of, 118–19, 150
   Islamic humanism of, 120
   links with *adabiyāt*, 148
   links with *edebiyat*, 139–40
   reinscription of as literature, 111, 117–18, 124–5, 131, 133, 135
   in relation to *sunna*, 119–20
   spectral traces of in the Middle Eastern novel, 51–2
   as superseded by the novel, 51
   term, 110–11
adabiyāt
   classical Persian as the literary language of, 148–9
   in the Constitutional era, 156
   genres of, 149
   links with *adab*, 148
   as Persian literary humanism, 149–50, 151
   reinscription of as literature, 111
   secularization of, 150–1
   term, 110–11
Adib-Moghaddam, Arshin, 277
Adorno, Theodor, 27, 28, 30, 31–2

aesthetic, notion of, 8–9, 304
Afghanistan, 276
Ahmed, Siraj, 90–1, 92
Akhundzade, Mirza Fath'ali, 51, 153
Allan, Michael, 134–5
Allen, Chadwick, 86–8
Allen, Roger
   adab as belles-lettres, 113, 114, 116, 117
   on the Arabic novel, 183
   literary historical work, x, 50, 51
   on Naguib Mahfouz, 177, 179
   on the *Nahda*, 122, 157
Alshaar, Nuha, xi, 50, 118, 119
The Ambassadors (Holbein), vi–viii
Amin, Samir, 16, 208
Amirrezvani, Anita, 269
Anam, Nasia, 263
Anderson, Benedict, 112, 127, 240
anglophone Iranian novel
   autobiografiction in relation to, 269–70
   autobiographies/memoirs by female authors, 266–7
   comparative Middle Eastern studies and, 261–2
   diasporic Iranian novels, 268–9
   as exploration of Revolutionary trauma, 266–7, 269–70
   feminist agency within Iran, 265, 293–4
   gender issues, 262
   ideological-based critiques of, 280–1
   Iranian relations with the West, 262
   marketing of, 267
   and the narrative of flight, 265, 286
   and the worlding of Iran, 262–3
   see also *Persepolis* (Satrapi); *Reading Lolita in Tehran* (Nafisi); *The Saffron Kitchen* (Crowther)

Apter, Emily, ix, 27, 237–8
Arab Spring, 208–9
Arabian Nights and Days (Mahfouz)
  English translation of, 196
  inversion of Orientalist logic, 196
  narrative overview, 191–2
  as political allegory, 192–3
  pre-modern form of, 183, 191, 193, 196, 197
  the reintegration of the past into modernity, 193–5
  spectrality of Gamasa al-Bulti, 194–5
Arabic language
  in the nineteenth century, 117–18
  Project of Translation from Arabic (PROTA), 179
  and the Qur'ān, 118
  standardization of, 127
Arabic novel
  first publication of, 127
  as an imported, modern, European construct, 157, 159–61
  indigenous tradition of, 157
  Naguib Mahfouz as the founding father of, 159, 162, 177, 183–4
  national contexts for, 158–9
  recognition by the Swedish Academy, 178–9
  riwāya, term, 158, 159–60
Arabic-Islamic culture
  adab in, 114
  displacement of literary heritage of, 112–13
  and *Don Quixote* (Cervantes), 44, 45–7
  Islamic consciousness of, 118–19
El-Ariss, Tarek, 50, 123, 124, 130, 159
Asad, Talal, 218, 250–1, 252
Ataç, Nurullah, 51, 146
Atatürk, Mustafa Kemal, 136, 143, 144, 145
autobiografiction
  concept of, 264, 269–70
  Reading Lolita in Tehran (Nafisi) as, 278–9, 283

Badawi, M. M., x, 50, 51, 53, 122–3, 157, 183
Badran, Margot, 277, 284–5
Bahar, Mohammad Taqi, 51, 156
Bakhtin, Mikhail, 41
Ball, Anna, 52
Barakat, Halim, 82
Bedouin
  'Ain Dar, Saudi Arabia, 99
  Mu'allaqāt, 91–2, 93
  Naqab Bedouin, Israel, 83–5
  nomadism as a threat to the nation state, 82, 83–5, 86
  nomadism/civilization dialectic, 81–2, 86
  oral literature, 89–90, 91
  reading the remains of desert camps, 88
  resurgent tribal identities, 82–3
  see also *Cities of Salt* (Munif)
Beeman, William, 276

belles-lettres
  adab as, 114, 116–18, 119
  Enlightenment humanism, 116–17
  Eurocentrism of, 116–17
Benjamin, Walter, 28, 38, 226, 241
Berman, Marshall, 8
The Black Book (Pamuk)
  cultural neo-Ottomanism, 218, 230, 239–40, 248–9, 253
  and the detective genre, 223–4
  domesticating translation, 234–5, 236–7
  English translations of, 217–18, 220, 231–8
  the face as Turkish cultural history, 245–8
  foreignizing translation of, 234, 236, 237
  hüzün, 226–8
  Istanbul setting of, 226–8
  as a *Künstlerroman*, 225–6, 243–4
  linguistic complexity, 217, 232, 233, 235–6
  linguistic dimension of Turkish identity, 218, 236
  the mannequin as Turkish cultural history, 240–4
  plot, characters, themes, 220–2
  political neo-Ottomanism, 229–30, 247–8
  as postmodern novel, 218, 223–5, 238–9
  postsecular/secular position in, 253
  structure, style, form, and genre, 222–6
  Sufism and Hurufism, 218, 221, 222, 225–6, 239, 245–8
  translatorial strategies for, 232–8
  treatment of Islam, 218, 221
  Turkish cultural identity, 222, 223, 225–6, 229–31
  Turkish political history, 228–31
  Turkish secular modernity, 217, 226
  untranslatability of, 236, 237
Blair, Hugh, 116, 117
Bloom, Harold, 41
Boehmer, Elleke, 265, 286, 287
Bonaparte, Napoleon, 120–1
Boullata, Issa, 73
Boyer, Dominic, 95, 96
Braudel, Fernand, 11
Brennan, Timothy, 179, 265, 286
Burton, Richard Francis, 195
Bush, George W., 270–1
al-Bustani, Butrus, 51, 127, 128–9, 130–3, 136

The Cairo Trilogy (Mahfouz)
  Egyptian political history, 187
  family saga form, 186–8
  the figure of al-Sayyid Ahmad, 188–9, 190
  inf(l)ected in spectral fashion, 182, 183
  narrative overview, 186–90
  as spectral Egyptian realism, 183, 186, 190
capitalism
  capitalist world-economy, 8, 12–13
  emergence in parallel with world literature, 8–10
  Marxist analysis of the commodity, 28–9
  Specters of Marx (Derrida), 33–4, 35

Casanova, Pascale, ix, 1, 2–3, 23–4, 178, 180
Cervantes Saavedra, Miguel de see *Don Quixote* (Cervantes)
Cheah, Pheng, 36, 37
Chomsky, Noam, 275
Cities of Salt (Munif)
  Anglophone critical reception of, 72–3
  the Bedouin community's destruction by petro-modernity, 77–9, 81, 88–9, 94, 97–8, 100
  compared to the European novel form, 72–3, 74
  interpretation of trace of Bedouin way of life, 88–9
  John Updike's review of, 72–3
  narrative overview, 72, 76–8
  parallels between Mooran and Saudi Arabia, 72, 78–9, 97–8
  portrayal of the oil encounter, 71, 96–7, 100
  the protagonist-assumption and, 72, 73, 74, 79–80, 101
  spectrality as resistance to incorporation, 93–4
  spectrality of Miteb al-Hathal, 74–5, 80–1, 100–4
  textualization of Bedouin oral poetry, 88–9
  traditional Bedouin culture, 77–8
Cohen, Hermann, 41, 42
Cohen, Walter, 45–6
colonialism
  colonial idea of Indian literature, 22–3
  English as the language of, 87–8
  in the Middle East, 50
  Orientalist philology and, 90–1, 92
  see also postcolonial literature
cooke, miriam, 82–3, 277–8, 286
Cooppan, Vilashini, 36
Crowther, Yasmin see *The Saffron Kitchen* (Crowther)

Dabashi, Hamid, 149–51, 209, 265, 280, 281
Damrosch, David, ix, 1, 183, 195, 278
Defoe, Daniel, 72, 127, 131
Dehkhoda, 'Ali Akbar, 51, 155
Deleuze, Gilles, 82
Derrida, Jacques
  on democracy as haunted, 103–4
  différance, 35
  logic of spectrality, x, 33–5, 103, 300
  on the rogue state discourse, 275–6
  trace, 35
Descartes, René, 135
El-Desouky, Ayman, 205, 206–7
Don Quixote (Cervantes)
  as an anti-Romance novel, 43, 45, 46
  Arabic-Islamic content, 44, 45–7
  Cide Hamete Benengeli, 44, 45, 46, 47
  as the first modern novel, 40–1, 72
  form/content relationship, 45
  as inflected by the specter of the Oriental other, 47
  literary impact of, 43–4
  metafictional devices in, 44–5
  as modernity in novel form, 41–4
  representation of empire in, 45–6

Eagleton, Terry, 8, 9, 304
Eckermann, Johann Peter, 3
edebiyat
  definitions of, 145
  Divan poetry, 139
  European-modelled literary and cultural modernization, 140
  genres of, 139
  links with *adab*, 139–40
  Ottoman literary and cultural sphere, 138–9
  reinscription of as literature, 111, 137
  term, 110–11
  yazın as alternative for, 146
Egypt
  amāra, 206, 208
  Free Officers Revolution, 201–2
  the French Campaign, 50, 120–1, 197
  key sites of Middle Eastern modernity, 51
  military modernization, 125, 147
  1990s generation of writers, 182, 205, 206–8
  printing, journalism, and translation technology, 125, 126–8
  state response to Naguib Mahfouz's Noble Prize, 181
  the Suez Crisis, 199–201, 204
  Tahrir Square and the Egyptian demos, 182, 205–6
  women's piety movement, 285
  see also Mahfouz, Naguib; *Nahda* (cultural renaissance)
El-Enany, Rasheed, 182, 185, 186, 192, 197
Engels, Friedrich, 3, 10
English, James, 178, 180
English language
  anglophone Arab/Middle Eastern novels, 260–1
  global anglophone concept, 263–4
  as the language of colonialism, 87–8
  see also anglophone Iranian novel
Enlightenment, 131, 132–3, 135
  Enlightenment humanism, 116–17
  Enlightenment liberalism, 252
Erdim, Esim, 236
Ersoy, Mehmet Akif, 51, 141–3
Ertürk, Nergis, 140, 146, 159

Fadel, Mohamed, *Nasser 56*, 204
Fazlallah of Astarabad, 245–6, 248
Felski, Rita, 300–4
form
  abstraction, mediation and crystallization of, 29, 30, 32
  adaptation of *ṭabaqāt* form (*Morning and Evening Talk*, Mahfouz), 183, 191, 197–9, 205
  concept of, 28–30
  Don Quixote (Cervantes) as an exemplary novel, 40–3, 45

INDEX | 335

family saga form of *The Cairo Trilogy* (Mahfouz), 186–8
Marx's analysis of the commodity, 28–9
the mediation of conflict in form, 28, 29–30
and the Middle Eastern novel, 159
pre-modern form of *Arabian Nights and Days* (Mahfouz), 183, 191, 193, 196, 197
in relation to the life-world concept, 32–3
and spectral life-world of modernity, 38–9
Fotouhi, Sanaz, 266–7, 269
Foucault, Michel, 41, 43
Frank, Andre Gunder, 16
Freely, Maureen, 217, 231, 232, 234–5, 236–7
French Campaign in Egypt and Syria, 50, 120–1, 197

Galland, Antoine, 195
German literature, 4, 5
Ghosh, Amitav, 94, 96, 97
Gibran, Khalil, 261
global anglophone concept, 263–4
global capitalist modernity
and the emergence of world literature, 8–10, 39
incorporation of the periphery into, 15–17, 19–20, 21
shift to in Western Europe, 8–9
in single-resource economies, 79, 80
term, 13–14
see also oil industry
Goethe, Johann Wolfgang von
"Book of Háfiz", 5
influence on Karl Marx, 7, 10
Künstleromane, 225
Weltliteratur concept, 3–6, 8, 10–11, 18
West-Eastern Divan, 4–6, 91
Gökalp, Ziya, 51, 143–4
Göknar, Erdağ, 217, 226, 239
Gommlich, Klaus, 236
Gordon, Joel, 204
Great Britain
GB-Iran relations, 262
Iranian diaspora, 260, 265–6
the Suez Crisis, 200–1
Grossman, Edith, 42
Guattari, Félix, 82
Gün, Güneli, 217, 231, 233–5, 236
Gunn, Giles, 263
Gürbilek, Nurdan, 231

Habermas, Jürgen, 32, 218, 251
Hafez, Sabry, 183, 187, 190, 206–7
Hafiz, 4, 5
Halman, Talat, 139
al-Hamadani, Badi' al-Zaman, 46, 115
Haqqi, Mahmoud Tahir, 158–9
al-Hariri of Basra, 46, 115
Hassan, Waïl, xi, 51, 159–61, 184, 261
Haykal, Muhammad Husayn, 127, 159
Hermes, Nizar, 45, 46–7
Hitchcock, Peter, 73, 96, 97

Home, Henry, 116–17
Hopkins, Terence, 15
Horta, Paulo, 183, 195
Hourani, Albert, 50, 121, 122, 132
Huggan, Graham, 265, 267, 286
Husayn, Taha, 51, 133–5
Husserl, Edmund
critiques of phenomenology, 31–2
life-world (*Lebenswelt*) concept, 30–2

Ibn al-Akfani, 120
Ibn al-'Arabi, 115, 119
Ibn Khaldun, 81–2, 119, 122
Ibn Qutayba, 115
Ibn Sina, 115
India, 22–3
indigenous cultures
global indigenous literary studies, 86–8
nomadism/civilization dialectic, 81–2
reproduction of through oral literature, 89–90
textualization of oral culture, 88–9, 91–2, 93
see also Bedouin
Iran
the Constitution of 1906, 154–5
critical Iranian studies, 277
emergent nationalist discourse, 153–4
human rights record, 272–3
Iranian diaspora, 260, 265–6
Islamic feminism in, 285, 286
Islamic Revival in, 250
literary and cultural modernization, 147–8, 152–5
military modernization, 147
nuclear program, 262, 273, 277
pre-Revolution, 283–4
printing, journalism, and translation technology, 151–2
radical version of Shi'a Islam, 272, 273
rogue state status, 264, 271, 272–5, 278
rumān, term, 158
standardization of Persian, 152, 153, 154, 155–6
US discourses of gender and, 276–7
US-Iran relations, 262, 270–2, 276
women's rights in, pre-Revolution, 284
see also *adabiyāt*; anglophone Iranian novel
Islam
as the episteme of *adab*, 118–19, 150
Islamic humanism of *adab*, 120
US discourses of gender and, 276–7
Islamic feminism
Iranian Islamic feminism, 285, 286
multiple roles of women, 286
in *Reading Lolita in Tehran* (Nafisi), 265, 281–2, 283
scholarship on, 277–8, 284–5
Islamic Revival, 249–50, 252
Isma'il, 121, 128
Israel, 83–5

Jabbur, Jibrail, 88
James, Laura, 201
Jameson, Frederic, 13–14, 28
Jay, Paul, 263
Jayyusi, Salma, 51, 157, 179, 183
Johnson, Rebecca, 130
Jones, William, 22–3, 90–2, 93
journalism, 127, 140

Kadir, Djelal, ix, 26, 48
Katouzian, Homa, 149
Kermani, Mirza Aqa Khan, 51, 153–4
Keshavarz, Fatemeh, 280
Khakpour, Porochista, 269–70
Khalidi, Rashid, xi, 165
Khan, Mirza Malkam, 51, 154
Kilito, Abdelfattah, xi, 50, 51, 118, 158, 160
Kilpatrick, Hilary, 112, 115–16, 183, 189
Klare, Michael, 274–5
Kyle, Keith, 201

Lacan, Jacques, viii
Lake, Anthony, 271–2, 275, 276
Lane, Edward William, 195
Latour, Bruno, 302, 304
Lawall, Sarah, 180
Lazarus, Neil, 80
Lebovic, James, 274
Leeuwen, Richard van, 196
life-world (*Lebenswelt*) concept
  concept of, 30–2
  critiques of, 31–2
  in relation to form, 32–3
  spectral life-world of modernity, 38–9
literary studies
  national literature paradigm, viii–ix
  postcritical turn in, 300–4
literature
  concept of, 3–10, 110, 179
  emphasis on the aesthetic experience, 9, 304
  national identity and, 22–3
  in relation to energy production, 94–5
  Romanticism, 8, 9, 304
Litwak, Robert, 274
Lockman, Zachary, xi, 163, 164, 165
Louis, William Roger, 201
Lukács, Georg, 27, 29, 41, 42, 43

Mahfouz, Naguib
  Children of the Alley (Mahfouz), 185, 191, 208
  as embodiment of Egyptian literary culture, 181–2
  as the founding father of the Arabic novel, 159, 162, 177, 183–4
  global literary recognition of, 177–8, 181–2
  indigenous/traditional phase, 182, 183, 185–6
  modernist techniques, 185
  Nobel Prize in Literature, 177, 178, 179–81
  oeuvre of, 182–3, 184–6
  as proponent of the Wafd Party, 204
  revolution of form against Egyptian modernity, 182, 208–9
  scholarship on, 185–6
  significance for world literature, 183
  spectral inf(l)ection in, 186
  see also *Arabian Nights and Days* (Mahfouz); *Morning and Evening Talk* (Mahfouz); *The Cairo Trilogy* (Mahfouz)
Mahmood, Saba, 252, 253, 277, 285
Makdisi, George, 150
maqāma, genre of, 46–7, 115
Marx, Karl
  on the commodity, 28–9
  influence of Goethe on, 7, 10
  Manifesto of the Communist Party, 3, 6, 8
  Specters of Marx (Derrida), 33–4, 35
  Weltliteratur concept, 3, 6–8, 10–11, 18
Massad, Joseph, 218, 252, 253
Mehrez, Samia, 205
Meyer, Stefan, 102
Middle East
  colonialism in, 50
  comparative Middle Eastern literary and cultural studies, 165–6
  dialectic of modernity in, 49–51, 111–12
  petro-modernity's impact on indigenous cultures, 77–9
  term, 52–3, 163, 165
Middle East Institute (MEI), 163
Middle East studies, x–xi, 52, 163–5
Middle East Studies Association (MESA), 163–4, 165
Middle Eastern novel
  anglophone Arab/Middle Eastern novels, 260–1
  Arabic literature post-*Nahda*, 122–3
  Arabic translations of Western fiction, 157
  engagement with *One Thousand and One Nights*, 196–7
  and the European concept of literature, 157
  exchange, 49–50, 111–12
  form and, 159
  global status, 53–4
  internalized appropriation, 21, 50–1, 111–12
  literary incorporation into modernity, 49–51, 112–13, 159–61
  national contexts for, 158–9
  national identity and, 112–13
  overview of, x–xii
  reproduction of modernity via the novel, 51, 111–12
  riwāya, term, 158, 159–60
  roman, term, 158
  rumān, term, 158
  spectral trace of *adab* in, 51–2
  spectrality in, 54–5, 161–2
  untranslatability of, 237–8
  see also anglophone Iranian novel; Arabic novel

Mitchell, Timothy, 76, 79, 98, 198
modernity
  Don Quixote (Cervantes) as the first modern novel, 40–3
  incorporation of periphery into, 17–18, 24–6
  literary forms of, x, 24, 25, 27, 110
  Middle East literary and cultural modernity, 49–51, 111–12, 159–61
  reproduction of modernity via the novel, 51, 111–12
  secularization/religiosity distinction, 251
  singular modernity, 13–14
  spectral analysis of, 36–7, 38
  spectral life-world of modernity, 38–9
  through *Nahda*, 121–2
  world literature as an agent of, 8–10, 27, 33, 39
  see also global capitalist modernity
Moretti, Franco, 28, 80, 159
  compromise in world literature, 25
  literary evolution, 21
  personal standing of, xiii–xiv
  theory of the novel, 47–8
  on world literature, ix, 1, 2
Morning and Evening Talk (Mahfouz)
  adaptation of *ṭabaqāt* form, 183, 191, 197–9, 205
  class identifications in, 203
  deconstruction of nationalism, 204–5
  Egyptian political history, 183
  familial collapse, 202
  history of Egyptian modernity, 197–8, 199–200, 203–5
  the Suez Crisis, 199–200, 202–3, 204
Moshiri, Farnoosh, 269
Muʿallaqāt, 91–2
Mubarak, Hosni, 181, 200, 204, 205
Mufti, Aamir
  critique of postsecularism, 252–3
  critique of world literature, ix, 24, 26–7, 92
  on Islamic feminism, 285
  literary exchange concept, 22
  on Orientalist systems, x, 18–19
Muhammad ʿAli, 121–2, 125–8, 198
Munif, Abdelrahman, 71–2, 77; see also *Cities of Salt* (Munif)
al-Musawi, Muhsin, x, 50, 117, 118–19, 124, 150

Nafisi, Azar see *Reading Lolita in Tehran* (Nafisi)
Naguib Mahfouz Medal for Literature, 177, 181
Nahda (cultural renaissance)
  Butrus al-Bustani's contribution to, 130–3
  European concept of literature, 128, 130
  following the French Campaign, 120–1
  Leg over Leg (al-Shidyaq), 129–31
  legacy of, 208–9
  Muhammad ʿAli's programme of, 121–2, 125–8
  new literary readings of, 123–4
  overview of, 50
  printing, journalism, and translation, 125, 126–8, 157
  role of Orientalist philology, 124
  Taha Husayn's contribution to, 133–5
  technological aspect of, 121, 122, 126
  in Turkey, 136–7
  Western literature's influence on, 122–3
  Western modernity and, 117, 122
Naqab Bedouin, Israel, 83–5
Nasser, Gamal Abdel, 199–202, 204
Nasser al-Din, 147–8
nation-state
  nation building through internalization of literature, 22–3, 51, 112
  national contexts for the Middle Eastern novel, 158–9
  nomadism as a threat to, 82, 83–5, 86
  postcolonial nations as spectral others, 37
  in world-systems theory, 37
national identity
  emergent nationalist discourses in Iran, 153–4
  literature and, 22–3
  Middle Eastern novel and, 112–13
  national literature paradigm, viii–ix
neoimperalism
  conscription of women's rights by, 286–7
  critiques of Islamic feminism, 277–8
  and the incorporation process, 16
  and *Reading Lolita in Tehran* (Nafisi), 281–2, 283
Nixon, Rob, 95–6, 97
Norris, H. T., 246
Noujaim, Jehane, 206
the novel
  absorption of oral culture by, 89
  Don Quixote (Cervantes) as an exemplary text, 40–3
  Moretti's theory of, 47–8
  spectral infl(l)ection in, 40
  see also anglophone Iranian novel; Arabic novel; Middle Eastern novel

oil industry
  Abdelrahman Munif's experience of, 71–2
  American oil industry, 96, 98, 99
  in the context of global culture, 75–6
  energy humanities and, 95
  fragmentation of Bedouin communities by petro-modernity (*Cities of Salt*), 77–9, 81, 88–9, 94, 97–8, 100
  invisibility of in modern literature, 94–7, 99–100
  the oil encounter in *Cities of Salt* (Munif), 71, 96–7, 100
  in Saudi Arabia, 97–8, 99–100
One Thousand and One Nights
  as a fantasy of the Orientalist imagination, 183, 195, 196
  within Middle Eastern literature, 196–7

One Thousand and One Nights (cont.)
   as source text for *Arabian Nights and Days* (Mahfouz), 191, 192, 193
   translations of, 195–6
oral culture
   absorption of by the novel, 89
   Bedouin oral literature, 89–90, 91
   textualization of Bedouin oral poetry, 91–2, 93
Orientalism
   Europe's Oriental Renaissance, 5–6
   and the French Campaign, 121
   in Goethe's *West-Eastern Divan*, 5
   Middle East studies and, 163–5
   world literature as a product of, 18–21
Orientalist philology
   the colonial process and, xi, 18–19, 90–1, 92
   influence on *Nahda*, 50, 124
   internalization of, 18, 93, 153, 161
   Jones's translation/transcription of the *Muʿallaqāt*, 91–2, 93
   reinscription of *adab* as literature, 111, 117–18, 124–5, 131, 133, 135
Ortega y Gasset, José, 41, 42
Osanloo, Arzoo, 278, 285
Ouyang, Wen-chin, 158, 183, 191, 192, 193, 199
Özyürek, Esra, 231

Paker, Saliha, 238
Palumbo-Liu, David, 15
Pamuk, Orhan
   as a 'born translated' writer, 216–17, 218
   connection with Istanbul, 217
   global literary image of, 215–17, 238–9
   involvement in the translation process, 235
   Istanbul: Memories and the City, 227–8
   The Museum of Innocence, 219–20
   Nobel Prize in Literature, 215
   oeuvre of, 219–20
   as postmodernist author, 216, 239
   Snow, 217, 219
   and the Turkish novel, 218–19
   as untranslatable, 218
   see also *The Black Book* (Pamuk)
Pasha, Ziya (Abdul Hamid Ziyaeddin), 51, 141
Peace of Westphalia, 12
Peeren, Esther, 35–6
Persepolis (Satrapi)
   graphic novel format, 291
   narrative overview, 290–1, 292–3
   the veil in, 291
   women's feminist agency in Iran, 265, 286–7
   women's resistance in, 292, 293
phantasmagoria, 38
Phillips, Christina, 199
philology
   contemporary relevance of, 93
   Indo-European language hypothesis, 90–1
   literary and cultural modernity, 111
   riwāya, term, 158, 159–60
   see also Orientalist philology

Pilar Blanco, María del, 35–6
Pizer, John, 4, 6
postcolonial literature
   critiques of, ix
   global anglophone concept and, 263, 264
   spectral theory applied to, 37
postcolonial theory, "empire-colony" model, 19–20
postcritique, 300–5
postsecularism
   concept of, 250–1
   critiques of, 252–3
   Islamic Revival's rejection of, 252
   plurality of faith and non-faith communities, 251–2
Prawer, S. S., 6, 7
Prebisch, Raúl, 13
Puchner, Martin, 6

qaṣīda (ode)
   form of, 88, 89
   Jones's translation / transcription of the *Muʿallaqāt*, 91–2, 93
Qazvini, ʿAref, 51, 156
qiṣṣa (folk tale), 89, 90, 158

Rabaté, Jean-Michel, 36–7
Radwan, Noha, 207
Rafat, Taqi, 51, 156
Rastegar, Kamran, 50, 123, 124, 130, 159
Reading Lolita in Tehran (Nafisi)
   appeal to a Western feminist readership, 265, 281–2
   as autobiografiction, 278–9, 283
   critical reception of, 280–1
   gendered violence in, 280, 282
   historical obfuscation in, 283
   ideological-based critiques of, 280–1
   on Islamic feminism, 283
   narrative overview, 279–80
   presentation of Iranian women, 282–3
Redhouse, James William, 145
Rhodes James, Robert, 200
Rihani, Ameen, 261
riwāya, term, 158
Robbins, Bruce, 15, 302–3, 305
Robinson Crusoe (Defoe), 72, 127, 131
Rogan, Eugene, 50, 122
Rogue States doctrine
   critiques of, 273–6
   deployment of by the US political establishment, 271–2, 274–5, 276
   Iran as a rogue state, 264, 272–3, 278
   women's rights in, 276–7
Romanticism, 8, 9, 41, 304
Rowe, John Carlos, 281, 283
Roy, Arundhati, 305–6
Rumi, 115, 119, 149, 221, 245

Sacks, Jeffrey, x–xi, 50, 117–18, 124, 130–1, 133, 135
The Saffron Kitchen (Crowther)
  experiences of migration, 286–7, 289–90
  feminist agency within Iran, 265
  narrative overview, 287–8
  on Western perceptions of Iran, 288–9
Said, Edward
  on *Cities of Salt* (Munif), 71, 94
  on the French Campaign, 121
  on Goethe's *West-Eastern Divan*, 4–6
  on Middle East studies, 163, 164
  on Orientalism, x, 164–5
  on scarcity of translations of Middle Eastern literature, 238
Sandberg, Mark, 241, 242
Satrapi, Marjane see *Persepolis* (Satrapi)
Saudi Arabia
  'Ain Dar, Saudi Arabia, 99
  oil industry in, 97–8, 99–100
  parallels between Mooran and Saudi Arabia, 72, 78–9
Saunders, Max, 264, 269–70
Schlegel, Friedrich, 41, 42
Schmidt, Rachel, 41
Schwab, Raymond, 5
secularism, 250–1
Sedghi, Hamideh, 277
Seyhan, Azade, 159, 217, 225, 234, 239
Shatz, Adam, 216, 239
Shaw, Wendy, 240
Sheehi, Stephen, 50, 123, 124, 130, 132, 159
al-Shidyaq, Ahmad Faris, 51, 128, 129–31, 136
singular modernity, 13–14
Smith, Derek, 274
Smith, Simon, 201
Sofer, Dalia, 269
Sowers, Jeannie, 205
spectral theory
  analysis of modernity, 36–7, 38
  in *Arabian Nights and Days* (Mahfouz), 194–5
  in *The Cairo Trilogy* (Mahfouz), 182, 183, 186, 190
  democracy as haunted, 103–4
  in literary studies, 35–6
  logic of spectrality (Derrida), x, 33–5, 103, 300
  overview of, x
  postcolonial nations as spectral others, 37
  rereading of modernity/modernism, 36–7, 38
  Specters of Marx (Derrida), 33–4, 35, 103
  spectral inf(l)ection in the novel, 40
  spectral life-world of modernity, 38–9
  spectral trace of *adab* in the Middle Eastern novel, 51–2
  spectrality in *Cities of Salt* (Munif), 74–5, 80–1, 100–4
  spectrality in the Middle Eastern novel, 54–5, 161–2
  in world literature, 36, 39, 81

Spivak, Gayatri, 33–4
Swedish Academy
  expansionist period, 178–9
  literary universality of, 180
  Naguib Mahfouz's Nobel Prize in Literature, 177, 179–81
  Orhan Pamuk's Nobel Prize in Literature, 215
Swift, Jonathan, 116
Szeman, Imre, 95, 96

ṭabaqāt, 183
al-Tahtawi, Rifa'a, 51, 121, 122, 125–6, 127
Tanoukhi, Nirvana, 15
Tanpınar, Ahmet Hamdi, 219
Taylor, Charles, 218, 251
Theroux, Peter, 71, 94
trace
  of the Bedouin way of life, 88–9
  spectral traces of *adab*, 51–2
  term, 35
transcendental idealism, 31
translation
  assessment of primary sources, xii
  domesticating translation, 234–5, 236–7
  Don Quixote (Cervantes), 42
  English translations of *The Black Book* (Pamuk), 217–18, 220, 231–8
  foreignizing translation, 234, 236, 237
  inverse sentences in Turkish, 232
  literary translation movement, Turkey, 140–1
  and the Middle Eastern novel, 157
  of the *One Thousand and One Nights*, 195–6
  of Orhan Pamuk's work, 216–17, 218, 235
  printing, journalism, and translation technology in Egypt, 125, 126–8
  printing, journalism, and translation technology in Iran, 151–2
  printing, journalism, and translation technology in Turkey, 140–1
  Project of Translation from Arabic (PROTA), 179
  scarcity of Turkish to English translations, 237–8
  translatability of world literature, 216
  untranslatability of *The Black Book* (Pamuk), 236, 237
  untranslatability of world literature, 237–8
  William Jones' philology, 90–1
  William Jones's translation/transcription of the *Mu'allaqāt*, 91–2, 93
Turkey
  economic liberalization of, 230–1
  European-modelled literary and cultural modernization, 136, 138, 141–4
  Istanbul's commercial mannequins, 241–2
  language reform, 136, 143–4, 145, 146
  military modernization, 147
  museum culture of, 240–1
  Nahda in, 136–7
  1980 *coup d'état*, 228–9

Turkey (*cont.*)
    printing, journalism, and translation
        technology, 140–1
    reform-era Ottoman Empire, 137–8
    Republican literature, 144–5
    roman, term, 158
    the Sufi orders, 245–7
    Tanzimat era, 131, 136, 138, 140, 141–2
    translation of Turkish literature into English,
        140, 237–8
    Turkish novelistic tradition, 144, 159
    see also *edebiyat*
Türkkan, Sevinç, 236

Unamuno, Miguel de, 41, 42
United States of America (USA)
    discourses of gender in Iran, 276–7
    global primacy of, 11
    Iranian diaspora, 260, 265–6
    Middle East studies in, 163–4
    oil industry and, 96, 98, 99
    as a rogue state itself, 275
    Rogue States doctrine, 264, 271–5, 278
    US foreign policy, post-9/11, 270–1
    US-Iran relations, 262, 264, 270–2, 276
Updike, John, 72–3

Venuti, Lawrence, 217, 232, 236
Vitalis, Robert, 99

Walkowitz, Rebecca, 216–17
Wallerstein, Immanuel, 11–13, 14, 15, 112
Watt, Ian, 41, 78
Weltliteratur
    defined, 10
    Goethe's concept of, 3–6, 10–11, 18
    Marx's concept of, 6–8, 10–11, 18
    in relation to capitalist modernity, 8–10
Western Europe
    concept of literature, xi, 6, 17, 23, 110, 128,
        140, 146, 157, 159–61, 179
    emphasis on the aesthetic experience, 9
    Eurocentrism of world literature, 23–4
    literary exchange with the Middle East, 49–50
    long sixteenth century, 12
    Oriental Renaissance, 5–6
    shift to capitalist modernity, 8–9
White, Ben, 84
Williams, Raymond, 8
women
    adoption of the veil in Iran, 277, 282
    in pre-Revolutionary Iran, 284
    US discourses of gender in Iran, 276–7
    Western universalist feminism, 281–2

women's piety movement, Egypt, 285
see also Islamic feminism; *Persepolis*
    (Satrapi); *Reading Lolita in Tehran* (Nafisi);
    The Saffron Kitchen (Crowther)
world literature
    as an agent of modernity, 8–10, 27, 33
    concept of/understandings of, 1–3
    critiques of, ix–x, 24, 26–7, 92
    and the emergence of capitalist modernity,
        8–10, 27, 33, 39
    "empire-colony" model, 19–20
    Eurocentrism of, 23–4
    The God of Small Things (Roy), 305–6
    Goethe's concept of, 3–6
    within literary studies, ix–x, 305–6
    Naguib Mahfouz's significance for, 183
    otherness in, x
    as peripheral modernity, 80
    as a product of Orientalism, 18–21
    in relation to the world markets, 7
    in relation to world-systems theory, 2
    spectrality in, 36, 39, 81
    translatability of, 216
    untranslatability of, 237–8
    as a world-historical process, 18, 20–1, 26–7
world-systems theory
    the capitalist world-economy, 12–13
    concept of, 11–13
    core and peripheral zones within, 13, 14
    exchange, x, 12–13, 21, 26
    exchange, literary, 22, 49–50, 111–12
    incorporation of the periphery into global
        capitalist modernity, 15–17, 19–20, 21–2
    internalization, x, 13–14, 17, 26
    internalization of literature, 23–4, 50–1,
        111–12
    literary exchange and incorporation in colonial
        India, 22–3
    methodological use of, xii
    nation state in, 37
    reproduction, x, 14, 26, 111–12
    reproduction of modernity in the periphery,
        17–18, 24–6
    state-centric criticism of, 14–15
    struggle for global literary dominance, 24–6
    world literature in relation to, 2

Xinos, Ilana, 73

Yaeger, Patricia, 94–5
Yıldız, Ahmet Günbay, 238

Zaydan, Jurji, 158
Zürcher, Erik, 137, 138

EU representative:
Easy Access System Europe
Mustamäe tee 50, 10621 Tallinn, Estonia
Gpsr.requests@easproject.com

www.ingramcontent.com/pod-product-compliance
Lightning Source LLC
Chambersburg PA
CBHW071826230426
43672CB00013B/2773